Romani
A Linguistic Introduction

Romani is a language of Indo-Aryan origin which is spoken in Europe by the people known as 'Gypsies' (who usually refer to themselves as *Rom*). There are upwards of 3.5 million speakers, and their language has attracted increasing interest both from scholars and from policy makers in governments and other organisations during the past ten years.

This book is the first comprehensive overview in English of Romani. It opens with a discussion of the historical and linguistic origins of the Romani-speaking population. An in-depth and detailed discussion is devoted to the changes in the sound system, grammatical structure, and lexicon that led to the formation of Proto-Romani and Early Romani. The book surveys current issues in the study of Romani by examining the phonology, morphology, syntactic typology, and patterns of grammatical borrowing in the language, drawing on a comparative survey of the principal dialects. It offers a new model of dialect classification, describes the sociolinguistic situation of Romani, examines its contribution to other languages and slangs, and discusses recent and current codification attempts as well as changes in function and status. The book provides an essential reference for anyone interested in this fascinating language.

YARON MATRAS is Senoir Lecturer in Linguistics at the University of Manchester. He as published numerous articles in academic journals on various aspects of language contact, linguistic typology, descriptive linguistics and sociolinguistics of Kurdish, Domari, Turkish, German dialects, and other languages. He has also published extensively on Romani including the monograph *Untersuchungen zu Grammatik und Diskurs des Romanes (Dialekt der Ke!deraša/Lovara)*, 1994.

Romani
A Linguistic Introduction

Yaron Matras
University of Manchester

CAMBRIDGE
UNIVERSITY PRESS

PUBLISHED BY THE PRESS SYNDICATE OF THE UNIVERSITY OF CAMBRIDGE
The Pitt Building, Trumpington Street, Cambridge, United Kingdom

CAMBRIDGE UNIVERSITY PRESS
The Edinburgh Building, Cambridge CB2 2RU, UK
40 West 20th Street, New York, NY 10011-4211, USA
477 Williamstown Road, Port Melbourne, VIC 3207, Australia
Ruiz de Alarcón 13, 28014 Madrid, Spain
Dock House, The Waterfront, Cape Town 8001, South Africa

http://www.cambridge.org

First published 2002

Printed in the United Kingdom at the University Press, Cambridge

Typeface Times 10/12 pt. *System* LaTeX 2_ε [TB]

A catalogue record for this book is available from the British Library

ISBN 0 521 63165 3 hardback

Contents

Figures

Tables

Acknowledgements

Several people accompanied and supported the emergence of this book. Pieter Muysken, Nigel Vincent, Peter Bakker, and Victor Friedman encouraged the idea of an introductory book on Romani, and backed my proposal. During the preparation of the manuscript I benefited from stimulating discussions with Viktor Elšík, through our collaboration on the project 'The morphosyntactic typology of European Romani dialects' at the University of Manchester. I am grateful to the Arts and Humanities Research Board, which provided a grant for this research project (1999–2000). Peter Bakker and Dieter Halwachs were a source of inspiration, helping with ideas and comments, sharing sources and materials, and often providing important moral support. The Faculty of Arts at the University of Manchester provided me with a research sabbatical from September 2000–January 2001 to complete the manuscript. In structuring certain parts of the book, I was inspired by Colin Masica's monumental work on *The Indo-Aryan Languages* (Cambridge University Press, 1991). Several students and research assistants contributed to the transcription of data, and to the compilation of some of the secondary data and bibliographical information: Christa Schubert, Ioanna Sitaridou, Beckie Sobell, Zoë Lewis, and Anthony Grant. Irene Sechidou and Sissie Theodosiou shared with me some of their unpublished fieldnotes on Romani dialects of Greece. I am especially grateful to Peter Bakker, Victor Friedman, Viktor Elšík, and Christa Schubert for their very helpful corrections, suggestions, and comments on an earlier version of the manuscript.

Abbreviations

ABL	ablative
ACC	accusative
AKT	aktionsart
ART	definite article
CAUS	causative
COMP	complementiser
COND	conditional
COP	copula
DAT	dative
DECL	declarative
F	feminine
FUT	future
GEN	genitive
OBL	oblique
INDEF	indefinite article
INSTR	instrumental
INTRANS	intransitive derivation
ITER	iterative
LOAN	loan verb adaptation marker
LOC	locative
M	masculine
MIA	Middle Indo-Aryan
NIA	New Indo-Aryan
NOM	nominative
OIA	Old Indo-Aryan
PERF	perfect
PFV	perfective
PL	plural
PRES	present
REFL	reflexive
REM	remote (tense)

SG	singular
SLASP	Slavic aspect
SUBJ	subjunctive
SUPER	superlative
TRANS	transitive derivation
JGLS	*Journal of the Gypsy Lore Society*
TURK	Turkish verb inflection

Dialect name abbreviations:

Ab	Abruzzian
Arl	Arli
AV	Agia Varvara
Boh	Bohemian
BR	Burgenland Roman
Brg	Bergitka Roma
Bsq	Basque
Bug	Bugurdži
Cr	Crimean
Erl	Sofia Erli
ES	East Slovak
Fin	Finnish
Grv	Gurvari
Gur	Gurbet
Hrv	Hravati/Croatian/Dolenjski/Sloveni/Istrian
Ib	Iberian (Spanish and Catalonian)
Ip	Ipeiros
Kal	Kalderaš/Kelderaš
Lat	Latvian/Estonian (Čuxni)
Lov	Lovari
LS	Lombard Sinti
M	Manuš
NR	North Russian (Xaladitka)
Pol	Polska Roma
Prl	Prilep
Prz	Prizren
PS	Piedmontese Sinti
Rmg	Romungro
Rum	Rumelian
Sep	Sepeči
Ser	Serres

Sin	German Sinti
Ukr	Ukrainian
VS	Venetian Sinti
W	Welsh Romani
WS	West Slovak
Xor	Italian Xoraxane

1 Introduction

The Rom are known to western culture as nomads and travellers (peripatetics, in anthropological terminology), while to southeastern European society they are familiar as the lowest and most stigmatised social stratum. Stereotypes also surround the image of *Romani*, which is often thought to be synonymous with argot, jargon, or a set of distinct and historically unrelated speech varieties, referred to as 'Gypsy languages'. While there is interface and even some overlap between Romani and argots, just as there is between the Rom and peripatetics, Romani is at its core a language like many others. The agenda of Romani linguistics is consequently similar to that of other fields of investigation in descriptive linguistics: it pursues questions relating to historical reconstruction and structural change, dialect diversification, discourse structure, language maintenance and loss, and more. This book sets out to introduce the structures of Romani and the current agenda of Romani linguistics; parts of it are also an attempt to introduce new ideas into the study of Romani.

Romani is the adjective (feminine singular) derived from *řom*, the historical self-designation of speakers of the language. As a language name, the adjective modifies *čhib* 'language', and so *řomani čhib* means 'language of the *řom*'. It is by far the most widespread term for the language in modern linguistics, and so the most practical cover-term for its various dialects. Speakers can be heard referring to their language as *řomani čhib*, *amari čhib* 'our language', *řomanes* lit. 'in a *rom* way', or by any one of several dozen group-specific names. For lack of any better cover-term for the population of speakers, I shall use the collective form *Rom* – avoiding both the integration into English plural inflection, and the adoption of the Romani plural *Roma* – regardless of individual group affiliation.

Romani-speaking populations are assumed to have settled in Byzantium sometime before the eleventh century (cf. Soulis 1961). References to 'Gypsies' or 'Egyptians' from the eleventh century are believed to relate to them, though we have no definitive evidence that those referred to were indeed Romani speakers. 'Gypsies' then appear in chronicles in other regions, allowing scholars to reconstruct an outwards migration from the Balkans beginning in the fourteenth century, and reaching northern and western Europe in the fifteenth century (Fraser 1992a). Although chronicle references during this period provide descriptions that match the general image and appearance of the Rom (dark-skinned, organised in family groups, pursuing itinerant trades and especially entertainment), no actual mention of the language is made, nor of their self-ascription. Documentation of the Romani language first appears in the form of wordlists in the early sixteenth century, by which time it is already very close to Romani as we know it today.

The earliest source on Romani is a list of 13 sentences with an English translation, published by Andrew Borde in 1542 under the heading *Egipt speche* (Miklosich 1874–8, IV; Crofton 1907). The State Archives in Groningen contain a manuscript by the magistrate Johan van Ewsum, who died in 1570, with 53 entries of Romani words and phrases accompanied by a Low German translation, under the heading *Clene Gijpta Sprake* (Kluyver 1910). In 1597, Bonaventura Vulcanius, professor in Leiden, printed a list of 53 Romani words with a Latin translation, entitled *De Nubianis erronibus, quos Itali Cingaros appellant, eorumque lingua* (Miklosich 1874–8, IV). The next known sample was collected in 1668 in the Balkans, in western Thrace, by Evliya Çelebi, and published in his well-known travel calendar *Seyāhat-nāme*. It refers to the people called *činganeler* or *qipṭīler*, and contains a brief wordlist and 21 short sentences in their language with a commentary and translation into Ottoman Turkish (Friedman and Dankoff 1991). Job Ludolf's wordlist appeared in Frankfurt in 1691, containing 38 items (Kluge 1901).

The eighteenth century hosted a lively discussion on Romani, and sources are already too numerous to list here. Law enforcement officers in western Europe took a close interest in the speech habits of travellers and minorities. In this context, it was established that Romani and argot (or 'thieves' jargon') were separate linguistic phenomena, and the two were kept apart in compilations such as the Waldheim Glossary of 1727 (reproduced in Kluge 1901: 185–90), the Rotwelsche Grammatik of 1755, and the Sulz List of 1787. In the late 1700s, an international circle of scholars[1] exchanged notes and ideas on Romani, eventually establishing its Indic (Indo-Aryan) origins by comparing it with other languages from around the world. Johann Rüdiger, professor in Halle, was the first to announce the sensational discovery, in April 1777.[2] He then published an article which contained the first grammatical sketch of a Romani dialect, along with systematic structural comparisons of the language with Hindustani (Rüdiger 1782; cf. Matras 1999a). Others followed with similar conclusions (Pallas 1781; Grellmann 1783; Marsden 1785; the latter based on Bryant's list from 1776, see Sampson 1910).

[1] Among them Christian Büttner, Hartwig Bacmeister, Peter Pallas, Johann Biester, and William Marsden; see Pott (1844: 7–16); also Ruch (1986), Matras (1999a).

[2] In his correspondence with his colleague Bacmeister of St Petersburg, though he gives credit to Büttner, who had come to a similar conclusion earlier (Rüdiger 1782: 62; see also Matras 1999a: 95–6; cf. also Ruch 1986: 119–23).

By the time August Pott compiled his comparative grammar and etymological dictionary of Romani (1844–5), he was able to draw on several dozen descriptive sources representing the diversity of European Romani dialects. Pott is usually referred to as the father of modern Romani linguistics, having established the historical and structural coherence of the language and having pointed out the layers of pre-European loan vocabulary, which in turn offered insights into the migration history of the Rom from India to Europe. His book remains the only monograph so far published that is devoted to a comparative and historical discussion of Romani as a whole. Pott's contribution was superseded a generation later, however, by a series of papers by Franz Miklosich (1872–80, 1874–8). This sixteen-part dialectological survey of the language includes a corpus of texts and songs recorded in various parts of Europe, and a comparative and historical grammar and lexicon. By comparing the dialects of Romani, and through the study of selected historical sources, Miklosich was able to reconstruct the migrations of the Rom within Europe, complementing Pott's enterprise.

Two additional landmarks dominate old-generation Romani linguistics. The first is the publication of the *Journal of the Gypsy Lore Society* (1888–; since 2000 under the name *Romani Studies*). However contested some of the social attitudes reflected in its earlier volumes may be, the *Journal* has, since its appearance, served as the principal discussion forum for scientific research on the Romani language as well as a source of data on Romani. The second landmark, closely connected with the *Journal*'s activities, was the appearance in 1926 of John Sampson's monumental grammar and etymological lexicon of the *Dialect of the Gypsies of Wales*, the westernmost variety of Romani, now considered extinct. Alongside these two enterprises, there are numerous other descriptive works from the late nineteenth and early twentieth century that continue to be important and reliable sources of information on the structures of Romani dialects.

Post-war Romani linguistics saw an extension of the research agenda to include issues of language contact and language use, as well as language status and language planning, much of it, during the 1970s and 1980s, embedded into the context of emerging Romani political and cultural activism. A major upsurge of interest in Romani began in the late 1980s and early 1990s, inspired and facilitated by the political transition in central and eastern Europe, where the bulk of the Romani-speaking population lives. The decade from 1990–2000 saw the publication of a large number of monographs, collections, and numerous articles. New fields of interest include grammar, discourse, and typology. During this period, the discipline benefited from funding from national research agencies and governments to promote Romani-related research, from extensive co-operation among specialists working in the field, and from the launch of the International Conferences on Romani Linguistics (first held in Hamburg in 1993).

Recent years have also seen the participation of an increasing number of native speakers of Romani in activities devoted to the study and promotion of their language. Still, the vast majority of linguists specialising in Romani are outsiders to the Romani community. They face the special ethical responsibilities of scholars investigating a society which has not been in a position to produce a scientific tradition of its own. In Europe and urban America, where fieldwork on Romani is typically carried out, such an extreme asymmetrical relationship between the community of investigators and the community that is being investigated is rather exceptional. Ethical responsibility means that one must be cautious of romanticising and of trying to exercise control, but also that one must not be tempted to patronise. Linguistics cannot undo social injustice, nor can it be expected to act primarily in order to promote the self-confidence of Romani communities. There is however a range of services which Romani linguistics can give to the community of speakers, including concrete support of language planning and language education measures. Descriptive linguistics can help replace stereotypical images with information, facts, and evidence.

2 Romani dialects: a brief overview

The present chapter provides a brief overview of the principal dialects of Romani that have been described in the linguistic literature, focusing in particular on the dialects that are cited in the following chapters. It does not pretend to offer a complete survey of dialect names or locations; for additional references to dialects of Romani see the list of dialects in Bakker and Matras (1997: xxiv–xxvi) and the dialect index in Elšík and Matras (2000: 229–32).

Speakers usually refer to their language as *romani čhib, romanes* 'Romani' or as *amari čhib* 'our language', or else derive the term from the individual group designation, using either a genitive compound – *lovarengi čhib* 'the language of the Lovara' – or an adverbial derivation – *sintitikes* 'the Sinti way (of speaking)'. In the descriptive literature, dialects are often referred to using either the group name in the plural – 'the *Xaladitka* dialect' –, or reinterpreting the name as a singular – *Bugurdži* lit. 'drill-maker', *Sinto* lit. 'a Sinto', *Arli* lit. 'settled person'. Terms for a single dialect may differ when two distinct groups speak dialects that are close enough to be considered one and the same by linguists. On the other hand, terms may overlap when two communities speaking distinct dialects share a name based on their religious affiliation, trade, or region of origin. In addition, internal designations used by groups often differ from external designations applied to them by other Romani-speaking populations.

There are several types of group names in Romani. A number of groups simply refer to themselves as *rom*, or use other specific ethnic designations such as *romaničel*, *kale*, *manuš*, *sinte* (cf. Wolf 1960a; see also chapter 3). This is the conservative pattern, and the one more widespread in western and northern Europe. In the Balkans and central-eastern Europe, group designations may be based on traditional trades, the actual terms being borrowed mainly from Turkish, Romanian, or Hungarian: *bugurdži* 'drill-makers' (Turkish *burgucu*), *sepeči* 'basket-weavers' (Turkish *sepetçi*), *kelderara/kelderaša* 'kettle-maker' (Romanian *căldărar*), *čurari* 'sieve-maker' (Romanian *ciurar*), *lovari* 'horse-dealer' (Hungarian *lo-v-* with a Romanian-derived agentive suffix), *ursari* 'bear-leader' (Romanian), and many more.

The distinction between itinerant Rom and settled Rom is highlighted in some group names (cf. Paspati 1870). A widespread term in the southern Balkans is *erli/arli* from Turkish *yerli* 'settled', used to denote mainly Muslim settled populations. Some groups associate themselves with the nation among which they have settled, often using a general term for non-Roma as an attribute: *gačkene sinte* 'German (< *gadžikane* 'non-Romani') Sinti, *xoraxane rom* 'Turkish/Muslim Rom' (< *xoraxaj/koraxaj* 'foreigner'). Many designations are more specific, denoting country of settlement – *polska roma* 'Polish Rom' –, the region of settlement – *bergitka roma* 'mountain Rom' (of the southern Polish highlands) – , the place of origin – *mačvaja* 'from the district of Mačva in Serbia (a group based in the United States, Russia, and Sweden) – or, as an external designation, the (often mistakenly) assumed origin – *romungri* 'Hungarian Rom' (Polish and Russian Rom as referred to by Lovara).

Since the following chapters refer to the structures of varieties of Romani as described by linguists, it seems preferable to repeat the terminology used by the individual authors. As a reference grid I shall be using in part the recent division into dialect groups, as outlined and employed in Bakker and Matras (1997), Bakker (1999), Elšík (2000b), Matras (2000a) and Boretzky (2001) (see also chapter 9).

We begin with the historical centre of Romani population diffusion, in the **Balkans**. The Romani dialects of the southern Balkans (Turkey, Greece, Bulgaria, Macedonia, Albania, Kosovo) are generally referred to as the 'Balkan' branch, which in turn is divided into two groups. The more conservative, southern group includes the Rumelian sedentary dialect described by Paspati (1870); the dialects of the Sepečides or basket-weavers of northern Greece and Turkey (Cech and Heinschink 1999); the dialects known as Arli or Arlije, which are spoken in Greece, Albania, Macedonia, and Kosovo (Boretzky 1996a), one of the major dialects of the region in terms of numbers and geographical distribution of speakers; the Erli dialect of Sofia, documented by Gilliat-Smith (1944, 1945; cf. Calvet 1982, Minkov 1997, Boretzky 1998a); the dialect of the Crimean Rom (Toropov 1994), which nowadays is spoken mainly in Kuban' and Georgia; the Ursari dialect spoken in Romania (Constantinescu 1878); and the dialects of Prilep (Macedonia), Prizren (Kosovo), and Serres (northern Greece), which are Arli-type but considered by Boretzky (1999b) as separate varieties. Recent work in Greece has documented additional dialects, some of them with very conservative features: the dialect of the *romacel* musicians, called *romacilikanes*, of the Ipeiros district (A. Theodosiou p.c.), an additional and distinct dialect of Serres (I. Sechidou p.c.), and the dialect of Pyrgos in the Peloponnese (N. Christodoulou p.c.). The conservative Balkan group also includes a number of closely related dialects spoken in northern Iran, which are clearly European dialects of Romani whose speakers migrated eastwards: the dialect of the Zargari in Azerbaijan (Windfuhr 1970), and the dialect called Romano in northeastern Iran (Djonedi 1996).

A second group within the Balkan dialects emerged in northeastern Bulgaria. They are referred to in the following as the **Drindari–Kalajdži–Bugurdži group**; Boretzky (2000b) has referred to them as Southern Balkan II. The group includes the dialect of the Drindari (also known as Čalgidžis or Kitadžis) of Kotel and Varna in northeastern Bulgaria (Gilliat-Smith 1914; also Kenrick 1967), the dialect of the Kalajdži tinners of Tatar Pazardžik, Bulgaria (Gilliat-Smith 1935), as well as what appear to be immigrant dialects in Macedonia and Kosovo, such as that descibed by Uhlik (1965) for Skopje, and the Bugurdži (or Rabadži) dialect described by Boretzky (1993a).

Both Balkan sub-groups are characterised by a continuous Greek influence that appears to have lasted longer than the Greek influence on dialects that left the southern Balkans, as well as by a strong Turkish influence. Many speakers of the Balkan dialects are Muslims, and many retain active knowledge of Turkish. Speakers of Arli varieties in particular, from Macedonia and Kosovo, are also found in western Europe, especially in Germany and Austria, where they settled as labour migrants or asylum seekers between the 1960s and 1990s, as well as in the United States.

Probably the most 'prominent' group of Romani dialects – in terms of numbers of speakers, geographical distribution, and the extent of documentation – is the **Vlax** branch. It is believed that Vlax emerged in Romanian-speaking territory. The dialects share extensive Romanian influence on vocabulary, phonology, and loan morphology, as well as a series of internal innovations. There were many migration waves of Vlax speakers from the Romanian principalities, some of them at least connected with the abolition of serfdom in Romania, which lasted until the second half of the nineteenth century. The branch is split into two groups.

The **Southern Vlax** dialects are documented mostly for migrant communities that have settled outside Romanian-speaking territory. The Southern Vlax dialects of Valachia/Muntenia (Constantinescu 1878) and of northeastern Bulgaria (Gilliat-Smith 1915) are closest to their original locations. Farther south, there are two divisions.

In the southeast, we find the Southern Vlax varieties of Greece. Some were spoken by Christian nomadic groups during the nineteenth century (cf. Paspati 1870). Others are spoken by Christian immigrants from Turkey who were resettled in the 1920s. These are known as Kalpazea, Filipidzía, and Xandurja. Large communities are reported in Dendropotamos near Thessaloniki (Tong 1983) and in Athens; the only thoroughly described variety is spoken in the district of Agia Varvara in Athens (Igla 1996).

In the southwest, we find dialects generally referred to in the literature as the 'Gurbet-type', based on the group name *gurbet* employed by some. Other names include *džambazi* and *das* 'Slavs'. Unlike the speakers of Balkan Romani dialects among whom they live, the Gurbet-type varieties are spoken mainly by Christians. Descriptions and documentations exist for Serbia and Bosnia (Ackerley 1941, Uhlik 1941 and elsewhere), Albania (Mann 1933, 1935), and Kosovo (Boretzky 1986). There are however also Muslim groups of speakers, such as the migrant group in Italy, which calls itself *xoraxane* ('Muslims') (Franzese 1986).

The **Northern Vlax** sub-branch includes two dialects on which we have fairly extensive documentation. The first is the dialect of the Kelderaš (or Kalderaš), which, alongside (Balkan) Ursari, is probably the most widely spoken Romani dialect in Romania. It has numerous sub-divisions, with names usually reflecting the very intact clan structure that exists among the group. An extensive text documentation and comments on grammar of the Bukovina dialects is included in Miklosich (1872–80, IV–V). Detailed grammatical descriptions of Kelderaš are based exclusively on migrant dialects: Gjerdman and Ljungberg (1963) for a variety spoken in Sweden, Boretzky (1994) for a dialect of Serbia, Hancock (1995a) for an American contact variety of Mačvaja (Serbian Northern Vlax) and Russian Kelderaš, and Matras (1994) for a contact variety of Lovari and Kelderaš originally from Transylvania, spoken in Poland, Germany, and Sweden. There are large communities of Russian Kelderaš speakers in Argentina and Brazil.

The second is the dialect of the Lovari, formed in Transylvania in contact with Hungarian. Lovari is now the main variety of Romani spoken in Hungary (e.g. Mészáros 1968). Lovari groups had already migrated into Austria and Germany in the nineteenth century (Ackerley 1932). Other communities have settled in Slovakia, Poland, Yugoslavia (Vojvodina), and Scandinavia. Descriptive outlines of Lovari include Pobożniak (1964) for southern Poland, and Cech and Heinschink (1998) for Austria. Recent collections of Lovari narratives are Gjerde (1994) for Norway, and Cech, Fennesz-Juhasz and Heinschink (1998) for Austria. There are other Northern Vlax dialects, such as Čurari, which are not very well described. A recent CD-collection of songs and narratives in various Vlax dialects of Hungary and Romania is available in Bari (1999; cf. also Bari 1990). A further dialect of Hungary, Cerhari (Mészáros 1976), represents a transitional variety, sharing a number of diagnostic features with both the (Northern) Vlax and the Central dialects. Also affiliated with the Vlax branch, but with some independent developments, are the dialects of southeastern Ukraine (Barannikov 1934).

The **Central** branch of Romani dialects is also divided into two groups. The **Northern Central** dialects include the now extinct Bohemian Romani (Puchmayer 1821), West Slovak Romani (von Sowa 1887), and East Slovak Romani (Hübschmannová et al. 1991). The latter is now the dominant variety in the Czech Republic, due to the massive immigration of eastern Slovak Roma to Bohemia in the late 1940s to early 1950s, and is the variety most widely used in text production in this country. Northern Central dialects are also spoken in southern Poland (Rozwadowski 1936, Kopernicki 1930), Moravia, and Transcarpathian Ukraine. The Northern Central dialects retain a layer of Hungarian influence.

The **Southern Central** dialects are sometimes referred to as the *-ahi* dialects due to their characteristic imperfect/pluperfect suffix. They are further sub-divided into two groups. The first, eastern, group is collectively known as Romungro ('Hungarian Rom'). In Hungary itself, Romungro is only spoken by a very small number of speakers, following a large-scale shift to Hungarian. Documentation includes Görög (1985). Other Romungro dialects are spoken in Slovakia (Elšík et al. 1999). The second, western, group is known as the Vend group, and includes dialects of western Hungary (Vekerdi 1984), the Prekmurje variety of northern Slovenia (Štrukelj 1980), as well as the Roman dialect spoken by the Rom in the Burgenland district of Austria (Halwachs 1998). All Southern Central dialects show considerable Hungarian influence. The Gurvari dialect of Hungary (Vekerdi 1971a) is a transitional variety which has absorbed many Vlax influences.

Several diverse dialect groups and individual varieties are sometimes referred to collectively as a **'Northern'** branch, although they are spoken not only in the north of Europe but also in the west and extreme south. 'Northern' will be used in the following chapters primarily in citation. Instead, the groups and isolated dialects will be referred to individually. In the centre of the so-called 'Northern' branch we find the closely related Sinti-Manuš varieties. They all share strong German influence and a number of innovations, and it seems that the group emerged in German-speaking territory, with sub-groups migrating to other regions. The first grammatical outline of a Romani dialect, by Rüdiger (1782), was devoted to a Sinti variety. There is extensive documentation of short texts and narratives in various German Sinti varieties, almost all from the pre-war period. Grammatical descriptions of German Sinti varieties include Liebich (1863), Finck (1903), and most recently Holzinger (1993, 1995). Closely related to German Sinti is the dialect of the Manuš of France (Jean 1970, Valet 1991). German Sinti varieties are also spoken in the Netherlands, Austria, as well as in Hungary (Vekerdi 1983), Bohemia, Slovakia, Russia, and Yugoslavia. There is in addition a southern branch of Sinti in northern Italy: the rather conservative Piedmontese Sinti (Franzese 1985), Lombard and Venetian Sinti (Soravia 1977), and the varieties of the Sinti Estrexarja or Austrian Sinti of South Tirol (Tauber 1999). It appears that *Manuš* and *Kale* are the older names used by the groups, whereas *Sinti* first appears in the eighteenth century (cf. Matras 1999a:108–12).

Related to Sinti is the Finnish dialect of Romani (Bourgeois 1911, Thesleff 1912, Valtonen 1972, van der Voort 1991, Koivisto 1994), which has only a very small number of speakers, perhaps just a few thousand. From historical records, and from the Swedish element in the dialect, it is clear that the Finnish

Rom or Kaale migrated via Sweden. The series of features that are shared with Sinti allows us to speak of a **Northwestern** group, with a historical centre in German-speaking territory. In the other Scandinavian countries, traces of Romani (apart from Vlax-speaking immigrant communities) remain only in the special vocabularies used by peripatetic populations (Etzler 1944, Iversen 1944, Johansson 1977). A dialect once spoken in northern Estonia by the Rom of Laiuse, or Lajenge Roma, now appears to be extinct (Ariste 1964), following the persecution and annihilation of most speakers under the Nazi occupation. While sharing some features with the neighbouring Baltic dialects, it has strong connections to Finnish Romani and the Northwestern group, including Swedish influences, which suggest that the dialect was once part of the Finnish sub-group.

A fairly coherent dialect branch is the Polish–Baltic–North Russian or **Northeastern** group. Best documented is the North Russian or Xaladitka dialect (Sergievskij 1931, Wentzel 1980). Closely related to this dialect is the dialect of central Poland, spoken by a group who refer to themselves as the Polska Roma (Matras 1999b). Latvian Romani, also known as the Čuxny dialect (a Russian term for Estonians) or as Lotfiko/Loftiko, is spoken by a small population in Lithuania and Latvia as well as in Estonia (Mānušs 1997; Kochanowski 1946). Little documentation exists on a further Baltic dialect, once spoken in eastern Latvia and Lithuania (Ariste 1964).

British Romani, an independent branch, is now considered extinct. The most thorough and extensive description is Sampson's (1926) monumental grammar of Welsh Romani or the Kååle dialect, which was still spoken by a number of families until the second half of the twentieth century (cf. Tipler 1957). English Romani appears to have become extinct towards the end of the nineteenth century, and survives only in the form of a special lexicon. Both forms of English Romani, termed the 'old' and the 'new' dialect, are described by Smart and Crofton (1875). It is possible that the oldest documentation of a Romani dialect by Borde in 1542 (see Miklosich 1874–8, IV; Crofton 1907) is based on British Romani.

Iberian Romani is also extinct, and survives only as a special lexicon in Spanish-based Caló (< *kalo* 'black'; Bakker 1995, Leigh 1998) and Basque-based Errumantxela (< *romaničel*; Ackerley 1929, Bakker 1991). Sources from the nineteenth century however allow us to reconstruct fragments of the variety of Romani that was spoken in Catalonia (Ackerley 1914).

Finally, there are two rather isolated groups of dialects. The first are the dialects of southern Italy–Abruzzian and Calabrian Romani (Soravia 1977) and Molisean Romani (Ascoli 1865). They are strongly influenced by Italian, and appear to be early offshoots of the Balkan dialects. The second is the Croatian dialect, for which there is no documentation from Croatia itself. Speakers of the dialect in Slovenia refer to themselves as Dolenjski Roma (i.e. from the lower province of central Slovenia), while a sub-group in Italy call themselves

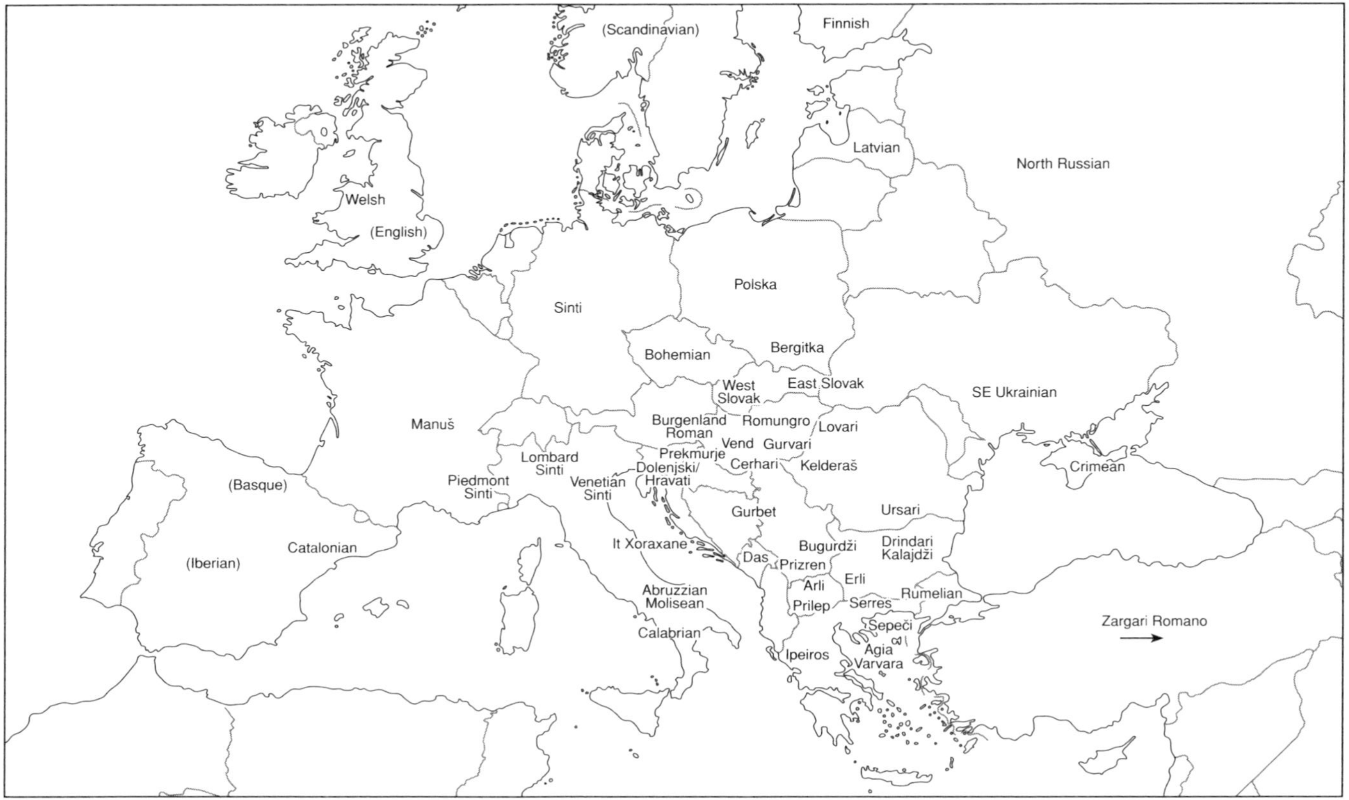

Figure 2.1 Location of the principal dialects of Romani

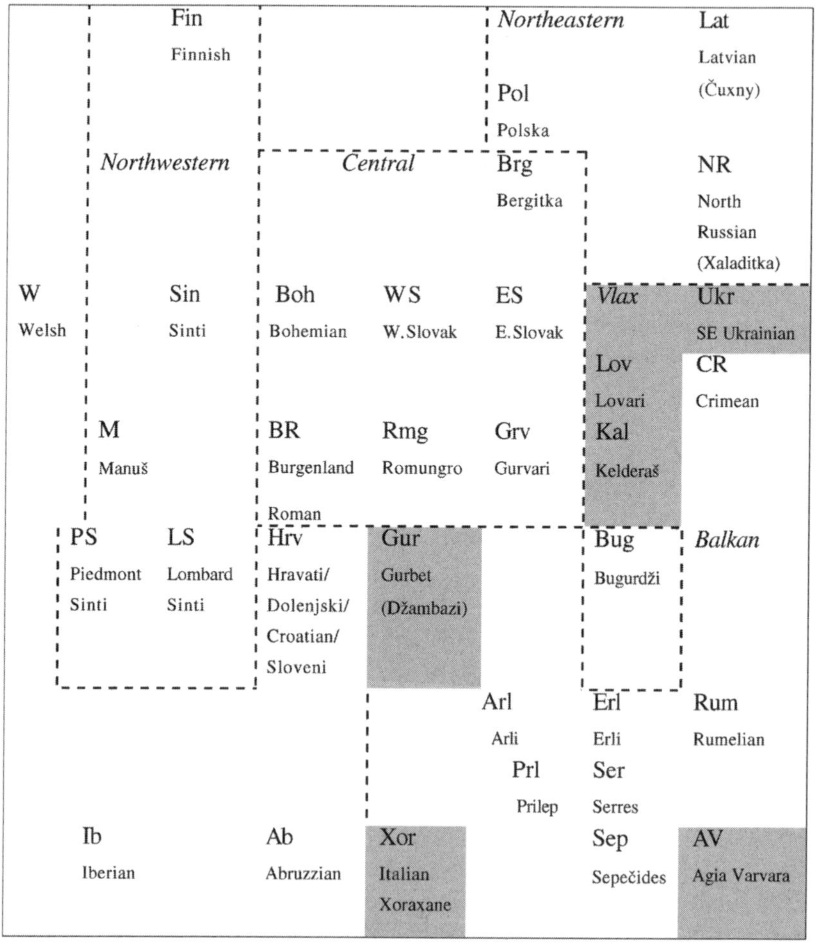

Figure 2.2 Abbreviations, abstract geographical position, and group affiliation of the principal dialects

Sloveni or Hravati/Havati, though their dialect has also been referred to as Istrian Romani (Cech and Heinschink 2001; Štrukelj 1980; Dick Zatta 1986, 1996; Soravia 1977). This dialect shows strong Croatian and Slovene influences. It also shares internal features with several distinct dialect groups which surround it geographically – Arli, Southern Central, and Sinti – making it a test case for dialect classification (see chapter 9).

Not included as dialects of Romani in this book are Domari, the language of the Near Eastern Dom (Matras 1999c, Macalister 1914), the special vocabularies of Near Eastern peripatetics that are based on Domari, or the special vocabulary of the Armenian Lom (Finck 1907). These are considered separate languages, and their historical ties with Romani will be dealt with in chapter 3.

In addition to dialects of Romani, we find the inclusion of extensive Romani vocabulary as well as some, mainly fossilised, grammatical structures, as a special lexicon in varieties of the majority language used mainly by communities with itinerant trades in various parts of Europe (so-called Angloromani, Scandoromani, Basque Romani, Caló in Spain, and more). These vocabularies have been widely discussed in the literature on Romani, as well as in connection with the secret languages employed by peripatetic communities, and with mixed languages or contact languages. In contemporary Romani linguistics the phenomenon is often referred to as **Para-Romani** (Cortiade 1991, Bakker and Van der Voort 1991, Matras 1998b). Para-Romani is dealt with in chapter 10, but occasional reference to individual features of Para-Romani vocabularies is made in the other chapters as well, since Para-Romani varieties sometimes allow us insights into the lexicon and phonology of dialects that are now extinct.

Figure 2.1 provides an overview of the locations of the principal dialects surveyed here and referred to in the following text. Some of the dialects, such as Kelderaš and Lovari, have large speaker populations outside the location in which they are assumed to have emerged and where they are positioned on the map. Dialects that are assumed to have emerged elsewhere but are only known from their present location, such as Gurbet, Das, Bugurdži, or Italian Xoraxane, are placed in the locations in which they are documented. In the case of some dialects, such as Arli in the Balkans, there is geographical overlap with neighbouring dialects; the position on the map reflects the location of the dialect dealt with in the sources consulted here.

Figure 2.2 gives a more abstract geographical display of a sample of the principal dialects, focusing on those that are taken into consideration in chapter 9 on dialect classification. The display of isoglosses in chapter 9 follows this type of representation, and employs the abbreviations introduced here.

3 Historical and linguistic origins

3.1 Theories on the origins of the Romani population

Although linguistic evidence has proved crucial in establishing India as the place of origin and in tracing early migration routes both within and outside India, it has generally not helped explain the reasons for the Romani migration or the social and ethnic background of the Rom's ancestral population. There is no known record of a migration from India to Europe in medieval times that can be connected indisputably with the ancestors of today's Romani-speaking population. Attempts to reconstruct the motivation for the westward migration have relied on piecing together loose descriptions of events that may have encouraged speakers of an Indo-Aryan language to migrate away from India and ultimately into Europe while retaining their ethnic and linguistic characteristics. That the discussion always had an emotional component can be seen already in the views taken by the two contemporaries Rüdiger (1782) and Grellmann (1783). Rüdiger, who sympathised with the Gypsies and regarded them as victims of society's oppression and prejudice (cf. Matras 1999a), suggested that their ancestors may have felt intimidated by invading armies and were forced to move away from their ancient homeland in times of social and political unrest. Grellmann, on the other hand, an advocate of enforced acculturation policies in Europe, who attributed the Gypsies' misery to their own refusal to integrate, argued for an origin in a population of Indian social outcasts, or Śudras. In some variation or other, both ideas continue to appear in present-day discussions.

Of central relevance to the discussion of Romani origins is the presence, since medieval times, of various populations of Indian origin outside of India, notably in the Near East and Central Asia. Like the Rom, they tend to specialise in peripatetic, service-providing economies, especially metalwork and entertainment. They are generally marginalised by the majority, mainstream or settled population, and their contacts with the latter are typically restricted to economic transactions. Some of these populations retain Indo-Aryan languages: the Dom, Karači, or Kurbati of the Near East (Syria, Palestine, Jordan, and in earlier times also Iraq, Iran and Azerbaijan) speak Domari (Pott 1846, Patkanoff

1907–8, Macalister 1914, Matras 1999c); the Parya of Tajikistan speak a form of Rajasthani (Oranskij 1977, Payne 1997); the Inku and Jat of Afghanistan also retain a Central Indian language (Rao 1995) as do the Ḍoma of the Hunza valley in northern Pakistan, who speak Ḍumāki (Lorimer 1939). Other populations of commercial nomads, from the Caucasus in the north and as far as Sudan in the south, have been reported to use secret vocabularies which consist either entirely or partly of Indo-Aryan lexical material. They include the Mıtrıp and Karaçi of Kurdistan (Benninghaus 1991), the Karači, Luti, and Kauli of Iran (Amanolahi and Norbeck 1975, Gobineau 1857) the Ghagar and Nawar of Egypt (Hanna 1993, Newbold 1856), the Bahlawān of Sudan (Streck 1996: 290–303), and the Poša or Lom of Armenia, whose speech is referred to as Lomavren (Finck 1907, Patkanoff 1907–8). This phenomenon suggests either loss of an ancestral Indo-Aryan community language and selective retention only of vocabulary, or else close contacts with speakers of Indo-Aryan languages that served as a source for secret lexical material. In either case we have evidence of well-established links between speakers of Indo-Aryan languages, and populations of commercial nomads outside of India.

It was Pott (1844: 42), following up on a suggestion by Hermann Brockhaus, who first drew attention to the possibility of a direct connection between the Rom and castes of commercial nomads in India itself. Pott cites the word *ḍombā*, which appears in medieval texts from Kashmir as a designation for members of a low caste of travelling musicians and dancers (see also Grierson 1888, Woolner 1913–14). The term *ḍom* continues to denote a caste-type affiliation in India today, and is used to refer to a variety of populations in different regions that specialise in various service-providing trades: smiths, basket-makers, cleaners of various kinds, including sweepers and corpse-burners, musicians, and dancers are among those cited most frequently (cf. Grierson 1922, XI: 143 ff.). The word *ḍom* is clearly an etymological cognate not only of the names *ḍom* (Hunza valley) and *dom* (Syria, Jordan, and Palestine), but also of *lom* (Armenia) and *řom* (Europe). Many of the groups broadly classifiable as commercial nomads of Indian origin also share a term for outsiders who are not part of the ethnic group: Romani *gadžo* 'non-Gypsy', Domari *kažža*, Lomavren *kača*. Grierson (1922, XI) notes cognate expressions in various languages of itinerant groups in India itself: Ḍom *kājwā*, Kanjari *kājarō*, Sasi *kajjā*, Nati *kājā*. The word is often found with the additional meaning 'settled' or 'farmer', reinforcing the impression of an historical self-identification as a non-sedentary group. This meaning led Pischel (1900) to derive it from Old Indo-Aryan (OIA) *gārhya* 'domestic', through Middle Indo-Aryan (MIA) **gajjha* (cf. Soravia 1988: 8). It has been suggested, mainly on the basis of their occupational profile and social status, but also because they are usually regarded by settled populations as 'dark-skinned', that the *ḍom* may be the descendants of Dravidian tribes from southern India who were absorbed into the Hindu caste system at a low and stigmatised level (cf. Woolner 1913–14; Grierson 1922, XI:5–11).

An early attestation of an Indian service-providing population migrating westwards, one which has received much attention in Romani studies, is the Persian poet Firdusi's *Šāhnāme* from the eleventh century. It includes the story of the Persian king Bahrām Gūr who, in or around 420 AD, invited a population of some 10,000 Indian musicians, called *luri*, to come to Persia and serve as official performers. After attempts to settle them failed, the Luri remained nomadic entertainers. The story receives confirmation in various Arabic and Persian chronicles, with at least one source, Ḥamza Iṣfahānī, pre-dating Firdusi (Grierson 1887). The immigration of various northern Indian populations to the Persian Gulf area during the reign of the very same Sassanide king Bahrām V is rather well described by Byzantine historians (cf. Wink 1990: 156). The Luri musicians have often been associated with the ancestors of the Rom, although no direct connection can be established. The name *luri* (also *luli* and *luti*) however surfaces in the self-appellations of various peripatetic communities in Iran, some of which are known to use secret lexicons containing Indo-Aryan vocabulary (cf. for example Amanolahi and Norbeck 1975).

The Dom hypothesis allows us to attribute the socio-ethnic profiles shared by groups like the *řom, lom, dom, luti*, or *kurbati* with the *ḍom* of India to ancient traditions, rather than view them as coincidental similarities or as features acquired by the respective groups separately in different places and at different times. It can also account for ethnonyms that are derived from caste names, some of them shared (*řom, dom, lom*), and for shared terms for outsiders, and it can furthermore accommodate westward migrations rather easily by allowing for repeated ventures by individual groups seeking employment opportunities in specialised trades. This has led some writers to take for granted a shared linguistic origin of the groups. Most outspoken in this respect were Sampson (1923, 1927), who regarded Romani, Domari, and Lomavren as derived from a single ancestral language, and Lesný (1941), who added Hunza valley Ḍumāki to the group. At the other end of the spectrum, linguistic differences have led Turner (1927) and later Hancock (1995, 1998) to express scepticism with regard to a common origin and history. What makes the Dom hypothesis attractive however is precisely the fact that it can explain similarities in social organisation and ethnic identity while allowing for linguistic diversity: Caste origin need not at all overlap with geographical or linguistic origin, beyond the mere fact that all the groups concerned come from India and speak Indo-Aryan languages. Thus the ancestors of the Rom, Dom, Lom and others may well have been a geographically dispersed and linguistically diverse population, sharing a socio-ethnic identity.

A further name that surfaces regularly in connection with commercial nomads of the Near East is *Jat* or in its Arabic form *Zuṭṭ*. These names are used with reference to various populations of Indian origin in the Arab world, at various times. They include Indian immigrant groups that appear in Persia, Mesopotamia, and Syria already in the fifth century, as well as slaves captured during Arab raids in the province Sindh in northwest India and deported to Iraq during the eighth and ninth centuries (Wink 1990: 156–73). *Jat* is the self-ascription of several groups of commercial nomads in Afghanistan (Rao 1995). *Zuṭṭ* is nowadays a derogatory term used by the Arabs, alongside *nawar*, to refer to the Dom of Syria, Jordan, and Palestine. The term is also found in Arab historical sources, denoting nomadic populations of Indian origin. It was also used by Ḥamza Iṣfahānī, writing in Arabic in the eleventh century, to refer to the descendants of Bahrām Gūr's Luri musicians (Grierson 1887). Bataillard (1875) consequently regarded the Jat as a tribe of nomadic musicians, and the Rom as their descendants, a view that has often been cited.

In a variation on the caste-origin hypothesis, de Goeje (1903, first published in 1875) viewed the Gypsies as a group of nomadic entertainers who had been camp-followers of the Jat or Zuṭṭ. The latter he regarded as a population of warriors originating from Sindh, who served in the Sassanide armies and were later resettled under the Arab 'Umāya dynasty in the seventh century. De Goeje refers to a twelfth-century text by the Arab historian Ṭabari, who describes the resettlement of a population of no less than 30,000 Zuṭṭ near the Byzantine border, to Syrian Ain Zarba, where they were taken prisoner during a Byzantine raid in the year 855. The date of the event and the size of the population, if at all accurate, might of course fit in quite nicely with the appearance of a Romani-speaking population of a significant size in Byzantium in the medieval period, to which the linguistic evidence testifies (see below).

A more direct link between early migrations and political unrest in medieval India as a result of the Islamic conquests was argued for by Pischel (1883). Carrying a similar argument yet further, activist scholars writing in the context of the Romani civil rights movement have more recently suggested that the Rom may in fact themselves be descendants of the warrior castes, or Rajputs, who resisted the Islamic invasions (see e.g. Kochanowski 1990, 1994, Hancock 2000; cf. discussion in Hancock 1988: 204). A connection has been suggested between the westwards migration of the ancestral Rom population and the defeat of the Rajputs in the battles against the Muslim Ghaznavid rulers based in Afghanistan in the twelfth century (see already Pischel 1883: 374). Rishi (cited in Soravia 1988: 8) even relates the word *gadžo* 'non-Gypsy' (and by interpretation 'stranger' and 'enemy') to the name of Maḥmūd of Ghazna, and Hancock (2000) adds to the proposed etymology from OIA *gārhya* 'domestic' the reading 'civilian', seeking a dichotomy between Rom as warriors and non-Rom civilians. The Rajput hypothesis creates, as Fraser (1992b: 143) points out, chronological difficulties: both historical records (cf. Soulis 1961) and linguistic evidence (notably a strong Greek element in all dialects of Romani) suggest that Romani presence in Byzantium began in the eleventh century at the latest; given the extent of Greek influence on the language, it must have lasted for a considerable period before the dispersal of individual Romani dialects across Europe from the thirteenth or fourteenth century onwards. It is furthermore generally accepted that the Persian and Armenian elements in Romani (see discussion below) testify to a prolonged presence of the Rom in the Near East prior to their migration to Byzantium. This, along with the lack of any significant Arabic influence on the language, could suggest an outward migration from India perhaps around the eighth or ninth century.

Kochanowski (1994) tries to resolve these chronological inconsistencies by proposing several waves of Indian migration, which met in Byzantium and converged there into a single population. In another attempt to reconcile a warrior origin, which Hancock (1988: 204) admits has a certain appeal to Gypsies themselves, with the social-economic characteristics of peripatetic Indian diaspora communities, Hancock (1991, 2000) proposes the following scenario: the Rajput population of mixed central Asian and Dravidian descent, accompanied by their camp followers of untouchable and low caste status, moved westwards into Persia as part of the military campaigns against Islam. Becoming more remote from their homeland, caste distinctions were then overcome and gave way to a shared Indian ethnic identity (see Kenrick 1993 for a somewhat similar view).

The question of how to reconstruct Romani origins and early migrations remains essentially a debate on how to interpret possible connections between linguistic features and socio-ethnic characteristics, such as traditional occupation profiles and ethnonyms. Inevitably, the issue touches on images and self-images of the populations concerned, and so it is likely to remain a point of controversy. Indisputable nonetheless is the century-old presence in the Near East of various populations of Indian origin – specialising in certain trades, retaining mobility, and preserving a distinct ethnic identity as well as linguistic features – prior to the appearance of the Rom in Byzantium, sometime around the eleventh century or earlier.

3.2 Proto-Romani and Early Romani

The dialects of Romani are characterised by a series of both conservativisms and innovations which set Romani as an entity apart from other New Indo-Aryan (NIA) languages, including other Indian diaspora languages such as Domari or Ḍumāki. The sum of the various developments that ultimately gave rise to the predecessor of all present-day dialects of (European) Romani will be referred to in the following chapters as **Proto-Romani**. The beginning of Proto-Romani is the point at which the language became sufficiently distinct from other related Indo-Aryan idioms to be classified as an entity in its own right. In the absence of any written records, this point is of course most difficult to locate in space and time. In order to reconstruct Proto-Romani we must therefore turn to older Indo-Aryan prototypes and their continuation into NIA, and compare them with their cognates in present-day dialects of Romani. We are not concerned here however with an attempt to provide a full hypothetical description of an ancient proto-language (but see Tálos 1999 on the phonology of what he calls 'Ancient Romani'). Proto-Romani is, rather, the sum of changes in the pre-European component of Romani. Some of those may have been shared with other languages of India, some perhaps with other Indo-Aryan diaspora languages such as Domari or the Lomavren vocabulary, while other changes are unique to the ancestor of present-day Romani dialects.

Proto-Romani forms are not directly attested, but may be derived from related present-day forms. We can reconstruct, for example, oblique demonstratives in M.SG **otas>oles* and F.SG **ota>ola*, despite the fact that *oles, ola* survive only in few dialects. This is possible on several grounds:(a) they appear in renewed demonstrative expressions such as *od-oles,od-ola*, (b) they survive in contracted forms in the oblique third-person pronouns *les, la*, and (c) they correspond to the Domari demonstratives M.SG *oras* and F.SG *ora* (cf. Matras 1999c), and of course (d) an Indo-Aryan demonstrative stem in *t-* is well attested, and the change of internal OIA /t/ to /l/ (in Domari to /r/) is regular. As a further example, Boretzky and Igla (1993: 14–15) reconstruct a process of reduction of OIA /a/ to a centralised vowel /*ʌ/ which later became decentralised to /e/, and hence a sound shift OIA *daśa* > Proto-Romani **dʌš* > Romani *deš* 'ten' (see also Tálos 1999: 218–19).

The developments which we refer to as 'Proto-Romani' are succeeded by an entity comprising structures for which we generally have wider attestation; I shall refer to this entity as **Early Romani**. Early Romani is characterised by the acquisition of productive Greek morphology used mainly in loanwords (so-called 'athematic grammar'), as well as through other structural innovations, some of them, such as the emergence of a preposed definite article, triggered through contact with Greek. It might be dated – though only tentatively, for lack of any written records – to the Byzantine period, from the tenth or eleventh century onwards. The period ends with the split into the predecessors of present-day dialects of the language, and their dispersal throughout Europe; historical accounts relating to Gypsies suggest that this took place from the thirteenth or fourteenth century onwards (see Fraser 1992a). Early Romani forms are archaic structures which we know existed, since they continue to survive today, though in some dialects they may have been lost or replaced; and they are structures which, we may assume, were shared by Romani as a whole just before the time of outwards migration from Byzantium and dispersal in Europe.

A likely example of an Early Romani structure is the demonstrative set in *adava/akava:* it is still attested, both in the westernmost Romani dialect of

Wales and in one of the easternmost dialects, Southern Balkan Arli. Various demonstrative sets which we find in other present-day dialects, such as *dava/kava* or *ada/aka*, can be explained as simplifications and reductions of the Early Romani forms. Others, such as *kado/kako*, are region-specific innovations (here: reduplication and adoption of adjectival inflection). In phonology, we may assume that the sound /ř/ as in *řom* 'Rom', which in many dialects has merged with /r/, reflects an Early Romani phoneme. Its phonetic quality is unknown, but it may either have been the uvular /ʀ/ that is still preserved today e.g. in Kelderaš, or perhaps the Proto-Romani retroflex /ḍ >*ḷ, *ṛ/ from which it is derived (cf. Indo-Aryan *ḍom*).

The fact that present-day Romani dialects shared structural features at various stages in their earlier development need not of course imply that Romani was entirely uniform, either in its Proto- or in its Early phase. One of the most challenging tasks facing comparative Romani dialectology today is to determine which elements of present-day variation within Romani might be traceable to variation within Early Romani, or indeed even Proto-Romani. On the other hand, a rather large inventory of forms and structures seems to have been carried over from the Early Romani period almost intact into the great majority of present-day dialects, and we shall refer to these forms as representing **Common Romani**. An example is the subjunctive complementiser *te*, a Common Romani form for which hardly any deviant cognates are found (Sinti and Sepeči *ti* being a marginal exception), or the word *oxto* 'eight' (< Greek *oxtó*), generally Common Romani, which in some dialects (Southern Central and Balkan) becomes *ofto* (either through regular sound change, or by analogy to *efta* 'seven').

In the following sections, and elsewhere in the book, I use Common Romani and reconstructed Early Romani forms when generalising about the occurrence of a lexical item, or when comparing the structures of Romani as a whole to those of genetically related languages. Naturally, the use of such notation runs the risk of simplifying dialectal variation somewhat, or perhaps even of creating the impression that some variants of the language are being preferred while others excluded. Variation, however, is dealt with in detail in the grammatical chapters. Common Romani and Early Romani notations seem a practical and convenient way to represent common points of departure in those sections of the text where shared origins and developments, and similarities, not differences, are in the foreground.

3.3 The Romani lexicon

3.3.1 *Core and inherited lexicon*

Romani dialects share an inherited lexicon, though its size appears to be small by comparison with other related non-literary languages (cf. Boretzky 1992a).

The Early Romani legacy amounts to around 1,000 lexical roots, beyond which Romani dialects each show various layers of lexical borrowings from individual European languages. The total number of pre-European lexical roots found in all dialects of Romani put together is estimated at around 800, though this number is rarely found in any single variety of the language. In addition, there are between 200 and 250 shared lexical roots of Greek origin. Of the 800 shared pre-European items, we find alongside the Indo-Aryan core around 70 Iranian and perhaps some 40 Armenian roots, as well as single items of various, in some cases unclear or controversial etymologies. The original Indo-Aryan component in the Romani lexicon thus amounts to somewhere between 650 and 700 roots, though figures may differ considerably for individual dialects. Vekerdi (1971b: 134) for instance claims that in Hungarian Lovari up to 80 roots of Indo-Aryan origin are missing, while Haarmann (1985: 68), basing his observations on Valtonen's (1972) dictionary of Finnish Romani, suggests a retention of only up to 450 Indo-Aryan roots.

Despite the successive layers of lexical borrowings, the **Indo-Aryan core** has remained the most significant component on which Romani dialects draw for basic vocabulary. Fraser (1992b) tests Swadesh's 100-item wordlist for three different dialect sources – Rumelian of Thrace (Paspati 1870), Welsh (Sampson 1926), and Kelderaš (Gjerdman and Ljungberg 1963) – and shows that between 15 and 20 items lack Indo-Aryan cognates in Romani. For Swadesh's longer list of 200 items, Boretzky (1992a) identifies between 33 and 37 that lack Indo-Aryan cognates in Romani (the fluctuation likewise reflecting different results for individual dialects).[1] The actual counting is distorted somewhat by the fact that some Romani roots may cover more than just one meaning given in the Swadesh list (e.g. *thulo* is used for both 'fat' and 'thick'), and that the entry 'with' corresponds in Romani to a grammatical ending (the instrumental case in *-sa*). One must also keep in mind some general problems of the list that help explain the absence of Indo-Aryan etymologies in Romani, such as the fact that distinct words for certain colours, specifically for 'blue' and 'yellow', are often missing from languages of the world, or that items such as 'because' or 'some' are in fact function words that are particularly prone to borrowing and so do not really belong in a list of basic vocabulary.

There are several possible interpretations of the notion of **inherited lexicon** in Romani. A broad view might include shared items of Byzantine Greek etymology, and so allow 'inherited' to correspond to the Early Romani period. There is some risk here of blurring or indeed even failing to identify distinctions between the shared Greek component that will have been acquired in

[1] Boretzky's (1992a) results for the 100-item list differ from Fraser's (1992b), and he only finds 8–9 items with no Indo-Aryan cognates. It appears that Boretzky was using a different version of the short list.

the Early Romani period (with gaps in individual present-day dialects resulting from partial loss of Greek-derived vocabulary in later periods), and Greek items acquired individually by dialects that had continuous contact with Greek. Boretzky (1992a) takes a narrower approach to the inherited lexicon, confining it strictly to the pre-European element. This is in line with the radical change in integration patterns of lexical loans that takes place during the Byzantine period, when portions of the Indo-Aryan nominal and verbal inflection cease to be productive and new loans are adapted with the help of borrowed Greek morphology (so-called 'athematic grammar').[2] Yet another possible reading of 'inherited lexicon', and one that will not be followed in the present discussion, is dialect specific, and pertains to the retention of lexical items from earlier contact languages to which speakers no longer have direct access, e.g. the retention of Romanian vocabulary in Vlax dialects outside Romanian-speaking territories, of Slavic vocabulary in western European varieties of Romani, or of German items in the Northeastern dialects. It was on the basis of these stable layers of European loans that Miklosich (1872–80) was able to reconstruct Romani migration routes across Europe that followed the Early Romani period (see chapter 9).

3.3.2 *Loan components in the inherited lexicon*

By far the largest loan component in the inherited Romani lexicon is the **Greek** layer. It is not entirely clear whether the Greek element is so strong simply because it is relatively recent and therefore well preserved, or whether the Greek impact was qualitatively more powerful, perhaps due to a longer period of contact. The fact that a transition from thematic (Indo-Aryan) to athematic (mainly Greek-derived) inflection productivity took place during the Byzantine period might point in the latter direction. The Greek lexical component includes up to 250 items, many of them basic semantic concepts such as *foro(s)* 'town' (Greek *fóros* 'market'), *drom* 'road' (Greek *drómos*), *zumin* 'soup' (Greek *zumí*), *kokalo* 'bone' (Greek *kókkalo*), *xoli* 'anger' (Greek *xolí*), *karfin* 'nail' (Greek *karfí*), *kurko* 'week' (Greek *kyriakí* 'Sunday'), *luludi* 'flower' (Greek *lulúdi*), *papu(s)* 'grandfather' (Greek *papús*), *skamin* 'chair' (Greek *skamní*), and more. Grammatical loans include adverbs and particles such as *pale* 'again' (Greek *pále*), *panda* 'more' (Greek *pánta* 'always'), *komi* 'still' (Greek *akómi*), *(v)orta* 'straight ahead' (Greek *orthá*), the numerals *efta* 'seven', *oxto* 'eight', and *enja* 'nine', and in many dialects all numerals above twenty. In addition to the lexical component, Greek has supplied a series of inflectional and derivational affixes which are applied to European-derived vocabulary of all declinable word classes: *-os*, *-o*, *-as*, and *-is* for the nominative of masculine nouns, *-a* for

[2] Arguably, Greek-derived grammatical inflection endings are also part of the inherited component of Romani, as they are shared by all dialects and were acquired before the dispersion of the dialects, i.e. in the Early Romani period (see chapters 5 and 6).

the nominative of feminine nouns, *-mos* PL *-mata* for abstract nouns, diminutive *-ici*, adjective derivation *-itiko* > *-icko*, *-to* for ordinals, *-is-*, *-in-*, and *-iz-* for verb derivation (loan root adaptation), *-(i)men* for participles, and more (see discussion in chapter 8). Many syntactic phenomena are equally attributable to Greek impact, most notably the emergence of pre-posed definite articles in Romani.

Iranian items in Romani are in part difficult to distinguish from cognates shared by Indo-Iranian as a whole. Precise etymologies are further obscured by the similarities among the Iranian languages. Persian cognates may be found for most items that are identified as Iranian, but Kurdish and Ossetian etymologies have also been proposed; at least for some items uncertainties as to the exact source remain (cf. Boretzky and Igla 1994b: 329–32, Hancock 1995b). There are of course several additional Iranian languages that could have contributed to Romani, given their geographical position, but which so far have not found any extensive consideration in the literature, among them Baluchi, Pashto, Luri, and others. A thorough investigation of the Iranian element in Romani from an Iranist's point of view is still missing.

Among the accepted Persian etymologies are *ambrol* 'pear' (Persian *amrūd*), *res-* 'to arrive' (Persian *ras-īdan*), *avgin* 'honey' (Persian *angubīn*), *diz* 'fortress, town' (Persian *diz*), *pošom* 'wool' (Persian *pašm*), and more. Items that offer both Iranian and Indo-Aryan etymologies include *kirmo* 'worm' (Persian *kirm*, OIA *kṛmi-*), *xer* 'donkey' (Persian *xar*, OIA *khara-*), *angušt* 'finger' (Persian *angušt*, OIA *anguṣṭha-*), and *bi-* 'without' (Persian *bī*, OIA *vi-*). Shared by Persian and Kurdish are among others *zor* 'strength', *tover* 'axe', *baxt* 'luck', *sir* 'garlic', and *xulaj* 'lord'. Hancock (1995b) lists as many as 119 items for which he suggests possible Iranian cognates. Some of these however are clearly Balkanisms whose immediate source is Turkish (e.g. *dušmano* 'enemy'),[3] for others an OIA etymology is straightforward (e.g. *džamutro* 'brother-in-law', OIA *jāmātr-; anav* 'name', OIA *nāma-; xa-* 'to eat', OIA *khāda-*).

The second largest contingent of pre-European loans comes from **Armenian.** They include a number of rather basic vocabulary items such as *bov* 'oven' (Armenian *bov*), *grast* 'horse' (Armenian *grast*), *kotor* 'piece' (Armenian *kotor*), *pativ* 'honour' (Armenian *patiw*), and *xanamik* 'co-parent-in-law' (Armenian *xənami*). Boretzky (1995a) maintains therefore that the ancestors of the Rom must have spent a certain period under the predominant influence of Armenian, and further that the inventory of Armenian-derived loans in contemporary Romani represents merely the remnants of a once much more extensive Armenian component. Some 20 items have so far been identified with certainty as Armenian. Hancock (1987) lists altogether 34 items, Boretzky and Igla (1994b) give approximately 40, and Boretzky (1995a) discusses altogether 51 items with possible Armenian connections. Many items for which an

[3] This particular word is identifiable as a European loan on the basis of its Greek-derived inflection as well as stress placement *(dušmán-o)*.

Armenian etymology has been suggested are in fact shared with Iranian, for example *arčič* 'tin' (Armenian *arčič*, Persian *arziz*), *mom* 'wax' (Armenian *mom*, Persian *mōm*). Similarly, there are shared items among the forms for which Iranian etymologies have been suggested, such as *zor* 'strength' (Persian *zōr*, Armenian *zor*), or *tover* 'axe' (Persian *tabar*, Kurdish *tavar*, Armenian *tapar*).

Boretzky (1995a) attributes the indefinite *či* to Armenian *čhi*, and the indefinite *čimoni* 'something' to *či*+Armenian *imən* 'something' (but see chapter 5 for an alternative explanation, based on Elšík 2000c). One must note however that *či* is widespread in the region (cf. Persian *ču*, Kurdish *čü* 'nothing', Modern Aramaic *ču-mindi* 'nothing'). A further grammatical borrowing from Armenian according to Boretzky (1995a) is the suffix *-eni*, which gives Romani *-in*, a derivational suffix forming the names of fruit trees (*ambrol* 'pear' > *ambrolin* 'peartree'). Boretzky also derives the nominal suffix *-ik* in Romani (*pošik* 'dust', alongside *poš*) from the Armenian diminutive; though here too we have a parallel in the Kurdish diminutive (*kurr-ik* 'boy', *keç-ik* 'girl').

Finally, there is an assembly of pre-European loans for which various etymologies have been suggested. A number of items have been identified as **Ossetian**, among them *vurdon* 'wagon' (Ossetian *wærdon*), and *orde* 'here' (Ossetian *ortä*). **Georgian** etymologies include *khilav* 'plum' (Georgian *khliavi*), and *čamčali* 'eyelash' (Georgian *çamçami*; cf. Friedman 1988). Berger (1959) suggests a number of **Burushaski** loans, among them *cer-d-* 'to pull' (Burushaski *car et-*).[4] Many etymologies proposed in the literature remain controversial (see for instance Tálos 1999), while a number of lexical items still lack a satisfactory derivation. Among the pre-European loans with unclear etymologies Boretzky (1992b) cites *ažuker-* 'to wait', *balamo* 'Greek', *džungalo* 'ugly', *ser- pe* 'to remember', *purum* 'onion', and more.

The historical and geographical settings in which pre-European loans were acquired are not entirely clear, either. The Iranian and Armenian components in the inherited Romani lexicon were first pointed out by Pott (1844–5) and later by Miklosich (1872–80). Both agreed that they represent layers acquired successively in time, and so also successively in geographical space. The mainstream view in Romani linguistics, relying on the present-day geographical location of Persian and Armenian, has since been that these successive

[4] Others are less convincing: *ciro* 'time' from Burushaski *cir* 'instance', is usually accepted as Greek *xairo* (but see Tálos 1999: 255 for an Indo-Aryan etymology); *kašuko* 'deaf' from Bur. *karútu* is given by Boretzky and Igla (1994b: 137) as *kan-šuko* 'dry-ear'; *xev* 'hole' from Bur. *qam* assumes the sound changes *q>kh>x*, *-m>-v*, and *a>e*, which would make this a very early loan, while Boretzky and Igla (1994b: 115) suggest OIA *kheya-* 'ditch' or alternatively Persian *xāvi* (the latter however is unlikely, since it is an Arabism); *dzi* 'soul' from Bur. *ǰi* is a contraction of *odzi, odži, ogi* and more likely to be Armenian *ogi*; *sapano* 'wet' from Bur. *hayum* is less attractive than Tálos's (1999: 251) OIA **sāpya-* as a variant of *āpya-* 'wet' (but Boretzky and Igla 1994b: 255 suggest *sap* 'snake' through 'slippery'); *gadžo* 'non-Rom' from *khǎjuná* 'external name for the Burušo' is likely to overestimate the importance of the Burušo in early Romani history.

layers reflect pre-European migration routes. But modern Romani linguistics has often failed to take into account the strong Greek and Armenian presence in Anatolia in previous centuries. Elsewhere (Matras 1996b) I have suggested that the Persian, Kurdish, Armenian, and indeed even the earlier Greek components could in principle have been acquired in close geographical proximity to one another, namely in eastern and central Anatolia. The Iranian and Armenian cognates referred to above might support such a theory.

The lack of Arabic influence in Romani – isolated items such as *dzet* 'oil' (Arabic *zēt* 'olive oil') can be explained as borrowings via Persian or Armenian – has generally been regarded as evidence either for an early migration preceding the Islamic conquests, or for a northern migration route through the Pamir, south of the Caspian Sea, through the Caucasus, along the southern Black Sea coast, and on toward Constantinople. A northern migration route receives support from the few items of Georgian and Ossetian origin, though one cannot entirely dismiss the possibility that these isolated loans were not actually acquired in situ but transmitted via other sources. Keeping in mind the significant non-Muslim (mainly Christian, but also Yezidi and Jewish) presence in eastern and central Anatolia until well into the twentieth century, and the fact that Anatolia was an integral part of Greek-speaking Byzantium, the northern route may well have led not westwards along the Black Sea coast, but south, to eastern Anatolia. There, Romani will have been subjected neither to Arabic nor, at the time, to Turkish influence.

3.3.3 *Semantic domains of the inherited lexicon*

A brief characterisation of the semantics covered by the inherited lexicon is of interest, especially since we are dealing with a comparatively small inventory of shared lexical items. We begin with items that relate to **human beings**. A striking feature of Romani is its consistent distinction between Rom and non-Rom. Terms for persons of Romani origin are used both for general reference, and as kinship designations: *rom* 'man, husband', *romni* 'woman, wife', *čhavo* 'boy, son', *čhaj* 'girl, daughter'. For persons of non-Romani origin we have *gadžo* 'man', *gadži* 'woman', *raklo* 'boy', *rakli* 'girl'. Ethnicity-neutral terms also exist: *manuš* 'person, man' and *manušni* 'person, woman' stress humankind-affiliation, while *murš* 'man', and *džuvli* 'woman' generally emphasise gender, and *dženo* 'person', *džene* 'people' usually refer to persons whose identity remains unspecified.

The system of **kinship terms** generally shows Indo-Aryan forms for consanguines that are first-level kin of the same generation (*phen* 'sister', *phral* 'brother'), for first-level and lateral kin one generation older *(dad* 'father', *daj* 'mother'; *kak* 'uncle', *bibi* 'aunt', the latter two are possibly Iranian loans), and for first-level kin one generation younger (*čhavo* 'son', *čhaj* 'daughter').

First-level kin two generations older are Greek loans (*mami* 'grandmother', *papu(s)* 'grandfather'). All other terms, notably those designating cousins, nephews, and grandchildren (same-generation lateral kin, one-generation younger lateral kin, and two-generation younger first-level kin), are European loans that differ among individual dialects. The rate of retention thus gives preference in the first instance to first-level over lateral kin, then to older over younger generation, and finally to proximate over remote generation. Significantly, there is a high rate of retention of pre-European vocabulary in the domain of affinal kin terminology. We find the Indo-Aryan forms *rom* 'husband', *romni* 'wife', *salo* 'brother-in-law', *sali* 'sister-in-law', *džamutro* 'brother/son-in-law', and *bori* 'sister/daughter-in-law, bride' (possibly an Iranian loan), *sastro* 'father-in-law', *sasuj* 'mother-in-law', and the Armenian loan *xanamik* 'co-parent-in-law'. Terms for lateral relations often co-exist alongside European loans. The word for 'marriage' is Indo-Aryan *(bijav)*, but 'family' is a European loan.

The system of terms for **nations** is of mixed etymology. Self-ascription may be layered: *rom* is widespread as a cover-ethnonym, and agrees with the name of the language *romani čhib.* Group-specific terms frequently follow geographical locations (in the Romani dialects of central Europe, the Baltics, and the Balkans), religion, and occupation (Romani dialects in the Balkans). Mainly in the west we also find the inherited self-ascription terms *manuš* ('person') in Germany and France, *kalo* ('black') in Iberia, Germany, Britain, and Finland, and *romaničal (romani* with a second component of unclear etymology) in Britain, the Basque country, Sweden, Finland, France, as well as *romacel* in the Greek district of Ipeiros. Characteristic of Romani is – alongside replications of nations' self-ascription (e.g. *sasitko* 'German', *njamco* 'German', *valšo* 'French') – the widespread use of inherited or internal names for nations. Thus we find *das* 'Slavs' (cf. OIA *dāsa-* 'slave'), a word play based on Greek *sklavos*; *xoraxaj/koraxaj* of unclear etymology, in the Balkans generally 'Muslim, Turk' and elsewhere 'foreigner' or 'non-Rom'; *gadžo* 'non-Rom' (see above). Other inherited words for non-Rom include *xalo* ('meagre, shabby'), also in the diminutive *xaloro* 'Jew', *balamo* and *goro* 'Greek, non-Gypsy'; *biboldo* 'Jew' ('unbaptised'), *čhindo* 'Jew' ('cut' = 'circumcised'), *trušulo* 'Christian' (cf. *trušul* 'cross'), *džut* 'Jew' (possibly Iranian). Names attached to foreign countries by individual Romani groups often refer to incomprehensible speech, based on either *lal-* 'dumb' or *čhib* 'tongue' (cf. Wolf 1958): *lallaro-temmen* 'Finland' and *lalero them* 'Bohemia' (= 'dumb land'), *lalero* 'Lithuanian', *čibalo/čivalo* meaning 'Albania' among Balkan Rom, 'Bavaria' among German Rom, and 'Germany' among Yugoslav Rom. More recently, *barvale thema* (lit. 'rich countries') has emerged as a designation for 'western Europe', *lole thema* (lit. 'red countries') for 'eastern, communist Europe'.

Internal creations of place names are common mostly among the northwestern dialects of Romani (cf. Liebich 1863: 90–2, Wagner 1937, Wolf 1958, and see also Matras 1998b: 17). They are frequently either translations, or semantic or sound associations based on the original place names: *nevo foro* lit. 'new town' for 'Neustadt', *xačerdino them* lit. 'burned country' for 'Brandenburg', *čovaxanjakro them* lit. 'witches' country' for 'Hessen' (German *Hexen* 'witches'), *kiralengro them* lit. 'cheese country' for 'Switzerland', *u baro rašaj* lit. 'the big priest' for 'Rome', *lulo piro* lit. 'red foot' for 'Redford', *baro foro* lit. 'big town' for capital cities of various countries (Helsinki, Stockholm, Belgrade).

There are few inherited words for **occupations and functions**. Semantically adapted Indo-Aryan etymons stand out for *rašaj* 'priest' (OIA *ṛṣi-* 'chanter of hymns'), and *raj* 'non-Romani official' (OIA *rāja-* 'king'). Among the few others are *lubni* 'prostitute', *lurdo* 'soldier', and the pre-European loans *xulaj* 'landowner' (Iranian *xuda/xula* 'Lord, God'), and *thagar* 'king' (Armenian *thagavor).* There is however a rich internal terminology for 'police(man)', including *klisto* (< 'mounted'), *xalado* (<'washed, tidy'), *čingalo* (<'quarrelsome'), *phuralja* (<'bothersome').

A strong Indo-Aryan presence in the lexicon is found in the domain of **body parts and bodily functions**. It covers most parts of the body, e.g. *šero* 'head', *bal* 'hair', *jakh* 'eye', *muj* 'face/mouth', *(v)ušt* 'lip', *nakh* 'nose', *kan* 'ear', *vast* 'hand/arm', *(an)gušt* 'finger', *peř* 'stomach', *pindřo* 'foot/leg' (cf. Boretzky 1992a; but see Haarmann 1985 for a discussion of European loans in this domain) – a rare loan being the superordinate 'bone' (Greek *kokalo)* – as well as body-related activities such as *sov-* 'to sleep', *xa-* 'to eat', *pi-* 'to drink', *mer-* 'to die', *xas-* 'to cough', and what might be classified as physical and mental states and conditions: *bokh* 'hunger', *dar, traš* 'fear', *ladž* 'shame', *doš* 'guilt', *dukh* 'pain', *truš* 'thirst', *khino* 'tired', *mato* 'drunk', *nasvalo* 'ill', *thulo* 'fat', *rov-* 'to cry', *as-* 'to laugh', *džan-* 'to know', *bistr-* 'to forget'. Rather mixed is the pre-European lexicon for **religious–spiritual** concepts. We find *devel* 'god' (OIA *devatā), beng* 'devil', *trušul* 'cross' (adaptation of OIA *triśūla* 'trident'), *rašaj* 'priest' (an adaptation of OIA *ṛṣi-* 'chanter of hymns'), *patradži* 'Easter' (of unclear etymology, possibly *patrin* 'leaf' + *dives* 'day'), *drabar-* 'to tell fortunes' (from *drab* 'medicine'), *arman* 'curse', and the pre-European loans *bezex* 'sin' (Persian *bazah* 'guilt'), *baxt* 'luck' (Persian *baxt), čovexano/ čovexani* 'ghost/ witch' (Armenian *čivag).* Of unclear etymology are *khangeri* 'church', and *kirvo* 'godfather, godson', while *kris* 'Romani court' is Greek *krísi* 'verdict'.

In the area of **nature**, **landscape**, **and time**, Indo-Aryan etymons dominate the terms denoting weather conditions (*kham* 'sun', *balval* 'wind', *iv* 'snow', *brišind* 'rain', *šil* 'cold', *tato* 'warm'), while basic landscape concepts are mixed: from Indo-Aryan we find *jag* 'fire', *pani* 'water', *kišaj* 'sand', *phuv* 'earth', *len* 'river', *bar* 'stone', *rukh, kašt* 'tree', *poš* 'dust'; alongside *veš* 'forest' (possibly Persian), *dorjav* 'river, sea' (Persian *daryā), paho* 'ice' (Greek *páɣos*). Time expressions include Indo-Aryan *ivend* 'winter', *nilaj* 'summer', *dives* 'day', *rat* 'night', *berš* 'year', *masek* 'month', but *kurko* 'week' (Greek *kyriakí* 'Sunday'), *ciros* 'time' (Greek *kairós*), *paraštuj* 'Friday' (Greek *paraskeví*), *tasja* 'tomorrow' (Greek *taxiá*). Various studies have pointed out the paucity of inherited words for **animals and plants**. Indo-Aryan words for domesticated animals include *guruv* 'ox', *guruvni* 'cow', *bakro* 'sheep', *buzno* 'goat', *balo* 'pig', *džukel* 'dog', *khajni* 'chicken', while pre-European loans appear for *grast* 'horse', *grasni* 'mare' (Armenian *grast*), *rikono* 'dog' (Armenian *koriwn*), *papin* 'goose' (Greek *papí*). There are even fewer inherited words for wild animals and insects: *ruv* 'wolf', *rič̌h* 'bear', *mačho* 'fish', *šošoj* 'hare', *čiriklo* 'bird', *sap* 'snake', *džuv* 'louse', *pišom* 'flea'. For plants only some rather basic and general terms appear, such as *rukh* 'tree', *kašt* 'wood', *kandřo* 'thorn', *patrin* 'leaf', *akhor* 'walnut', *khas* 'hay', *čar* 'grass', while the cover-term *luludi* 'flower' is Greek. Indo-Aryan forms appear also for basic foods: *mas* 'meat', *mandřo* 'bread', *thud* 'milk', *ařo* 'flour', *andřo* 'egg', *khil* 'butter', *goj* 'sausage', *lon* 'salt', *kiral* 'cheese', *mol* 'wine', *drakh* 'grape', *džov* 'barley', *giv* 'wheat', and more.

Terms for **dwellings and places** are poorly represented in the inherited lexicon. Only the very basic are Indo-Aryan – *kher* 'house', *gav* 'village', *than* 'place', *mal* 'field'– with few pre-Europen additions like *diz* 'town' (Persian *diz* 'fortress'), *foro(s)* 'town' (Greek *fóros* 'market'), *them* 'land' (Armenian *them* 'district', possibly from Greek), *drom* 'road' (Greek *drómos*). The domain of **tools and artefacts** also relies heavily on pre-European loans. Alongside Indo-Aryan *čhuri* 'knife', *roj* 'spoon', *xandřo* 'sword', *suv* 'needle', *kangli* 'comb', *lil* 'paper, letter, book', *love* 'money', *sastri* 'iron', *sumnakaj* 'gold', *rup* 'silver', *čaro*, 'bowl', *moxto* 'box', *khoro* 'pitcher', *gono* 'sack', *gad* 'shirt', we find'*angrusti* 'ring' (Persian *anguštarī*), *desto* 'handle' (Persian *daste*), *mom* 'wax' (Persian *mōm*), *poxtan* 'cloth' (Persian *paxte*), *pošom* 'wool' (Persian *pašm*), *taxtaj* 'glass' (Persian *tašt*), *tover* 'axe' (Kurdish *tavar*), *vordon* 'wagon' (Ossetian *wærdon*), *zen* 'saddle' (Persian *zēn*), *avsin* 'steel' (Kurdish *avsin*), *arčič* 'tin, lead' (Armenian *arčič*), *bov* 'oven' (Armenian *bov*), *karfin* 'nail' (Greek *karfi*), *klidi* 'key' (Greek *kleidí*), *petalo* 'horseshoe' (Greek *pétalo*), *skamin* 'chair' (Greek *skamní*).

Finally, Indo-Aryan **numerals** cover *jekh* 'one', *duj* 'two', *trin* 'three', *štar* 'four', *pandž* 'five', *deš* 'ten', *biš* 'twenty', *šel* 'hundred', with *šov* 'six' being a possible Dardic loan (cf. Kashmiri *śeh*, Shina *ša*, Gawar-Bati *šo*, Maiya *šoh* < OIA *ṣáṭ*; see Turner 1926: 174). All Romani dialects have Greek-derived items for *efta* 'seven', *oxto* 'eight', *enja* 'nine'. Numerals between ten and twenty are combinations (lit. 'ten-and-X', with various expressions for 'and'). Numerals between twenty and one-hundred are either internal combinations, such as *trin-var-deš* lit. 'three-times-ten' for 'thirty' etc., or Greek borrowings (*trianda* 'thirty', *saranda* 'forty', etc.), or, in some cases, European loans (cf. section 8.2.2).

We are left with the question whether the semantic structure of the inherited lexicon has any significance for attempts to reconstruct ancestral Romani culture. The expectation that the composition of the ancient lexicon should reflect an ancient habitat, ancient traditions, or forms of social organisation is a working hypothesis borrowed from traditional Indo-European studies; but it is not one that is necessarily valid in our context, as can be seen from the contrasting interpretations that are sometimes given to the lexical data. The division between Rom and non-Rom in terms referring to human beings, for instance, is sometimes interpreted as reflecting the prominence of the opposites purity vs. pollution, preserved in the culture of some Romani groups. But while some connect this with the Hindu caste system (cf. Hancock 1991), others regard it in the more specific context of peripatetic cultures (Sutherland 1975: 258–61). As another example, kinship terminology is generally expected to reflect the system of social obligations in the family (see e.g. Sutherland 1975: 139–80). Cohn (1969) regards the practice of bride-price as the key to understanding the system of Romani kin terminology. Thus *bori*, both 'sister-in-law' and 'daughter-in-law', is viewed as having the basic meaning of 'woman acquired through marriage', with the male *džamutro* 'brother/son-in-law' merely mirroring the same concept. Cohn also explains the survival of the pre-European *xanamik* 'co-parent-in-law' (of Armenian origin) in terms of the procedures of negotiating bride-price, in which would-be co-parents-in-law play the key role. But on the whole it can be said that Romani follows universals in its replacement of kin terminology through more recent loans, with proximity at the level of genealogical relationship and generation correlating with term stability. Other lexical universals are reflected in the retention of terms for body parts, and of the basic numerals one to five and ten.

The use of internal names for nations, as well as the creation of internal place names, might on the other hand be regarded as a reflection of a cryptolectal or secretive function of Romani. This is reinforced by the presence of multiple names for 'police', typical of the lexicon of marginalised minorities. The very dialects that show an overwhelming tendency to use cryptolectal place names, notably the western European dialects of Romani, are also those that often prefer internal derivations of inherited nouns (e.g. *pimaskri* 'cigarette' from *pi-* 'to drink') over loans, perhaps another indication of the function of these dialects as secret languages (cf. Matras 1998b, and see chapter 10). Controversial is the position of terms for agriculture, wildlife, tools, and artefacts. It has been argued that the paucity of Indo-Aryan vocabulary in particular domains testifies to the lack of the respective notions in the ancestral, pre-migration culture of the Rom. Hancock (1992: 39, 2000) for example argues against a specialisation in handicraft and service economies before the migration out of India, referring to the lack of Indo-Aryan words for smithery, metals, and tools, while Vekerdi (1981: 250) adds to these the relatively small number of Indo-Aryan terms for agricultural products and the lack of Indo-Aryan terms for agricultural tools or processes (such as 'to plough' or 'to plant'), and concludes from this that the ancestors of the Rom were dependent on the producing society from which they received food in return for services, without having a structured economy of their own.

While culture-related hypotheses are diverse and often contradictory, what is clearly reflected in the Romani lexicon is a century-old multilingual reality: borrowings generally reflect the domains of activities which typically involve contact with the surrounding majority-language community. Lexical retention, on the other hand, is more typical of the intimate spheres of interaction that remain the domain of the family. We might thus expect that words for trades, social functions and offices, and economic resources would be more likely to be shared with neighbouring languages, while body, state of mind, kin, and core resources remain stable and resistent to loans. In this respect, Boretzky's (1992a) conclusion that the Rom retain a comparatively small inherited vocabulary chiefly in order to flag resistance to assimilation might be supported.

3.4 Historical phonology

A first systematic attempt at an historical phonology of Romani is found in Beames's (1872–9, I) *Comparative Grammar of the Modern Languages of India*, though Beames's sources on Romani were few and the language was not his primary object of interest. Probably the most detailed discussion of Romani historical phonology to date is Sampson (1926: 28–67), who bases much of his work on Miklosich (1872–80, IX), while Turner's (1926) paper on the 'Position of Romani in Indo-Aryan' is groundbreaking in the contribution it makes to locating changes in time and space. A concise summary of these works is provided by Hancock (1988: 193–9).

Of more recent date is Boretzky and Igla's (1993: 13–20) attempt to accommodate historical changes in Romani phonology to the framework of naturalness and markedness theory. Their attention is focused on the predictability of change, which they examine in relation to processes such as the devoicing of aspirated consonants (reduction of the marked cluster features '+voice' and '+aspirate'), the overall reduction in the number of consonant clusters, transfer of aspiration to initial positions (which already require intensified articulatory energy), and the loss of marked retroflex dentals. Hamp (1990), in a somewhat comparable approach, points out the consistency of historical developments in Romani phonology, which he describes with the help of a formula indicating a general shift in distinctive features from [−contin.] to [+contin.]/[obstruent front] (for instance *ḍ>r, t>l, m>v*).

3.4.1 *Changes shared with subcontinental MIA and NIA*

Proto-Romani participates in a series of changes that generally characterise the shift from OIA to MIA, as well as that from MIA to NIA. Perhaps the oldest of those is the loss of OIA syllabic /r̥/, a process that begins already in OIA and is attested in the Rigveda. In Romani, as in the Central languages of the subcontinent, /r̥/ is replaced by a vowel /i/ or /u/: OIA *mr̥ta*, Romani *mulo* 'dead' (cf. MIA *muda*, Hindi *muā*, Domari *mra*), OIA *vr̥ttiḥ*, Romani *buti* 'work', OIA *mr̥ṣṭaḥ*, Romani *mišto* 'good' (Domari *[na]mišta* 'ill'), OIA *hr̥dayam*, Romani *(j)ilo* 'heart' (Domari *xur*); but OIA *kr̥t-*, Romani *kerd-* 'done' (Domari *kard-*). A series of simple consonant reductions follows. Medial consonants are often dropped: OIA *lavana*, MIA *loṇa*, Romani *lon* 'salt' (Domari *lon*, Lomavren *nol*), OIA *bhaginī*, MIA *bahiṇī*, Romani *phen* 'sister' (Domari *bēn*). Initial /y/ becomes /j/ (for OIA/NIA I use the transcription common in Indology, whereby *j* indicates /dž/ and *y* indicates /j/): OIA *yā-*, MIA *jā-*, Romani *dža-* 'to go' (Domari *dža-*, Lomavren *dž-*), OIA *yuvatīḥ*, Romani *džuvel* 'woman' (Domari *džuwir*). Medial /p/ becomes /v/: OIA *svap-*, MIA *suv-*, Romani *sov-* 'to sleep'.

Characteristic of the MIA changes is the reduction of OIA consonant clusters. Generally the development from OIA to MIA sees the progressive assimilation of clusters and the emergence of geminates, with subsequent reduction of this geminate in the transition to NIA: OIA *rakta*, MIA *ratta*, Romani *rat* 'blood', OIA *tapta*, MIA *tatta*, Romani *tato* 'hot' (Domari *tata*), OIA *śuṣka*, MIA *sukkha*, Romani *šuko* 'dry', OIA *varkara*, MIA *vakkara*, Romani *bakro* 'sheep', OIA *sarpa*, MIA *sappa*, Romani *sap* 'snake' (Domari *sap*). The reduction of the geminate is accompanied in subcontinental NIA by compensatory vowel lengthening (Hindi *rāt* 'blood', *sāp* 'snake'), which is missing in Romani (*rat, sap*), perhaps due to loss of length at a later stage.

Several clusters show more specific simplifications. In initial position, /sth/ is simplified to /th/: OIA *sthūla*, MIA *thulla*, Romani *thulo* 'fat'. The group /kṣ/ is replaced by an aspirated cluster, later simplified: OIA *bubhukṣa*, MIA *buhukkhā*, Romani *bokh* 'hunger' (Domari *bka-*, Lomavren *bug-*), OIA *akṣi*, MIA *akkhi*, Romani *jakh* 'eye' (Domari *iki*, Lomavren *aki*), but exceptionally OIA *kṣurikā*, MIA *churī*, Romani *čhuri*, Domari *čuri* 'knife' (possibly a loan from a non-Central MIA dialect). The groups /tm, tv/ result in /p/: OIA *ātman*, MIA *appā*, Romani *pe(s)* (reflexive pronoun), OIA *-itvana*, MIA *-ippaṇa*, Romani *-ipen* (nominal abstract suffix). The cluster /sm/ is simplified via aspiration and metathesis to /m/: OIA *asmnán*, **tusme*, MIA *amhe, tumhe*, Romani *amen, tumen* 'we, you(pl)' (Domari *eme, itme*). Further special cases include OIA *vaḍra*, MIA *vaḍḍa*, Romani *baro* 'big' (Lomavren *voro-*), OIA *karṇa*, MIA *kaṇṇa*, Romani *kan* 'ear' (Domari *kan*), and OIA *parśva*, MIA *pāsa*, Romani *paš* 'half', where the palatal sibilant is preserved; the overall process in all these cases however is well in line with Central NIA cluster simplification.

The presence of older phonological innovations that are shared with the Central languages of India led Turner (1926) to postulate an ancient origin of Romani in the Central group. The closest other relation is found with the

Table 3.1 *Romani innovations shared with Central languages (following Turner 1926)*

OIA	Northwest	Southwest	Central	Romani	East	South
r̥	ri	a	i, u	i, u	a?	a
tv	tt	tt	pp	pp	pp?	tt?
sm	sp, ss	mh?	mh	mh	mh	mh?
kṣ	c̣c̣h	cch	kkh	kkh	kkh	cch?
y-	y-	j-	j-	j-	j-	y-

Eastern languages (e.g. Bengali), though Romani is separated from those by its treatment of OIA /r̥/, and possibly also of /tv/ (see table 3.1).

Later changes that are characteristic of the transition to NIA include the reduction of semi-vowels and nasals following stops: OIA *rūpya*, Romani *rup* 'silver' (Domari *rup*), OIA *agni*, Romani *jag* 'fire' (Domari *ag*); and the emergence of /ng/: OIA *mārg-*, MIA *magg-*, Romani *mang-* 'to beg' (Domari and Lomavren *mang-*).

Three additional processes are paralleled in Central NIA languages, but could also have been completed independently in Romani, with similar results. The first is the shift from /u/ to /o/, as in OIA/MIA *ru(v)-*, Hindi *ro-*, Romani *rov-* 'to cry' (Domari *rɔw-*), OIA *upari*, MIA *uppari*, Hindi *ūpar*, Romani *opre* 'above'.

The second involves the shift from labial fricative to stop in initial position, or /v/>/b/: OIA *varṣa*, MIA *varisa*, Hindi *baras*, Romani *berš* 'year' (but Domari *wars*), OIA *viś-*, Hindi *baiṭ-*, Romani *beš-* 'to sit' (but Domari *wēs-*, Lomavren *ves-*). The fact that this development is not shared with Domari, which has /w/, or with Lomavren, which retains /v/, led Sampson (1926: 36) to interpret it as a later innovation that took place in Byzantine Greece, long after the split of what he assumed had been branches of a single ancestral idiom. Turner (1926) however pointed out that Romani has an early Iranian loan *veš* 'forest' which is not affected by the change (cf. also Ossetian-derived *vurdon* 'wagon'). In subcontinental Indo-Aryan, some Dardic languages of the extreme north also show /v/>/b/; in the northwest /v/ is either retained or it becomes /w/. The change /v/>/b/ in the Central and Eastern languages is argued by Turner to be a rather late development. The shift in Romani could therefore have occurred independently, though the evidence provided by Iranian loans suggests that it preceded the outwards migration from India.

Finally, we find a shift of /m/ to /v/ in medial position: OIA *grāma*, MIA *gāma*, Hindi *gā̃v*, Romani *gav* 'village'. The change is regular in Romani (cf. also OIA *nāman*, MIA *nāma*, Romani *nav* 'name', OIA *bhūmi*, Romani *phuv* 'earth'), but is not attested in Domari: Turner (1926) regarded Domari *nām* 'name' as a Persian loan (cf. also Hindi *nām*). For the Domari 1SG present concord marker *-mi* (OIA *-ami* Romani-*av*) Turner suggested a possible pronominal origin.

3.4.2 *Conservative features of Romani*

While the changes outlined in section 3.4.1 portray a close affinity between Romani and the Central NIA languages, a set of conservative features already separates Romani from MIA developments in the Central regions. The most remarkable of those is the preservation of the cluster in a dental+/r/: OIA *trīṇi*, MIA *tiṇṇi*, but Romani *trin* 'three', OIA *pattra*, MIA *patta*, but Romani *patrin* 'leaf', OIA *drākṣa*, Hindi *dākh*, but Romani *drakh* 'grape'. This preservation of the cluster has been a source for controversy in Romani linguistics. Some considered Romani to be of Dardic or Northwestern origin, since the Dardic languages, and some of the Northwestern languages (e.g. Sindhi), appear to be the only groups that have likewise preserved this OIA archaism (cf. Miklosich 1872–80, Pischel 1883, Grierson 1908). Turner (1926) however was unable to reconcile a Dardic origin of Romani with the impressive inventory of innovations shared with the Central MIA languages. Instead, he concluded that Romani must have originated in the Central group, with which it shared earlier innovations, but migrated to the north before the reduction of the clusters dental+/r/. Since the change is already documented in the Aśokan inscriptions of the fourth century BC, Turner suggested an ancient migration from the central area at a point preceding this period. Noteworthy is the fact that this conservativism is shared with Domari (*taran* 'three', *drakh* 'grape'), providing a clue to an ancient close affinity among the two languages (corresponding items are unattested in Lomavren). Somewhat less outstanding is the preservation of an initial cluster in a labial+/r/. It is attested in OIA *bhrātṛ-*, MIA *bhāda*, Hindi *bhāi*, but Romani *phral* 'brother', though we also find OIA *bhruma* MIA, *bhūmi* Romani, *phuv* 'earth'. Unlike the clusters with an initial dental, the one in a labial+/r/ is not shared with either Domari (*bar* 'brother') or Lomavren (*phal* 'brother'), though it is shared with Northwestern NIA languages such as Kashmiri and Lahnda.

A further archaic cluster in Romani is the sibilant+dental in medial position: OIA *miṣṭa*, MIA *miṭṭha*, Hindi *mīṭhā*, but Romani *mišto* 'good', OIA *hasta*, Hindi *hāth*, but Romani *v-ast* 'hand'. Again we find agreement between Romani and Domari, which has *(na-)mišta* 'ill', *xast* 'hand' (comparable forms are unattested in Lomavren), but also with Kashmiri. Medial and final dental stops that are generally simplified in MIA, and disappear in the transition to NIA, are preserved in Romani as dental liquids: OIA *bhrātṛ-*, MIA *bhāda*, Hindi *bhāi*, but Romani *phral* 'brother', OIA *gatáḥ*, Hindi *gayā*, Romani *gelo* 'gone'. Here too, Romani agrees with Lomavren (*phal* 'brother') and Domari (*bar* 'brother', *gara* 'gone'), but also with Dardic Kalaša, which likewise has /l/ (Turner 1926: 165).

Finally, Romani has two dental sibilants which directly succeed the original OIA inventory of three: Romani /s/ continues OIA /s/, as in OIA *sarpa*, Romani *sap* 'snake', while Romani /š/ continues both OIA /ś/ as in OIA *śata*, Romani *šel* 'hundred', and OIA /ṣ/ as in OIA *varṣa*, Romani *berš* 'year' (cf. Hamp 1987). The preservation of an inherited distinction between dental sibilants is another archaism, shared to some extent with the Northwestern languages of India (Kashmiri, Western Pahari, Kamauni; cf. Masica 1991: 98–9), but not with Domari, which except for the medial cluster in /št/ has /s/ throughout (*sap* 'snake', *siy-yak* 'hundred', *wars* 'year', but *ušt* 'lip').

Clusters in which nasals are followed by stops are retained, whereas in Central NIA the nasal is reduced to a nasalised vowel: OIA *danta*, Hindi *dā̃t*, Romani *dand* 'tooth' (Domari *dand*), OIA *pancan*, Hindi *pā̃c*, Romani *pandž* 'five' (Domari *pʌndžes*), OIA *gandha*, Romani *khand-* 'to stink' (but Domari *gan-*, Lomavren *gian-*).

3.4.3 *Romani innovations*

Romani shows a series of distinct and in some cases unique innovations. Beginning with the vowel system, we find first a loss of the historical length distinction. It is usually assumed that vowel length disappeared as a result of Greek or Balkan influence (see von Sowa 1887: 18, Miklosich 1872–80, IX:24; cf. also Boretzky and Igla 1993). Lesný's (1916) suggestion (later revised; see Lesný 1928, 1941) that long vowels that are shared among several Romani dialects, and correspond to historical OIA long vowels, are in fact a continuation of OIA length distinction, was made primarily on the basis of data from Central dialects and from Sinti, which Boretzky and Igla (1993: 35–8) have shown to have developed vowel length independently in similar environments (see chapter 4).

The second noteworthy vowel development involves the continuation of historical /a/. We find in Romani occasionally /o/ in medial positions, mainly in the environment of labials, as in OIA *dhāv-*, Romani *thov-* 'to wash', OIA *svápa-*, Romani *sov-* 'sleep', but also in OIA *śaśáḥ*, Romani *šošoj* 'rabbit'. A general shift to /o/ appears in final positions where the vowel represents the M.SG nominative inflectional ending, as in OIA *kr̥ta*, MIA *kada*, Romani *kerdo* 'done', Hindi *baṛā*, Romani *baro* 'big', Hindi *aṇḍā*, Romani *andro* 'egg'. Preceding simple consonants, historical /a/ is represented in Romani by /e/, and in some cases by /i/: OIA *kar-*, Romani *ker-* 'to do', OIA grammatical ending-*asya*, Romani *-es*, OIA *gaṇaya*, Romani *gen-* 'to count'. Historical /a/ is retained however in positions preceding an historical consonant cluster: OIA *gharma*, Romani *kham* 'sun', OIA *taptáḥ*, Romani *tato* 'hot', OIA *danta*, Romani *dand* 'tooth'. Boretzky and Igla (1993: 14–15) explain the shift to /e/ as a retention, in an initial stage, of /ā/ in the system, and a lengthening of /a/ to /ā in positions preceding clusters (thus *danta* > **dānd* 'tooth'). At the same time, /a/ is reduced to /*ʌ/ in other preconsonantal positions (thus *daśa* > **dʌš* 'ten'). At a later stage, length is reduced, giving **dānd* > *dand*, while decentralisation of /ʌ/, possibly as a result of contact influence, leads to the emergence of /e/ in affected positions (**dʌš* > *deš*). A somewhat similar scenario, reconstructing the reduction of short /a/ in open syllables to /ə/ with a later shift to /e/, is proposed by Tálos (1999: 218–19).

Other vowel developments include the change from historical /i/ to /e/ as in OIA *śiras*, Romani *šero*, and the appearance of /u/ through regressive assimilation, as in OIA *jakuṭa*, Romani *džukel* 'dog', OIA *triśula*, Romani *trušul* 'cross'. None of the innovations affecting vowels in Romani is shared with Lomavren or Domari, with the exception of the backing of /a/ to /o/ around labials (OIA *dhāv-*, Romani *thov-*, Lomavren *tov-*, Domari *dɔw-* 'to wash').

In the consonantal domain, Romani shows devoicing of aspirated stops: OIA *bhaṇ-*, Romani *phen-* 'to say', OIA *dhāv-*, Romani *thov-* 'to wash', OIA *ghāsa-*, Romani *khas* 'grass'. Sampson (1926: 34), operating on the assumption that Romani, Lomavren, and Domari must have left India as a single language, treated this as an innovation that occurred in Persian territory, since it is shared with Lomavren (*tov-*, *qas*), but not with Domari (*dɔw-*, *gas*). He used the devoicing isogloss to coin the terms *phen*-Gypsy (Romani and Lomavren) and *ben*-Gypsy (Domari), referring to reflects of OIA *bhaginī* 'sister'. But the split could likewise be interpreted as evidence against a single entity at the time of the outwards migration from India. The absence of a voiced aspirate series is a regional feature common among the northern languages, such as Kashmiri and Dardic, Panjabi, Lahnda, and some Western Pahari dialects (Masica 1991: 102). In Lomavren, devoicing might indeed be an independent process resulting from the incorporation of Indo-Aryan vocabulary into an Armenian grammatical and phonological framework. Turner (1959) showed quite convincingly that the devoicing of voiced aspirates occurred independently in Romani and Lomavren. In Romani, transfer of aspiration, which constitutes an independent Romani development that is not shared with Lomavren, took place before devoicing: OIA *duddha* > **dhud* > Romani *thud* 'milk', but *duddha* > **du(t)tha* > Lomavren *luth;* OIA *bandh-*, Romani *phand-* 'to shut', but Lomavren *banth.*

The inventory of initial voiceless aspirate stops is significantly increased in Romani through transfer of aspiration. The process took place when the original initial consonant was voiced, and the internal aspirated consonant or consonant group was also voiced, and led at a later stage to the devoicing of the initial consonant: OIA *dugdha*, Romani *thud* 'milk', OIA *bandh-*, Romani *phand-* 'to shut', OIA **br̥ḍḍhah*, MIA *buḍḍha*, Romani *phuřo* 'old man', OIA *gandha*, Romani *khand* 'smell', OIA *jihvā*, Romani *čhib* 'tongue'. Turner (1959) observed that aspiration is not transferred to initial sonorants – OIA *vr̥kṣá-*, MIA *rukkha*, Romani *rukh* 'tree' – nor is it transferred when the original internal aspirated consonant is voiceless – OIA *duḥkhá-*, MIA *dukkha*, Romani *dukh* 'pain', an exception being OIA *pr̥cch-*, MIA *pucch-*, Romani *phuč-* 'to ask'. As mentioned, transfer of aspiration is not shared with either Domari or Lomavren.

Initial aspiration is lost in the case of /kh/, which in Romani becomes /x/ (sometimes attributed to Iranian influence): OIA *khād-*, Romani *xa-* 'to eat', OIA *khara-*, Romani *xer* 'donkey', OIA *khakkh-*, Romani *xox-* 'to tell a lie'. Fricativisation is shared with Lomavren (*xath-* 'to eat', *xar* 'donkey'), but not with Domari (*qa-, qar*; but OIA *mukha-* MIA, *muha* Romani *muj* 'mouth', Lomavren *muh*, Domari *muh*). Non-aspirated original /k/ may undergo a similar, albeit irregular development in Romani: OIA *kās-*, Romani *khas-*, alongside *xas-* 'to cough', OIA *śāka*, Romani *šax* 'cabbage'. Another development involving initial aspiration is the partial loss in Romani of initial /h/, as in OIA *hima*, Romani *iv* 'snow', partly compensated for at a later stage through prothetic consonants, as in OIA *hr̥dayam*, Romani *(j)-ilo* 'heart', OIA *hasta*, Romani *v-ast* 'hand'. Here, Domari has initial /x/ (*xur* 'heart', *xast* 'hand'), while in Lomavren we find *hath* alongside *ath* for 'hand'. Romani preserves initial /h/ however in OIA *haḍḍa* 'bone', Romani *heroj* 'leg' (Domari *xar*), while variation is found for OIA *hasa-*, Romani *(h)asa-* 'to laugh' (Domari past-tense stem *xas-*, Lomavren *xas-*).

The fate of internal (medial and final) dental stops in Romani is a striking example of both archaism (preservation of a consonant that is typically lost in MIA), and innovation. The specific results of the process are as follows: internal historical /t/, /d/, /th/, and /dh/ become /l/: OIA *bhrātr̥-*, Romani *phral* 'brother' (Lomavren *phal*, Domari *bar*), OIA *hr̥dayam*, Romani *(j)ilo* 'heart' (Domari *xur*), OIA *gūtha-*, Romani *khul* 'dung', OIA *madhu*, Romani *mol* 'wine' (the historical aspirates are unattested in Domari and Lomavren). The retroflex set shows a more complex development. Internal /ḍ/, which appears as /l/ already in MIA, is retained as /l/: OIA *krīḍ-*, MIA *khel-*, Romani *khel-* 'to play' (Lomavren *qel-*, Domari *kel-*). Internal /ṭ/ (via MIA /ḍ/), as well as /ṭh/ (via MIA /ḍh/), /ḍ/, /ḍḍ/, and /ḍr/ (via MIA /ḍḍ/) are succeeded by /r/: OIA *ciṅghāṭa*, Romani *čingar* 'battle', OIA *beḍā*, Romani *bero* 'boat, OIA *piṭharī*, MIA *piḍhara*, Romani *piri* 'pot', OIA *haḍḍa* 'bone', Romani *heroj* 'leg' (Domari *xar)*, OIA *vaḍra*, MIA *vaḍḍa*, Romani *baro* 'big' (Lomavren *vor-*).[5] Internal /ṭṭ/ (as well as OIA /ṭ/ > MIA /ṭṭ/) and /ḍḍh/, and initial /ḍ/ (as well as OIA /d/ > MIA /ḍ/), appear as /ř/, which in some dialects is preserved as uvular [ʀ] or long trill [rr], occasionally as [l] or even a retroflex, and elsewhere is reduced to /r/: OIA *aṭṭa-*, Romani *ařo* 'flour' (Lomavren *ara*, Domari *aṭa*), OIA *peṭa*, MIA *peṭṭa*, Romani *peř* 'belly' (Lomavren *per*, Domari *peṭ*), OIA **vr̥ddhah*, MIA *buḍḍha*, Romani *phuřo* 'old man' (Domari *wuda*), OIA *ḍom*, Romani *řom* 'Rom' (Lomavren *lom*, Domari *dom*), and OIA *darva*, MIA *ḍōva*, Romani *řoj* 'spoon'.

The development from stop to liquid appears to have its roots already in OIA vernaculars and the Prākrits (Beames 1872–9, I:238; Pischel 1900: 238, 240).

5 An exception is OIA *jakuṭa* Romani *džukel* 'dog', which however is likely to be a loan, perhaps of Iranian origin (cf. Hancock 1995b: 35).

Table 3.2 *Retention and shift of historical dental and dental retroflex stops in Romani, Lomavren, and Domari*

OIA>MIA	Romani	Lomavren	Domari
Group 1: internal ḍ>l	l	l	l
Group 2: internal t, d, th, dh	l	l	r
Group 3: internal ṭ>ḍ, ṭh>ḍh, ḍ, ḍḍ, ḍr>ḍḍ	r	r	r
Group 4: internal ṭ>ṭṭ, ṭṭ, ḍḍh	ř	r	t̺, d
Group 5: initial ḍ, d>ḍ	ř	l	t̺, d
Group 6: initial d	d	l	d

It later affects the series of retroflex dental stops, which in NIA are often continued as /ḷ/ or /ṛ/ (cf. Turner 1926). Sampson (1926: 35–6) argued that in Romani the shift must have taken place after emigration from India, since it takes on a different course in each of the 'Gypsy' languages. Turner (1926) agreed with the separateness of the Romani development, mainly on the grounds of relative chronology, arguing that the conservative features of Romani prove that it must have parted from the Central languages before the loss of medial retroflex dental stops; the latter development therefore cannot be shared with Central NIA. A comparison of the three languages Romani, Lomavren, and Domari (table3.2), illustrates the layered character of the process.

All three languages continue the shift from /ḍ/>/l/ already attested in MIA (Group 1), where they agree with much of subcontinental NIA. The non-retroflex dental stops in internal position (Group 2) develop regularly to /l/ in Romani and Lomavren, and to /r/ in Domari. They are thus preserved as consonants in all three languages, whereas elsewhere in NIA (and already in MIA) they are generally lost, as are most simple consonants in internal position. Retroflex dental stops, on the other hand, are divided into three classes (Groups 3–5). The first (Group 3) is represented in Romani, and apparently also in the two other languages (though attestation is incomplete), by /r/. The others (Groups 4–5) appear as /ř/ in Romani, as /r/ and /l/ respectively in Lomavren, and as pharyngealised or plain dental stops /t̺, d/ in Domari. In subcontinental NIA, all three classes of historical retroflex stops continue as retroflexes, but tend to be, likewise, differentiated. This concerns first the distinction between MIA initial /ḍ/ (Group 5), which usually remains /ḍ/, and MIA internal /ḍ/ (Group 3), which tends to shift to /ṛ/ or /ḷ/ (Turner 1926). Turner recognised the distinction in Domari between initial /d/ and internal /r/; but he also added the Lomavren distinction between initial /l/ and internal /r/ to the same pattern, though in actual fact the picture in Lomavren merely overlaps with a separate phenomenon, namely the shift of initial voiced dentals /d/ and /ḍ/ to /l/ (Group 6). As for Romani, Turner failed to identify the Early Romani opposition between /r/, and /ř/, which is indeed obliterated in the majority of present-day dialects, but is obviously of key importance to historical reconstruction, as it reveals the systematic and layered character of the shift away from retroflex stops. Groups 3 and 4, which Turner lumped together for Romani, are similarly differentiated, both in Romani and Domari.

The picture conveyed in table 3.2 suggests that the shift from stop to liquid affected the various groups of consonants separately, and, although it was obviously posterior to the MIA period, it appears to have followed more or less the same layered progression as in the subcontinental languages: changes in the groups at the top end of the table preceded changes in the groups at the lower end, the latter showing more archaic features. This applies to Romani, where /ř/ is still in transition from an actual retroflex (cf. Gilliat-Smith 1911).[6] Archaisms are especially evident in Domari, where the shift from stops to liquids comes to a halt before reaching Groups 4–5, where although the retroflex quality is lost, the stops remain. Here, pharyngealisation might be interpreted as an attempt to compensate for the loss of the old retroflex feature by replacing it by a new distinctive quality, acquired through contact with Arabic.

The loss of retroflex consonants in all three languages is likely to be a result of contact with languages that lack retroflex consonants, and so it is in itself of little significance to the reconstruction of linguistic origins. A rather late development in Romani appears to be the loss of retroflex quality in the cluster /ṇḍ/. Its only regular reflex is in the word OIA *pāṇḍu*, Romani *parno* 'white' (Domari *prāna)*, which is found in this form in all dialects and can therefore be taken to represent an Early or even a Proto-Romani development. Elsewhere, Romani dialects are highly diverse. Typical successor forms are /ndř/, /nd/, /ngl/, /nř/, /ř/, /řn/, and /n/ (/ř/ merging with /r/ in many dialects): OIA *maṇḍa*, Romani *mandřo, mando, manřo, mařno, mařo, mano* 'bread' (Domari *mana*, Lomavren *mala*), OIA *aṇḍa*, Romani *andřo, anřo, ařno, ařo, ano* 'egg' (Domari *ana*, Lomavren *anlo*) (see chapters 4 and 9). It is thus likely that /ṇḍ/ remained a cluster – possibly /ndř/ – well into the Early Romani period. Historical /nd/ is simplified to /n/: OIA *candra*, MIA *canda*, Romani *čhon* 'moon'. The historical clusters /nt/ and /nc/ show voicing of the second component: OIA *danta*, Romani *dand* 'tooth' (Domari *dand*), OIA *pancan*, Romani *pandž* 'five' (Domari *pʌndžes*). A rather complex and multilayered innovation in Romani is consonant prothesis involving /j/ and /v/ (see chapter 4).

The principal sound changes that distinguish Romani can be summarised as follows (table 3.3). Vowel length is lost. Short vowels are on the whole retained, though *a* changes to *e* in positions preceding simple consonants and to *o* in inflectional endings. OIA *r̥* becomes *u* or *i*. Non-retroflex stops are generally retained, but voiced aspirates are devoiced, and medial dental stops

[6] For (Proto-)Romani too, Boretzky and Igla (1993: 16–17) postulate a retroflex liquid */ṛ/ or */ḷ/ at an intermediate stage, with subsequent differentiation.

Table 3.3 *Principal sound correspondences between OIA and Romani*

OIA	Romani	
a	a	preceding consonant clusters: *gharma* > *kham* 'sun'; *taptáḥ* > *tato*
	e	preceding simple consonants: *daśa* > Romani *deš* 'ten'; *-asya* > Romani *-es* (case ending); *varṣa* > *berš* 'year'
	o	in M.SG nominative endings: *kāla* > *kalo* 'black' medial: *bhava-*> *ov-* 'to become'; *śaśáḥ* > *šošoj* 'hare'
	u	through regressive assimilation: *jakuṭa* > *džukel* 'dog' (perhaps loan)
	i	isolated, preceding sonorant in unstressed position: *varṣana* > *biršin* 'rain'
ā	a	*ānī-* > *an-* 'to bring'; *grāma* > *gav* 'village'
e	e	*peṭa* > *per* 'belly'
ē	e	*dēvata* > *devel* 'God'
i	i	*hima* > *iv* 'snow'
	e	*śiras* > *šero* 'head'
	u	through regressive assimilation: *triśula* > *trušul* 'cross'
ī	i	*śita* MIA *sīta* > *šil* 'cold'
o	o	*goṇa* > *gono* 'sack'
ō	o	*cōra* > *čor* 'thief'
u	u	*dugdha* > *thud* 'milk'; *yuvatíḥ* > *džuvel* 'woman'
ū	u	*rūpya* > *rup* 'silver'; *mūtra* > *mutar* 'urine'
r̥	u	*vr̥ttiḥ* > *buti* 'work'; *śr̥ṇ-* > *šun-* 'hear'
	i	*hr̥dayam* > *ilo* 'heart'
	(a)	*r̥śi* > *rašaj* 'priest' (according to Turner 1926, MIA dialectal loan)
r̥t	erd	*kr̥ta* > *kerdo* 'done'
(r̥m)	(irm)	*kr̥mi* > *kirmo* 'worm' (according to Turner 1926, Iranian loan)
p	p	initial: *pānīya* > *pani* 'water'
	ph	through transfer of aspiration: *pr̥cch-* > *phuč-* (alongside *pučh-*) 'to ask'
	v	medial: *apara* > *aver* 'other', *āpaya-* > MIA *āv-* > *av-* 'to come'; *svapa-* > *supa-* > *sov-* 'to sleep'
t	t	initial: *tale* > *tele* 'down'; *taruṇa* > *terno* 'young'
	l	medial: *bhrātr̥-* > *phral* 'brother'; *-ati* > *-el* (3SG present concord marker)
k	k	*kāla* > *kalo* 'black'
tt	t	*vr̥ttiḥ* > *buti* 'work';
b	b	*bubhukṣa* > *bokh* 'hunger'
	ph	through transfer of aspiration: *bandha-* > *phand-* 'to shut'
	v	*bahis* > MIA *vāhira* > *avri* 'out'
d	d	initial: *divasa* > *dives* 'day'
	th	through transfer of aspiration: *dugdha* > MIA *dudha* > *thud* 'milk'
	l	medial: *hr̥dayam* > *ilo* 'heart'
g	g	initial: *goṇa* > *gono* 'sack'
	kh	through transfer of aspiration: *gandha* > *khand-* 'to stink'
	–	medial: *bhaginī* > *phen* 'sister'
ph	ph	*phalaka* > *phal* 'pale'
th	th	initial: *(a)tha* > *thaj* 'and'

(*cont.*)

Table 3.3 (*cont.*)

OIA	Romani	
	l	medial: *gūtha-* > *khul* 'dung'
kh	x	*khād-* > *xa-* 'to eat'; *khakkh-* > *xox-* 'to tell a lie'
	j	*mukha* > MIA *muha* > *muj* 'mouth, face'
bh	ph	*bhaṇ-* > *phen-* 'to say'; *bhaginī* > *phen* 'sister'
dh	th	initial: *dhāv-* > *thov-* 'to wash'
	l	medial: *madhu* > *mol* 'wine';
gh	kh	*gharma* > *kham* 'sun'
tth	št	*utthā (ud+stha-)* > *ušt-* 'to arise'
ṭ	r	*ciṇghāṭa* > *čingar* 'battle'
	ř	*peṭa* > MIA *peṭṭa* > *peř* 'belly'
	(l)	*jakuṭa* > *džukel* 'dog' (possibly dialectal or Iranian loan)
ḍ	ř	initial: *ḍom* > *řom* 'Rom'; *darva* > MIA *ḍōva* > *řoj* 'spoon'
	r	medial: *beḍā* > *bero* 'boat'
	l	*krīḍ-* > MIA *khel-* > khel- 'to play'
ṭh	r	*piṭharī* > *piri* 'pot'
ṭṭ	ř	*aṭṭa-* > *ařo* 'flour'
ḍḍ	r	*haḍḍa* 'bone' > *heroj* 'leg'
ḍḍh	ř	**vr̥ddhah* > MIA *buḍḍha* > *phuřo* 'old man'
c	č	*caru* > *čaro* 'bowl'
	š	preceding voiceless stop: *catvari* > *štar* 'four'
j	dž	initial: *jānā-* > *džan-* 'to know'
	čh	transfer of aspiration: *jihvāi* > *čhib* 'tongue'
	i	medial: *rājan* > *rai* 'lord'
jj	dž	*lajjā* > *ladž* 'shame'
ch	čh	*chin-* > *čhin-* 'to cut'
v	b	initial: *viṃśati* > *biš* 'twenty'; *varṣa* > *berš* 'year'
	v	medial: *nava* > *nevo* 'new'; *yuvatíḥ* > *džuvel* 'woman'
	–	medial: *lavana* > MIA *loṇa* > *lon* 'salt'
h	–	initial: *hima* > *iv* 'snow'; *hr̥dayam* > *ilo* 'heart'
	h	initial: *haḍḍa* 'bone' > *heroj* 'leg'; *hasa-* > *(h)asa-* 'laugh'
	-	medial: *gohūma* > *giv* 'wheat'
m	m	initial: *miṣṭa* > *mišto* 'good'
	v	medial: *hima* > *iv* 'snow'; *nāman* > *nav* 'name'
n	n	*nāman* > *nav* 'name'
ṇ	n	*goṇa* > *gono* 'sack'; *lavana* > MIA *loṇa* > *lon* 'salt'
r	r	*rājan* > *rai* 'lord'; *śiras* > *šero* 'head'
l	l	*lajjā* > *ladž* 'shame'; *vāla* > *bal* 'hair'
s	s	*sarpa* > *sap* 'snake', *divasa* > *dives*
ś	š	*śata* > *šel* 'hundred', *śr̥ṇ-* > *šun-* 'to hear'; *viś-* > *beš-* 'to sit'
	s	in promixity of internal aspirate: *śīghrá-* > *sigo* 'quick'; *śapátha-* > *sovel* 'curse'
ṣ	š	*varṣa* > *berš* 'year'; *manuṣaḥ* > *manuš* 'person'
y	dž	*yā-* > *dža-* 'to go'; *yuvatíḥ* > *džuvel* 'woman'; *hyáḥ* > *hiyyo* > *idž* 'yesterday'
pt	t	*tapta* > *tato* 'hot';
kt	t	*rakta* > *rat* 'blood'

Table 3.3 *(cont.)*

OIA	Romani	
pr	p	*prat-* MIA *patt-* > *pat-* 'to believe'
tr	tr	*trīṇi* > *trin* 'three'; *pattra* > *patrin* 'leaf'
kr	kh	*krīḍ-* > MIA *khel-* > *khel-* 'to play'
dr	dr	*drākṣa* > *drakh* 'grape'
bhr	phr	*bhrātṛ-* > *phral* 'brother'
	ph	*bhruma* MIA *bhūmi* > *phuv*
ḍr	r	*vaḍra* > *baro* 'big'
tv	p	*-tvana* > *-pen* (abstract nominal suffix);
	t	*bahutva* > MIA *bahutta* > *but* 'much, many'
tm	p	*ātman* > *pe(s)* (reflexive pronoun)
gn	g	*agni* > *jag* 'fire'
kṣ	kh	*bubhukṣa* > *bokh* 'hunger'; *akṣi* > *jakh* 'eye'
	(čh)	*kṣurikā* > *čhuri* 'knife'; *r̥kṣaḥ* > *rič͏h* 'bear' (according to Turner 1926, probably loans from other IA dialect)
py	p	*rūpya* > *rup* 'silver'
nt	nd	*danta* > *dand* 'tooth'
nd	nd	*gandha-* > *khand-* 'to stink'
nc	ndž	*pancan* > *pandž* 'five'
ndr	n	*candra* > *čhon* 'moon'
ṇḍ	ndř, nř, nd, rn, r, etc.	*maṇḍa* > *manřo, marno, mandřo, maro, mano, mando* etc. 'bread'; *aṇḍa-* > *andřo, anřo, ařno, aro etc.* 'egg'
ṃs	s	*māṃsa* > *mas* 'meat'
rp	p	*sarpa* > *sap* 'snake'
rk	k	*varkara* > *bakro* 'sheep'
rg	ng	*mārg-* > *mang-* 'to beg'
rṇ	n	*karṇa* > *kan* 'ear'
rs	s	*gharṣ-* MIA *ghaṃs-* > *khos-* 'to wipe'
rś	š	*parśva* > *paš* 'half'
st	st	*svastha* > *sasto* 'healthy'; *hasta* > *(v)ast* 'hand'
sth	th	*sthūla* > *thulo* 'fat'; *sthāna* > *than* 'place'
sm	m	*asmnán, *tusme* > > *amen, tumen* 'we, you(PL)'
ṣṭ	št	*mr̥ṣṭah* > *mišto* 'good'; *kāṣṭhám* > *kašt* 'wood'
ṣk	k	*śuṣka* > *šuko* 'dry'

are replaced by *l*. New initial voiceless aspirates emerge through transfer of aspiration from medial positions in the word. Retroflex stops are replaced by *r*, *ř*, or *l*. Sonorants are continued. From the original three sibilants a two-way distinction between *š* and *s* is retained. Most clusters are simplified, but those in dental or labial and *r* (*tr* etc.) as well as those in a sibilant and dental (*st* etc.) and in a nasal and dental (*nd* etc.) are continued, with *ṇḍ* taking diverse shapes through what appears to be a relatively recent development.

3.5 Historical morphology

3.5.1 *Direct continuation of OIA/MIA productive morphology*

Inherited derivational morphology in Romani is productive primarily within the pre-European lexicon, and its extension to European loans is limited. In direct continuation of OIA nominal derivation morphemes we find the abstract nominalisers *-ipen (sasto* 'healthy', *sastipen* 'health'), from OIA *-itvana* > MIA *-ppaṇa*, and *-iben*, most likely from OIA *-itavya* > MIA *-iyavva* and contamination with *-pen* (cf. Schmid 1968). The diminutive suffix in *-oř- (kher* 'house', *kherořo* 'little house') continues MIA *-ḍ-* from OIA *-r-*. From OIA *-nī* we find *-ni* forming animate feminine nouns *(manuš* 'man', *manušni* 'woman'; *grast*, from Armenian *grast*, 'horse', *grasni* 'mare'). Other nominal formation suffixes that derive from OIA word-formation patterns are confined to individual lexical items and are only marginally productive. Sampson (1926: 79) mentions for example *-ikl-* in *čiriklo* 'bird', *marikli* 'cake' (cf. *maro* 'bread'), as connected to OIA *-ika.*

There is a series of productive adjectival derivation suffixes: OIA *-āl-*, Romani *-al- (bokh* 'hunger', *bokhalo* 'hungry'; *baxt*, from Iranian *baxt*, 'fortune', *baxtalo* 'happy'), OIA *-n-*, Romani *-an- (rom* 'Rom', *romano* 'Romani'), OIA *-ika* + *-n-*, Romani *-ikan- (gadžo* 'non-Gypsy', adjective *gadžikano)*, OIA *-vat*, giving rise to MIA *-va*, Romani *-(a)v- (ladž* 'shame', *ladžavo* 'shameful') and (MIA *-vāl-*) Romani *-val- (xandž* 'itching', *xandžvalo* 'itching, greedy'), OIA *-tvan-*, Romani *-utn- (palu(t)no* 'later, last', from *pal* 'behind'; also *-un-* in *angluno* 'first', from *angl-* 'before'). The possessive suffix *-ir-/-iř-* continues a MIA adjectival possessive suffix in *-ra (< kara)*, thus *mindřo (mißo* etc.) 'my', *tiro* 'your', *amaro* 'our', *tumaro* 'your', the earlier form surviving in the genitive ending *-kero (les-kero* 'his', *čhaves-kero* 'of the boy').

In its verb derivation, Romani continues the OIA primary causative suffix OIA *-paya-*, MIA *-va-*, Romani *-av- (naš-* 'to escape', *našav-* 'to drive s.o. away'; cf. Hübschmannová and Bubeník 1997: 135). Another older marker of causativity is found in the transitiviser or intensifier affix *-ar-*, possibly from OIA/MIA *kar-* 'to do'. Participial suffixes in *-t-* and *-(i)n-* are continued in Romani as *-t-, -d-, -l-* and as *-in-* respectively (*bešto* 'seated', *kerdo* 'done', *mukhlo* 'deserted', *dino* 'given'). In fixed adverbial expressions we find preservation of OIA locatives in *-e, -i* (*andr-e* 'inside', *upr-e* 'above', *avr-i* 'outside'; cf. also *khere* 'at home' to *kher* 'house', which is widespread in other NIA languages), which is productive with names of days of the week (*lujin-e* 'on Monday'), and of ablatives in OIA *-āt* giving Romani *-al: avr-al* 'outside', *tel-al* 'down below'.

The vocalic inflection markers on nouns and adjectives are shared with other NIA languages: M.SG *-o* continues OIA declension classes in *-a* (masculine and neuter), F.SG *-i* is usually regarded as continuing OIA feminines in *-ikā*, MIA *-iyā*, and possibly also OIA *-ī* (see Tagare 1948: 337): M. *baro*, F. *bari* 'big', *raklo* 'boy', *rakli* 'girl' (cf. Hindi *baṛā, baṛī* and *laṛkā, laṛkī*; Domari *lača, lačī*). Romani pronouns are a continuation of late MIA stems: 1SG (oblique) *m-* (Romani *me/man*), 2SG *t-* (Romani *tu/te*), 1PL *am-* (Romani *amen*), and 2PL *tum-* (Romani *tumen*). The OIA reflexive pronoun *ātman* > MIA *appa-* is Romani *pe-*. Deictic stems in *ta-* are continued as *l-*, deictics and interrogatives in *ka-* are continued in *kon* 'who', *kaj* 'where', *kana* 'when', *keti* 'how much'.

While most of this material is preserved in NIA as a whole, Romani also shows unique morphological conservativisms in its nominal and verbal inflection. In the nominal inflection, it preserves the consonantal endings of the oblique case markers M.SG *-es* PL *-en*, from OIA genitives M.SG *-asya* PL *-ānām*, which are reduced in most other NIA languages. A consonantal form in *-s* for the M.SG oblique is also preserved in Kashmiri and other Dardic languages such as Kalaša and Pašai (cf. Grierson 1906: 32), forms in *-n* for the PL oblique are preserved in Dardic as well as in Kumauni, Sindhi, Awadhi, Bhojpuri, and Sinhalese. Romani shares both features with Domari (M.SG *-as*, PL *-an*).

Perhaps the most striking conservativism in Romani is its preservation to a considerable degree of the OIA/MIA present verb conjugation: OIA SG *-ami* > Romani *-av*, OIA 2SG *-asi* > Romani *-es*, OIA 3SG *-ati* > Romani *-el*, OIA 1PL *-āmas* > possibly Romani *-as*, OIA 3PL *-anti* > Romani *-en*, by analogy also spreading to the 2PL *-en*. Preservation of this primary set of personal concord markers seems characteristic of NIA fringe languages; it is found to some degree in the Dardic languages to the north (Grierson 1906), and in Sinhalese to the south, while some conservative forms in *-s* for the 2SG and in *-n* or *-t* for the 3PL can be found in various languages (Bengali, Oriya, Konkani, Marathi). Once again the similarities between Romani and Domari are striking; Domari shows 1SG *-ami*, 3SG *-ari*, and 3PL *-andi*, with innovations for 2SG *-ēk*, 1PL *-ani* and 2PL *-asi* (see chapter 6).

3.5.2 *Innovations shared with other NIA languages*

Romani shares a number of significant morphological innovations that are widespread in Northwestern and Central NIA and beyond, and which therefore do not at all conflict with its profile, in many respects, as a conservative 'fringe' or 'frontier' language. The historical three-way gender distinction is reduced to a two-way masculine/feminine system; here Romani goes along with Hindi, Panjabi, Sindhi, Kashmiri, Nepali, as well as Domari. The historical OIA/MIA case declension system is reduced to a plain nominative/oblique opposition, alongside a vocative. As elsewhere in NIA, the oblique forms derive from OIA genitive endings in *-asya* (M.SG), *-yāḥ* (F.SG), and *-ānām* (PL).

Characteristic of the transition from late MIA to the early NIA period is the loss of the historical inflected past tense and the generalisation of the past participle, which then forms the basis for new past tenses. This is connected to the emergence of ergativity and the generalisation of oblique marking of transitive subjects. Present-day Romani dialects of southeastern Europe continue to show active past participles with adjectival agreement in the 3SG past tense of intransitive, especially unaccusative, verbs (*gelo* 'he went', *geli* 'she went'). This structure has largely retreated outside the Balkan regions, and has been replaced by a person-inflection marker *-a(s)*, which is also the general 3SG past-tense termination with transitive verbs. Domari retains adjectival agreement even with transitive verbs (*gara* 'he went', *garī* 'she went'; *karda* 'he did', *kardī* 'she did'), employing the ending in *-os* with pronominal object clitics (*kardos-is* 'he/she did it'). Given the participial base of all past-tense verbs, even those with person-inflected terminations, Proto-Romani may be assumed to have relied primarily on active participles for past-tense formation (see chapter 6). Further evidence that links Proto-Romani with the emergence of the ergative construction of early NIA is the generalisation of the oblique 1SG pronoun *me*, cf. Hindi *mɛ̃*, Domari *ama* (see discussion in Bubeník 2000).

Compensating for the loss of the historical nominal case declension is the emergence of Layer II case markers. These constitute a closed set of invariant, usually semantically abstract affixes that are attached indirectly to the nominal base, mediated through the remnants of the OIA case system, namely the oblique forms of Layer I (cf. Masica 1991: 232). This development too characterises the NIA period, and for some languages it is only documented as late as the fourteenth century (see Bubeník 1998: 99). On the whole the Romani inventory of Layer II elements matches that of other NIA languages, in particular the Central and Eastern languages: genitive *-kero*, from the MIA genitive preposition *kera* and OIA adjectival participle *kārya* 'done' (Maithili *-ker*, Hindi *-kā*, Bengali *-er*,); dative *-ke*, which Bubeník (2000: 225) traces to Apabhraṃśa *kehiṃ* 'for'[7] (Hindi *-ko*, Bengali *-ke*, also Domari *-ke*), instrumental/ sociative *-sa*, from OIA *samam* 'with', MIA *samau* and *sahũ* (Hindi *-se*, Domari *-san*). Less straightforward etymologically are the locative suffix *-te* and the ablative suffix *-tar.* Locative *-te* has cognates in a series of NIA languages, often in dative meaning (see Masica 1991: 244–5), including Domari *-ta* and Bengali *-te*, and it could be derived from OIA *artha* 'purpose', or *sthā-* 'stand' (see Bloch 1970: 208–9).

The renewal of the NIA case system also sees the emergence of a set of adpositions, or Layer III case markers, derived from adverbial location expressions. This too is found in Romani: *andre* 'in' and *andar* 'from' < OIA *antar-*, Romani *angl-* 'before' < OIA *agr-*, *paš* 'near' < OIA *pārśva-*, *pal-* 'after' < OIA *par, pe* 'on' < MIA *piṭṭh-*, *avr-* 'outside' < OIA *bahis*, *opre* 'above' < OIA *upari*, and more.

In the verb, OIA *bhuv-* 'to become' gives rise to a copula and to copula auxiliaries, which in present-day Romani survive in the subjunctive form of the copula *ov-* (cf. Boretzky 1997). Finally, Romani shares the development of

[7] Rather than to OIA *kakṣā* 'side', as proposed by Sampson (1926: 134).

secondary concord markers of the verb in the past tense, based on the attachment of either finite auxiliaries or pronominal forms to the participle (see chapter 6). Romani carries this development to the extent of full synthetisation of the new set of concord markers, agreeing on the whole with Domari: 1SG *-om* (Domari *-om*), 2SG *-al*>*-an* (Domari *-or*), 3SG *-a(s)* (Domari *-os*), 1PL *-am* (Domari *-ēn*), 2PL *-an* (Domari *-es*), the 3PL form remaining participial *-e* (Domari *-e*).

3.5.3 *Romani-specific innovations*

Apart from the emergence of past-tense secondary concord markers, Romani agrees with Domari in a number of further developments. The first is the loss of gender agreement in the plural. Another is the synthetisation of Layer II affixes. Here, Domari remains somewhat more conservative, allowing pronominal object clitics to intervene between the nominal base and the Layer II affix (*kury-im-ta* 'to my house'). Romani on the other hand shows partial phonological assimilation of the affix to the oblique base, thus *les-ke* 'for him', *len-ge* 'for them'. Both languages also develop external, agglutinative tense markers that follow personal concord affixes. The Romani forms are *-as* and *-ahi*, possibly derived from a Proto-Romani **-asi*. They form the imperfect by attaching to the present (*kerav* 'I do', *kerav-as* 'I used to do') and the pluperfect/counterfactual from the past (*kerdom* 'I did', *kerdom-as* 'I used to do').

Innovations that are unique to Romani include the grammaticalisation of *ov-* from OIA *bhuv-* 'to become' as a passive marker that is attached to the passive participle to form synthetic or composed passives (*kerdjovel* 'it is being done', from **kerdo+(j)ovel*), the grammaticalisation of *-ker-* < *ker-* 'to do' and of *-d-* < *d-* 'to give' as transitive derivation markers, and the development of *av-* 'to come' and of the copula into passive auxiliaries. Further morphosyntactic innovations that are characteristic of Romani are the shift to verb-medial word order and the prepositioning of Layer III case markers, the lack of relativisers in *y-* and the development of subordinating conjunctions based on interrogatives, the loss of most non-finite forms, the lack of converbs of the NIA type, and the emergence of preposed definite articles.

3.6 The position of Romani, Domari, and Lomavren

Romani displays a series of conservative traits in phonology and morphology. The fact that many of these features are also found in Northwestern NIA and Dardic led early scholars of Romani to postulate its origin in northwestern India, or in the region known as the Hindu Kush (Miklosich 1872–80, III:3, VI:63, IX:4, Pischel 1883: 370, 1900: 28, Grierson 1908; cf. above). Since Romani also participates in a series of morphological innovations that are characteristic of the NIA period as a whole, most notably the reduction of the case system, it has been viewed as having parted from India during the transition period to NIA, which can only be dated rather vaguely to medieval times, perhaps between the eighth and tenth centuries AD (see Miklosich 1872–80, III:3)

The most reliable key to reconstructing sub-group affiliation within a language family is of course the presence of shared innovations that are typical of that particular sub-group. Shared conservativisms, on the other hand, do not provide straightforward evidence: there may be various reasons why a language might remain conservative, and why related offshoots of an ancient parent language might preserve shared inherited traits in different geographical locations. Geographical isolation could be one of those reasons. Social isolation might indeed be another, though it appears not to have been considered so far, despite ethnographic evidence linking the ancestral Rom population with the socially isolated peripatetic castes of Indian *ḍom*. Emigration from India as early as the fourth century BC was suggested by Kaufman (cited in Hancock 1988 and in Fraser 1992b), but it is hardly reconcilable with the series of innovations that stem from the transitional period between MIA and NIA. A geographical origin of Proto-Romani in the northwest, on the other hand, does not account for the early innovations which it shares with the Central languages.

Turner's (1926) analysis of the relative chronology of early changes in Romani has not yet found a serious challenger. The inventory of early innovations that are shared with the Central group is impressive. Moreover, they are found not just in Romani, but also in Domari and Lomavren. It is thus likely that all three languages originated in the Central group. Most of the conservative features of Romani are shared by Domari and Lomavren as well: the preservation of internal dentals as liquids, the preservation of the clusters /st, št, dr, tr/,[8] and, shared with Domari, conservative traits in nominal and verbal morphology. These archaisms do not of course stand in the way of postulating an early origin in the Central group, since the languages will have left the region before some of the later phonological changes took place, and before the breakdown of the old morphology. But they do indicate that all three languages became isolated from the Central group at a rather early stage. Turner assumed that separation had occurred by the fourth century BC, at which point the breakdown of the above clusters is already attested in Central MIA.[9]

[8] Contrary to Lesný's (1941) impression, none of these features are shared with Hunza Valley Ḍumāki as described by Lorimer (1939), which reduces internal dentals (*mō* 'wine', Romani *mol; gōwa* 'horse', Romani *khuro*, Domari *gori*) as well as clusters (*ōte* 'lip', Romani *ušt*, Domari *ušt; kot* 'stick', Romani *kašt*), but preserves retroflexes (*ḍom*, Romani *rom*, Domari *dom; hoṭ* 'bone', Romani *her*, Domari *xur*).

[9] Turner's theory receives support from Fraser's (1992b) glottochronological calculations, according to which the distance between Romani and Kashmiri reflects a split that took place around 1700 BC, that is around the time of the formation of OIA in India, while the difference between Romani and Hindi reflects a split from around 390 BC. On the other hand, Turner's dating was criticised by Woolner (1928), who doubted that the Aśoka inscriptions could form an accurate point of reference, since they are not likely to reflect contemporary vernacular usage.

Turner's suggestion of a migration to the northwest sought to account for the preservation of conservative features that resist change in this region, while allowing for continuing participation in the morphological changes that are typical of the overall transition to the early NIA period, notably the collapse of the old nominal declension. Turner cites a number of lexical items that could have been borrowed from the Northwestern languages, though this lexical evidence remains marginal and largely inconclusive. Noteworthy is the fact that there are hardly any phonological innovations that are shared with the Northwestern languages: the voicing of dental stops in the historical clusters /nc, nt/ in all three languages may be seen as a predictable outcome of what is essentially a conservative trait, namely the preservation of the cluster itself (as opposed to its simplification through loss of the nasal in the Central languages). The devoicing of /bh, dh, gh/ occurred independently in Romani and Lomavren (see section 3.4.3), and is lacking altogether in Domari.

The devoicing isogloss had led Sampson (1923) to coin the terms *phen*-Gypsy (Romani and Lomavren) and *ben*-Gypsy (Domari). Sampson's labelling of the 'branches' reflects just one single feature, rendering the impression of an otherwise tightly bound entity. But there are at least two additional distinctive features separating the groups: the preservation of old internal dentals as either /l/ or /r/, and the treatment of historical /bhr/. The three representative features are all reflected in OIA *bhrātr̥-* 'brother', for which all three idioms have cognates. The three languages are therefore better labelled the '*phral*-group' (Romani), the '*phal*-group' (Lomavren), and the '*bar*-group' (Domari). Sampson's idea was that the two 'branches' split while in Iranian-speaking territory. But Hancock (1995b), based on the paucity of loans of Iranian origin that are shared by all three languages, suggested that the three groups passed through Iranian territory independently. This can be taken to imply that the split into not just two, but into three branches must have already occurred in India.

While the inventory of conservative features shared by the three languages seems to favour their separation from Central MIA at a rather early period, it is not imperative that this separation should have occurred in the form of a shared migration within India, leading to the northwest and ultimately out of India. The three languages share few innovations that followed the separation from the Central group. In the treatment of OIA internal dental stops and of MIA dental retroflex stops there are similarities, but also differences (see above). There are also differences in the evolution of MIA medial /v/ (Romani /v/, Domari and Lomavren /w/) and of MIA medial /p/ (Romani /v/, Domari and Lomavren /u/), in the preservation of the OIA dental sibilants /s, ś, š/ (Romani /s, š/, Lomavren and Domari /s/), and in the treatment of OIA initial /kh/ (Romani and Lomavren /x/, Domari /q/) and of OIA initial /h/ (Romani /ø/ or /h/, Lomavren /h/, Domari /x/). Neither Lomavren nor Domari share the most outstanding Romani innovations, namely the shift /a/>/e/ preceding simple

Table 3.4 *Some lexical correspondences: Romani and related languages*

	Romani	Lomavren	Hindi	Domari
'big'	baro	voro-	baṛā	tilla
'house'	kher	kar	ghar	kuri
'above'	opre	ubra	ūpar	atun
'inside'	andre	anraj, mandž	andar	mandža
'to take'	l-	–	le-	par-
'work'	buti	kam	kām	kam
'what'	so	kē	kyā	kē
'village'	gav	lehi	gā̃v	dē(h)
'blood'	rat	nhul	rat	nhīr

consonants, the shift /a/>/o/ in grammatical endings, transfer of aspiration, the shift of initial /v/>/b/ and of internal /m/>/v/.

The patterns of lexical correspondences between the languages present a contradictory picture. There is some evidence in favour of an ancient separation of Domari (see the first group of words in table 3.4), while on the other hand Romani stands out in a number of features, and Domari and Lomavren in turn share some items, some of them, such as Kurdish *dē-* 'town', being Iranian loans.

Striking nonetheless are the grammatical similarities between Romani and Domari: the synthetisation of Layer II affixes, the emergence of new concord markers for the past tense, the neutralisation of gender marking in the plural, and the use of the oblique case as an accusative. A morphological innovation that both Romani and Domari share with some Northwestern languages is the emergence of a new past-tense set of concord affixes, derived from pronominal affixes. Areal contacts and morphosyntactic convergence among related languages remain a necessary part of our scenario of historical reconstruction.

In conclusion, one must at least allow for the possibility that the archaisms that the three languages display are tokens not of a shared geographical relocation, but rather of a collapse, at some point in time of the network of contacts with territorially based languages, and its replacement by a network of alternative contacts with groups sharing a similar socio-ethnic affiliation – in other words, of the formation of non-territorial languages. On the other hand the grammatical and morphological similarities could be the outcome of shared areal developments at a later stage. The linguistic affinity between Romani and Domari (and, as far as documented, Lomavren) might therefore be accounted for in terms of their shared ancient origin and subsequent similar social and geographical history, rather than as a token of continuous genetic ties in the form of a linguistic sub-branch within the Indo-Aryan languages.

4 Descriptive phonology

4.1 Consonants

4.1.1 *Stop positions and articulation*

Three basic stop positions are inherited from Indo-Aryan and retained in all dialects of Romani: labial /p/, dental /t/, and velar /k/. To those one might add a palatal position, which is an inherited feature of other NIA languages (cf. Masica 1991: 94–5). The status of the palatal positions in Romani is somewhat problematic. In quite a few dialects /č/ behaves differently from other stops, showing loss of aspiration /čh/>/č/, loss of plosiveness /čh/>/ś/>/š/, /dž/>/ź/>/ž/, or substitution of its fricative quality through palatalisation /dž/>/d'/. These tendencies toward simplification suggest greater complexity than other stop positions, which in turn seems to recommend a separate classification of /č/ as an affricate. Palatalisation as an articulatory attribute can on the other hand accompany consonants (not just stops) in various positions. It makes sense therefore to separate three groups: genuine palatal stops, palatalised consonants, and affricates.

Genuine palatals are recent developments (cf. Boretzky 2001). They emerge either through the effects of inherited palatalisation of dentals in selected lexemes, as in Lovari *dźes* < **d'ives* 'day', *bući* < **but'i* 'work' (also in Northern Central dialects), or through contact developments, as in Arli and Gurbet varieties of Macedonia and Montenegro, affecting velars in positions preceding /i/ and /e/: *ćher* < *kher* 'house', *ćin-* < *kin-* 'to buy'. Finnish and Laiuse Romani show similar palatal mutation of velars, as a result of earlier contact with Swedish: *čhēr* < *kher* 'house'. In Bugurdži, palatals emerge through the reduction of the clusters /šti/ and /kli, gli/: *ući-* < *ušti-* 'to stand up', *kandźi* < *kangli* 'comb'.

Palatalised consonants are more widespread, though they are generally restricted to dialects in areas where the contact languages also have palatalised consonants, and so synchronically at least this feature can be considered areal in Romani. The background is similar: palatalised consonants may emerge internally, drawing on inherited variable palatalisation of dentals in selected lexemes: Northern Vlax *d'es* < **d'ives* 'day'. This development may lead to substitution of the palatalised dental through a palatalised velar: Kelderaš *g'es* < **d'es* < **d'ives*. The reverse process is found in the northern group of the Southern Central dialects (southern Slovakia and northern Hungary): *t'in-* < *kin-* 'to buy', *d'il-* < *gil-* 'to sing'. Palatalisation is triggered especially through contact with North Slavic languages in the Central and Northeastern groups. In the North Russian (Xaladitka) dialect (Wentzel 1980), palatalisation accompanies most consonants in positions preceding /i/ and /e/ as well as in jotated positions: *g'ind'a* < **gindja(s)* 'he read', *g'il'a* < **gilja* < **gili-a* 'songs', *phuv'ja* 'lands', *gad'a* < **gadžja* < *gadži-a* 'women'. It also has distinctive phonemic status, e.g. *sïr* 'how' but *sïr'* 'garlic'. Both the aspirated and non-aspirated voiceless postalveolar affricates merge in a palatalised affricate /č'/: (*ač'-* < *ačh-* 'to stay', *č'aj* < *čhaj* 'daughter', *č'ar* < *čar* 'grass'). In the Central dialects, palatal mutation of dentals is encountered occasionally, while the sonorants /n,l/ are particularly prone to the process, leading to the palatal sonorants /n', l'/.

Apart from the various effects of palatalisation and palatal mutation, stops are generally stable in Romani. Stops may assimilate to nasals: *khamni* < **khabni* 'pregnant', *lumni* < *lubni* 'whore'. The reverse process, i.e. the dissimilatory emergence of /nd/ from /n/, is attested in Welsh and in Finnish Romani: *mend* < *men* 'neck', *lond* < *lon* 'salt'. In the Sinti group, labial stops emerge from fricatives in final position: *lab* < *(a)lav* 'word', *job* < *jov* 'he'.

4.1.2 *Sonorants*

The basic inventory of sonorants includes a labial nasal /m/, a dental nasal /n/, a dental lateral /l/, and a dental trill /r/. The lateral /l/ is partly velarised in most dialects, the Sinti group being an exception. In dialects of Romani in Poland belonging both to the Northeastern and the Central groups, strong velarisation to /ł/ with ultimate substitution through a semi-vowel /w/ is found in the environment of all vowels except /i/, a development that is borrowed from Polish (*łove* = /wo've/ < *love* 'money'). Another contact effect is the substitution of the trill in the Sinti–Manuš group through a uvular /ʀ/, as a result of German and French influence.

Early Romani had a sonorant /ř/, which represented the historical retroflexes /ḍ/ in initial position, and /ṭṭ, ḍḍh/ in internal position, as well as part of the historical cluster /ṇḍ/ (in some dialects /ř/ replaces the cluster). The great diversity of forms that continue the historical cluster /ṇḍ/ in present-day dialects, and the reported presence of a retroflex sound in the Rhodope dialect of Bulgaria (Igla 1997: 152), are indications that Early Romani /ř/ may have still been a retroflex (cf. Gilliat-Smith 1911). In some Balkan dialects, historical /ř/ becomes /l/. It is continued as a uvular /ʀ/ in Kelderaš, and as a long or geminate trill /rr/ in some Gurbet varieties, in the southern Italian dialects (Soravia 1977: 84–5), and in western Northern Central dialects (Western Slovak Romani, as well as Bohemian and Moravian dialects; Elšík et al. 1999: 304; cf. Boretzky 1999a: 214). Elsewhere, /ř/ has merged with /r/. There is a tendency in some dialects to preserve a distinct reflex of historical /ř/ in the word **ařo* 'flour', to distinguish it from **andřo > ařo > (j)aro* 'egg' (see chapter 9): Northeastern *jažo/jaržo/jārlo*, Sinti-Manuš *jaxo/jarro*.

Sonorants are often unstable and subject to substitution through other sonorants, or metathesis. In some grammatical morphemes, final /n/ is often lost: *tume < tumen* 'you (PL)' in some dialects (Lovari, Welsh Romani, the Northeastern group), the abstract nominal suffix *-ipe < -ipen* (in dialects of southeastern Europe), the Greek-derived participle ending *-ime < -imen*.

4.1.3 *Fricatives and semi-vowels*

The inventory of fricatives derives to a considerable extent from recent innovations. Early Romani fricatives included labials /f, v/, a velar /x/, a glottal /h/, dental sibilants /s, z/ and postalveolar sibilants /š, ž/. Of those, /z/ first entered the language with the Iranian component, and /f/ with the Greek component; Boretzky (1999b: 27) even omits /f/ from his inventory of 'conservative' phonemes.[1] The velar /x/ is not inherited from OIA/MIA either, but constitutes a Proto-Romani innovation /kh/ > /x/, which however must have been an early development, as it preceded devoicing in initial aspirates *ghar > kher* 'house'. In many conservative dialects, its articulation is closer to a voiceless uvular /χ/, and it is possible that this reflects the earlier articulation, while the shift to a velar /x/ is contact-induced. Both /h/ and /ž/ are marginal in the pre-European component; the latter may even be regarded as rare (*užo* 'clean' < MIA *ujju-* being an isolated example), the former in initial position is frequently a recent prothetic development (cf. Polska Roma *hučo < učo* 'high').

The uvular fricative /ʀ/ could have been an Early Romani innovation substituting for the historical retroflex (see above), though it could just as well have emerged separately in individual dialects. As a continuation of historical /ř/, the uvular is attested in Kelderaš and a number of Balkan dialects. The uvular in the Sinti group is a late contact-related development, which replaces the inherited trill. In North Russian Romani, a voiced velar fricative /ɣ/ can continue /h/: *ɣeroj < heroj* 'foot', *ɣazd- < hazd-* 'to lift'.

New palatal sibilants /ś, ź/ have emerged as a result of the reduction of the affricates /čh, dž/. Kelderaš and Lovari show both processes, while Ursari and Drindari as well as the Vend dialects have only /dž/>/ź/ (cf. Boretzky and Igla 1993: 22–3). For Welsh Romani, Sampson (1926) notes that /č/ interchanges with /š/.

[1] *feder* 'better' is the only occurrence of /f/ in the pre-European component.

The alternation and variation of /x/ and /h/ is a contact development. In Arli and Bugurdži of Kosovo and Macedonia, the two often merge into /h/, in all likelihood due to Albanian, Turkish, and/or South Slavic influence: *ha-* < *xa-* 'to eat'. A similar development can be noted for the Southern Central dialects, due to Hungarian influence. The reverse process, a merger into /x/, appears in the Northeastern dialects under the influence of Russian and Polish: *xać(ker)-* < *hać(ar)-* < *ać(ar)-* 'to understand'. Velarisation of the glottal fricative in these dialects also affects the articulation of aspirated stops and affricates (*pxen-* < *phen-* 'to say'). The velar fricative /x/ in Welsh Romani is often replaced by /h/ or /k/.

The shift of /s, z/ > /š, ž/ is reported for individual varieties of the Northern Central group in the Štítnik river area of southern Slovakia (Elšík et al. 1999: 302–3): *šo* < *so* 'what'. The reverse development is found in Romani dialects in contact with Greek, such as Agia Varvara and Dendropotamos Vlax, where under Greek influence the postalveolars /š, ž, č, čh, dž/ are currently undergoing merger with dentals /s, z, c, ch, dz/ respectively: *sil* < *šil* 'cold'. A specific development of Finnish Romani is the shift /š/ > /h/, as in *heero* < *šero* 'head', triggered through contact with Swedish. In the Southern Central dialects, a sibilant emerges in the cluster /st/ < /xt/: *bast* < *baxt* 'fortune'.

Semi-vowels have a somewhat marginal position in the Romani phonological system. In the older layer representing Early Romani, /j/ appears mainly in positions following vowels. Otherwise its presence is limited to morphophonological jotation phenomena: *dikhjom* < *dikhljom* 'I saw', and to prothetic positions: *jon* < *on* 'they', in Northern and Northern Central dialects. In Arli of Kosovo and Macedonia, /j/ surfaces as a glide compensating for the reduction of morphological /s/ in intervocalic position: SG instrumental ending *-eja* , *-aja* (also *-ea*, *-aa*) < *-esa*, *-asa*. Labial /w/ in the inherited component is only found in dialects which, under Polish influence, have velarised /l/ to /ł/ and then to /w/ in most positions except those preceding /i/.[2]

4.1.4 *Affricates*

The Early Romani inventory of affricates included postalveolar /č/ and /dž/, which continue the MIA palatals, a voiceless aspirated postalveolar /čh/ through a Proto-Romani innovation (transfer of aspiration and initial devoicing of aspirates), and a dental /c/ (=[ts]) in the Greek loan component.[3] Both the inventory

[2] Dialects of English Para-Romani (=Angloromani) show /w/ replacing /v/ in initial position: *wast* < *vast* 'hand'.

[3] An isolated pre-European item in /c/, with unclear etymology, is *cird-* 'to pull', though the presence of *tird-* in Northeastern dialects suggests that the affrication is secondary and late. Unclear also is the origin of an additional affricate /dz/ in isolated Armenian or Iranian words, such as *dzet* < *zet* 'oil', which interchanges with /z/; this affricate seems more likely to be a late development.

of affricates and their frequency are increased through recent innovations in individual dialects.

The affricates /c/ and /dz/ can continue inherited palatalised dentals in selected lexemes: Catalonian Romani *dzives* < **d'ives* 'day'; western European dialects *keci* < **ket'i* 'how much'; Vlax, eastern Northern Central, and eastern Balkan *cikno* < **t'ikno* 'small'; all dialects except Northeastern *cird-* < **t'ird-* 'to pull'. The process is particularly widespread however in Vlax and the Northern Central dialects. In the Northern Central group the process may also affect /ki-/: *cin-* < *kin-* 'to buy'. In Burgudži, /c/ and a voiced counterpart /dz/ (optionally /z/) emerge in positions preceding /i/ from /k, g/, from medial /-t-, -d-/, and from the cluster /st/, as well as from the palatals /ć, dź/ in jotated positions: *buci* < *buti* 'work', *gozi* < *godzi* < *godi* 'mind', *kerdzum* < **kerdźum* < **kerd(j)um* 'I did'.

As mentioned above, recently emerged palatals show a tendency to merge with affricates: Montenegro Gurbet *džive* < *dźive* < **d'ives*, *čin-* < *ćin-* < *kin-* 'to buy'. A voiced postalveolar /dž/ emerges from /z/ in Finnish Romani: *džummi* < *zumi* 'soup'. A voiceless postalveolar /č/ emerges under Hungarian influence from initial /j/ in the Vend sub-group of the Southern Central group: *čak* < *jakh* 'eye'.

Dentalisation of postalveolar affricates /č, dž/>/c, dz/ is an ongoing process in dialects in contact with Greek (Agia Varvara and Dendropotamos Vlax). A similar process is found in several of the Northern Central dialects in the Štítnik river area of southern Slovakia (Elšík et al. 1999: 302–3). A palatalised articulation of the dental plosive component, in free variation with both affricates, is often characteristic of this transitional stage. The reverse development affects the voiceless dental /c/ in Sepeči, which under Turkish influence is substituted by /č/: *čip-* < *cip-* 'to scream'.

4.1.5 *Voicing*

Voice opposition is a general feature of stops, affricates, labial fricatives, and sibilants. There are dialects with no voiced counterpart for /c/ (e.g. Sinti; or Vlax, except in contact with Greek) or for /ć/ (Lovari and Kelderaš), and some with none to /č/ (Vend, Ursari, Drindari, Kelderaš, Lovari). In some dialects, notably Kelderaš varieties, /ř/ might be considered the voiced counterpart of /x/, both being uvulars. In Xaladitka, voice opposition is found in velar fricatives /x:ɣ/.

Voice alternation is found in some grammatical endings. All Romani dialects have inherited the pattern by which Layer II case suffixes in *-t-* and *-k-* are voiced following /n/: *leske* 'for him', *lenge* 'for them'. The voicing of velar and dental stops in positions following /n/ can be seen in connection with Proto-Romani innovations that may be connected to changes in the Northwestern languages of

India. The causative affix *-ker-* has a voiced variant *-ger-* in the Vend group of the Southern Central dialects. These exist in addition two variants of a nominal suffix, *-ipen*/*-iben*, for which Schmid (1963) however has argued in favour of two distinct OIA etymologies. For Welsh Romani, Sampson (1926: 21) mentions voice alteration in lexical items.

The most common development affecting voice is the devoicing of stops in word-final position, a tendency in Romani dialects in contact with European languages that display this phenomenon: Czech, Slovak, Polish, Russian, German, Turkish, and partly Macedonian: *dad* > *dat* 'father'. Boretzky and Igla (1993: 45) suggest that the absence of a word-final devoicing of stops in Welsh Romani reflects the fact that the ancestors of the Welsh Roma passed through central Europe before devoicing had become widespread in the local contact languages. Initial devoicing is a feature of the Finnish and Laiuse (Estonian Romani) dialects: *tād* < *dad* 'father'. In Burgenland Roman, voiced /z/ merges with /s/ under Austrian German influence.

4.1.6 *Aspiration*

Distinctive aspiration operating within the set of voiceless stops and distinguishing them into two classes, aspirated and non-aspirated, is perhaps the most remarkable phonological feature of Romani as a language that is territorially based in Europe, and the most outstanding phonological feature marking it out as a NIA language. In general, voiceless consonants have aspirated counterparts for all three major stop positions – /ph, th, kh/ –, as well as for the dental-postalveolar affricate – /čh/. The latter is the weakest member of the set of aspirates. Where /č/ shifts to /c/, for example under Greek influence, the change is also reflected in the aspirate set /čh/>/ch/. Distinctive aspiration may disappear in the affricate position, as in Welsh Romani or Sinti, which only retain /č/; the aspirated affricate may be replaced by a palatalised affricate /č'/ as in Xaladikta, or be reduced to a palatal sibilant /ź/, as in Northern Vlax. Other instances of loss of aspiration are documented only in a fragmented manner, with contradictory notations in the sources, and so it is not quite clear whether aspiration is indeed disappearing in the language. In Northeastern dialects, velarisation of the aspirated articulation leads in effect to loss of aspiration and to the emergence of a new set of clusters /px, tx, kx, čx/.

4.1.7 *Geminates*

Gemination is a recent development and is confined to individual dialects. Only in the case of the geminate trill /rr/, which represents Early Romani /ř/, as in Gurbet and in some Central dialects, might gemination be regarded as the continuation of an older opposition. Elšík et al. (1999: 311) mention consonant assimilation leading to gemination in the Southern Central dialects: *od'd'a* < *on'd'a* 'there', *gullo* < *gudlo* 'sweet'. In the Abruzzi dialect of southern Italy, gemination through assimilation is found in word boundaries where object pronouns are cliticised: *dikáttə* < *dikhav tu* 'I see you'. In both varieties, what appear to be internal assimilation processes leading to gemination are in fact supported, if not indeed motivated, by contact-induced gemination in lexical items as well, thus Abbruzzi *akkana* < *akana* 'now', Southern Central *gáddžo* < *gadžo* 'non-Gypsy, farmer', alternating with *gádžo*. Gemination triggered by contact with Turkish is found in the Romani dialects of Iran, Zargari and Romano (Windfuhr 1970, Djonedi 1996): *butti* < *buti* 'work', *tatto* < *tato* 'hot'. In Finnish Romani, gemination appears to compete with vowel lengthening, thus *davva* < *dava* 'this' but *čāvo* < *č(h)avo* 'boy', while in Finnish long vowels may be followed by either simple or geminate consonants. Boretzky and Igla (1993: 40–1) suggest that the process was triggered through earlier contact with Swedish, where in words with more than one syllable a stressed vowel is either long and followed by a simple consonant, or short and followed by a cluster or geminate.

4.1.8 *Consonant clusters*

The inventory of initial clusters in the Early Romani legacy comprises just four initial clusters that are inherited from OIA, /tr, dr, phr, št/ – *trin* 'three', *drakh* 'grape', *phral* 'brother', *štar* 'four'. The Greek component adds a significant number of initial clusters: /sf, sk, sp, str, vr, kr, mr, hr, pr/. The inventory of medial and final consonant clusters on the other hand is extensive and varied. It allows for combinations of most stop, fricative, and nasal positions with a following liquid /r, l/, of dental and postalveolar sibilants with most stop and fricative positions (though not with other dental or postalveolar sibilants or affricates, e.g. */šč/), and of nasals and to some extent also liquids with most stop and fricative positions. The emergence in initial position of new clusters and the reduction of old ones are local, dialect-specific processes. Clusters may emerge in initial position through metathesis: *breš* < *berš* 'year', *brišind* < *biršind* 'rain'. In internal position, new clusters are typically the outcome of syllable reduction, common especially in the Sinti group: *leskro* < *leskero* 'his'.

Cluster reduction may involve pure simplification (Welsh Romani *phal* < *phral* 'brother', *gras* < *grast* 'horse', Welsh Romani and Arli *baval* < *balval* 'wind'), assimilation (Finnish Romani *phannel* < *phandel* 'shuts', Bugurdži *angruci* < *angrusti* 'ring'), metathesis (*turšul* < *trušul* 'cross'), or syllable addition (*baravalo* < *barvalo* 'rich'). Initial clusters are sometimes eliminated through Turkish influence in Sepeči and other dialects of Turkey (*ištar* < *štar* 'four') and through Azeri and Persian influence in Zargari and Romano (*derom* < *drom* 'road').

4.1.9 *Types of consonant systems*

Tables 4.1–4.7 present an overview of the consonant phonemes of selected dialects, beginning with the reconstructed consonant systems of Proto-Romani and Early Romani.

Table 4.1 *Proto-Romani consonant phonemes*

Retroflex dental/nasal are still preserved in the cluster /ṇḍ/; retroflex liquids /ḷ/ and /ṛ/ continue MIA medial dentals and retroflex dentals, respectively. Iranian and Greek loan phonemes do not yet appear.

p	t	k		č			
ph	th	kh		čh			
b	d	g		dž			ḍ
m	n						ṇ
		x	s	š		h	
v				(ž)			
	l						ḷ
	r						ṛ
					j		

Table 4.2 *Early Romani consonant phonemes*

Palatalised dentals are allophonic. The palatal is marginal. Phonemes in square brackets represent possible realisations of historical retroflexes.

p	t(t')	k	c	č			
ph	th	kh		čh			
b	d(d')	g	(dz)	dž			[ḍ]
m	n						[ṇ]
f		x	s	š		h	
v			z	(ž)		**[R]**	
	l						[ḷ]
	r						[ṛ]
					j		

Table 4.3 *Consonant phonemes in Kelderaš and Lovari*

Affricates are reduced to fricatives. Palatalised velars in Kelderaš, jotation-triggered in (rj), elsewhere tendency to merge with affricate /č/ and alveopalatal sibilants /š, ž/. Uvular /**R**/ is maintained only in Kelderaš.

p	t	k(k')	c	č	(ć)	
ph	th	kh				
b	d	g(g')			(dź)	
m	n					
f		x	s	š	(ś)	h
v			z	ž	(ź)	(**R**)
	l					
	r					
	(r')					
					j	

Table 4.4 *Consonant phonemes in Sinti*

No palatals. Reduction of aspiration in the affricate. The dental trill/flap is usually replaced by a uvular.

p	t	k	c	č		
ph	th	kh				
b	d	g		dž		
m	n					
f		x	s	š		h
v			z	ž		**R**
	l					
	(r)					
					j	

Table 4.5 *Consonant phonemes in Gurbet*

Velar stops become palatals in positions preceding front vowels. Palatalised consonants are restricted to /l', r'/. Historical /ř/ is a geminate trill /rr/.

p	t	k	c	č	ć	
ph	th	kh		čh	ćh	
b	d	g		dž	dź	
m	n					
f		x	s	š		h
v			z	ž		
	l					
	l'					
	r rr					
	r'					
					j	

Table 4.6 *Consonant phonemes in North Russian (Xaladikta)*

Most consonants have palatalised counterparts in distinctive distribution. The historical affricates /čh, č/ merge in a palatalised affricate. Velar fricatives show voice opposition.

p	t	k	c			
p'	t'	k'		č'		
ph	th	kh				
	t'h	k'h				
b	d	g	(dz)	dž		
b'	d'	g'				
m	n					
m'	n'					
f		x	s	š		h
		x'	s'			
v		ɣ	z	ž		
v'		ɣ'				
	l					
	l'					
	r					
	r'					
					j	

Table 4.7 *Consonant phonemes in Sepeči*

Dental affricates become postalveolar. The voiced velar fricative appears in Greek loans.

p	t	k		č		
ph	th	kh		čh		
b	d	g		dž		
m	n					
f		x	s	š		h
v		(ɣ)	z	(ž)		
	l					
	r					
					j	

4.2 Vowels

4.2.1 *Vowel quality*

The basic, Early Romani system of vowels appears to have encompassed just five vowels /a, e, i, o, u/. The introduction of additional vowel qualities is a contact-related phenomenon. Sampson (1926: 6–11) mentions a back vowel /å/, phonetically apparently [ɔ] and [ɑ], in Welsh Romani, resulting from Welsh and English influence, as well as an unrounded /ʌ/. It arises mainly in the environment of velar consonants, sibilants, and sonorants, in stressed syllables: *jåg* < *jag* ‘fire’, *påårnō* < *parno* ‘white’. Elšík et al. (1999: 309) report on the backing of the vowel /ā/ to [ɒ:] in some cases, in dialects of southern Slovakia: [akɒ:n] < *akan(a)* ‘now’. In some Arli varieties of Macedonia, as spoken in Muslim or Xoraxane communities where Turkish is widespread alongside Romani, /u/ is rounded in jotated grammatical endings: *dikhlüm* < *dikhljum* ‘I saw’.

Centralisation of /e/ to /ə/ and of /i/ to /ɨ/ occurs in Vlax, mainly in the environment of sibilants as well as /x/ and /ʀ/: *šəl* < *šel* ‘hundred’, *sɨ* < *si* ‘is’; these vowels are decentralised in Lovari. Boretzky (1991) suggests the possibility that centralisation coincided with the same development in Romanian dialects, as it appears in more or less the same phonetic environments. The change was triggered by the adoption of Romanian loans, following which the general pattern of distribution of /e, i/ versus their centralised counterparts was copied into the Romani inherited lexicon. This in turn is followed by a loosening of the conditions on distribution, and a spread of /e/>/ə/ to other environments such as velars (*khər* < *kher* ‘house’) and additional lexemes (*bərš* < *berš* ‘year’). A centralised vowel /ə/ is borrowed from Bulgarian into neighbouring Romani dialects, as in Rhodope *javər* < *aver* ‘other’, and occurs as a variant in some dialects in contact with Macedonian. In the Northeastern dialects we find replacement of /i/ through centralised /ɨ/ as a result of contact with Russian and Polish: *ɨsɨ* < *(i)si* ‘is’. In Welsh Romani, centralised vowels [ə] and [ʌ] appear as variants of short /a e i o/ in unstressed positions: *əkáj* < *akáj* ‘here’ (Sampson 1926: 10).

4.2.2 *Vowel length*

Vowel lengthening in Romani is an areal contact feature. The dialects of the Balkans, belonging to the Vlax and Southern Balkan groups, generally lack vowel length, while on the other hand Northern and Central dialects, and Vlax dialects in continuing contact with Hungarian, tend to show some form of vowel lengthening, although its phonemic status is often debatable.

It is clear that long vowels in Romani do not continue OIA/MIA length oppositions (cf. already Miklosich 1872–80, ix: 24). The partial agreement among Romani dialects in the distribution of vowel lengthening, mentioned by Lesný (1916) and Ariste (1978) as possible evidence for such historical continuation, is rather a result of similar, recent processes of lengthening. Boretzky and Igla (1993: 36) attribute the acquisition of length to the similarities among the patterns of vowel lengthening found in Hungarian,

Slovak, and Czech. These developments are considered to have triggered, through contact, vowel lengthening in the Central dialects, in the Sinti group, in Finnish Romani, and perhaps also in Welsh Romani. Length is independent of stress, and the correlation of the two features in Sinti, Laiuse, and elsewhere, is argued to have emerged only at a later stage, following shift in stress patterns.

The source of long vowels is often compensatory lengthening: Baltic and Central *dēl* < *devel* 'God', cf. *del* 'he gives'; Southern Central *āri* < *avri* 'out'; Welsh Romani *džunā* < *džunava* 'I know'. Non-compensatory acquisition of length is also apparent, however. It is often characterised by a tonal lengthening: Lovari (*čāčó*) < *čăčó* < *čačó* 'true'. On the whole, lengthening may affect the first vowel in the pattern CVCV (*čāvo* 'boy', *bāro* 'big'), though not usually in CVCCV (*moxto* 'box', *tikno* 'small'; but in Welsh Romani *mištō* 'well'). In three-syllable words or those of the patterns CVCVC the second vowel is occasionally lengthened (*kokōro* 'alone', *šukār* 'pretty'). Monosyllabic roots show lengthening in positions preceding sonorants as well as /v/: *džān-* 'to know', *thōv-* 'to wash' (cf. Boretzky and Igla 1993: 36–8).

Vowel length can be functionalised grammatically. Morphological endings such as the terminations of demonstratives (Southern Central and Welsh Romani) or plural markers may show consistent lengthening. Elšík et al. (1999: 311) report on the functionalisation of vowel length in some Southern Central dialects, where adjectives have length only in non-attributive position: *čāčo* 'right', but *čačo va* 'right hand'.

4.2.3 *Other processes affecting vowels*

Vowel reduction is characteristic of unstressed positions in Sinti (*šúkər* < *šukár* 'pretty'), where it is frequent due to the frequent shift away from final stress, and optionally in Welsh Romani (*əkáj* < *akáj* 'here'). The process often leads to syllable reduction in Sinti, especially in the environment of sonorants which are allowed to combine into new clusters: *rómnes* < *romanés* 'Romani', *léskro* < *léskero*, *pre* < *opre* 'up', *vri* < *avri* 'out'. In Gurbet, the emergence of syllabic /r/ is modelled on Serbian: *brš* < *berš* 'year', *mrno* < *mirno/minro* 'my'. Bohemian Romani also has a syllabic /r/, modelled on Czech.

Vowel raising arises independently in various dialects. For Drindari, Boretzky and Igla (1993: 40) relate it to the influence of Bulgarian dialects in unstressed positions (*rumjá* < *romnjá* 'women'), but note its spread to stressed positions as well (*ternú* < *ternó* 'young', *sastipí* < *sastipé* 'health'). A similar phenomenon occurs in Welsh Romani (*čuripén* < *čoripén* 'poverty, misfortune', *mándi* < *mánde* 1SG locative pronoun) and in Laiuse (*čāvu* < *čavó* 'boy'), as well as in Latvian Romani.

Vowel harmony is attested for individual lexical items (Sepeči *šoro* < *šero* 'head', resulting in distinct stems for different agreement markers: M.SG *polo* 'fell', F.SG *peli*, genitive with masculine agreement *-koro*, with feminine heads *-kiri*, and elsewhere), as well as for grammatical morphemes (Gurvari 2SG future ending *-ehe* < *-eha*). Historical umlaut arising through the effect of jotation is characteristic of the 1SG copula and the perfective concord marker in Vlax: *dikhlem* 'I saw' < **dikhljöm* < **dikhljom*. A similar process occurs in Kalajdži and Drindari: *bev* < *bjav* 'wedding', *sev* < *sjav* 'mill'.

The fronting of /u/ to /i/ occurs in Romano and Zargari under regional influence (*maniš* < *manuš* 'person').

4.2.4 *Diphthongs*

Romani diphthongs are generally difficult to distinguish from sequences of vowels and a consonant /j/, which usually emerge historically through consonant elision: *muj* < **muja* < **muha* (cf. Domari *muh*) < OIA *múkha-* 'mouth', *naj* < OIA *nákha-* 'finger', *čhaj* < **čhavi* 'girl', cf. *čhavo* 'boy' (cf. Kostov 1960). The diphthongs in these words are shared by the dialects, and so we can assume that they reflect the Early Romani forms. There are further cases of shared forms, including lexical items such as *řoj* 'spoon', *šošoj* 'rabbit', *heroj* 'leg', and the deictics *odoj* 'there', *adaj* 'here', *akaj* 'here'.

The elision and contraction processes that give rise to these so-called diphthongs are still ongoing in individual dialects, mainly affecting terminations in /n, l, v/: *bokoj* < *bokoli* 'cake'. An enclitic copula can attach to vowel endings rendering forms like *mišto-j* < *mišto-i* < **mišto-hi* 'it is good', *na-j* < **na-hi* 'it is not'. The most common combinations are /oj/ and /aj/, /uj/ being rather rare: *duj* 'two', alongside *muj* 'face'. Seldom do we find /aw/ and /ej/. The first appears in Kelderaš and Sinti, as well as in a number of Central dialects, where final /v/ becomes a glide: *kamaw* < *kamav(a)* 'I want'. The second is found in Northern Vlax *phej* < *phen* 'sister', in assimilation to jotation phenomena affecting feminine nouns. A bi-syllabic structure is preserved however in Lovari *paï* < *pani* 'water', and perhaps also Welsh Romani *xoï* < *xoli* 'anger'. Boretzky and Igla (1993: 38–9) report on the diphthongisation of vowels following shift of stress in Prekmurje: *máoto* < *mató* 'drunk', *phéjnel* < *phenél* 'says' . Similar developments may be found in some Northern Vlax dialects and in the easternmost Northern Central varieties.

4.2.5 *Types of vowel systems*

Tables 4.8–4.12 illustrate the addition, to the Early Romani inventory, of vowel qualities and vowel quantity in selected dialects.

Table 4.8 *Vowels in Arli, Gurbet, Sepeči*

i	(y)	u
e	(ə)	o
		a

Table 4.9 *Vowels in Kelderaš*

i	ɨ	u
e	ə	o
		a

Table 4.10 *Vowels in the Polska Roma and North Russian (Xaladitka) dialects*

i	ɨ	u
e		o
		a

Table 4.11 *Vowels in Welsh Romani*

i i:			u u:	
e e:	ə	ʌ	o o:	
			a a:	ɔ ɔ:

Table 4.12 *Vowels in Sinti*

i i:		u u:
e e:	ə	o o:
		a a:

4.2.6 *Stress*

Early Romani had word-level grammatical stress, which is preserved in contemporary Romani in what Boretzky and Igla (1993) call 'conservative' stress patterns. In the pre-European ('thematic') component, stress is on the final position of lexical roots, in the absence of grammatical affixes, or on older grammatical affixes: *sastó* 'healthy', *sastipén* 'health', *čhavó* 'boy', *čhavoř́ó* 'little boy', *čhavořés* 'little boy.OBL', *bikináv* 'I sell', *bikindóm* 'I sold'. Only a limited class of younger grammatical affixes is unstressed. This includes Layer II case markers (*čhavés-ke* 'for the boy'), the vocative marker (*devél* 'God', but *dévl-a!* 'God!'), the extension to the present conjugation in *-a*, which in some dialects serves as a future marker (*bikináv-a* 'I shall sell'), and the remoteness tense marker in *-as/-ahi* which forms the imperfect and pluperfect (*bikináv-as* 'I used to sell'). We can therefore generalise that conservative stress in the pre-European (thematic) component falls on Layer I inflectional endings in nominal and nominalised categories (nouns, pronouns, possessives, adjectives, participles, demonstratives), on person inflection in finite verbs, and on the final component of indeclinables (*anglál* 'in front', *ketí* 'how much').

This pattern in fact also applies to the European (athematic) component, insofar as European loan elements are assimilated into Indo-Aryan inflectional morphology: *foróske* 'to the town', < Greek *fóros*, *hramosardóm* 'I wrote', Greek *ɣrámma*). With no pre-European inflectional morphology, i.e. in the nominative form of nouns, in adjectives, and in indeclinables, European loans usually retain the original stress: *fóro(s)* 'town', *lavutári(s)* 'musician', *lúngo* 'long', *pánda* 'still' < Greek *pánda* 'always'.

Compound verbs in *-d-* (from *d-* 'to give') usually have stressed roots: *bóldav* 'I turn, transform', *vázdav* 'I open'. In some dialects, such as Sepeči, they are adapted to normal stress patterns and show stressed person inflection markers, while elsewhere the stress patterns of compounds are extended by analogy to similar verbs (Vlax *trádel* 'he drives'). Intransitive derivations (mediopassives) have stress on the lexical root position (though shift of stress to the person inflection marker by analogy to active verbs is common): *dikhél* 'he sees', but Lovari *díčhol* 'it is seen'.

Distinctive stress in the pre-European component of Romani is rare. In some cases, homophonous grammatical affixes with differing stress features may result in minimal pairs: *džan-ás* 'we know (=know-1PL)', vs. *džá-n-as* 'they used to go (=go-3PL-REM)'. In Lovari, the remote demonstrative *kak-ó* with adjectival inflection contrasts with *káko* 'uncle'; the latter appears to be an Iranian loan (cf. Kurdish *kak-* 'uncle'), but follows loan-noun integration patterns (oblique *kakós-*; see chapter 5). In the nominal inflectional paradigms of loans, it is not unusual to find case distinctions expressed through shift of stress, as a result of the selective assimilation of European loan nouns to conservative or inherited stress patterns in oblique forms: *bába* 'the grandmother (nominative)' vs. *babá* 'grandmother (oblique)'. For Welsh Romani, Sampson (1926: 23–8) mentions that nouns and adjectives take final stress when used in predicative constructions, but initial stress elsewhere, and that demonstratives have penultimate stress in attributive positions but final stress in pronominal function: *kóva dives* 'that day' but *ková* 'that one'. This is not an inherited feature, however, but one that is connected to the contact-induced shift in stress patterns.

A tendency toward shift of stress to early positions in the word, penultimate or initial, is found in Romani dialects in contact with languages that have initial or penultimate stress, either generally or in high frequency. There are two main centres for this development. The first is in central Europe, and encompasses Romani dialects in historical contact with Hungarian and Slovak, as well as, at a later stage in their history, with German, Italian, English, Swedish, and Finnish: the affected Romani dialects are the Central branch, Sinti, Welsh, and Finnish Romani. The second centre is in the Balkans. Here the trigger is likely to be in the complex patterns of Albanian, which often result in penultimate stress. The affected dialects include varieties of Bugurdži, Arli, and others. In both groups, the process still appears to be ongoing and stress is subject to variation. Consistent shifts are reported for the Terzi Mahale dialect of Prizren (penultimate) and for Finnish Romani (initial). While some Central dialects are consistent in showing initial stress, in Eastern Slovak Romani, the tendency is to preserve the conservative, grammatical stress in Layer I endings that precede Layer II endings, thus exempting forms like *roméskero* 'of the man' from the shift toward penultimate stress. Sinti is even more conservative and retains stress on both Layer I case endings and on personal endings of the finite verb. Its conservativism, compared with the Central branch, leads Boretzky and Igla (1993: 33) to assume that shift of stress in Sinti is not the outcome of German influence, but rather of earlier influence, possibly by Hungarian, a process which actually lost some of its momentum following the migration into German-speaking territory.

4.3 Phonological and morphophonological processes

4.3.1 *Historical ṇḍ*

Romani dialects show striking variation in the successor forms of the historical retroflex cluster in /ṇḍ/, suggesting a rather recent development. All forms however can be derived from an Early Romani cluster */ndř/, and so it is possible to take this as an abstract point of departure; abstract, since the precise quality of the component /ř/ remains unknown.

The most common reflexes of the cluster in contemporary Romani are /r/ and a form akin to /nr/. The latter may take on the form /nř/, showing the conservative sonorant that continues a number of historical retroflex sounds, or else a metathesised form in /rn/. Further forms include /ndr/ and /nd/, and less frequently also /ngl/ and /nl/. A rare simplified form is /n/ (Dendropotamos

Vlax *mano* 'bread'). Assimilation to /ř/, which derives from other retroflex sounds, is also found.

Although there are only few lexical items that contain reflexes of the historical cluster, their presence is nonetheless conspicuous as they include some items belonging to the most stable basic vocabulary: **mandřo* 'bread', **andřo* 'egg', **mindřo* 'my', **pindřo* 'foot', **kandřo* 'thorn', as well as **mandřikli* 'cake', **mindřikli* 'necklace', and **xandřo* 'sword'. Exempted from the variation is the word *parno* 'white' (OIA/MIA *paṇḍu*), which appears to be uniform in Romani and where the cluster therefore must have undergone a shift already in Proto-Romani;[4] this impression is reinforced by Jerusalem Domari *prana* (alongside *parna*), but *mana* 'bread' (OIA *maṇḍa*) and *ana* 'egg' (OIA *āṇḍa*). A further Romani regularity is *xarno* 'short' (OIA *khaṇḍa*), possibly through an early attempt to distinguish it from **xandřo* 'sword' (OIA **khaṇḍaka*).

Not all dialects are consistent in their treatment of the cluster across individual lexical items. Eastern Slovak Romani for instance has forms in /r/ for *maro* 'bread', *xaro* 'sword', and *miro* 'my', but /ndr/ in *jandro* 'egg', *kandro* 'thorn', and *pindro* 'foot'. In southeastern Europe especially, dialects differ in their treatment of the cluster: Kalderaš Vlax has generalised /nř/, while individual varieties of Gurbet Vlax have either /rn/ or /nr/; in the southern Balkan group, Prilep and Ipeiros have /nd/, Arli has /r/, Erli has /ř/, and Sepeči shows /ndr/ (see also Boretzky 1999b: 29). This seems to contradict Boretzky and Igla's (1993: 24) impression that the development of /ṇḍ/ constitutes an old, pre-European development which is suitable for the reconstruction of very early pre-European (genetic) dialect groupings (see chapter 9). Not suprisingly, the most extreme diversity is found in the Balkans, the historical centre of diffusion for European Romani. Variation appears to diminish as one moves toward the northern/northwestern parts of the continent, where dialects typically show /r/ in all or most items that are otherwise prone to variation. This again seems to support a late development, one that is contained within the European settlement patterns of the various dialects and groups.

4.3.2 *Prothesis and truncation*

The insertion of initial consonants and vowels, and removal of initial vowels, in lexical roots is an inherited Early Romani development which continues and expands in contemporary dialects. The typical prothetic consonants are /j-/ and /v-/, with individual cases of prothetic /h-/, /f-/, /r-/, and rarely also /l-/ in some dialects. The initial vowel that is prone to both prothesis and truncation is /a-/, with isolated cases of truncated and prothetic /u-/, /i-/, and /o-/.

[4] The only exception so far attested is Iranian Romani *panro*; a late development, either analogous to *vanro* 'egg' or a plain metathesis, cannot be excluded for this isolated variety.

A genuinely phonological prothetic development would be the insertion of palatal /j/ in positions preceding front vowels /i/ and /e/, and of labial /v/ preceding back vowels /o/ and /u/. However, the only three items that share prothetic consonant forms in all Romani dialects do not support this prediction: *vast* 'hand' (OIA *hásta*), *jakh* 'eye' (OIA *ákṣi*), and *jag* 'fire' (OIA *agní*). Turner (1932) proposed that the early insertion of initial *j-* and *v-* was not at all phonologically conditioned, but rather a morphological assimilation of preposed determiners in M.SG **ov* and F.SG **oj* with masculine and feminine nouns, respectively, as well as with adjectives. The pattern of gender distribution (M. *vast* 'hand', F. *jakh* 'eye', *jag* 'fire') was, according to Turner, later disrupted through analogous developments, resulting in dialect specific variants (M. *ařo* 'flour', alongside both *jaro* and *varo*). Turner's theory is supported by the forms *ovaver* < *ov-aver* 'the other' in the Prilep dialect, *vaver* 'other' in the dialects of northwestern Europe, and *kaver* 'other' < *ekh aver* 'an-other' in Lovari Vlax, the latter demonstrating the plausibility in principle of morphological assimilation of this kind. This consonant insertion must have followed the emergence of a preposed definite article **ov*, **oj*, but preceded the reduction of the article to the vowel forms that are attested today, e.g. *o*, *i*. This places the beginning of the development in the Early Romani period.

The subsequent spread of phonological and analogous prothesis affects Romani as a whole, too, but its specific outcomes are particular to individual dialects. Of the items that attract /v/, most go back to a form with initial back vowels. They include not just pre-European items – *vušt* < *ušt* 'lip', *vučo* < *učo* 'high' (alongside *hučo*), but also Greek and European loans – *vorta* 'straight' < Greek *ortha*, *vodros* 'bed' < Slavonic *odrŭ*. Only a minority of items that attract /j/, on the other hand, have initial front vowels (*jilo* < *ilo* 'heart', *jekh* < *ekh* 'one', *jiv* < *iv* 'snow'). Those however are found to be more widespread in cross-dialectal comparison.

A conspicuous prothetic development affects third-person pronouns. Early Romani forms in *ov, oj, on* continue in the Balkan branches and in the Southern Central group. Prothetic *v-* (*vov, voj, von*) is distinctive of Vlax (though it also appears in Sepeči, presumably through Vlax influence), and prothetic *j-* (*jov, joj, jon*) is distinctive of the dialects of western and northern Europe. Typical of northwestern European dialects are in addition the developments in *jaro* < *a(nd)řo* 'egg', and to a lesser extent *vaver* < *aver* 'other' (see chapter 9). Additional developments are dialect-specific, and may show contradictory patterns. In the Northeastern dialect of the Polska Roma, for example, the overall tendency is to avoid initial *a-*, and truncation of *a-* operates in a manner that is complementary to *j*-prothesis (*jamen* < *amen* 'we', alongside *maro* < *amaro* 'our').

The fluctuation of initial /a-/ has its roots in two separate and fairly recent developments, namely the truncation of etymological /a-/ in forms like *av-* 'to come', *ačh-* 'to stay', *avri* 'out', *amen* 'we', *anglal* 'in front' and *akana* 'now', and the addition of prothetic /a-/ to forms which etymologically possess an initial consonant, such as *res-* 'to arrive', *šun-* 'to hear', *rakh-* 'to find', *nav* 'name', *lav* 'word', *bijav* 'wedding'. Truncation is overwhelmingly a tendency of the dialects of northwestern Europe, in particular of the contraction processes that are common in Sinti (*čela* 'he stays', *vri* 'out', *mer* 'we', *glan* 'in front'), while in the Northeastern group avoidance of initial /a-/ is complemented by extensive consonantal prothesis of /j-/: Polska Roma *čheł* 'he stays', *głan* 'in front', *kana* 'now', but *jamen* 'we'. By contrast, the tendency to insert prothetic /a-/ is overwhelmingly Vlax, and partly Balkan. While individual dialects of the Balkans may preserve conservative forms (cf. Sepeči *bijav* 'feast', *šun-* 'to hear', *res-* 'to suffice', but *anav* 'name', and *arakh-* alongside *rakh-* 'to find'), a number of items, such as *ašun-* 'to hear', or *abijav* 'wedding', are lower-ranking on the hierarchy of *a*-prothesis, and are confined to Vlax. The Southern Central group shows partial affinity with Vlax in this regard, and has *alav* 'word' and *anav* 'name', but *bijav* 'wedding', *res-* 'to arrive', and *šun-* 'to hear' (see chapter 9).

Other fluctuations of initial consonants and vowels are generally of local relevance only (cf. *žužo, ružo* < *užo* 'clean'; *furj-, hurj-* < *urj-* 'to dress'; *vazd-, azd-, hazd-* 'to lift').

4.3.3 *Jotation*

Morphophonological jotation is a feature of the following categories: the copula *som* ~ *sjom* 'I am'; the inflection of feminine nouns *buti* 'work' > PL *butja* > *but'a* > *buča*, *phuv* 'land' > PL *phuvja*; the formation of mediopassives (de-transitives) *kerel* 'he does' > *kerdjol* 'it is done'; and the past-tense conjugation *kerdom* ~ *kerdjom* 'I did', though not in forms that directly continue historical participles (*kerde* 'they did', *kerdo* 'done').

The process has several triggers. The first is the feminine singular inflectional ending in *-i*. The attachment of additional inflectional affixes leads to jotation in the relevant segments, on pure phonetic grounds – adjacency to a front vowel: *romni* 'woman' > PL *romnja* ~ *romn'a*. The resulting fluctuation then leads to analogous alternations that infiltrate other feminine paradigms as well, where no front vowel appears (*phuv* 'land' > PL *phuvja*). This development is shared and well-established, and appears to be of Proto-Romani origin. De-jotation leading to forms such as *romna* 'women' is encountered sporadically.

Jotation in the perfective concord endings was presumably triggered by a connecting particle, which mediated between the participle and person marker (see chapter 6): **ker-do-jo-me* > **kerdjom* 'I did'. The third trigger for jotation is the attachment of the grammaticalised passive auxiliary *(j)ov-* (OIA *bhav-* 'to become') to the participle to form the synthetic intransitive derivation (mediopassive): **kerdo-(j)ovel* > *kerdjovel* > (*kerdjol*) 'it is being done'. The origin of initial yod here remains unclear; perhaps we are dealing with a case of selective prothesis.

The development of jotation can follow one of several paths:

1. a sequence of a consonant+glide: *sjom* ~ *sinjom* 'I am', *kerdjom* ~ *kergjom* 'I did'; this is quite rare, and found mainly in the Balkans.
2. palatalisation or palatal mutation of the consonant preceding morphological yod: **kerdjom* > *kerd'om* > *kerdźom* 'I did', **dikhtjom* > *dikht'om* > *dikhćom* 'I saw', **kerdjol* > *kerd'ol* > *kerdźol* 'it is done'; this is the preferred outcome for past-tense verbs and mediopassives in most dialects of Romani that are in contact with palatalising languages (Northeastern, Central, and some Balkan dialects).
3. assimilation and ultimate replacement of the preceding consonant – primarily sonorants – by yod: *phenja* > *pheja* 'sister (ACC)', **geljom* > *gejom* 'I went'. In nouns it appears to be confined to individual lexemes in individual dialects, with strong tendencies in Vlax. In verbs, the process is widespread and includes the Sinti group, Welsh Romani, Northeastern, southern Italian Romani, the Central dialects, and the Bugurdži–Drindari group.
4. convergence of *yod* and the following vowel (Umlaut): **kerdjom* > *kerdem* 'I did', **sjom* > *sem* ~ *sim* 'I am'; this is typical of Vlax.
5. de-jotation: most frequently in *som* 'I am', but also *kerdom* 'I did', *kerdol* 'it is done'; this is found in the Balkans, and alongside option 3 in Sinti and Welsh Romani.

4.3.4 *s/h alternation in grammatical paradigms*

In grammatical paradigms in Romani, /s/ may alternate with /h/. A secondary development is the shift of intervocalic /h/ to /j/ or zero, and the loss of initial /h/ in dialects in contact with French, Italian, Macedonian, and Greek. The process is not a straightforward phonological one, since it usually skips lexical morphemes.

There are several kinds of patterns. First, there are dialects that have /s/ in all positions: the Northeastern group, Welsh Romani, the Bugurdži–Drindari group, Sepeči, Rumelian, Lovari, and the southern Italian dialects. In some dialects, there is fluctuation in intervocalic positions only (instrumental SG and long present conjugation): Transylvanian Kelderaš (optionally) and South Ukrainian *laha* 'with her', *keresa/kereha* 'you will do'. A number of dialects have complete sets of the copula in /h/ or zero – *(h)om*, *(h)inum* 'I am' etc. Of those, the *h*-copula appears in variation with a copula paradigm in /s/ in Arli (*sijum/hinum*) and Piedmontese Sinti (*som/om*). In some dialects, copula

Table 4.13 *s/h alternation in selected Romani dialects (interr=in interrogatives, pres=in the present tense, interv=in intervocalic position)*

	verb interv	INSTR	REM interv	COP3 pres	COP3 past	COP1,2	interr
Sinti (Germany)	h	h	–	h	h	h	h
Sinti (Piedmontese)	s	s	–	s/h	s/h	s/h	s
Finnish	h	h	–	h	s	s	s
Northern Central	h	h	–	h	s/h	s	s (h)
Southern Central	h	h	h	h/s	s	s	s
Hravati/Dolenjski	h	h	–	h	h	h	s
Cerhari	h	h	–	h	h	h	s
Gurvari	h	h	–	h	h	h	s
Southeast Ukrainian	s/h	h	–	s	s	s	s
Montenegrian	–	h	–	h	s	s	s
Serres	h	h	–	h	h	h	s/h
Arli	h	h	–	s/h	s/h	s/h	s

forms in /h/ are limited to the third person: Central dialects *hi(n)* 'is', West Slovak *ehas* 'was'. In some of those /h/ only appears in the present tense. Sinti, finally, also shows /h/ in all interrogatives and some determiners with histori cal /s/: *ho* 'what', *ha* 'all', *hako* 'every'. Some Northern Central dialects show this selectively, for some forms: *havo* 'which' but *so* 'what'.

There is a clear hierarchy in the distribution of /h/ in grammatical paradigms (table 4.13) (cf. Matras 1999d): at the very top of the table we find intervocalic positions (including the remoteness tense marker in the Southern Central dialects *-ahi*). This is followed by the third-person copula present, then past. Next is the complete copula set in /h/, optionally alongside /s/, then the extension to selected interrogatives, and finally the extension to all interrogatives as well as determiners in historical /s/.

The dynamics of the process can be explained through the regularisation of inherited variation from Early Romani, with Proto-Romani roots representing variation in late MIA. According to Bubeník (1996: 104–10), variation in Apabhraṃśa begins with the 2SG future *-issasi* > *-ihisi*, triggered through dissimilation, then spreads to the 2SG present-tense marker in *-asi* > *-ahi*. This is likely to be the source of variation in the Romani 2SG long present conjugation (*-esa/-eha*), spreading by analogy to the 1PL (*-asa/-aha*), and to the instrumental SG (*-esa, -asa/-eha, -aha*). In addition, Early Romani appears to have inherited two sets of the copula, in *s-* and in *h-* (cf. Boretzky 1995b). This latter state of affairs is preserved in the conservative dialects Arli and Piedmontese Sinti.

The present distribution of the forms is conditioned by analogies and in part by a functional hierarchy of markedness, based on selection among the inherited variation (Matras 1999d): Only dialects that generalise /h/ in intervocalic

Table 4.14 *Treatment of final -s in various dialects*

	athem. M.SG	3SG past	REFL	ACC.M.SG	adverb	short verb	'day'
Sepeči, Bugurdži, Erli, Welsh, Finnish	-os	-as	pes	-es	-es	-s	dives
Sinti	-o(s)	-as	pes	-e(s)	-es	-s	dives
Northern Central	-os	-as/-a	pes	-es	-es	-s	d'ives
Latvian	-os	-a	pes	-es	-es	-s	dives
North Russian, Polish	-o	-a	pes	-es	-es	-s	dives
Lovari	-o	-as	pe	-es	-es	-s	dźes
Kelderaš	-o	-a	pe	-es/-eh	-es	-s/-h	dźes
Southern Central	-o	-a	pe	-e	-e	-s	di(ve)
Gurbet	-o	-a	pe	-e	-e(h)	-h/Ø	d'ive(h)
Arli, Hravati	-o	-a	pe	-e	-e	Ø	dive

position also select *h*-forms in the copula; the least marked form of the copula is most likely to be selected (cf. also Boretzky 1995b); consistent selection of *h*-forms among the inherited options may trigger extension of *s* > *h* to yet another grammatical paradigm, namely interrogatives (Sinti and Northern Central). This extension is a kind of structural syncretisation of the grammatical apparatus, with phonology serving as a token for the functional position of the relevant items. The developments tend to cluster in a geographical area comprising the central part of Europe (see chapter 9).

4.3.5 *Final -s*

A separate, recent change affects /s/ in final positions. Here too there are several different processes involved, one of which is phonological, others are simplification strategies that are confined to individual grammatical forms.

Potentially affected by the loss of final /s/ is a series of morphological endings (table 4.14): the Greek-derived nominative masculine ending of loan nouns in *-os* (also *-us* and *-is*), the 3SG past-tense ending of verbs *-as*, the reflexive pronoun *pes*, the masculine singular oblique ending *-es* serving as an accusative ending in final position, as well as the oblique ending in preconsonantal position preceding Layer II case endings (*leske* 'for him' etc.), the adverbial ending *-es*, and final /s/ in the short present forms of the verb in the 2SG (*-es*) and 1PL (*-as*). Phonological loss of final /s/ also affects some lexical items, represented here by *dives* 'day' (but not e.g. monosyllabic *mas* 'meat').

The conservative stage shows full preservation of /s/ in final positions. This is found in dialects that are in the geographical extremes: Southern Balkan I and II in the south, Welsh Romani in the west, and Finnish in the north. In various dialects of central and northern Europe we find loss of /s/ in the masculine nominative ending of European loan nouns (M.SG 'athematic' ending). Possibly, this is a result of a competition between two distinct forms that are borrowed from Greek, namely the masculine ending *-os* (Greek *fóros* 'town') and the neuter ending *-o* (Greek *kókkalo* 'bone'). In Romani, both are treated as masculine, and Romani dialects tend to be consistent in their choice of just one ending: *foro, kokalo*, or *foros, kokalos*. Selective phonological reduction of /s/, however, rather than competition among Greek-derived endings, cannot be ruled out. In southern dialects of Romani, the distinction is blurred through the general reduction of final /s/.

Likewise affected by a process of selective reduction is the third-person singular past-tense marker *-as*, in the Northeastern and the Southern Central groups, with variation in the dialects of eastern Slovakia belonging to both the Northern and Southern Central groups. There is no obvious connection between this development, and the reduction of the nominative ending of European loan nouns. Marginally we find, in some Sinti dialects, a loss of /s/ in the masculine singular accusative ending. Northern Vlax shows mixtures, Lovari being somewhat more conservative than Kelderaš, which shows fluctuation among individual varieties.

A general, articulatory loss of /s/ in final position is found in the Southern Central dialects, and among a cluster of dialects in the southwestern Balkans including Kosovo and Macedonian Arli, Gurbet-type Vlax dialects of Albania, Montenegro, and Serbia, and Hravati/Dolenjski (see also chapter 9).

5 Nominal forms and categories

5.1 Inherent properties of the noun

The present chapter surveys primarily the morphology of nominal entities and their modifiers. The Romani noun has a number of 'inherent' properties that are not assigned either at the sentence level (case), or at the discourse and information level (definiteness), but accompany the selection of a noun as a lexical entry. The least ambiguous of those is grammatical **gender**. Romani belongs to those NIA languages which have simplified the historical gender classes into just two grammatical genders, masculine and feminine. Gender is relevant first to the classification of nouns by inflectional paradigms, and further to the agreement patterns between the nominal head and its modifiers. As Elšík (2000a) points out, gender in Romani consistently coincides with inflection class, as noun classes are either exclusively masculine or exclusively feminine. Loans may be assigned gender based on the natural sex of the animate noun, on the grammatical gender of the loan in the source language or the grammatical gender of the original noun which it replaces, or else on the phonological shape (usually the ending) of the loan. At the syntactic (agreement) level, the prominence of gender in Romani, compared to other NIA languages, stands out in the obligatory selection of gender with both pronouns and articles. Romani (like Domari) is exceptional among the NIA languages in neutralising gender agreement in the plural of adjectives. Although gender is primarily an inherent property of the noun, it is often structurally inferrable from patterns of semantic gender derivation, both those that are still productive – *rom* 'man', *romni* 'woman' – and those that are historical – *čhavo* 'boy', *čhaj* (< **čhavi*) 'girl'.

A particular feature of the Romani noun is **animacy**. Animacy is more of a challenge, since its triggers and its effects are less easy to identify. The most obvious animacy-related split is in the case marking of the direct object (see discussion below), with inanimates taking the default nominative while animates take an oblique marker. Individual dialects may also show animacy splits with other case markings, as well as with pronominal reference: personal pronouns may refer only to animates, while demonstratives are used when reference is made to inanimates. In fact, in differentiating between third-person pronouns and demonstratives, Romani stands out among the NIA languages, and the animacy split might be regarded as a contributing factor to this state of affairs (cf. Plank 2000).[1] What exactly constitutes an animate noun can, for some nouns, be subject to dialectal or even stylistic variation. Holzinger (1993) postulates an animacy hierarchy in which expressions of kin figure most prominently (i.e. they are statistically most likely to be treated differently from prototypical inanimates), followed by other humans and domestic animals, and finally by animals such as 'fish' or 'worm', whose animacy status may be ambiguous or more variable. Hancock (1995a) suggests that body parts may be treated as animates (cf also Igla 1997: 155), and Boretzky (1994: 102) speaks of 'transfer of animacy' to inanimate nouns that might contain humans (or are otherwise closely associated with humans). It seems therefore beneficial to consider animacy in the broader pragmatic context of **topicality** and **referential prominence**, rather than in the literal sense of animate properties. We return to the relevant parameters below, when discussing the Independent Oblique and Synthetic Case Stability.

The final and, in cross-linguistic perspective, most unique inherent property of the Romani noun is its so-called **thematic status**. The choice of term is inspired by Indo-Aryan linguistics, but its use in Romani linguistics has no operational relation to its use in the former. In Romani, 'thematic status' pertains to the split in the morphological treatment of pre-European vocabulary and European loans. The morphological patterns that apply to pre-European vocabulary and to some early European loans have been labelled 'thematic'. The thematic grammatical formants are mainly of Indo-Aryan stock. By contrast, subsequent loans receive so-called 'athematic' morphology, largely borrowed from Greek as well as from later contact languages.This terminology appears by now to be well-established at least in recent anglophone works on Romani linguistics (see Kaufman 1979, Hancock 1995a, Bakker 1997b, Elšík 2000a), while most German-language publications seem to avoid the term, referring instead simply to morphological distinctions between 'inherited' ('Erbwort') and 'borrowed' ('Lehnwort') vocabulary (Boretzky 1989, 1994, Igla 1996, Halwachs 1998, Cech and Heinschink 1999).

Historically, the split goes back to the Early Romani period and the adoption of an inventory of productive Greek morphological endings: nominative inflection in nouns, adaptation affixes of inflectional origin in verbs, both derivational and inflectional suffixes in adjectives. In Early Romani, these Greek morphemes became the principal productive morphological pattern in the language. They were then assigned to all words that were subsequently acquired, while the conservative morphology remained productive only for lexical derivation within

[1] Jerusalem Domari (Matras 1999c) however shows no animacy split in case marking, but equally differentiates third-person pronouns from demonstratives.

the limits of the pre-European lexical component. The fact that we are dealing with a distinction that manifests itself in more than just one grammatical domain justifies the notion of an athematic 'grammar' (see examples of paradigms below, and cf. chapter 6). Moreover, there is evidence that the Greek morphology that was adopted into Romani for the purpose of loanword integration in fact constituted a pattern of morphological adaptation that was applied to words of foreign origin already in Greek. Romani may therefore be said to have borrowed a Greek borrowing pattern (Bakker 1997b). Although all Romani dialects show a thematicity split, many have replaced some of their nominal athematic morphology of Greek origin through later loan morphology, especially nominative plural endings. Variation is found even in the distribution of the Greek-derived nominal morphology itself. Some Greek morphemes appear only in particular dialects, others are subject to various processes of levelling within and among inflectional paradigms.

5.2 Derivation patterns of nouns and adjectives

Nominal and adjectival derivation in Romani shows overwhelmingly suffixed morphology. Pre-European suffixes are only partly productive, and are supplemented by a series of productive loan affixes that are attached predominantly to European loans. The principal derivation strategies for nouns involve deverbal and deadjectival suffixes, to a limited extent compounding, and genitive derivations.

5.2.1 *Nominal derivation affixes*

The most common and most productive derivational morphemes of pre-European origin are the abstract nominal suffixes *-ipe(n)* and *-ibe(n)*. They were believed to be variants of the same suffix (Sampson 1926, see also Kostov 1965), but Schmid (1968, also 1963) has convincingly argued that they derive from two distinct morphemes: *-ipen* continues the deadjectival affix OIA *-itvana-* (which appears as deadjectival *-pa* etc. elsewhere in NIA), while *-iben* continues the deverbal suffix OIA *-itavya* (which renders infinitival forms in *-b-* in various NIA languages). The non-etymological extension *-en* in *-iben* is explained by Schmid (1968) as a contamination through *-ipen*. This contamination in structure parallels a tendency of the two affixes to merge functionally as well. In some dialects, such as the Southern Central group (Elšík et al. 1999: 29–30) or Xaladitka (Wentzel 1980: 56), a tendency is maintained for *-iben* to specialise in deverbal abstracts (*mariben* 'fight', from *mar-* 'to strike'), while *-ipen* is predominantly deadjectival (*barvalipen* 'prosperity', from *barvalo* 'rich'). Elsewhere, the two functions may merge in either *-iben* (Welsh Romani) or *-ipen* (Sinti). From this it seems that the structural contamination and possibly also the begining of the functional merger can be dated to Early Romani, while the actual fate of the affixes is a late development that is confined to individual dialects (rather than to dialect branches) in their present-day locations.

A further complication is the borrowing into Early Romani of the Greek deverbal affix *-(s)imo*, PL *-(s)imata* (Greek *gráfo* 'I write', *to grápsimo* '(the) writing'). It appears in Romani as a masculine ending *-imo* (alongside *-imos*, by analogy to Greek masculine nominal endings in *-os*) PL *-imata*, the original initial *s-* having been reanalysed as part of the Greek verbal root (see Schmid 1968: 215–16), apparently by analogy to Greek aorist formations. In some dialects, the inherited abstract nominaliser is gradually replaced by the Greek-derived form. In some dialects this affects all positions with the possible exception of the nominative singular: Lovari *čačipe* 'truth' alongside *čačimo*, but plural *čačimata* 'truths' and oblique *čačimasa* 'truthfully'. In others, *-imo(s)* occurs exclusively (e.g. Taikon's Kalderaš; Gjerdman and Ljungberg 1963). A general exception to these developments is the word *xabe(n)* 'food' (from *xa-* 'to eat'), where the deverbal affix *-(i)be(n)* tends to be retained (though Vlax tends to form the plural in *xabemata*, elsewhere *xabena*). The distribution of *-imos* – it is found in the east in the Vlax branch, and in the west in Welsh and Iberian Romani – points to an Early Romani innovation, which appears to have declined in the dialects of central and southeastern Europe.

The abstract nominalisers are rather unique in their distribution: on the one hand Indic-derived *-ipe(n)* and *-ibe(n)* are not restricted to the pre-European lexicon but can be productive within the earlier (Greek) European loan component as well (e.g. *xasaripe* 'loss', from *xasar-* 'to loose'; Greek *xano* 'I loose', aorist *éxasa*), while on the other hand they compete with Greek loan morphemes over productivity within the pre-European lexicon.

Another productive word-formation affix within the pre-European component is the nominal diminutive in *-oř-*, which takes vocalic inflectional endings: *raklo* 'boy', *raklořo* 'little boy', PL *rakloře*; *rakli* 'girl', *rakloři* 'little girl', PL *raklořja*. There are some productive formations in *-eli/-ali*, as in *momeli* 'candle' from *mom* 'wax', *dudali* 'window' from *dud* 'light' (Polska Roma). Rarely productive are *-ikl-* as in *marikli* 'cake' from *maro* 'bread' (cf. *čiriklo* 'bird'), and *-no*, originally a participial and adjectival ending, used for nominal derivation, as in *xoxano* 'liar' from *xoxav-* 'to lie' (Welsh Romani), *bucarno* 'worker' from *buci* <*buti* 'work' (Bugurdži). Still productive in later stages of Proto-Romani and applied to pre-European loans are the feminine derivation in *-ni* (*grasni* 'mare', from *grast* 'horse' of Armenian origin; cf. *řom* 'man', *řomni* 'woman'), and an ending denoting fruit trees in *-in* (*ambrolin* 'pear tree', from *ambrol* 'pear' of Persian origin; cf. *akhor* 'hazelnut' and *akhorin* 'hazelnut tree'). Traces of the latter's continuing productivity may still be found, e.g. in Vlax *prunin* 'plum tree', from Romanian *prună* 'plum'. Numerous other Indo-Aryan word-formation terminations (cf. Sampson 1926: 68ff.) are merely inherited with the Indo-Aryan lexicon, with no indication for their productivity within Romani (cf. section 3.5.1).

European loan morphology in the domain of nominal derivation encompasses mainly agentives and diminutives, as well as some abstract and feminine suffixes. A general nominaliser is the Greek-derived *-in* which shows a tendency to substitute for other endings (cf. Sampson 1926: 70): *papin* 'goose' (Greek *páppia*), *filicin* 'castle' (Greek *filakí*), but also *patrin* 'leaf' (OIA *pattra*). A further loan affix with general distribution in Romani, whose productivity extends to the pre-European component, is the agentive *-ar-*, corresponding to Romance and Slavic endings: *rechtsprechari* 'judge' (Sinti, from German *Rechtsprecher*), but also Xaladitka *butari* 'worker' from *buti* 'work', *rakiribnari* 'storyteller' from *rakiriben*, nominalised form of *rakir-* 'to tell'. The diminutive *-ic-* is widespread in the Balkans (Greek, Slavic, and Romanian), and is found throughout Romani, as are the Slavic diminutive affix *-ka* and the Greek diminutive *-ela* (of Romance origin). All three appear to be restricted to European loans. Other affixes enter the language along with borrowed lexical items. Examples are Slavic feminines in *-ajka*, *-ojka*, *-inka*, Turkish agentives in *-dži-* found in Southern Balkan dialects, and the Hungarian abstract nominaliser *-(i)šag-* found in the Southern Central group (see also section 8.2.2).

5.2.2 *Nominal compounding and genitive derivations*

Plain nominal compounding is on the whole rather rare in Romani. Exceptions are dialect-specific innovations such as *phrala phena* 'siblings' (*phrala* 'brothers', *phena* 'sisters'), Šóka and Farkašda (Southern Central) *kańhajaro* 'egg' (*kańhi* 'hen', **jaro* 'egg'), or the title of the community leader of the Polska Roma, *šéro róm* 'head Rom' (*šero* 'head'). More common are collocations that rely on genitive compositions. These involve coining a lexical entry by placing a genitive noun in attributive position, showing adjectival inflection agreement with the head (see below): *bakr-esk-o mas* lit. 'lamb-GEN.M.SG-M meat = meat of a lamb' for 'lamb'. As in plain compounding, the normal word-order pattern for genitive compositions is one in which the modifier precedes the head, in accordance with the default order of other attributes in the noun phrase (lexical adjectives, and attributive possessives and demonstratives). Occurrences of modifiers following the head in genitive compositions are also attested, however. In Lovari *kher le dil-eng-o* lit. 'house ART.OBL.PL crazy-GEN.PL-M = crazy people's house' for 'mental institution', reversal of the order modifier–head indicates the generic nature of the compound, as opposed to *le dilengo kher*, which would denote a specific house belonging to the possessor *e dile*. Koptjevskaja-Tamm (2000) however cites head–modifier compositions from Lovari that could equally be regarded as default generics (note the absence of a definite article): *kirčimi kuxenge* 'cake restaurants', *čor khanjango* 'chicken thief'.

Speakers often resort to such coinings spontaneously, and although nominal genitive compositions are likely to be understood by speakers with access to the general contextual setting in which they emerge, they remain largely confined to the established lexicon of individual dialects. Thus, although lexical creation through genitive composition is clearly a Common Romani structural resource, the actual number of shared lexical entries that are formed by drawing on this resource remains small.

Many dialects make use of genitive compositions for euphemistic in-coinings, as in Sinti *mulengro kher* lit. 'dead people's house' for 'coffin', including the creation of cryptic place names, such as *kiralengro them* lit. 'cheese country' for 'Switzerland' (see section 3.3.3). Although such composition strategies are attested throughout Romani, they are particularly productive among the northwestern European dialects. This might be regarded as a conservativism, reinforced by the extreme social isolation and overwhelmingly nomadic lifestyle of the respective groups, leading to a reliance on Romani for purposes of internal, concealed communication, and so resulting in a preference for internal coining over loans (cf. Matras 1998b).

It is also in the dialects of northwestern Europe that lexical creation through genitive derivation is most productive. Sampson (1926: 87–91ff.) cites a great variety of such items for Welsh Romani, and many more can be found in vocabularies of other northwestern European dialects. Especially common are agentives denoting professions or officials, but also everyday consumable objects. The format for genitive derivations is either a genitive of a plural noun – *grajengro* 'horsedealer' (from *graj* 'horse'), *masengro* 'butcher' (from *mas* 'meat'), *mumliengere* 'candlesticks' (from *mumeli* 'candle'), a genitive of a singular noun – *rateskero* 'leech' (from *rat* 'blood'), or, most commonly, the genitive of an abstract deverbal nominalisation – *pimaskeri* 'cigarette' (from *pi-* 'to drink', 'to smoke' > abstract nom. *piben*), *dikimangeri* 'mirror' (from *dikh-* 'to see', nom. *dikhiben*). While agentives are typically masculine, quite often inanimate nouns are feminine (though masculines like *phuvjengero* 'vegetable' also exist).

5.2.3 *Adjectival derivation*

The series of inherited Indo-Aryan adjectival formants includes *-alo*, *-valo*, *-ano*, *-ikano*, *-no*, *-uno*, *-utno*, *-avno/-amno*, most of which are denominal formations that are productive within the pre-European lexicon. The suffix *-no* often extends to European loans as well. Denominal adjectives may figure in lexical compositions that compete with nominal genitive compounding: thus *balikano mas* 'pork' (from *balo* 'pig' and *mas* 'meat'), or Roman *čiriklano por* alongside *čiriklakero por* 'a bird's feather' (*čirikli* 'bird', *por* 'feather'; Halwachs 1998: 107). Exceptional and less productive derivational suffixes include *-ver* in *god'aver* 'clever' from *godi* 'mind'. Of Proto-Romani origin is also the productive derivation of negative adjectives through prefixation of *bi-* 'without', the only Common Romani productive derivational prefix: *bilačho* 'bad' (*lačho* 'good'), *bibaxtalo* 'unlucky' (*baxtalo* 'lucky', Iranian *baxt* 'luck'). The prefix may also attach to genitive nouns and pronouns (*bilesko* 'without him/it', *bilovengro* 'with no money'), providing potentially a means of lexical derivation of adjectives (*bithemengo* 'stateless'). Like most nominal genitive derivations, those in adjectival function are usually local in-coinings that are particular to individual dialects. Among the loan-derivational affixes, Greek-derived *-icko*, *-itko*, *-itiko* stand out in their productivity with European loans. Incorporated into the pre-European component is Greek-derived *-to* which forms ordinal numbers (*eftato* 'seventh', Greek *eftá*, but also *dujto* 'second', *trito* 'third' etc.).

Adjectival compounds, like nominal compounds, are peripheral. We find *budžanglo* 'wise, experienced' (from *but* 'much' and *džanglo* participle of 'to know'), in a modifier–head formation, while *punřango* 'barefoot' (*punřo* 'foot', *nango* 'bare') is exceptionally head–modifier, perhaps reflecting the inalienable possession associated with body parts. Comparative and superlative formations frequently rely on the inherited suffix *-eder* (whose origin may be either Indo-Aryan, or Iranian), or on the preposed loan particles such as *po-* (Slavic), *maj* (Romanian), or *da(h)a* (Turkish) (see also section 8.2.2). We find the retention of *-eder* in virtually all dialect branches except Vlax, where *maj* dominates. Slavic-derived *naj-* often competes with *-eder* within individual dialects in the Balkans, the Central and the Northeastern dialects, while *maj* may equally be found sporadically among the Central dialects.

5.3 Nominal inflection

5.3.1 *Case layers*

As elsewhere in NIA, the system of nominal case in Romani is composed of three distinct **layers**, referred to here following Masica (1991: 232ff.) as Layers I, II, and III. 'Inflection' will refer here to the interplay of all components, whether inflective, agglutinative, or analytic. Historically the various layers arose in NIA to compensate for the loss of the earlier case inflection system of OIA/MIA. In their origin and partly in their function and typology, Romani markers of the various layers correspond in principle to those of the other NIA languages. This is perhaps one of the clearest pieces of evidence for a shared development of Romani and the subcontinental languages up to the NIA period, roughly around the tenth century AD. However, Romani case layers also show some unique characteristics when compared to NIA as a whole. The nature and position of the markers belonging to Layers I, II, and III in Romani make the distinction between them more straightforward than in most NIA languages.

Layer I inflective elements function as nominative and oblique endings that attach directly to the nominal base. They are stressed (except in dialects that have undergone a radical shift of stress placement), and they form distinct declensional classes. Gender, number, and thematic status are distinguished at this level. The nominative endings have been affected by renewal at various historical development stages. As in other NIA languages, the oblique endings are remnants of the older (OIA/MIA) nominal declension, though the surviving forms may have changed considerably in function as well as in form and distribution. Romani stands out in preserving archaic consonantal forms of the masculine singular and plural oblique markers *-es* and *-en* respectively, which are generally thought to go back to OIA genitives in *-asya* and *-ānām* (cf. Domari as well as Kashmiri *-as* and *-an*, elsewhere often reduced, respectively, to vowels or to nasalised vowels). They function in Romani, as elsewhere in NIA, as general oblique forms which mediate between the nominal base and Layer II case formations, though in Romani they may also occur independently of Layer II markers, assuming a variety of functions (see below). Since their principal role is to extend the nominal base to form an 'oblique stem' to which additional case markers are attached, they are transcribed below in a hyphenated form (nominative *manuš* 'person', oblique *manušes-*, dative *manušeske*, etc). Supplementing the inventory of Layer I markers are unstressed nominative inflectional endings that are borrowed from European contact languages (so-called 'athematic' endings), and which are rather diverse and subject to considerable dialect variation (see below).

Layer II is a closed set of unstressed agglutinative markers, derived from OIA/MIA postpositions and postposed adverbs, and, in the case of the genitive, from a postposed adjectival particle of participial origin (see below). They are identical for the various declension classes. Here too Romani shares the basic inventory with other NIA languages. The unique feature of Romani Layer II markers is their advanced stage of integration with the extended nominal base in its oblique form (or the 'oblique stem'). Unlike in some other NIA languages, where Layer II affixes are clitics that modify the entire noun phrase and often appear just once at the end of a complex nominal construction, in Romani they are inseparable from the individual noun (cf. discussion in Friedman 1991). Moreover, they show voice assimilation to the oblique endings of the noun to which they attach (dative *-ke/-ge*, locative *-te/-de*, ablative *-tar/-dar* etc.).

Layer III consists of analytic adpositions, which constitute a more open set that is subject to more frequent and so also more recent renewal. The inherited material from which Layer III elements are recruited is similarly shared to a considerable extent with other NIA languages, though Romani also has internal innovations as well as borrowings. The unique feature of Romani in NIA is the preposed position of Layer III markers, an outcome of the general shift in word-order typology which Romani has undergone.[2]

Alongside the three layers we find **vocative** forms, usually in masculine *-a*, *-éja*, more seldom *-o* or *-e*, feminine *-(j)a*, *-(j)e* and more seldom *-(j)o*, and plural *-ale(n)*. The vocative forms connect directly to the nominal base without Layer I mediation, but unlike Layer I markers they are unstressed, indicating a rather late formation. The origin of the vocative endings is unclear. Boretzky (1994: 93) proposes to derive them from interjections. There are however occurrences of forms in *-ole* and *-ale*, attested in Xaladitka (Wentzel 1980: 67) and in the Southern Balkan dialects (Boretzky 1999b: 41) for more frequently used feminine singular vocatives *da-le/do-le* 'mother!', *bib-ole* 'aunt!'. They correspond to the plural form in *-ale(n)*, which could suggest that the forms in *-al-/-ol-* are more archaic forms deriving from deictic expressions (see below), perhaps from a postposed form of the oblique demonstrative or definite article. The widely distributed singular vocative marker *-(j)a* might be related to the emphatic endings of personal pronouns in *-a*, and perhaps also to a Proto-Romani deictic form **-a* (see discussion below).

5.3.2 *Layer I declension classes*

Romani declension classes are distinguished at the level of Layer I markers. A series of factors have contributed to the present shape of the declension paradigms. The most detailed discussion to date is provided by Elšík (2000a), who distinguishes four stages in the historical development of Romani nominal paradigms. The Proto-Romani declension system, or Stage 1, is the historical outcome of a combination of three essential components. The most conservative of those are the oblique markers that are inherited from the OIA/MIA nominal declension, and which classify singular nouns by gender (cf. *rom* 'man', oblique *romes-*, *romni* 'woman', oblique *romnja-*). A somewhat more recent layer are the nominative markers, which derive largely from OIA/MIA nominal derivation endings (*čhav-o* 'boy', *čirikl-i* 'bird'). Finally, processes of partial phonological assimilation and analogies, most conspicuously jotation, contribute to further differentiation among the paradigms (cf. the feminines *džuv* 'louse', oblique *džuva-*, but *suv* 'needle', oblique *suvja-*, analogous to *romni* 'woman', oblique *romnja-*). Pre-European loans, as well as a considerable number of early loans from Greek, are adapted into the Proto-Romani declension patterns (cf. *drom*, 'road', plural *droma*, oblique *dromes-*, from Greek *drómos*, to the inherited pattern of the type *rom* 'man', plural *roma*, oblique *romes-*; or *kurko* 'week', plural *kurke*, oblique *kurkes-*, from Greek *kyriakí* 'Sunday', to the pattern *čhavo* 'boy', plural *čhave*, oblique *čhaves-*).

2 A similar shift in word-order patterns occurs in Domari, though adpositions are all borrowed from Arabic.

The second stage is the later Early Romani period. It sees the adoption of productive loan morphology from Greek at the expense of the productivity of some of the inherited nominal morphology. This involves essentially the borrowing of nominative endings (*fóros* 'town', plural *fóri*, Greek *fóros-fóri*; *kókalo* 'bone', plural *kókala*, Greek *kókkalo-kókkala*). Romani oblique endings on the other hand probably remained productive for quite some time before partial restructuring occurred (as in the oblique masculine singular **forés* > *forós*, while the Common Romani oblique plural remains *forén*, and only in some dialects did it later become *forón*; see below). The Greek nominative endings (and the oblique analogies that are based on them) then take over, and are assigned to all subsequent loans, including later European borrowings into the individual dialects. This results in so-called 'athematic' morphology, which, as Elšík (2000a) remarks, forms a pattern that marks out a nominal class of loan nouns.

The third stage coincides with the decline of the Early Romani period and the split into individual dialects and dialect branches. New loans are generally accommodated into the Greek model and assigned gender and a corresponding declension class membership. But additional morphology is also acquired, mainly endings marking agentives, diminutives, feminines, and nominative plurals. In some cases, there is selective backwards diffusion of newly acquired plural markers at the expense of Greek markers, though rarely at the expense of thematic markers. Thus Vlax acquired the Romanian plural *-uri*, which it assigns to words with penultimate stress in the base form, such as *foruri* 'towns' (Greek *fóri*), but not to *kókala* 'bones' (**kokaluri*), nor to thematic nouns such as *roma* 'men' (**romuri*), nor to thematically inflected, earlier Greek loans, such as *droma* 'roads' (**dromuri*). This stage is also characterised by various dialect-specific processes of levelling, such as the emergence of analogous athematic plural oblique forms *forón-* 'towns' (by analogy to singular oblique *forós-*), from *forén-*.

The final and most recent stage involves the loss of inflection markers, such as the disappearance of Greek-derived nominative masculine *-is* in many dialects, and further analogies between athematic and thematic classes (see below). Acquired athematic morphology that is retained, whether of Greek or of later origin, remains productive for subsequent loans. Thus Vlax dialects in Germany assign the Romanian-derived plural in *-uri* to German loans, as in *ofentaluri* 'residence permits' (German *Aufenthalt* 'stay'), and Balkan dialects that acquired Greek plurals in *-es* and *-Vdes* through prolonged contact with Greek after the Early Romani period also apply the pattern to Turkish loans (*sepečides* 'basket-weavers', Turkish *sepetçi*).

Synchronic membership in a particular declensional class is sensitive to a series of factors: the historical phonology of the base form (vocalic versus consonantal stems), analogies and shifts between classes, and the intrinsic properties of the noun, namely gender and thematic status. Animacy is often considered an additional factor. Sensitive to animacy is, in particular, the opposition between subject and direct object inflection: animates are differentiated for the two cases at the level of Layer I (subject *manuš*, direct object *manušes* 'person'), while inanimates are not (subject *kher*, direct object *kher* 'house'). Numerous descriptive grammars of Romani varieties postulate separate declension classes for animates and inanimates. For the animate class, an accusative is postulated that is identical with the general oblique. For the inanimate class, the accusative is regarded as identical with the nominative. Such multiplicity of declension classes is redundant however if one views animacy as a phenomenon that is external to the declension paradigms, or 'hyperparadigmatic', as Elšík (2000a) puts it. In diachronic terms, the animacy split reflects the beginning decline of synthetic case marking, with animates showing a tendency to retain more conservative patterns.[3] This applies not only to the case of the direct object, but also to other cases, where analytic case marking is often preferred for inanimates (see below). At the strict level of declension classes, namely the Layer I level, which indicates nominative and general oblique (as a base for Layer II case formations), animates and inanimates are actually treated alike as far as the shape of the forms is concerned. They differ in their likelihood to be assigned synthetic case altogether, including an independent oblique that is not accompanied by Layer II elements (see below).

There is no widely accepted standard for labelling Romani declension classes. Descriptions tend to list or number them, with masculines preceding feminines, consonantal stems preceding vocalic stems, and thematics preceding athematics (cf. Wentzel 1980: 71–9, Boretzky 1994: 31–45, Halwachs 1998: 62–82). An attempt to formalise the relevant classificatory criteria into declension class symbols is introduced by Elšík (2000a): {*} denotes athematics, {M/F} denotes gender, {ø} denotes consonantal (=zero-vowel) stems, while nominative endings containing vowels are indicated through the respective vowel {o/i/u/a}, and non-derivable pre-European plural modifications figure as {-ø} for zero-plurals, {-a} for *a*-plurals, {-A} for the specific forms of Abstract nouns in *-ipen/-iben*, and finally {-J/-U}, respectively, for Jotated and Unmodified consonantal feminine stems. The notation takes for granted derivable default formations, namely plurals in *-e* for thematic masculines in *-o*, and plurals in *-ja* for both thematic masculines and feminines in *-i*. It further allows for variation in athematic plural endings, and it disregards nominative endings that are based on European derivational affixes, and those based on European inflectional affixes that are borrowed after the Early Romani period, which likewise vary (table 5.1).

Nominative forms show the highest diversity, while oblique forms, and especially oblique plurals, tend towards greater regularity. The most common

[3] Domari shows no animacy split: subject *laši* 'girl', direct object *lašya*, subject *kuri* 'house', direct object *kurya*.

Table 5.1 *Early Romani nominal declension classes, adapted from Elšík (2000a)*

Class	Symbol	Example	NOM SG	NOM PL	OBL SG	OBL PL
Thematic (pre-European):						
zero-masculines	Mø-a	*kher* 'house'	–	*-a*	*-es-*	*-en-*
	Mø-A	*čačipen* 'truth'	–	*-a*	*-as-*	*-en-*
	Mø-ø	*vast* 'hand'	–	–	*-es-*	*-en-*
o-masculines	Mo	*šero* 'head'	*-o*	*-e*	*-es-*	*-en-*
i-masculines	Mi	*pani* 'water'	*-i*	*-j-a*	*-j-es-*	*-j-en-*
zero-feminines	Fø-U	*džuv* 'louse'	–	*-a*	*-a-*	*-en-*
	Fø-J	*suv* 'needle'	–	*-j-a*	*-j-a-*	*-j-en-*
i-feminines	Fi	*piri* 'pot'	*-i*	*-j-a*	*-j-a-*	*-j-en-*
Athematic (European):						
o-masculines	*Mo	*foros* 'town'	*-o(s)*	*-i*	*-os-*	*-en-*
u-masculines	*Mu	*papus* 'grandfather'	*-u(s)*	*-i*	*-us-*	*-en-*
i-masculines	*Mi	*sapunis* 'soap'	*-i(s)*	*-ja*	*-is-*	*-en-*
a-feminines	*Fa	*cipa* 'skin'	*-a*	*?*	*-a-*	*-en-*

oblique plural ending is the inherited *-en* (with the effect of jotation *-j-en*). Occasionally, most notably in Vlax, oblique plurals are renewed, and one finds *romnjen-* > *romnjan-* 'women', *foren-* > *foron-* 'towns'. Boretzky (1994: 33) regards this as an analogy to the nominative plural *romnja*, though such analogy is much less obvious for the athematic *foron-*. Elšík (2000a) points out a similar process affecting the athematic oblique singular already in the Early Romani period: nominative *fóros* 'town', oblique *forós* by analogy to the nominative form, from an original thematic oblique singular **forés*. This Early Romani development is shared by all dialects, while the plural analogies are dialect-specific. It is therefore possible that the general drift towards levelling is continued in individual dialects, but that the specific development of oblique plurals is now modelled not on the nominative plural, but on the oblique singular: *romnja-* 'woman', *forós-* 'town'.

Oblique feminines end in *-a-* (jotated to *j-a-*). Athematic feminines, which have unstressed *-a* in the nominative, are adapted into the same pattern and form their oblique by changing the stress position (*bába* 'grandmother', oblique *babá-*). With pre-European feminines ending in a consonant, jotation is analogous, and hence often irregular (thus oblique *suva-* 'needle', alongside *suvja-*). Special cases affected by phonological assimilation and contraction processes vary among individual dialects; examples are *phen* 'sister', oblique *phenja-* alongside *pheja-*; *daj* (Vlax *dej*) 'mother', oblique *da-* alongside *daja-*.

Oblique masculines are somewhat more diverse. The inherited ending for most pre-European nouns is *-es-* (jotated to *-j-es-*). Pre-European masculines ending in *-i* or *-j* belong essentially to the same class (*rašaj* 'priest', oblique *rašajes-*), but may show structural simplification processes that give rise to contracted endings (*graj* 'horse', oblique *gres-* or *gras-*; *muj* 'face', oblique *mos-* alongside *mujes-*, etc.). A unique feature of the class of abstract nouns ending in *-ipen/-iben* is the retention of a conservative masculine singular oblique form in *-ipnas/-ibnas*, rather than the expected **-ipnes/*-ibnes* (though the latter does appear as a result of a secondary development, by analogy to the general masculine oblique formation, cf. Roman *-ipes*). Noteworthy is the partial assimilation of the Greek-derived abstract nominal ending *-imo(s)* into this particular oblique inflection, giving rise to oblique forms in *-imas-*. A superficial similarity even emerges between the borrowed affix, and the inherited form in some dialects where the stop undergoes assimilation to the adjoined nasal in oblique positions, giving *-ibnas* > *-imnas* and finally *-imas*.[4]

With athematic masculines, the Greek-derived endings in *-s* (*-os*, *-us*, *-is*) are retained in the oblique, although they are often lost in the nominative. This suggests reanalysis of the segment *-s-* as a potential oblique marker, by analogy with the inherited (thematic) oblique (cf. Elšík 2000a). The pattern has become productive, and it is also applied to masculine European loans ending in *-a*, as in *sluga* 'servant' (Slavic *sluga*), oblique *sluga-s-* (cf. Kostov 1989), as well as to borrowed agentive suffixes such as *-ár-*, as in *butári* 'worker', oblique *butarís-*. Partial erosion of the pattern takes place in dialects that show a tendency to aspirate preconsonantal /s/, as in some Southern Vlax varieties. As is the case with athematic feminines and plurals, in athematic masculines the oblique ending carries the stress (in dialects with conservative stress patterns). Full assimilation of athematic masculines to thematic oblique formations characterises Welsh Romani, and is under way in the Southern Central dialects (Elšík 2000a, Halwachs 1998), thus oblique *grofós-* alongside *grofés-*, to nominative *grófo* 'count'.

Many pre-European nouns lack distinct nominative endings in the singular. Nominative endings that are of relevance to declensional classes are the abstract marker *-ipen/-iben* (with a unique oblique formation), the vocalic masculine ending in *-o* (with a unique plural formation), forms in *-i*, which trigger jotation, and those in *-j*, which may show contracted oblique forms. Athematic singulars, on the other hand, are normally assigned athematic nominative inflection

[4] Kostov (1965) postulates the reverse development, namely *-pnas* > *-mnas* > *-bnas* and hence the emergence of *-ben* by analogy to *-pen*, to which he adds, relying on Pobożniak (1964), the emergence of an analogous nominative form *-mo*. This hypothesis has been convincingly rejected by Schmid (1968), who identified the Greek origin of *-mo(s)*.

endings which reflect gender. Examples are Common Romani masculine *prezidento(s)* 'president', Northeastern feminine *felda* 'field' (German neuter *Feld*), Bugurdži masculines *bahčas* 'garden' (Turkish *bahçe*) and *bugurdžis* 'drill-maker' (Turkish *burgucu*).

The inherited nominative plural ending is generally *-a* (jotated to *-j-a*). Masculines ending in *-o* regularly take *-e* in the plural, matching the pattern of adjectival inflection (masculine *terno čhavo* 'young boy', PL *terne čhave*). A closed class of masculine nouns with consonantal stems shows neutralisation of number marking; this class is however subject to considerable dialectal variation and renewal. Among the possible candidates for number neutralisation are first quantifiable masses – *thud* 'milk', *khas* 'hay', but also nouns denoting time – *dives* 'day/s', *čhon* 'month/s' –, parts of the body – *vast* 'hand/s', *bal* 'hair', *dand* 'tooth/teeth' –, and human beings – *rom* 'man/men', *manuš* 'person/s' (the latter however often marks collectives, which co-exist with plurals). Dialect-specific additions to the group of nouns lacking plurals may also include nouns from feminine classes, likewise uncountables such as *baxt* 'luck', or *bokh* 'hunger' (cf. Halwachs 1998: 81).

Highly diverse are the nominative endings of athematic plural nouns. For Early Romani or the Greek period, Elšík (2000a) postulates *-i* for the plural of masculine loans. Plural endings of feminine loans vary among the dialects, and we find *-e*, *-i*, *-y*, and *-es* as well as assimilation to thematic endings in *-a*. Individual Romani dialect branches continued to borrow plural endings after the Early Romani period, and we find Slavic-derived *-ovi*, *-i* and *-e* in various dialects, Romanian *-uri* in Vlax, and Greek *-des* in the Balkans (see also section 8.2.2). Fairly common are contaminations of borrowed endings with the inherited plural marker *-a*, giving rise to forms such as *-oja*, *-(i)ja*, *-urja*, and *-da*. Borrowed derivational suffixes may retain their own plural forms, the most widespread example being the Greek-derived abstract nominaliser *-imos* PL *-imata*.

5.3.3 *The independent oblique*

Layer I oblique endings may sometimes occur 'independently', that is unaccompanied by Layer II elements. This is most conspicuous in the marking of the animate direct object. Only in some dialects, where final /s/ is lost but pre-consonantal /s/ is retained, do we find discrepancies in the masculine singular between the form of the general oblique, and that of the independent oblique that marks the animate direct object: Roman *rom* 'man', oblique *romes-*, direct object case *rome*. The use of the oblique as an independent case that is not followed by a Layer II element is an archaism which Romani inherits from MIA, and which it shares with Domari, where it likewise represents the accusative case, and with Kashmiri, where it is used for the dative (cf. Bubeník 2000: 215).

The identity-in-principle between the oblique and the case of animate direct objects results in a tendency in grammatical descriptions to describe the independent oblique as an accusative case. Depending on the analysis, the accusative is either viewed as restricted to animates (Elšík 2000a), or as having different forms for animates and inanimates, the inanimate accusative being identical in form to the nominative (see above).

Occurrences of the independent oblique generally coincide with high referential status or topicality of the noun. Thus, all pronouns pattern with animates in their marking of the direct object. In some dialects, animate direct objects take the independent oblique only if they are definite, while indefinite animates, like inanimates, appear as default (nominative). Consider the independent oblique marking of the indefinite animate noun in the following: Polska Roma dialect *me lav romes* 'I take a man.OBL = I am getting married', but Lovari *me lav [mange] rom* (cf. Matras 1997a: 76; see also Boretzky 1994: 101 for Kalderaš examples).

Apart from marking the definite/animate direct object, the independent oblique also serves additional functions. It is the case of the possessor in the existential possessive construction with *si/hi* '(there) is', irrespective of the possessor's animacy status. This is widespread among dialects that are not related, such as Vlax, Roman, and Sinti, and it is likely to reflect the Proto-Romani state of affairs (cf. Boretzky 1997: 123); the assignment of the dative to the possessor appears to be a more recent, contact-related development. The same pertains to the benefactor of 'to give', which appears in the independent oblique in various unrelated dialects (Vlax, Central, Sinti). Both the possessor and the 'give'-benefactor are highly topical roles that prototypically involve animates. Parallel developments of more limited distribution include the oblique marking of the experiencer in the Sinti dialect (*man hi rōpaske* 'I feel like crying'; cf. Holzinger 1995: 11), and of animate prepositional objects: *ko kakes* 'to the uncle'.[5]

The independent oblique might therefore be interpreted as consistently encoding the **non-agentive referent** that is **high on the topicality scale**. Occasionally it figures in opposition to the default nominative, which encodes non-topical (inanimate or indefinite) entities in parallel syntactic roles (direct and prepositional object). Elsewhere it indicates that the non-agentive role is normally reserved for topical entities (possessor and experiencer). Its primary function in semantic-pragmatic terms is to alert the hearer to the discrepancy between the referent's topicality status, and the appearance of this referent in a non-agentive role. With some variation, this function is grammaticalised in Romani.

[5] This form is already attested in Evliya Çelebi's seventeenth-century Balkan sample (Friedman and Dankoff 1991).

Viewed in this perspective, Romani may be said to lack a genuine accusative case altogether. The inanimate direct object is the default, since its patient role is consistent with its non-topical semantics. Its nominative case marking reflects this default status. The animate direct object (or in some dialects, the definite animate direct object) is assigned the case marking that is generally reserved for topical non-agents, namely the independent oblique. The higher-ranking status of topical entities on the hierarchy of case marking suggests itself in universal terms, and the interplay between case marking and topicality, animacy, and definiteness is particularly reminiscent of other NIA languages. For Romani, viewing the independent oblique as a kind of agent/topic discrepancy case marking has the advantage of reconciling the facts of animate/topical direct-object marking with other occurrences of the independent oblique inflection in the language.

5.3.4 *Forms and functions of Layer II markers*

Romani Layer II markers are generally cognates of the respective markers in other NIA languages (see section 3.5.2). Missing from the Romani inventory is a locative in *-m-* (Hindi *-mẽ*, Domari *-ma*), which may have been taken over by the original dative-directional *-te*. Romani linguistic tradition since Sampson (1926) has adopted the terms 'locative' for the marker *-te*, and (in accordance with NIA linguistics) 'dative' for *-ke*, which in Romani is in effect the benefactive case. Layer II markers are regular and agglutinative, though their voice assimilation to preceding consonants renders the superficial impression of a singular/plural split (*romes-ke* 'man.DAT', *romen-ge* 'men.DAT'; but also *tu-ke* 'for-you', *man-ge* 'for-me'). Their shape and especially their position as postposed elements leaves no room for ambiguity as to the dividing line between Layer II and Layer III markers. Modern grammatical descriptions of Romani varieties occasionally still refer to Layer II elements as 'postpositions' (see Hancock 1995a). The arguments against such a view have been summarised by Friedman (1991): Layer II elements are not detachable from the noun base, they partly assimilate to the preceding consonant, and the overall typological features of Romani are those of a prepositional language, which justifies viewing postposed markers as inflectional elements (in the broad sense, including agglutinative inflection) rather than as adpositions.

Although phonological changes may affect the actual shape of the forms in individual dialects, almost all Romani dialects maintain an opposition between five distinct Layer II markers (see table 5.2). A rare exception is the Polska Roma dialect (Matras 1999b), in which the locative *-te* has disappeared and all its functions are taken over by the ablative *-tyr* (<*-tar*). In Zargari, the dative and genitive appear to have merged.

Table 5.2 *Forms of Layer II markers in some dialects* (SG/PL)

	dative	locative	ablative	instrumental	genitive
Early Romani	*ke/ge	*te/de	*tar/dar	*sa/ca	*ker-/ger-
Bugurdži	ke/ge	te/de	tar/dar	sa/ca	k(V)r-/g(V)r-
Arli	e/dže	te/de	tar/dar	(j)a/ca(r)	(k)Vr-/(g)Vr-
Gurbet	e/dź-	te/de	tar/dar	ha/ca	k-/g-, ć-/dź-
Lovari	ke/ge	te/de	tar/dar	sa/sa	k-/g-
East Slovak	ke/ge	te/de	tar/dar	ha/ca	k(e)r-/g(e)r-
Sinti	ke/ge	te/de	tər/dər	ha/sa	kr-/gr-
Polska Roma	ke/ge	–	tyr/dyr	sa/ca	kyr-/gyr-
Welsh	kī/gī	tī/dī	tē/dē	sa/sa	k(er)-/g(er)-

The **dative** appears in Romani as *-ke/-kə/-k'e/-ki/-će/-e* (with voice assimilation to preceding consonants). Its original and still primary meaning is benefactive, and it has no directional use in the spatial sense (cf. Boretzky 1994: 104). The dative marks the benefactive indirect object of particular verbs, such as 'to say' or 'to show'. In some dialects it also takes over the functions of the benefactor of 'to give', or of the possessive in the existential possessive construction (*si mange* '[there] is to-me'). One of its most widespread usages is as a dative-reflexive, which entails a benefactive reading: *džav mange* 'I am going away' (with the implication of a benefit), *kinav mange* 'I buy (for myself)'. With deverbal nouns, the dative can express modality, such as necessity or ability (Sinti dialect *man hi tšādepaske* 'I am going to be sick', *man hi phenepaske* 'I have the say', *man hi rōpaske* 'I feel like crying'; Holzinger 1995: 11). The dative of purpose is conventionalised in the expressions *soske* 'what for' and *adaleske* 'therefore'.

The **locative** marker is *-te/-t'e/-ti* (likewise, with voice assimilation). As an independent marker it expresses both stative location and movement towards a location (dative in the strict sense). The locative also serves as a default prepositional case accompanying most inherited Layer III prepositions (*pašal amen-de* 'next to us'). This is shared and quite clearly a Proto-Romani legacy. It is reminiscent of the use of the oblique genitive/possessive as a base for Layer III elements in subcontinental NIA (Hindi *hamare pās* '1.PL.POSS.OBL next = next to us'). In Romani the reading is not of possessive incorporation, but of a further specification of the local relation that is already expressed by the locative (thus literally 'with-us, on the side'). It is likely to derive from the intermediate stage of grammaticalisation of Layer III elements from independent postposed adverbials, which became postpositions and were later preposed in conjunction with the overall changes in word-order patterns in the late Proto-Romani stage (**amende, pašal* > **amende pašal* > *pašal amende*). Unlike the genitive/possessive base for Layer III markers in languages like

Hindi (or Domari, which uses the genitive–ablative *-ki* as a prepositional case), the origin of the Romani construction is clearly locative in meaning. As a prepositional case the locative is incompatible with spatial ablatives; *andar amende* with an ablative preposition cannot mean '*from us', but rather 'about us/ for our sake'. Although the locative is the only inherited prepositional case, other Layer II elements may accompany Layer III items in dialects where the case system is renewed through extensive borrowing of Layer III markers, the best example being the Sinti dialect: *fir tumenge* 'for you.DAT', *fon tumendar* 'from you.ABL', *mit tumenca* 'with you.INSTR' (from German *für*, *von*, *mit*).

The **ablative** marker *-tar/-tər/-tir/-tɨr/-tyr/-ta* (with voice assimilation) expresses spatial and material origin and source, and the object of comparison and reason. The **instrumental** forms are *-sa/-ssa/-sar/-ha/-ja/-a/-ʀa, -ʀe/ -he* in the singular. Plural forms of the instrumental vary, showing *-ca/-sa/-car/ -dža(r)* and more. The shape of the instrumental is less symmetrical than that of the other Layer II markers, both because of the different kind of phonological assimilation that affects the dental sibilant in the position following /n/ in the oblique ending (often a dental affricate), but also due to the processes that affect intervocalic /s:h/ in grammatical endings. Thus it is not unusual to find an instrumental singular ending in *-ha* alongside the instrumental plural in *-ca*. Apart from the actual instrumental function (*čhurjasa* 'with a knife'), the instrumental case also functions as a sociative/comitative (*tumensa* 'with you') and in fixed constructions as an expression of location or mode (*dromesa* 'on the road').

The final and most problematic Layer II marker is the **genitive** in *-ker-/ -kr-/- kəri,-koro/-kər-/-k-/-r-*. Only Vlax has exclusively 'short' forms lacking *-r-*, but there are dialects in which forms with and without *-r-* may co-occur. Sampson (1926: 86–8) even mentions a tendency toward a functional differentiation in Welsh and Finnish Romani, with 'long' forms indicating nominal formations and predicatives (*butiakero* 'servant', *iveskero* 'January', *me dakero s'o than* 'the tent is my mother's'), while short forms indicate adjectives and attributives (*sunakesko* 'made of gold', *ivesko* 'snowy', *me dako than* 'my mother's tent'). The original genitive derives from the participle of the verb **kar-* 'to do'. In subcontinental NIA, similar diversity in the genitive formations can be found, with forms in *-r-*, in *-k-*, and in *-ker-/-kr-*. It is possible that Romani inherited two forms for the genitive, which were either interchangeable or functionally differentiated. Structural simplification of the 'long' forms could also be a Romani-internal development (cf. Boretzky1999b: 39).

Like its cognate morphemes elsewhere in NIA, the Romani genitive occupies a special position in the case system. On the one hand it attaches to the genitive noun, figuring in paradigmatic relation to all other Layer II case markers, while on the other hand it shows morphological agreement in gender, number, and case with its head, which makes genitives look like adjectives (Vlax examples):

(1) a. le rakles-k-i dej
ART.M.OBL boy.OBL-GEN-F.NOM mother
'the boy's mother'
b. la raklja-k-i dej
ART.F.OBL girl.OBL-GEN-F.NOM mother
'the girl's mother'
c. le rakles-k-e phrala
ART.M.OBL boy.OBL-GEN-PL brothers
'the boy's brothers'
d. le rakles-k-o dad
ART.M.OBL boy.OBL-GEN-M.NOM father
'the boy's father'
e. le rakles-k-e dade(s)-sa
ART.M.OBL boy.OBL-GEN-M.OBL father.OBL-INSTR
'with the boy's father'

The Romani genitive is thus an example of 'double case' or 'Suffixaufnahme' (Plank 1995, Payne 1995). The morphological composition of genitives has syntactic and semantic implications. Genitives often maintain word-order flexibility, occurring both before and after the head noun (*le rakleske phrala* 'the boy's brothers', but also *e phrala le rakleske*). Koptjevskaja-Tamm (2000) discusses their range of semantic productivity, which includes both an anchoring referential function, characterising entities via their relations to other entitites (*le raklesko dad* 'the boy's father'), as well as non-anchoring classifying or qualifying functions (*bakresko mas* lit. 'sheep meat' = 'lamb'). The latter may indicate qualifying features such as material, source, age, measure, time, location, purpose, object, or more general properties such as eye or hair colour (*kale jakhengeri čhaj* 'a girl with black eyes'). As indicated above, this semantic productivity makes genitives the most common resource for lexical derivation in the language.

The affinity between genitives and adjectives in structural agreement patterns and in their functions of semantic attribution raises the question whether Romani genitives might in fact be classified as adjectival postpositions. There are however important morphological differences between genitives and adjectives in distribution (see Koptjevskaja-Tamm 2000, Grumet 1985): genitives attach to noun phrases through the mediation of oblique affixes, while derivational adjectives attach directly to the noun stem. By attaching to the oblique affixes, genitives can be said to inflect for gender, number and case. Like the other Layer II case affixes, the genitive marker is sensitive to voice alternation conditioned by the phonological environment. Genitives also control agreement with articles, adjectives, possessives, demonstratives, or other genitives, in much the same way as nouns, while adjectives do not.

According to Koptjevskaja-Tamm (2000), a major syntactic difference between genitive adnominals and adjectives in most dialects of Romani is the fact that a genitive that precedes the head noun is incompatible with possessors or articles that are attached to the head:

(1) a. *le rakleski e dej
ART.M.OBL boy.OBL-GEN-F.NOM ART.F.NOM mother
b. *e [le rakleski] dej
ART.F.NOM ART.M.OBL boy.OBL-GEN-F.NOM mother
but
c. e dej le rakleski
ART.F.NOM mother ART.M.OBL boy. OBL-GEN-F.NOM
'the boy's mother'

This suggests that preposed genitives have determiner status, rather than adjectival status. Some dialects may show a breakdown of this system, however, either admitting articles, as in (2a), or showing agreement between the article and the head, rather than the possessor (*o raklesko kher* with a nominative definite article, rather than *le raklesko kher*, where the definite article is in the oblique). It seems then that the adjectival affinity of the genitive has a reality in actual patterns of language use.

5.3.5 *Layer III adpositions*

The collapse of the OIA/MIA nominal inflection system led to the gradual extension of the grammaticalised inventory of analytic markers of case, which are recruited from adverbial material (often of nominal origin). Romani shares this general development, as well as part of the inventory of Layer III analytic markers, with other NIA languages. Many of the older adpositions retain an adverbial form, and are still also used as adverbs, though some dialects make use of derivational morphemes *-e/-i* and *-al/-il* to differentiate adpositions, stative adverbs, and directional adverbs (Vlax *angla amende* 'in front of us', *tordžul anglal* 'it stands in front/ahead', and *džav angle* 'I go forwards'). The basic adpositions are inherited from Proto-Romani. Nonetheless, there are differences between the inventories of Layer III markers in individual dialects. Common to most dialects are *angle/angla/anglal/glan/ang'il* 'in front', *pal/pala/pała/pale* 'behind', *paš/paša/pašal* 'next to', *andre/ande/de/ane/dre* 'in/into', *tela/tel/tala/tała* 'under/below', *upre/opre/pre/pro* 'above', derived from adverbs, and *pre/pe/pa* 'on', *dži/žiko* 'until' from original adpositions. Of more limited distribution are *andar/dran/andral/ andal/anda* 'from/out of', *ke/ki/ka/kaj/kije/kija* 'at/to', *maškar/maškir* 'between', *vaš* 'for', *truja/utruja/tru/tur/* 'past/around', *perdal/pirdal/pedar* 'across'. They appear to belong to the original inventory, but were lost in individual dialects or dialect branches.

A younger group of adpositions, similarly of limited distribution, goes back to recent grammaticalisations, perhaps during the Early Romani period. Of those, relatively widely distributed is *karing/karig/krik* 'towards', from **akaja-rig* lit. 'this-side'. More seldom is *mamuj/mamujal* 'against/opposite', which includes the component *-muj* 'face'. Two additional prepositions replicate Layer II elements: the ablative *katar/kotar/tar* 'from', and the locative *te/ti* 'at'. The continuing grammaticalisation of adpositions might be seen as part of the gradual trend to rely more heavily on an analytic expression of case, though the use of prepositions does not always entail reduced productivity of synthetic case markers (see below). To varying degrees, Romani dialects also borrow prepositions. This however is a recent phenomenon that follows the split into dialect branches. There are no borrowed prepositions that are Common Romani, and none that go back to the Early Romani period. Perhaps the most common borrowed preposition is Slavic *pretiv/protiv* 'against'. The most extensive borrowing of prepositions is found in the Sinti dialect, where *fon* 'from', *mit* 'with', *fir* 'for' and more are adopted from German (see also section 8.2.2). In the Balkans, some dialects have borrowed the Turkish postnominal positioning of adpositions and show optional postpositions: Rhodopes Romani *katar o voš* alongside *o voš katar* 'from the forest' (Igla 1997: 153). Postpositioning of inherited adpositions also occurs in Finnish Romani.

5.3.6 *The stability of synthetic case markers*

Synthetic case marking in Romani – the use of Layer I and II inflection markers to express case relations – is on the whole stable and well preserved in all present-day dialects (with the exception of the dialects of southern Italy), but it competes nonetheless with a tendency toward analytic expression of case through exclusive use of Layer III adpositions. The outcome of this competition depends on a variety of factors. First, the resources available to express individual case relations are not always symmetrical: all dialects possess at least one, and usually two prepositions with a locative meaning (inessive/illative *andr-* 'in', and adessive/allative *k-* 'at'). These compete with locative and sometimes also with dative Layer II markers. But there is no inherited or shared preposition with an instrumental or sociative meaning which could compete with the Layer II instrumental marker. Some dialects however have borrowed comitative/instrumental prepositions from current or recent contact languages. Synthetic case stability thus depends both on the resources available for individual case relations, and on the structural resources and solutions adopted in individual dialects. Generally, the distribution of synthetic case is sensitive to a hierarchy of referential prominence. Pronouns always take synthetic case. Full nouns show variation: topical entities, animates, and definites are more likely to take synthetic case marking than non-topical entities, inanimates, and indefinites. All these factors interact to determine the balance between synthetic and analytic case marking (cf. Matras 1997a).

The most extreme decline of synthetic case is exhibited by the Abbruzzian and Molisean dialects of Italy (Soravia 1972, Ascoli 1865), where the system virtually disappears, as well as by the now extinct variety of English Romani documented by Smart and Crofton (1875). Vlax varieties show fairly extensive use of analytic case expression at the expense of Layer II markers. Prepositions are regularly used with full nouns for most ablative and locative relations, for some dative relations (*phendem ko raklo* 'I said to the boy'), and often to paraphrase the genitive (*o kher katar muro dad* 'the house of [from] my father'). This is however a rather recent development, and present-day variation across generations is clearly detectable. Northern dialects tend to be more conservative in their reliance on synthetic case markers.

Among the Layer II markers themselves, the locative is generally low on the hierarchy of synthetic case productivity, a fact that coincides with the availability of locative prepositions in all dialects. Constructions such as *kadale thaneste* 'this.OBL place.LOC = at this place' are thus quite likely to be abandoned in Romani as a whole in favour of *ande kadava than* 'at this place' (in the nominative case). Less prone to renewal is the ablative. The synthetic ablative may stand in semantic opposition to an ablative preposition: Eastern Slovak Romani *khatar o phike* 'from the shoulders (downwards)', but *phikendar* '(grabbed) by the shoulders'. In the Northeastern dialects there is no ablative preposition at all, and the synthetic Layer II ablative expresses all ablative relations.

Renewal of the inventory of prepositions does not necessarily mean reduction of the productivity of synthetic case marking, however. In the Sinti dialect, borrowed prepositions often accompany synthetic markers, rather than substitute for them: *fir o dadeske* 'for the father.DAT' (German *für*), or *fon o phalester* 'from the brother.ABL' (German *von*). Both the genitive and the instrumental lack obvious competitors among Layer III markers. The former may be paraphrased through an ablative preposition. The latter is reinforced by a borrowed preposition in the Sinti dialect. A more recent development is the substitution, with full nouns, of the instrumental through a borrowed preposition from the current contact language in various dialects (German Lovari, Argentinian Kalderaš, Greek Vlax and Arli, Slovene Romani as spoken in Italy, and others): *mit/kon/me (to) muro phral* 'with my brother'.

The topicality/animacy continuum and its effects on synthetic case representation were already addressed above. The independent oblique may be the clearest instance of a correlation between synthetic case marking and topicality or referential prominence, since here there is no competition with a Layer III element and resource availability is therefore irrelevant. But referential prominence is relevant for synthetic case stability with other case relations as well. The locative serving as a prepositional case is rarely found with inanimates: conservative dialects may have *pašal e manušeste* 'next to the person.LOC', but always *pašal o kher* 'next to the house.NOM'. For the ablative, dialects may show a hierarchical split within the group of animates, with close kin more likely to take synthetic case than other animates: Sinti *pučas peskri dater* 'he asked his mother.ABL' but *pučas fon peskre mala* 'he asked [from] his friends.NOM' with the preposition *fon* (German *von*), Lovari *manglas mure dadestar* 'he asked my father.ABL', but *manglas katar muro amal* 'he asked [from] my friend.NOM' (cf. Matras 1997a: 75). The dative expresses a benefactive meaning, which in general is associated with topical referents. Dative-marked nominals that are low on the referential hierarchy are therefore rather rare. This correlation with referentiality places the dative higher on the hierarchy of synthetic case stability than the locative or ablative. Pronominals can be accommodated on the hierarchy of referential prominence in their capacity as placeholders for established entities. With personal pronouns, synthetic case marking is obligatory. But with other pronouns, animacy may play a role: Vlax *kodolestar* 'from this.ABL [person]', but *anda kodo* 'from [=because of] this.NOM [fact or state of affairs]'.

5.4 Adjective inflection

Adjective inflection in Romani is generally sensitive to the inflectional properties of the head noun: gender, number, and Layer I case inflection. There is even some symmetry in the form of the inherited adjectival endings compared to the nominal endings of vocalic declensions. Early Romani declinable adjectives, such as *baro* 'big', had the nominative endings M.SG *-o*, F.SG *-i*, and plural *-e*, and the oblique endings M.SG *-e*, F.SG *-a* and plural *-e*. Noteworthy is the uniform shape of the plural ending, which neutralises both gender and case agreement. Adjectives thus normally end in an inflectional stressed vowel, both in attributive and in predicative position (*phuro rom* 'old man', *ov si phuro* 'he is old'). The same patterns of inflection apply to the agreement between genitives and their heads, and to the possessive adjective. There is only a very small group of indeclinable adjectives ending in consonants, such as *šukar* 'pretty'. Only nominalised adjectives may take full nominal inflection (*e phureske* 'for the old [man]'). A unique exception are attributive adjectives in the Hravati (Croatian) and Xaladitka (North Russian) dialects, which may copy nominal inflection: North Russian Romani *tikne čhavensa* 'with small children', alongside *tiknensa čhavensa* (Wentzel 1980: 81). Case neutralisation with inanimate nouns generally entails case neutralisation in adjectival agreement as well: *ande baro kher* 'in-the big.NOM house'.

Table 5.3 *Early Romani adjective inflection (after Elšík 2000a); athematic singular endings are unstressed*

	NOM SG.M	SG.F	PL	OBL SG.M	SG.F	PL
thematic	*-o*	*-i*	*-e*	*-e*	*-a*	*-e*
athematic	*-o*	*-o*	*-a*	*-on-e*	*-on-a*	*-on-e*

Recent erosion of the adjectival inflection can be detected in individual dialects. Gender distinction is often neutralised in the oblique, resulting in a uniform shape of the oblique adjective in *-e*. The process is still ongoing in some dialects (cf. Lovari *phure romnjake* 'for the old woman', alongside the conservative form *phura romnjake*). In some dialects, there is a tendency to neutralise agreement with predicative adjectives, with the masculine singular nominative form in *-o* taking over: Hamlin Sinti *jōb/joi/jōn hi gusevo* 'he/she/they is/are clever'; Holzinger 1995: 15).

Relatively few Greek-derived adjectives survive in Common Romani. Nonetheless, as with nouns, it was a Greek pattern of adjective inflection that was adopted into Early Romani as the productive pattern for the integration of subsequent loans. Here, too, the Greek endings are copied in the nominative, based on the Greek neuter forms: singular *-o*, with no gender distinction, plural *-a*, both unstressed. In the oblique, an extension *-on-* is added to the base and is followed by thematic adjectival endings, which are stressed. This is the pattern that accompanies the Greek-derived adjectival derivational endings, such as *-itko* etc. (see above), which in turn are often assigned to subsequent loan adjectives. The Greek-derived nominative plural ending *-a* survives only in some dialects, such as Xaladitka and the Northern Central group. In the Vlax and Balkan dialects, the tendency is for the oblique plural form *-one* to replace the nominative plural, thereby simplifying the paradigm and increasing the symmetry between thematic and athematic inflections. A development toward full integration of loan adjectives into the inherited inflection is attested in the Southern Central dialects (Elšík et al. 1999: 334). Loan adjectives ending in a consonant may in some dialects be treated like inherited indeclinable adjectives, e.g. Sinti *hart* 'hard' (German *hart*).

A further adaptation pattern for loan adjectives involves the selection of an inflectional prototype from the source language. In Roman, recent German-derived adjectives have a uniform ending in *-i*, a generalisation of dialectal German *-i* which in the source language is the most frequent and so most salient adjectival marker (nominative plural and feminine singular, and all oblique positions). Quite often one encounters a tendency to retain adjectival inflection with adjectives taken from the current contact language, as in Serbian Kalderaš *but dosadni sî le* 'they are very bothersome' (Boretzky 1994: 48), with the Serbian plural inflection *-i*.

Pre-European numerals in attributive position take, in principle, conservative adjectival inflection: *trin-e berš-en-go* 'three-M.OBL year-PL.OBL-GEN = three years old'. There is however considerable erosion of agreement with numerals, triggered at least in part through the infiltration of Greek numerals in positions above 'six'.

5.5 Deictics and related forms

5.5.1 *Definiteness and indefiniteness*

Romani is unique among the NIA languages in having a fully developed definite article. Although assumptions that Romani actually borrowed its article forms *o, i* from Greek must be rejected (for the diachrony of the article see below), it is nevertheless quite clear that the emergence of the preposed definite article was triggered through contact with Greek, and so it must go back to the Early Romani period. There are striking structural similarities between the Romani and Greek articles (cf. Boretzky 2000a): they are preposed, they are usually vocalic in the nominative but often consonantal in the oblique, there are no stressed forms, and there is no deictic use of the article. Moreover, there are similarities in semantic uses, such as the attachment of the article to proper nouns (see below). Boretzky (2000a) points out that there are no other languages with preposed definite articles between India and the Balkans that could have served as a model for the emergence of articles in Romani.[6] The other Balkan languages have postposed articles (Albanian, Balkan Slavic, Romanian). Romani articles therefore definitely developed before the dispersion of the dialects, that is, again, during the Early Romani period. Romani is thus a good example of the tendency of definite articles to show areal rather than genetic clustering (cf. Boretzky 2000a). The Northeastern dialects of the Polska Roma and Xaladikta, and the Hravati/Dolenjski dialects, which are in contact with languages that have no articles, have largely lost both the definite and the indefinite articles. Traces of the definite articles remain in the gender agreement between some prepositions that incorporate the historical article, and the nouns they modify: Polska Roma *pašo kher* 'next-to.M [the] house', *paši tyša* 'next-to.F [the] table' (Matras 1999b: 9–10).

Like other nominal modifiers, the definite article inflects for gender, number, and case at the Layer I level (nominative/oblique), gender agreement being neutralised in the plural. There are tendencies to simplify the paradigm of definite

[6] Southern Kurdish (Sorani), however, has a postposed definite article *-ak*, a reanalysis of an indefinite article deriving from the numeral 'one'.

Table 5.4 *Forms of the definite article in dialect groups*

	NOM S.GM	SG.F	PL	OBL S.GM	SG.F	PL
Northeastern	*o*	*i/e*	*o*	*e*	*e*	*e*
Northwestern	*o*	*i/e*	*i/o*	*i/e*	*i/e*	*i/e*
Northern Central	*o*	*e*	*o*	*(l)e*	*(l)a*	*(l)e*
Southern Central	*o*	*i*	*o*	*(o)le*	*(o)la*	*(o)le*
Vlax	*o*	*i/e*	*(l)e/əl/ol*	*(l)e*	*(l)a/e*	*(l)e/o(l)*
Bugurdži group	*o/u*	*i*	*o/u*	*e*	*e/i*	*e*
Southern Balkan	*o*	*e/i*	*o*	*e*	*e*	*e*

articles, and forms of the definite article show considerable cross-dialectal variation. Thus most present-day forms are not directly inherited from Early Romani, but are the outcome of later, dialect-particular innovations. The only form that is consistent across all dialects is that of the nominative masculine singular in *o* (with occasional phonetic variant *u*). The nominative feminine singular tends to have *i* or *e*. Oblique forms, and partly plural forms, tend to be more conservative, sometimes showing consonantal forms in *-l-*. This is typical of the innovation patterns within the Romani inventory of deictic and anaphoric expressions, where renewal usually begins in the nominative forms (see below). The most archaic forms that provide the best clues for reconstructing the original forms of the definite article are those that have preserved both the stem consonant and the initial vowel, namely those in *ol-*. Table 5.4 shows how conservative consonantal forms cluster in a geographical pattern comprising the Central and Vlax dialects (see also chapter 9).

As illustrated in table 5.4, the minimal system differentiates between two article forms (Southern Balkans), but systems can have up to five different forms (Southern Central). Articles are often integrated into prepositions: *ande* + *o* > *ando* 'in-the.M', *ka* + *e* > *ke* 'at-the.PL', etc. The definite article occupies the first position in the noun phrase, preceding attributive adjectives: *o phuro rom* 'the old man'. Adjectives in appositional function are generally treated as nominals, for case inflection as well as determination, and they may be introduced by a definite article, rendering the impression of a postposed definite adjective: *o rom o phuro* 'ART man ART old = the old man'. In some dialects of the Vlax and Balkan groups, definite articles may combine with demonstratives: *kadava o rom* or alternatively *o rom kadava* 'this man' (cf. Igla 1996: 40). Both options appear to be modelled on Greek, though the second also matches a Romanian model (cf. Boretzky 1994: 55). It appears that such combinations are not attested outside the Balkans, and so we are dealing with a late Balkanism.

The pragmatic uses of the definite article in Romani seem to be in line with universal usages of the definite article: it accompanies identifiable entities, introduced either in the previous discourse context or accessible through the speech situation, through general knowledge, or via a relation that has been established to a separate identifiable referent (a nominal or a relative clause). As in Greek (but also in dialects of German), proper nouns in Romani are also accompanied by a definite article. Semantic usages of the Romani article are more specific. Boretzky (2000a) argues for a close affinity to semantic uses of the article in Balkan languages and especially in Greek. Among them are generic reference, for instance to nations, as in *o gadžo* '[a/any] non-Rom', time quantification, as Bugurdži *pal o duj zis* 'after ART two days', contrastive and comparative reference, as in Agia Varvara Vlax *severim tut sar o sekeri* 'I love you like ART sugar', material source, as in Bugurdži *katar o zlatos* 'of ART gold', including origin, *porja katar e khanji* 'feathers of ART hen'. Institutions and habits that are known from general knowledge and experience can also be definite in a semantic sense, without pragmatic definiteness (prior introduction to the discourse): Slovak Romani *sar e Monika gel'a avri andal e škola* 'when Monika left ART school', Bosnian Gurbet *vov lija e džukle thaj gelo* 'he took the dogs and left', where the dogs are only identifiable through general experience that people may possess dogs (Boretzky 2000a: 51–4).

Overt marking of indefiniteness in Romani is facultative. The indefinite article *jekh/ekh/ek* is based on the numeral 'one', and is inflected (*dikhlas jekhe gažes* 'he saw a.OBL man.OBL'). It usually accompanies newly introduced topical entities: Kalderaš *sas haj sas jek gaźo čořo* 'there was a poor man' (Boretzky 1994: 229). Another function of the indefinite article is to demarcate events and locations by singling out referents from a potential group: Kalderaš *sas duj phral and ek foro* 'there were two brothers in a [particular] town' (Boretzky 1994: 236). Indefinite entities that are not topical or potentially ambiguous, and merely serve an anchoring or attributive function for the proposition as a whole, do not typically take the indefinite article: Lovari *traisardam kothe, sas ame kher, muro dad puterdas kirčima* 'we lived there, we had [a] house, my father opened [a] pub' (Matras 1994a: 47; cf. also discussion there).

5.5.2 *Personal pronouns*

Like nouns, pronouns in Romani have a layered structure, with nominative and oblique forms, the latter serving as a base for further case formations through the attachment of Layer II markers. First- and second-person pronouns continue OIA/MIA forms. At least for the first-person singular nominative pronoun *me*, an origin in an oblique form can be postulated. This suggests that Proto-Romani had passed through a stage of ergative morphology (cf. Bubeník 2000; see also Woolner 1915), which in turn supports an outwards migration from

India not earlier than in medieval times. The second-person singular nominative pronoun *tu* however derives from an historically nominative form. In having third-person pronouns that are distinct from demonstratives, Romani stands out among the NIA languages, but it also differs from Greek, its principal early contact language in Europe. The inventory of third-person pronouns testifies to repeated processes of renewal, and at least three stages can be reconstructed based on present-day forms (see below).

The Early Romani forms of the first- and second-person pronouns are as follows: first-person singular nominative *me*, oblique *man-*, independent oblique/clitic often *ma*; second-person singular nominative *tu*, oblique *tu(t)-*, the *-t-* generally assimilates to Layer II markers and is retained only in the independent oblique, and not in all dialects. The plural forms – first-person *amen* and second-person *tumen* – are in principle identical in the nominative and oblique, though reduction of the ending in *-n* is common in forms that are not followed by Layer II markers, especially in the nominative. In the Northern dialects, the first-person plural pronoun often undergoes truncation to *me(n)* or prothesis to *jamen* or even *lame(n)* (Abbruzzian Romani). Exceptional is the formation of the plural pronouns in the Istrian variety of the Sloveni/Hravati dialect *meamen, tuamen* (for details see Elšík 2000b: 70–1). Emphatic suffixes for the first- and second-person pronouns are found in a number of dialects. They include *-(a)ja*, which is found in various dialects, and *-ni* (Sloveni/Hravati, Erli), which may have given rise to an emphatic form in *-j* (cf. Sepečides *mej* 'I', *tuj* 'you').

Possessive forms of the first- and second-person pronouns are based on the attachment of a possessive suffix *-r-* (which is adjectival and agrees with the head in gender, number, and case). Unlike nominals and third-person pronouns, possessive markers of the first- and second-person pronouns do not attach to the general oblique forms, but to what Elšík (2000b) calls the 'base stems' of the pronouns: first singular *m-*, second singular *t-*, first plural *(a)m-*, and second plural *tum-*. It is important to note however that the processes by which the adjectival-possessive suffix attaches to these base forms are not identical for the various pronominal forms. It is possible that Proto-Romani already inherited a differentiation between singular forms, where the possessive affix was **-ir-* (first singular **mir-*, second singular **tir-*), and plural forms, which had **-ar-* (first plural **amar-*, second plural **tumar-*). For the first singular possessive, it is possible to continue to reconstruct a late Proto-Romani form **minř-* (cf. Elšík 2000b), which could well have emerged from the historical **mir-* by analogy to the oblique form *man-* (see table 5.5). It is likely that the change in the quality of the *r*-sound from *r* > *ř* was triggered by the proximity to the nasal, at a time when the retroflex cluster *ṇḍ* was undergoing shift to *ndř* and other forms (see chapter 4; cf. also Boretzky 1999b: 60–1). This makes the emergence of the present-day forms of the first singular possessive a rather young phenomenon, which accounts for the high diversity of forms.

Table 5.5 *(Common) Romani personal pronouns*

	NOM	OBL	POSSESSIVE
1 SG	*me*	*man-*	*mi(nd)řo/ mu(nd)řo*
2 SG	*tu*	*tut-*	*tiro*
1 PL	*amen*	*amen-*	*amaro*
2 PL	*tumen*	*tumen-*	*tumaro*
3 SG.M	*(v-/j-) ov*	*les-*	*les-k(er)o*
3 SG.F	*(v-/j-) oj*	*la-*	*la-k(er)o*
3 PL	*(v-/j-) on / ol*	*len-*	*len-g(er)o*
REFL	–	*pes*	*pesk(er)o / piro*

According to Elšík's (2000b) scenario, in the Vlax dialects the original second singular possessive was retained (*tiro* > *ćiro*), while the first singular possessive underwent labialisation of the vowel to *-unř-* (*munřo*, *mundřo*, *muřo*). Elsewhere in Romani, there is a later tendency toward uniformity in the possessive affixes of the two singular forms, favouring one of the patterns, thus either *miro/tiro* (Northern), or *minro/tinro* (Rumelian), *mindro/tindro* (Sepečides), *mindo/tindo* (Prilep) and other variants. A more recent development is the emergence of possessive forms that are analogous to the third-person and nominal possessive. They are based on the oblique stem of the pronoun with the possessive affix *-k-/-ker-*. We find singular forms in *mango*, *tuko* in some Kelderaš variants and in Rumelian, and plural forms in *mengro*, *tumengro* in Romani dialects of Italy (cf. Elšík 2000b). Various dialects show short forms of the possessive pronouns in *mo* and *to* (Vlax *ćo*).

The nominative forms of **third-person pronouns** are masculine singular *ov*, feminine singular *oj*, and plural *on*. The original forms survive in the Balkan and Southern Central groups, while elsewhere we find prothetic forms: initial *v-* (*vov*, *voj*, *von*) is predominantly Vlax (but also Sepečides), while forms in *j-* are found in northwestern Europe (Welsh, Northwestern, and Northeastern groups) and the Northern Central dialects. Specific phonological developments include changes to the consonants in the masculine singular pronoun (*jof*, *job* from *jov*, and *ōv*, *vo* from *vov*). Plural forms may have extensions in *-ne/-ni* and *-nk*. In some cases we find plurals in *ol/ole/ola* (see discussion below). Under the influence of the genderless languages Hungarian and Finnish, some dialects of Romani have neutralised gender distinctions and generalised one of the two forms for both genders. According to Elšík (2000b), the original masculine is now used in Vend, some Lovari varieties, and variants of Finnish Romani, and the original feminine in Hungarian Lovari, in Cerhari, and in most Romungro dialects. The oblique forms have stems in *l-*, which testify to their historical affinity to oblique demonstratives and oblique forms of the definite article (see below). Their inflection matches that of full nouns: masculine singular *-es-*, feminine singular *-a-*, and plural *-en-*. Possessive forms are formed in the same way as nominal genitive-possessives, that is with the suffix *-ker-/-k-*: *lesk(er)o, lak(er)o, leng(er)o.*

Romani possesses a **reflexive** pronoun, deriving from OIA *ātman* MIA *appā*. Forms vary between *pe* and *pes*; the quality of the vowel suggests that *pe* is a contraction of the independent oblique form *pes*. The reflexive may appear with reflexive or reciprocal verbs (*kerel pe* lit. 'does itself = becomes', *maren pen* 'they hit one another = they quarrel'). It can equally be a full thematic constituent (*vov daral anda peste* 'he fears for himself'), a pseudo-constituent with an epistemic-evaluative reading (*vov džaltar peske* 'he is going away [for himself]'), or a reflexive possessive (*areslo ande pesko kher* 'he arrived in his [own] house'), in all of which the anaphoric referent is identical with the subject of the clause. The reflexive generally inflects like pronouns, although many dialects show neutralisation of number agreement favouring the singular forms. The wide distribution of the possessive forms *pesk(er)o* allows us to reconstruct this as an Early Romani form, though in the Balkan forms analogous to the first and second singular possessive dominate (*pindro, piro, po*), in some even an analogy to the second-person plural may be found in the reflexive plural possessive *pumaro*.

5.5.3 *Clitic pronouns*

Third-person oblique pronouns have occasionally been referred to as 'clitics'. Although they generally tend to occupy the position most proximate to the verb, at least when expressing the direct object, their paradigmatic relation to possessive pronouns, and their availability for topicalisation strategies in some dialects – *les si duj čhave* 'he.OBL has [=is] two children' – must lead us to reject their general classification as clitics. Partial cliticisation however is apparent in the emergence of reduced forms of the oblique pronouns in the first and second person. In possessive constructions, they are clear counterparts to the topicalised full pronouns: *man si ma duj čhave* '1.SG.OBL is 1.SG.CL two children = me, I have two children'. Elšík (2000b) mentions the appearance of reduced, cliticised pronouns as prepositional objects: Sloveni/Hravati *smek ma* 'in front of me', Eastern Slovak Romani *pal ma* alongside locative-marked *pal mande* 'after me'. The most radical development is found in Abbruzian Romani, where clitics have fused with the verb to give rise to object agreement markers: *dikkēmə'* < *dikhel-ma* 'she sees me'.

Common in Romani, however, and clearly an Early Romani legacy, are post-posed third-person subject clitics. In structure they parallel the oblique forms of the third-person pronouns: their stem is *l-*, their endings are the nominative vocalic endings found in the vocalic nominal declension as well as in adjectival agreement inflection: masculine singular *lo*, feminine singular *li*, plural *le*.

Subject clitics appear to be an archaism in Romani. They are most productive in the Sinti–Manuš dialect groups, as well as in Roman. Conservative varieties show frequent occurrences of postposed subject clitics following various word classes, especially attaching to verbs, often just shortly after the first mentioning of the full referent: Manuš *o biboldo dikas-lo ku kova* 'the Jew looked.CL at that' (Valet 1991: 130). In other varieties of the Sinti group, clitics that attach to verbs are reduced to vocalic suffixes *-o*, *-i*, *-e*, while full clitics attach to non-verbal elements: Hamlin Sinti *vajas-o pal mende, rodēs men-lo* 'he.came.CL [looking] for us, he.searched us.CL' (Holzinger 1993: 320). Holzinger (1993: 308) places the consonantal clitics higher on the scale of topic continuity than the reduced suffixes. In part, the distribution of the two forms in the Sinti corpus can be accounted for on structural grounds (cf. Matras 1999e: 152–3). Postverbal subjects are generally expressed as suffixes; their occurrence in Sinti is to a considerable extent formalised through partial adoption of the German rules on subject–verb inversion. The placement of clitics that do not attach directly to the verb, and so appear in a consonantal form, on the other hand, is not formalised. In Roman, the position of clitics is similarly flexible, and their use is probably closest to their original function as non-emphatic anaphoric pronouns: *Bečiste but bombn tel čikerde taj lo odoj mulo* 'they threw many bombs on Vienna and he died there' (Halwachs 1998: 192).

Full subject clitics are also common in the other Northwestern dialects (notably Finnish Romani), Welsh and English Romani, Slovene/Croatian Romani, with traces in Caló (Spanish Para-Romani), as well as in Romungro. In all these dialects, however, they have retreated and are confined primarily to existential predications, usually attaching directly to the person-inflected copula: *si-lo* 'he is', etc. Yet a further stage in the decline of subject clitics is attested in Vlax dialects. Here, subject clitics are marginal, attaching only to deictics and interrogatives:, *eta-lo!* 'there he is!', *kaj-lo?* 'where is he?'. The pattern of retreat formed by subject clitics constitutes a predictable hierarchy, whereby pronominal copulas may appear in equatial predications, while non-verbal predications are restricted to deictic locatives (see Hengeveld 1992: 208–12). Subject clitics appear to have disappeared completely in an area comprising the Northeastern and Northern Central dialects. In some Balkan dialects, functionally similar subject clitics in *t-* are found. In the Prizren dialect, the clitic form in *t-* follows existential predications: *hi-to* /*si-to* 'he is' (Boretzky and Igla 1994b). In Arli (Boretzky 1996a: 23), a form in *-tano/-tani/-tane* appears, which may attach, like in Sinti, to existential, deictic, and regular verbal predications (*trin ine-tane* 'there were three', *kaj-tano* 'where is he', *ake-tani* 'there she is', *dželo-tano* 'he went'). The *t*-forms suggest continuous presence of a deictic stem in initial *t-* in Romani, in addition to the form deriving from the medial *-t-* in reconstructed demonstrative **ata* > **alo* > *lo* (see below). The *t*-deictic is likely to have been the original subject clitic, later replaced by a weakened form of the demonstrative. A case for comparison is Domari, where subject clitics in *t-* are, like in many Romani dialects, restricted to deictic predications (*kate-ta* 'where is he', *kate-ti* 'where is she', *hatta-te* 'there they are', *hatta-ta* 'there he is'). The regular deictic in Domari is cognate with Romani (oblique masculine *oras* 'that one', Romani *-oles*).

5.5.4 *Demonstratives*

Romani demonstratives show extreme cross-dialectal diversity, although the principal structural patterns of their formation are shared. Undoubtedly the most striking feature of Romani demonstratives from a typological perspective, especially in the context of the neighbouring European languages, is the fact that they typically form a four-term system. Only sporadically do we find varieties where the original paradigm has been reduced to a two-term system (some Sinti dialects). Demonstratives show a consonantal stem in *-k-*, *-d-* or a reduplicative combination of the two (*k_d-* or *k_k-*, and rarely *-d_k-*). The consonantal stems appear to derive from location deictics used to reinforce earlier demonstrative forms (see below), and are cognate with the present-day location deictics *akaj/adaj* 'here', *okoj/odoj* 'there'.

The deictic stem combines with vowels that carry semantic distinctions, termed 'carrier vowels' (Matras 2000a). They indicate the source of knowledge about a referent: *-a-* indicates that the referent is part of the extra-linguistic speech situation or the here-and-now, and so it is visible or audible to the speaker and the listener, while *-o-/-u-* refers to an entity that has been or will be introduced in the intra-linguistic context of the discourse. The latter thus constitutes a grammaticalised discourse or textual deixis in the sense of Levinson (1983; see discussion in Matras 1998a). The distinction only partly overlaps with a proximate/distal opposition. Carrier vowels may be reduplicated within a demonstrative expression: *adal-*, *odol-*, *akad-*, *okod-*, etc.

The final position in the demonstrative expression is reserved for inflection markers. Demonstratives generally inflect for gender, number, and case, like other nominals and attributives. But they show a unique series of nominative inflection markers, which are not found with other nominals: masculine singular *-va*, feminine singular *-ja*, plural *-la*. In a number of dialects, however, demonstrative inflection undergoes partial analogy to the adjectival inflection paradigm. This is a geographical development, affecting Lovari, Cerhari and some Romungro varieties (masculine singular *-o*, feminine singular *-i*, plural *-la*), and partly also Kalderaš (masculine singular *-o*, feminine singular *-ja*, plural *-la*). Occasionally one also finds such analogy in the plural *-le*. Inflectional endings are sometimes reduced, and the result is often the simplification of the masculine singular as a base form: Manuš *ka, kaj, kal*. In most Northern Central dialects and in Roman, simplification results in the disappearance of

Table 5.6 *Format layout of demonstrative expressions (with examples)*

Reduplicated carrier vowel	stem	carrier vowel	stem	carrier vowel	inflection	gloss
a-	*k-*	*a-*	*d-*	*a-*	*va*	SG.M.NOM
o-	*k-*	*o-*			*ja*	SG.F.NOM
	k-	*u-*	*k-*	*o-*	*len*	PL.OBL
a-	*d-*	*a-*			*les*	SG.M.OBL
	k-	*o-*	*d-*		*i*	SG.F.NOM
	d-	*a-*			*la*	PL.NOM
	k-	*a-*			*l*	PL.NOM

Table 5.7 *The four-term demonstrative system in selected dialects (*M.SG *forms)*

	plain (non-specific) situation	discourse	specific situation	discourse
Welsh, Arli, Sepečides	*adava*	*odova*	*akava*	*okova*
Northeastern	*dava*	*dova*	*adava*	*odova*
Sinti, Finnish	*dava*	*dova*	*kava*	*kova*
(west) Northern Central	*ada(va)*	*od(ov)a*	*akadava*	*okodova*
Roman	*ada*	*oda*		*ka*
East Slovak	*(k)ada*	*(k)oda*	*aka*	*oka*
Agia Varvara	*adava*	*odova*	*(a)kadava*	*(o)kodova*
Lovari	*kado*	*kodo*	*kako*	*kuko*
Kalderaš	*kadava*	*kodova*	*kakava*	*kukova*
Bugurdži	*kada*	*koda*	*kaka*	*kuka*
Gurbet	*kava*	*kova*	*akava*	*okova*
Erli	*adavka*	*odovka*	*akavka*	*okovka*

the original consonantal stem in all but the masculine form: *ada, aja, ala*. In Rumelian Romani, the masculine form serves as the base for further extensions and inflections: *akavka, akavkja, akavkle*. The oblique forms of the demonstrative are usually based on an extension in *-l-*, which corresponds to the oblique form of the third-person pronoun: e.g. masculine nominative *kadava*, oblique *kadales*, feminine nominative *kadaja*, oblique *kadala* (table 5.6).

Distinctive reduplication of the carrier vowel, or reduplication or substitution of the consonantal stem *-d-* with the stem in *-k-*, results in a marked complexity of the demonstrative expressions. This is exploited iconically to represent the semantic feature of 'specificity': an intensified deictic reference procedure. The combination of the oppositions 'discourse context/speech situation' and '+/– specificity' renders the typical four-term system (table 5.7).

The feature 'specificity' is used to single out intended referents from a group of potential referents, that is, for disambiguation or even explicit contrast. Forms marked for intra-linguistic specificity are often lexicalised to mean 'the other': Roman *ka*, Agia Varvara Vlax *okova*, East Slovak Romani *oka*, Lovari *kuko*. In Lovari, the extra-linguistic, +specific *kako* can be used as a filler for a missing word. A reduced form of the specific intra-linguistic demonstrative, *kova*, is often used as an indefinite filler or as an expletive or completive tag (meaning 'something', 'things', 'and so on'). Being the marked component of the system, it is specificity that is lost when the paradigm is reduced, as in some Sinti varieties, to just a two-term system.

The demonstrative is usually inserted to retrieve a referent from the speech situation or discourse context. It is considered lower on the scale of referent continuity than personal pronouns, but higher than full nouns, either definite or indefinite (cf. Holzinger 1993: 308, Matras 2000a: 113). In the majority of dialects, however, demonstratives are obligatory when anaphoric reference is made to inanimate entities: thus *dikhlom odova* 'I saw it/this', but *dikhlom les* 'I saw him/*it'. When used as pronominals, demonstratives carry nominal inflection, including Layer II and Layer III markers. In attributive use, they are assigned adjectival-type inflection, though the inflectional markers are distinct. Like adjectives, the attributive demonstrative normally precedes the noun. Emphatic use of postposed demonstratives is quite frequent in some dialects, though here demonstratives carry nominal inflection and are compatible with definite articles, and so they may be regarded as appositions (*e romeske kodoleske* 'ART man.DAT that.DAT = for that man'; cf. *kodole romeske*).

Despite the diversity of demonstrative expressions, their geographical distribution shows fairly consistent patterns. Diversification appears to be a rather recent development, consisting partly of simplification, partly of innovative extensions of the original forms. For the Early Romani phase, we can assume forms in *adava/odova* and *akava/okova*. The full original paradigm survives in the westernmost Romani dialect, that of Wales, and in the rather conservative, extreme southeastern Arli dialect of Kosovo and Macedonia, as well as elsewhere in the Balkans. Selective retention of parts of the original paradigm is widespread. The reductions that occurred involve the complete loss of the initial or 'reduplicated' carrier vowel in the group of Northwestern dialects comprising Sinti–Manuš and Finnish Romani, as well as in Northern Vlax and the Bugurdži–Drindari groups, and its partial loss in the Northeastern and Southern Vlax dialects. Inflection markers are reduced in the Central dialects and in Lovari/Cerhari, where adjectival inflection is partly adopted. In the Northern Central, Vlax, and the Bugurdži–Drindari groups, a reduplicated combination of stems in *k_d-* emerged. Yet another combination, *k_k-*, is restricted to the Northern Vlax and Bugurdži–Drindari groups. An external stem extension in *-ka* appears in the Balkans. Changing resources allowed for the formation of new opposition pairs within the paradigm while still preserving a four-term system. In some dialects, reduced forms coexist alongside longer forms (Serbian

Table 5.8 *Deictic and anaphoric expressions: Proto-Romani Stage 1*

	Nominative			Oblique		
	SG.M	SG.F	PL	SG.M	SG.F	PL
Demonstratives:						
proximate	**ata* > **alo*	**ati* > **ali*	**ate* > **ale*	**atas* > **ales*	**ata* > **ala*	**atan* > **alen*
remote	**ota* > **olo*	**oti* > **oli*	**ote* > **ole*	**otas* > **oles*	**ota* > **ola*	**otan* > **olen*
Third-person pronoun:	based on remote demonstrative					
Definite article:	non-existent					

Kalderaš, Northern Central dialects), and possibly also inherited forms alongside borrowings from neighbouring dialects (Bugurdži, Sepečides), resulting in an increased and occasionally even in a double inventory of demonstrative expressions.

5.5.5 *The historical development of deictic and anaphoric expressions*

Our reconstruction scenario outlines the historical development of demonstratives, third-person pronouns, pronominal subject clitics, and definite articles. It assumes movement from the deictic paradigm into the anaphoric one, and from there into the definite article paradigm. The loss of deictic properties coincides with the structural reduction of the forms. This in turn is followed by a compensatory renewal of the deictic paradigm itself.[7] On this basis it is possible to reconstruct several cycles of renewal of the deictic/anaphoric paradigm. The stages are numbered to indicate relative chronology.

The point of departure (table 5.8) is the MIA demonstrative set in *-t-*, which in Proto-Romani gives consonantal stems in *-l-*. For the Proto-Romani Stage 1, the reconstruction of oblique forms is supported by the attestation of the same forms in later stages, in particular in the oblique endings of present-day demonstratives (*k-ales*, *d-olen* etc.) and third-person pronouns (*les*, *la*, *len*). The paradigm is also supported by the Domari oblique forms *ēras, ēra, ēran* (proximate) and *oras, ora, oran* (remote) (see Matras 1999c).[8] The dental stop

[7] For a universal discussion of cyclical developments in the deictic system see Diessel (1999).

[8] Turner (1928) derives *les* from OIA *ta-*, and argues for a special development of initial sounds in pronominals, a development attested in other languages as well. In this he returns to an etymology offered by Miklosich (1872–80, XI:15), while rejecting Sampson's (1926: 161) proposal that *-l-* represents intervocalic **-t-* and so a regular development, and in its current form a contraction

Table 5.9 *Deictic and anaphoric expressions: Proto-Romani Stage 2*

	Nominative			Oblique		
	SG.M	SG.F	PL	SG.M	SG.F	PL
Demonstratives:						
proximate	*alo-a*	*ali-a*	*ale-a*			
	>*alova*	>*alija*	>*alea*			
	> *ava*	> *aja*	> *ala*	*ales*	*ala*	*alen*
remote	*olo-a*	*oli-a*	*ole-a*			
	>*olova*	>*olija*	>*olea*			
	> *ova*	> *oja*	> *ola*	*oles*	*ola*	*olen*
Third-person pronoun:	*(o)lo*	*(o)li*	*(o)le*	*oles*	*ola*	*olen*
Definite article:			non-existent			

of the original OIA/MIA deictic stem thus shifts to a lateral (in Domari a trill), final *a* in the SG.M ending becomes *o*, and medial *a* becomes *e*. For the third-person pronoun we can assume a form that is based on the remote or anaphoric demonstrative, which would allow Proto-Romani to pattern with the other NIA languages. Like other NIA languages, Proto-Romani will have had no definite articles.

At a later stage in the Proto-Romani period (Stage 2; table 5.9), the unmarked and frequently used nominative third-person pronouns are simplified and their initial vowel becomes optional, giving rise to pronominal forms that are later to become enclitic (*lo*, *li*, *le*). The oblique forms of the personal pronouns are more likely to have remained conservative at this stage, as forms with an initial vowel are still encountered in some present-day dialects, especially in the Balkans (for instance Ipeiros Romani *ov*, *oj* 'he, she', oblique *oles-*, *ola-*). The use of demonstratives as third-person pronouns carries with it a reduction of their deictic function. This is compensated for through renewal of the nominative demonstrative paradigm.

There is, of course, no textual evidence on which to base our reconstruction of this renewal process. However, one can assume a point of departure as depicted as Proto-Romani Stage 1. There, we have a set of demonstratives with cognates in other MIA/NIA languages, and which allow us to explain the present-day enclitic pronominal set *lo*, *li*, *le* (as an archaism in the nominative pronominal system, and hence in decline), the oblique endings of present-day demonstratives, and the oblique forms of present-day personal pronouns. But the demonstratives shown for Proto-Romani Stage 1 have the common

from *oles*. Turner rejects this, among other arguments, on the ground that in Syrian Romani (i.e. Domari) 'no demonstrative or pronominal stem with *l* appears to be recorded'. The oblique forms of the Domari demonstrative were only recorded very recently (Matras 1999c).

nominal-adjectival gender/number inflection. For the renewal pattern, we need to reconstruct a development which would eventually lead to the present-day demonstratives and their unique forms of gender/number inflection, namely M.SG *ava/ova*, F.SG *aja/oja*, PL *ala/ola*. Since we are dealing with a position in the cycle in which the deictic function of the demonstratives is being reinforced, it is likely that the 'new' forms emerged through complex formations, adding a deictic morpheme to the older forms (deictic reduplication; cf. German *der da*, Swedish *den här*). All three forms share the suffix *-a*, which also appears in the emphatic form of personal pronouns in a number of present-day dialects (*me-a* 'me' etc.), and perhaps also in the M.SG vocative (*čhav-a!* 'boy!'). We can conclude from this that the older inflected forms were reinforced by a deictic suffix *-a*. Although the trigger for the reinforcement of the demonstratives was the weakening of the remote or anaphoric set following its shift into the third-person pronoun functional slot, symmetry of the demonstrative paradigm as a whole is retained, and both the remote and the proximate sets are renewed.

The combination of the deictic reinforcement suffix *-a* with the earlier inflected demonstrative forms will have rendered, through sound changes, the forms attested in present-day dialects: the combination creates an epenthetic labial consonant after the back vowel *o* in the M.SG (**alo-a* > **alova* > **ava*), a palatal consonant after the *i* of the F.SG (**ali-a* > **alija* > **aja*), while in the plural assimilation of the two adjoining vowels to *a* takes place (**ale-a* > **alea* > **ala*) . In the singular forms, the consonantal *-l-* stem is subsequently weakened, and we are left with new shortened forms for the nominative, and so with a synchronically suppletive nominative-oblique paradigm: M.SG *ava/ales*, F.SG *aja/ala*. The nominative plural being more conservative, this seeming suppletion does not appear, and plural forms preserve structural symmetry, albeit with the odd inflectional marker *-a* in the nominative: *ala/alen*.

The demonstrative forms as reconstructed for Proto-Romani Stage 2 are attested in Romani, although in present-day dialects they are normally preceded by consonantal affixes (*k-ava*, *d-ava* etc.), derived from location deictics 'here' and 'there' (see below). However, traces of the independent vocalic forms are found in the conservative Southern Balkan dialects, in forms such as *av-dives* 'today', *aj-rat* 'tonight', Iranian Romano *ava-berš* 'this year' as well as *ava* PL. *ala* 'this'. The contracted remote forms *ov*, *oj*, *ol* move into the anaphoric field and figure as third-person pronouns. Individual occurrences of the proximate forms *av*, *aj* as pronouns are also attested, notably in the Rumelian dialect (cf. Boretzky 1999b: 57).

The second restructuring cycle brings us to the latest stage in the Proto-Romani period (Proto-Romani Stage 3; table 5.10). For third-person pronouns we can reconstruct, based on the distribution in present-day dialects, two nominative forms: an older form *lo, li, le*, and a newer emphatic form based on

Table 5.10 *Deictic and anaphoric expressions: Proto-Romani Stage 3*

	Nominative		Oblique			
	SG.M	SG.F	PL	SG.M	SG.F	PL
Demonstratives:						
proximate plain	**adaj-ava* > *adava*	**adaj-aja* > *adaja*	**adaj-ala* > *adala*	**adaj-ales* > *adales*	**adaj-ala* > *adala*	**adaj-alen* >*adalen*
proximate specific	**akaj-ava* > *akava*	**akaj-aja* > *akaja*	**akaj-ala* > *akala*	**akaj-ales* > *akales*	**akaj-ala* > *akala*	**akaj-alen* >*akalen*
remote plain	**odoj-ova* > *odova*	**odoj-oja* > *odoja*	**odoj-ola* > *odola*	**odoj-oles* > *odoles*	**odoj-ola* > *odola*	**odoj-olen* >*odolen*
remote specific	**okoj-ova* > *okova*	**okoj-oja* > *okoja*	**okoj-ola* > *okola*	**okoj-oles* > *okoles*	**okoj-ola* > *okola*	**okoj-olen* >*okolen*
Third-person pronoun:						
new set (emphatic)	*ov (av)*	*oj (aj)*	*ol (*al)*			
old set	*lo*	*li*	*le*	*oles*	*ola*	*olen*
Definite article:			non-existent			

the contracted demonstrative, usually on the remote demonstrative **ova > ov, *oja > oj, *ola > ol*, and in some cases on the proximate forms **ava > av, *aja > aj*. Once more, then, we have a shift in the nominative forms from the demonstrative set to the set of personal pronouns, carrying with it a structural reduction. In the oblique pronouns there is no renewal, and so a synchronic suppletion in the singular forms of the emphatic set: M.SG *ov/oles*, F.SG *oj/ola*.

To compensate for the erosion in the deictic function of demonstratives, the demonstrative set is again renewed, again through morphological extension, with increased complexity representing reinforcement of the deictic function. This time, reinforcement comes through prefixation of the place deictics 'here' and 'there' – *adaj, akaj, odoj, okoj*. The unique feature of the set of place deictics is their marking for specificity (*adaj* 'here', *akaj* 'precisely here'; *odoj* 'there', *okoj* 'precisely there'), which, figuring as deictic prefixes, they transfer to the demonstrative set, resulting in the four-term system carried over into Early Romani and later into the dialects. The compound forms with prefixed deictic expressions – **adaj-ava* 'this one here', **odoj-ova* 'that one there', etc. – are then simplified, giving rise to the integrated demonstrative forms attested today: *adava, odova* etc. The new formation covers both nominative and oblique forms of the demonstrative.

Early Romani thus inherited a complex four-term system of demonstratives (table 5.11). The set was passed on to the dialects, and survives in full in dialects

Table 5.11 *Deictic and anaphoric expressions: Early Romani*

	Nominative			Oblique		
	SG.M	SG.F	PL	SG.M	SG.F	PL
Demonstratives:						
proximate plain	*adava*	*adaja*	*adala*	*adales*	*adala*	*adalen*
proximate specific	*akava*	*akaja*	*akala*	*akales*	*akala*	*akalen*
remote plain	*odova*	*odoja*	*odola*	*odoles*	*odola*	*odolen*
remote specific	*okova*	*okoja*	*okola*	*okoles*	*okola*	*okolen*
Third-person pronoun:						
new set	*ov (av)*	*oj (aj)*	*ol,on (*al)*			
old set	*lo*	*li*	*le*	*(o)les*	*(o)la*	*(o)len*
Definite article:	**ov > o*	**oj > i*	*ol*	*(o)le*	*(o)la*	*(o)le*

as geographically remote from one another as the Welsh dialect and Kosovo Arli. It subsequently underwent regional simplifications, most notably the reduction of the initial syllable (*akava > kava* etc.), or the selection of just one consonantal set (in *-d-* or *-k-*), as well as regional innovations, such as further reduplication (Northern Vlax and Bugurdži–Drindari *k_k-*, Erli *adav-ka*) or the adoption of adjectival inflection (Northern Vlax *kad-o, kad-i*) (see discussion above). In the system of third-person pronouns, Early Romani inherits the two sets, but the older set *lo, li, le* begins its retreat, later becoming an enclitic pronoun and a marker of high topical continuity, and is ultimately confined in most dialects to existential and non-verbal predications. The new set in *ov, oj, ol* retains its emphatic function in Early Romani, which is still attested in those dialects where *lo, li, le* remain widespread, but later becomes the general pronominal form in most dialects. The plural pronoun will have had a variant *on* in Early Romani, which in present-day Romani is the predominant form outside the Balkans.[9] The Early Romani forms *ov, oj, ol/on* are continued in the Balkan and the Southern Central dialects. Elsewhere, the entire set undergoes phonological innovation, namely the addition of prothetic *j-* in the west (Northern and Northern Central dialects) and of prothetic *v-* in the Vlax dialects.

[9] Boretzky (1999b: 57–8) reviews the possibilities of analogical formations within the pronominal paradigms which might explain the two variants, but leaves the question of which form is the older unanswered. Two possible analogical formations that might explain the acquisition of final *-n* and which are not considered by Boretzky are the analogy among plural personal pronouns – 3PL *ol > on* adapting to 1PL *amen* and 2PL *tumen* – and the interparadigmatic analogy of *ol* to the 3PL present-tense concord marker *-en*. Elšík (2000b) views *ol/ole/ola* as recent forms that are based on demonstratives.

The oblique forms of the third-person pronouns remain conservative, and are in effect carried over from the Proto-Romani period, with isolated attestations of the older long forms with an initial vowel (*oles*) even in some present-day dialects (see above). In all likelihood, there is no functional differentiation within the oblique set that would parallel the distinction between emphatic *ov* and non-emphatic/enclitic *lo*. The position of pronominal objects in the sentence provides a clue that in Early Romani they continued to have a residual deictic function: despite the overall convergence with Greek word-order rules, Romani pronominal objects follow the verb, while Greek pronominal objects precede the verbs (see also chapter 7). But Greek oblique demonstratives also follow the verb, hence it is possible that Romani speakers associated Romani object pronouns with Greek demonstratives, rather than with Greek anaphoric pronouns.

The most outstanding development of the Early Romani period is the emergence of the definite article. A connection between the definite article and demonstratives had been suggested already by Sampson (1926: 152), who, however, relied on Macalister's (1914: 8) incorrect impression that the Domari demonstrative set *aha, ihi, ehe* was used in contracted form as a 'superdefinite article' (see discussion in Matras 1999c). Sampson however also cites the preservation of *-l-* in the oblique as evidence of native pronominal origin. The affinity between the article and demonstratives in Romani has more recently been discussed by Boretzky (2000a: 54–9). Boretzky points out the similarities between the more conservative oblique and plural forms of the definite article in *(o)l-*, and corresponding short forms of the demonstratives (in *ol-*), but concedes that such short demonstratives are only rarely attested. While strongly hinting in the direction of a derivation from pre-forms of the short pronouns, namely **ova, *oja, *ola*, Boretzky does not exclude a combination of origins either. In conclusion he proposes two alternative scenarios: one according to which the oblique forms of the article in *(o)l-* are the oldest forms, and another by which the nominative, short forms (*o*, *e*) are older, possibly deriving from cognates of the Domari demonstratives *uhu*, *ihi*, *ehe*, and where the oblique forms were introduced later, based on demonstratives, in order to reinforce the system. The latter scenario however contradicts the tendencies of the system to undergo simplification in the nominative rather than the oblique set, and consequently to undergo renewal in the nominative, rather than in the oblique.

The etymological dilemma can be resolved through the reconstruction model of the cyclic renewal of the entire deictic/anaphoric system. The natural candidate for the forerunner of the definite article is the reduced plain remote demonstrative *ov, oj, ol*. Before the demonstratives are renewed through prefixation of place deictics (Proto-Romani Stage 3), the plain remote demonstrative *ov* etc. shifts into the person-pronominal paradigm, where it serves as an emphatic third-person pronoun. Functionally, we might interpret this form as a marker of contextual accessibility, which, on the scale of topic continuity, figures in between the older pronoun *lo* etc. and the renewed demonstrative in *odova* etc. This position in the system allows it to copy the functional scope of the Greek definite article, once Early Romani becomes exposed to Greek impact. Subsequently, as the article function stabilises, there is a tendency to reduce its nominative forms (in line with the overall cyclical development). The M.SG form is reduced from **ov* > *o*. A structural similarity thus emerges between the article and the nominal/adjectival M.SG inflection marker *-o*, as well as between the Romani article and the Greek M.SG article *o*. Syncretism at both levels may have triggered an analogy to the F.SG, leading to the replacement (rather than plain reduction) of **oj* by *i*, agreeing with the F.SG inflection marker *-i*, and the Greek F.SG article *i*, possibly with a variant *e*. Postulating the renewal of the nominative singular forms as an Early Romani development thus allows us to account for the only form of the article that is shared by all dialects, namely M.SG nominative *o*, and possibly also for F.SG nominative *i/e*.

Nominative plural as well as oblique forms will have remained conservative for a longer period, and forms in *(o)l-* are still attested today (see above). As for the nominative singular forms, there may be indirect attestation of the earlier forms in the gender-specific prefixing of some nouns, which Turner (1932) has argued was morphologically motivated: thus we find in all dialects, and so in Early Romani, *v-* in masculine *vast* 'hand' from **ast* < *hast-* (Domari *xast*), but *j-* in feminine *jag* 'fire' from **ag* < *agni* (Domari *ag*) and *jakh* 'eye' from **akh* < *akkhi* (Domari *iki*). The likely Early Romani forms were therefore *ov-ast* 'the hand > hand', *oj-ag* 'the fire > fire', and *oj-akh* 'the eye > eye'.

Later renewals in the article system are largely regional developments (see above), and can be explained on the basis of analogies within the paradigm, such as the spread of *e* and sometimes *o* at the expense of other forms, and reduction of the more complex forms (*la* > *a*, *ole* > *le, e, ol*, etc.).

5.5.6 *Other pronouns*

Romani **interrogatives** have two sources. Corresponding to other NIA languages we find the set of interrogatives in *k-*: *kon* 'who', *kaj* 'where', *kana* 'when'. The personal interrogative *kon* 'who' preserves a conservative oblique inflection *kas* in most Balkan, Vlax, and Central dialects, while Northern dialects tend to have a secondary, regular oblique form *kon-es*. The other source for interrogatives is the set in *s-*. Romani is an exception among the NIA languages in not having a *k*-form for 'what'.[10] The form for 'what' is *so* (*ho*, *o*), which has traditionally been interpreted as deriving from the MIA *kassa/kasō* < OIA oblique *kasya* (cf. Boretzky and Igla 1994b: 326). Derived from this form in *s*- are *sar* (also *sir/syr*, *har*, *ar*) 'how', which combines *so* with an old ablative, and the adjectival form *sav*- (*hav*-, *av*-) 'which', apparently a combination of *so* with a Proto-Romani deictic expression, adapting to adjectival inflection. The latter competes in some dialects with other determiners, notably with the Romanian loan *če* (Northern Vlax) and with *kaj* (Southern Balkan), as well as with the secondary derivation *sosk*- 'what kind of' (Lovari; from *so* 'what' + genitive ending). Interrogatives expressing goal ('what for') and reason ('why'/ 'for which reason') are usually recent derivations of *so*-: dative *soske/sose*, ablative *sostar/sostir*, prepositional locative *anda soste*, prepositional dative *vaš soske*, or locative *soste/sohte*. Greater diversity is found among the forms of the quantitative interrogative 'how much'. The older inherited form appears to have been *keti/ket'i/keci*, with early palatalisation, which survives in all dialect branches. Regional innovations are Northern Vlax *sode*, (primarily Southern) Vlax and Balkan *kazom/kozom*, as well as the indefinite *kabor/kobor /ambor* used as an interrogative.

Romani dialects generally make use of the interrogatives *kaj*, *so* (*ho*), *sav*- (*hav*-) and *kon* as **relativisers**. The most widely used is *kaj*, while *so* is normally restricted to inanimate objects, *sav*- to animate agentives, and *kon* usually appears in a non-nominative form, referring to head nouns that assume non-subject roles in the relative clause (*kas* 'whom', *kaske* 'to whom', *kasko* 'whose', *kasa* 'with whom', etc.). In drawing on interrogatives for relativisers, rather than on the older relativisers in *y*-/*j*-, Romani is an exception among the NIA languages, along with Sinhalese, and, more significantly, most Dardic languages and Domari, and we might therefore assume an areal development during the northwest-Indian stage of Proto-Romani. Alternatively, the employment of interrogatives as relativisers could have been part of the Balkanisation process in Early Romani.

The system of **indefinites** is highly complex and prone to dialect-specific and regional innovations as well as to extensive borrowing. Elšík (2000c) reconstructs the original, Early Romani system as relying heavily on the inherited indefinite marker *kaj-/khaj*-, which one can comfortably interpret as a cognate of the NIA indefinite markers in *k*-, with the addition of the impersonal indefinite expressions *či*, in all likelihood of Iranian origin, an indefinite suffix -*ni* of obscure origin, and finally a 'free-choice' modifier -*moni*, in all likelihood a restrictive focus particle of Greek origin (*monos* 'alone'). Against alternative

[10] Only Romani appears to have forms in *s*-. Masica (1991: 253) cites as other exceptions Gujarati *šu*, Sindhi *chā*, and Shina *jēk*. Domari, like the majority of NIA, has *kē/kī*.

etymologies for *moni* (OIA *manaḥ* 'mind', Persian *mānā* 'like', Armenian *imən* 'something'), Elšík argues that the restrictive function of the original form is reconcilable with the universal path of possible grammaticalisation of 'universal concessive conditional' markers to free-choice indefinite markers, as discussed by Haspelmath (1997).

Traces of the indefinite in *kaj-/khaj-* are found throughout the dialects. The plain form in determiner function, *kaj/haj* 'some, any', is only attested in Bugurdži and Agia Varvara Vlax. Quite common in determiner function is the compound form *kajek/kijek/kajke/kajk/kek/ček/tek* from **kajek* < **kaj-jekh* 'any-one-(thing)'. In the Northwestern dialect branch, *kek* undergoes a development which Elšík (2000c) refers to as the 'negative cline': from a non-indicative indefinite in imperative constructions (Piedmontese Sinti *pen kek lava!* 'tell some words!'; Formoso and Calvet 1987: 50), through interrogative indefinite function (Piedmontese Sinti *na in kek akaj?* 'isn't there anybody here?' ibid.), on to indirect negation (Welsh Romani *mankē kek mūrš sas arō them* 'before ever a man was on earth'; Sampson 1926: 140) and finally direct negation, either in combination with the negative particle *na*, or relying strictly on the indefinite-turned-negator: Welsh Romani *naj man kek* 'I don't have' (Tipler 1957: 13), Sinti *kamau tek* 'I don't want' (Holzinger 1993: 64). The compound **kajek* also figures in the temporal indefinite *ka-jekhvar* 'sometime, anytime' (cf. *jekh-var* 'one time'), in the Northwestern dialects similarly with a negative cline: Sinti *kekvar*, Finnish Kaale *čekkar* 'ever, never', Welsh Romani *kekār* 'never'. In local indefinites, *kaj* figures alongside *-ni* in Sinti *kajni*, Finnish Romani *čēni*, Southern Vlax *kajnikaj* 'nowhere'. Other location indefinites with *kaj* are Vlax *khatinde* and *khati* 'somewhere', 'anywhere'.

The origin of the impersonal marker *či* in an Iranian indefinite is supported both by the presence of a cognate indefinite/interrogative expression in Iranian (and contiguous languages, notably Neo-Aramaic), and by the tendency of present-day Romani to borrow indefinites. As an independent indefinite ('something, anything'), *či/čhi* survives mainly outside the Balkans (Northwestern and Northeastern groups, Welsh Romani, Abruzzian, Bohemian), most commonly in a negative indefinite function: Polska Roma *nani men čhi* 'we have nothing'. In Scandinavian Para-Romani varieties, *či* functions as the principal negator, by appearing first as a postposed negative indefinite, then copying the function of the postposed principal negator of the Scandinavian grammaticiser languages. A somewhat similar development occurs in Northern Vlax, where *či* first acquires independent focal properties ('neither, nor, not even'), is then used for the negative coordination of constituents and phrases, and ultimately, in all likelihood under the influence of Romanian *nici . . . nici*, becomes an independent preposed principal negator (*či kamav* 'I don't want') (cf. Elšík 2000c). Elsewhere, *či* is usually attached to other indefinite markers, either inherited or borrowed. Among the inherited forms we find Bugurdži–Drindari *kači* < **kaj-či* 'something, anything, nothing' and Vlax *khanči* < **khaj-ni-či* 'nothing'.

Elšík (2000c) finds traces of a further Early Romani indefinite particle **ni* in Vlax *khanči* < **khaj-ni-či* 'nothing', in Vlax *khonik* 'somebody' oblique *khanikas-* < **khaj-ni-kon* oblique **khaj-ni-kas-*, in Sinti *kajni*, Finnish Romani *čēni*, Southern Vlax *kajnikaj* 'nowhere', in the emphatic forms of the personal pronouns *me-ni* 'me', *ti-ni* 'you' in the Croatian and some Southern Balkan dialects, and in the focus particle *ni-na* 'not even > even, too' (Sinti, Latvian Romani). Possibly, *-ni* was also assimilated into the marker *-moni*. As for *-moni* itself, Elšík interprets it as a likely Greek borowing into Early Romani, where its function as a restrictive focus particle is drawn on in free-choice indefinite constructions of the type **kon-moni* 'whoever', **kaj-moni* 'wherever', and so on. Such constructions involving a bound focus/indefinite marker and an interrogative or another indefinite as a semantic specifier will have set the pattern for further renewal of the system of indefinites through borrowing of bound indefinite markers in the southeastern European dialects of Romani. Compounds in *-moni* survive mainly in the fringe areas, in particular in western Europe: Sinti, Catalonian Romani, and British Romani *čimone/čimoni/čomoni* < **či-moni* 'something, anything', Welsh Romani, Finnish Romani, and Piedmontese Sinti *komoni(s)* < **kon-moni* 'somebody, anybody'. A recently attested form from the Arli variety of Florina – *čumuni* 'something' – testifies however that the form is old.

Especially the eastern and southeastern dialects of Romani are affected by recent renewal of the system of indefinites through borrowings. The most widespread, and possibly the earliest borrowing of an indefinite marker is *vare-* from Romanian *oare-*, whose diffusion ranges far beyond the Vlax dialects to include the Northern Central and Northeastern dialects as well as British and Iberian Romani. We are thus dealing either with a Romanian borrowing into Early Romani, or with a very early, and if so unique, interdialectal diffusion of a borrowing.[11] Like subsequent borrowed indefinite markers, *vare-* attaches to interrogatives as semantic specifiers: *vareso* 'something', *varekon* 'somebody', *varesavo* 'some (kind of)', *varekaj* 'somewhere', *varesar* 'somehow', *varekana* 'sometime'. Other borrowed indefinite markers and borrowed indefinite expressions derive mainly from Slavic languages, Hungarian, and Albanian (see section 8.2.2).

The overall picture then is that of a system of indefinites that is prone to renewal, especially in the eastern and southeastern European dialects of Romani, while the western and northern areas retain more conservative forms. Western

[11] Victor Friedman (in p.c.) suggests as another possibility that this is a unique Aromanianism/ Balkan Romance borrowing from the Byzantine period; this would explain the dialectal diffusion and still keep the chronology of contact consistent.

and northern archaisms are the free indefinite *či* and the Greek-derived bound marker *-moni*, as well as combinations in *kaj-* such as *kajni* and *kajek/kek*. The Northern Vlax dialects form another conservative centre, retaining *kaj-* combinations and a free negator *či*. The Central and Balkan dialects on the other hand have retained little of the Early Romani system as reconstructed by Elšík (2000c), relying instead on borrowings.

6 Verb morphology

6.1 The basic blueprint for the Romani verb

The Romani verb, perhaps more than any other grammatical category, reflects the historical changes that have shaped the language: person inflection on the verb is a unique combination of OIA archaism in the present tense conjugation, and a synthetic morphology based on past participles in the past tense, giving what Bubeník and Hübschmannová (1998: 42) describe as a 'Prakrit-like typology' of Romani. Derivation patterns are highly synthetic and partly agglutinative and reminiscent of present-day subcontinental Indo-Aryan. Derivation and the structure of tense–aspect–modality are also sensitive to recent contact developments, however; some dialects show a wholesale adoption of productive aktionsart morphology from the contact languages, most notably from Slavic. A remarkable characteristic feature of the Romani verb, like the Romani noun, is the systematic and productive replication of Greek inflectional morphology, which serves to adapt and so also to mark out European loans.

The core of the verb is the lexical root (see table 6.1). Verb morphology is suffixed, with the exception in some dialects of calqued and borrowed aktionsart prefixes (AKT/SLASP). Borrowed lexical roots are followed by loan-adaptation affixes (LOAN). Derivational extensions – INTRANS, TRANS, CAUS, ITER – mark valency alteration, as well as, in some cases, aspectual distinctions such as iterativity or intensity. They typically attach to the lexical root or to the adapted loan root; derivations that draw on historical participles follow a perfective stem extension that is no longer productive for aspect. The sum of all positions in the verb layout up to and including derivation markers can be regarded as the derivational part of the verb, or the verb stem. The perfective aspect is marked by an extension to the verb stem (PFV). The stem is followed by different sets of subject concord markers for present and past tenses (person concord). External to the person inflection we find the expression of remote tense (marking out the pluperfect and imperfect), and modality (subjunctive versus indicative, or alternatively declarative/intentional or future): FUT, REM, DECL, Ø=subjunctive. The verb layout thus ranges from the simplest form, found in the

Table 6.1 *The basic layout of the Romani verb (with gloss abbreviations)*

(aktionsart/Slavic aspect)(AKT/SLASP)
+ lexical root
+ (loan adaptation)(LOAN)
+ (perfective stem: derivational extension)(PFV)
+ (transitive/intransitive derivation)(INTRANS, TRANS, CAUS, ITER)
+ (perfective stem: aspectual)(PERF)
+ person concord
+ (tense/modality)(FUT, REM, DECL, Ø=subjunctive)

imperative and present subjunctive of plain inherited verbs, to the most complex derivations:

(1) dža! (common)
go
go!

(2) si te dža-v (common)
is COMP go-1SG-Ø
'I must go'

(3) phur-ju-diil-o (Finnish Romani)
old-INTRANS-PFV-M
'he has grown old'

(4) ker-d-jov-el-a (Vlax)
do-PFV-INTRANS-3SG-FUT
'It will become/be done'

(5) pod-šun-en-ys (Polska Roma)
SLASP-hear-3PL-REM
'they were listening'

(6) bekleti-s-ker-d-an (Sepečides)
wait-LOAN-CAUS-PFV-2SG
'you have made (somebody) wait'

(7) bikin-ker-av-en (East Slovak Romani)
sell-ITER-CAUS-3PL
'they often have (something) sold (by somebody)'

External to the actual verb morphology is a series of particles and auxiliaries that may precede or follow the verb, expressing future tense (*ka*, *ma*, *l-*, *jav-*), stative present (*s-*), remote or perfect tense (*sin-*, *ther-*), and conditional and quotative modality (*te*, *bi*, *li*).

6.2 Verb derivation

6.2.1 *Word formation and compounding*

Word formation in the Romani verb relies primarily on grammatical derivation, which is exploited for purposes of lexical creation. For example, the verb root *ker-* 'to do' has an intransitive (mediopassive) derivation, *ker-d-(j)o(v)-*, which can have either a lexical meaning 'to become', or a grammatical passive meaning 'to be done'. Intransitive and transitive derivations from the obsolete root **sikh-* render *sikh-l-(j)o(v)-* 'to learn', and *sikh-l-(j)ar-* 'to teach'. There are some traces of archaic compounds inherited from OIA, such as *bikin-* 'to sell' (OIA *vi-krī-*; cf. *kin-* 'to buy'), *rakir-/vaker-* 'to speak' (from **vraker-*, OIA *pra-kr̥-*, cf. *ker-* 'to do'), or *prindžan-* 'to recognise' (cf. *džan-* 'to know').

Resources for word derivation that have been productive in the language continuously since the Proto-Romani stage are limited to two verb roots: *d-* 'to give' and *ker-/kir-* 'to do'. Through compounding, both derive transitive verbs from non-verbs. In older formations they are suffixed: *trad-* 'to drive/ to send' (subsequently evolving in some dialects into an intransitive verb 'to drive'), *rod-* 'to search', *kid-* 'to gather', *phurd-* 'to blow', *adžuker-/udžaker-* 'to wait', *čaker-* 'to tread', *pariker-* 'to thank'. The pattern also encompasses a number of pre-European loans such as *hazd-/lazd-/vazd-* 'to raise', *cird-* 'to pull'. The incompatibility of formations in *-d-* with transitive derivational morphology suggests that *-d-* was originally a transitiviser. Compounds that are analysable, i.e. those that include a component that is lexically productive, may be taken to represent a later developmental stage: *čumid-* 'to kiss' (*čumi* 'kiss') or *kand-* 'to listen' (*kan* 'ear'). Quite often, they have analytic variants (*d- čumi*). Other formations in *d-*, including those based on European nominal loans, are overwhelmingly analytic: *d- armana* 'to curse', *d- mindže* 'to have intercourse', *d- duma/d- vorba* 'to speak'.

The development of *ker-* is similar in some dialects, and we find analytic compounds such as *ker- buti* 'to work' (cf. *buti* 'work'), alongside, in the Northeastern dialects, *butiker-*. In some dialects, *ker-* undergoes grammaticalisation as a marker of transitive derivation (causative, iterative), a development which probably began in Early Romani (see below). Productive compounding on a similar basis with other verbs, of the type *molpij-* 'to drink wine' (North Russian Romani; Wentzel 1980: 130), is rare.

6.2.2 *Transitivity and intransitivity*

An outstanding New Indo-Aryan feature of Romani, uncommon in the languages of Europe, is the presence of productive synthetic morphology that allows the altering of the valency of verb roots. Traditionally, valency alteration had been treated in descriptions of Romani either under the heading of word formation, or as part of the classification of verb inflection or conjugation groups. A number of modern studies have adopted the view that valency alteration, or transitive and intransitive derivation, constitutes the primary dichotomy in the verbal system. Attention has been devoted to the productiveness of valency alteration especially in studies by Cech (1995/1996) on the Sepečides dialect, by Igla (1996) on the Agia Varvara Vlax variety, by Hübschmannová and Bubeník (1997; also Bubeník and Hübschmannová 1998) on Eastern Slovak and Hungarian Romani (Romungro), and by Mori (1999) on Xoraxane Vlax. Not coincidentally, most of these studies survey dialects that are heavily influenced by neighbouring agglutinating languages: Turkish in the cases of Sepeči and Agia Varvara, and Hungarian in the case of Eastern Slovak Romani and Romungro.

Contact has clearly reinforced the productivity of valency alteration, turning it into a device that is fully productive rather than lexically contained, and exploiting the inherited morphological resources for new functions such as the second (or 'double') causative, as well as for aspectual functions (iterative, intensifier, non-durative). Nonetheless, valency alteration must be seen as an inherited productive device in Romani which continues a late MIA legacy. This device is best characterised as a series of morphological resources the function of which is to alter the valency of the core lexical root of the verb by deriving from the core a secondary verbal stem. I will therefore continue to refer to the phenomenon as a whole as **valency alteration,** and to the participating morphological operations and the types of stem formations which they produce as **transitive and intransitive derivations.**

There is no standardised terminology in Romani linguistics for the phenomenon of valency alteration. Bubeník and Hübschmannová (1998: 43) generally refer to the intransitive derivations as mediopassives, and to transitive derivations as causatives (see also Mori 1999). But the specific semantic and syntactic functions that are the outcome of the derivational process are not uniform, and are only partly predictable (see Cech 1995/1996). We normally find varying semantic relations between the pairs of derivations or base and derivation, such as active:reflexive, active:reciprocal, active:unaccusative, active:passive (cf. Igla 1996: 138–41).

Intransitive derivations from adjectives, adverbs and nouns generally render inchoatives, denoting transitions between states: *bar-(j)o(v)-* 'to grow' < *baro* 'big', *mat-(j)o(v)-* 'to become drunk' < *mato* 'drunk', *paš-(j)o(v)-* 'to approach' < *pašal* 'close', *rat-(j)o(v)-* 'to become night' < *rat* 'night'. Intransitive derivations from verbal roots can render either synthetic passives such as *kin-d-(j)o(v)-* 'to be sold' < *kin-* 'to sell', or lexicalised intransitives such as *dikh-(j)o(v)-* 'to appear' < *dikh-* 'to see', in the Northeastern dialects also *res-(j)o(v)-* 'to arrive'

< *res-* 'to achieve'. Some derivations from intransitive roots may be considered reflexives or reciprocals: *sikh-l-(j)o(v)-* 'to learn', *gara-d-(j)o(v)-* 'to hide', *mar-d-(j)o(v)-* 'to be hit/to hit one another'. They are often derivations of stems that are themselves formed through transitive derivation: *gara-d-(j)o(v)-* 'to hide (intr.)', < *garav-* 'to hide (tr.)' < _*gar-_. The latter class may be extended in dialects that rely more heavily on grammatical valency alteration. In Eastern Slovak Romani, intransitive derivation assumes an aspectual non-durative or 'semelfactive' function (Bubeník and Hübschmannová 1998), modelled on Slavic aktionsart distinctions: *dema-d'-o(v)-* 'to hit oneself (accidentally)' < *dem-av-* 'to pound/hit repeatedly' < *dem-* 'to hit'; *asa-nd'-o(v)-* 'to smile' < *asa-* 'to laugh'. In the dialect of the Sepečides, intransitive derivations may be used to describe indirect affiliation to the primary meaning of the verb root: *xa-l-jo(v)-* 'to be edible' < *xa-* 'to eat'.

Transitive derivations have similarly a range of semantic and syntactic functions. Transitive verbs deriving from nouns and adjectives are referred to by Hübschmannová and Bubeník (1997) as 'factitives': *bar-ar-* 'to raise, to grow' < *baro* 'big'; *dand-er-* 'to bite' < *dand* 'tooth'; *gilj-av-* 'to sing' < *gili* 'song'. Those deriving from productive verbal roots are generally labelled 'causatives'. Some however, whose base is in an unaccusative intransitive verb, have a primary transitive meaning with weak semantic causation: *dar-av-* 'to frighten' < *dara-* 'to fear'. These often include transitive derivations from verb stems that are themselves intransitive derivations: *sikh-l-(j)ar-* 'to teach' < *sikh-l-(j)o(v)-* 'to learn' < _*sikh-_. Plain or first causatives can be derived from intransitive roots, where the causee is the subject-agent of an intransitive verb (*ačh-av-* 'to make somebody stay' < *ačh-* 'to stay'), or from transitive roots or from transitive derivations, the causee being the subject of a transitive verb (Romungro *an-av-* 'to make somebody bring' < *an-* 'to bring'). 'Second causatives' (also called 'double causatives' or 'causatives of higher valency'; cf. Shibatani 1976, Comrie 1981) are common mainly in dialects with grammaticalised valency alteration (see below). They derive causatives from causatives: Romungro *dar-av-av-* 'to make somebody frighten' < *dar-av-* 'to frighten' < *dara-* 'to fear'.

Despite the productive potential of valency alteration, symmetry is often disturbed by the loss of some base-forms (see also discussion in Igla 1996: 138–41). For instance, from the obsolete _*sikh-_, we find a transitive derivation *sikh-av-* 'to show', which mirrors the intransitive derivation *sikh-l-(j)o(v)-* 'to learn' in structure, but not in meaning. A secondary transitive derivation is formed based on the intransitive one: *sikh-l-(j)ar-* 'to teach'. In the Agia Varvara dialect, where second causatives are productive, a further transitive derivation is encountered: *sikh-l-ar-d-ar* 'to make (somebody) teach'. On the other hand, symmetry may be restored for obsolete roots: transitive *gar-av-* 'to hide (something)' from _*gar-_, forms the base for intransitive *gar-a-d-(j)o(v)-* 'to hide (oneself)'.

The primary position of the valency dichotomy in the verbal system is also illustrated by the assignment of verbs to past-tense inflection classes on the basis of their argument structure, which is visible in the form of the third-person singular. This Early Romani state of affairs is still observable in the southern European dialects. Derived intransitives (mediopassives and inchoatives) form their past tense by attaching an adjectival derivation marker M *-ilo* F *-ili* (OIA *-illa* etc.) to the perfective stem (or to the non-verbal root, in the case of inchoatives): *ker-d-il-o* 'was done', *gara-d-il-o* 'hid', *bar-il-o* 'grew'. Two intransitive verbs of motion are added to this class: *av-il-o* 'came', *ačh-il-o* 'stayed'. The verb *ov-* 'to become' has a contracted past, *u-l-o*. A further extension of the class encompasses psych verbs, usually with stems terminating in *-a*: *dara-jl-o* 'feared', *asa-jl-o* 'laughed' (also *asa-nd-il-o* with a perfective extension). Mori (1999) comments on the parallel formation in Xoraxane Vlax (as in other dialects of southeastern Europe) of unaccusative verbs (or 'ergative' as she calls them), though here we do not find the adjectival extension *-il-*, but merely the survival of the active participle (OIA *-(i)t-*; see discussion below): *ge-l-o* 'went', *mu-l-o* 'died'. The retention of adjectival inflection in the third-person singular past tense in all these types of intransitives can be regarded synchronically as an inflectional representation of argument structure. By contrast, analytic reflexives, which have transitive argument structure, also behave like transitives in their inflection: *dikhljas pe* 'saw himself/herself'. The distinction is levelled in western, central, and northern Europe, where consistent person inflection in *-a(s)* replaces the older pattern of adjectival inflection in *-o/-i* (see below).

6.2.3 *The historical development of valency-alteration markers*

The oldest valency-changing morpheme in the language is the **transitive** marker *-av-* (also *-ev-*). It goes back to OIA *-yá-* and *-áya-*, which, with an epenthetic consonant, gives *-āpaya*, resulting in MIA *-āvē* (cf. Masica 1991: 315–20, Hübschmannová and Bubeník 1997: 135). The Romani marker has cognates in *-āv-/-āu-/-āb-/-ā-* in subcontinenal NIA. The Domari cognate is the extented form *-n-aw-*, which agrees with Kashmiri *-(an)āw-*. A series of verbs in *-av-* are shared by all dialects of Romani, and so in all likelihood they are inherited from the Proto-Romani stage, during which the marker had been fully productive. They include mainly transitive derivations from intransitive roots, such as *naš-av-* 'to expel' < *naš-* 'to escape', *dar-av-* 'to frighten' < *dara-* 'to fear'. Less common are derivations from transitive roots – *ker-av-/kir-av-* 'to cook' < *ker-* 'to do' – and from nominals – *gil(j)-av-* 'to sing' < *gili* 'song'. A significant portion of the older formations in *-av-* derive from roots that have become obsolete in the language: *sikh-av-* 'to show' from **sikh-*, *gar-av-* 'to hide (something)' from **gar-*, *phirav-* 'to open' from **phir-*, *bičh-av-* 'to send' from

**bičh-*. Others indicate early transitive verbal formations from non-verbal roots that have likewise been lost: *xox-av-* 'to tell a lie', *mal-av-* 'to find', *zum-av-* 'to try'. Both features further testify to the archaic character of the marker.

Nevertheless, *-av-* appears to have preserved some productive potential in the Early Romani stage. Its fate thereafter varies somewhat among the individual dialects. On the whole, its productivity declines, and we find *-av-* confined to older, primarily lexicalised formations in Vlax, in the Balkan groups, in the Northeastern group, and in Welsh Romani. On the other hand, its use expands in the Northwestern (Sinti-Finnish) group, where it is used for purposes of word formation (German Sinti *but-ev-* 'to work', from *buti* 'work'), for loan-verb adaptation (German Sinti *denk-ev-* 'to think' < German *denk-*; Finnish Romani *heng-av-* 'to hang' < German/Swedish *häng-*), and as a frequent replacement for the historical factitive marker *-ar-* (German Sinti *phag-ev-* 'to break (something)', elsewhere *phag-ar-*). In the Northern Central dialects, *-av-* is employed as a grammaticalised iterative marker, modelled on Slavic aspect distinctions (Bohemian Romani *čhiv-āv-* 'to throw (frequently)' < *čhiv-* 'to throw'). In the zone of Hungarian influence comprising the Southern Central dialects (with the exception of Roman), *-av-* is fully grammaticalised as a causative marker, deriving causatives from both intransitive and transitive roots (Southern Central *ker-av-* 'to make (somebody) do' < *ker-* 'to do'). The continued productivity of *-av-*, albeit in different functions, thus forms a geographical pattern encompassing the dialects of central Europe.

It is likely that the gradual decline of *-av-* had begun already in the later Proto-Romani stage, when that suffix entered into competition with the transitive marker *-ar-* (also *-er-/-yr-*, occasionally *-al-* following sibilants). The OIA etymology of *-ar-* remains obscure, but it is common in northwestern NIA (Kashmiri, Shina, Sindhi; cf. Masica 1991: 318), and as a transitiviser and intensifier in Domari. From this it seems that the marker was adopted into Proto-Romani during its later, northwestern Indian period. Derivations in *-ar-* are found with a number of obsolete roots: *akh-ar-* 'to call', *bist-ar-* 'to forget', *put-ar-* 'to open'. An early denominal formation is *dand-ar-/dand-er* 'to bite' < *dand* 'tooth'. The marker's principal impact on the typology of the language is to allow transitive verbs to derive from adjectives ('factitives'): *bar-(j)ar-* 'to grow/raise' < *baro* 'big', *kal-(j)ar-* 'to blacken' < *kalo* 'black', *dil-(j)ar-* 'to drive crazy' < *dilo* 'crazy'. The optional presence of jotation could indicate an expansion of the more general phenomenon of jotation in morphological boundaries in Proto-Romani, or perhaps a more specific infiltration of the intransitive (inchoative) derivation in *-(j)o(v)-*, as in *bar-(j)o(v)-* 'to grow', serving as a base for deadjectival factitives.

Shared deverbal derivations in *-ar-* are not very common. Already in Proto-Romani the productive use of *-ar-* in deverbal formations appears to have involved the attachment of the affix to the past participle: *m-u(n)d-ar-* 'to kill' (cf. *mer-* 'to die', past *mul-*). Participial morphology is less apparent in *phab-ar-* 'to burn', similarly an older formation, but this verb may have had a plain, unsuffixed participle; the intransitive formation *phab-(j)o(v)-* similarly lacks overt participial morphology (for a discussion of 'plain' participles in Proto-Romani cf. Bubeník and Hübschmannová 1998: 33).

The tendency to attach to the participle rather than to the verbal root is characteristic of the primarily factitive (deadjectival and denominal) function of *-ar-*. In the Balkan dialects (and to a more limited extent, in the Central dialects), *-ar-* attaches to the participle of some intransitive verbs: Erli *beš-l-ar-* 'to make (somebody) sit' < *beš-* 'to sit', past *beš-l-*. Irregular verbs may be regularised for this purpose: Eastern Slovak Romani *rov-l'-ar-*, Bugurdži *rov-j-ar-* 'to make (somebody) cry' < *rov-* 'to cry', past *r-und-/rov-d-*. In dialects under heavy and recent Turkish influence, *-ar-* can attach to the participle of transitive verbs to form causatives: Agia Varvara Vlax *an-d-ar-* 'to cause to bring' < *an-* 'to bring', past *an-d-*; Sepečides *ker-d-ar-* 'to cause to do' < *ker-* 'to do', Azerbaijanian Zargari *čor-d-ar-* 'to cause to pour' < *čor-* 'to pour'. (This development may have been reinforced by the Turkish causative marker *-dIr-/-tIr-*.) In Vlax and in Welsh Romani, *-ar-* is a loan-verb adaptation marker which attaches to the borrowed Greek aorist marker *-(i)s-*: Vlax *ažut-is-ar-* 'to help' (Romanian *ajut-*), Welsh Romani *ke-s-er-* 'to care'. A generalisation of *-er-* at the expense of *-ev-* is found in some eastern dialects of German Sinti, where it forms transitive verbs (*but-er-* 'to work') and serves as a loan-verb adaptation marker (*denk-er-* 'to think').

Denominal formations in *-ar-* are productive in Welsh Romani, where they serve as a principal resource for verbal derivation: *baxt-er-* 'to bless' < *baxt* 'luck'. In the Northeastern group, on the other hand, *-yr-* is restricted to older, irregular denominal formations in **-er-* (*dand-yr-* 'to bite', cf. elsewhere *dand-er-*). Its deadjectival and deverbal (departicipial) derivational functions are taken over by *-(a)kir-*: Xaladikta *mat'-k'ir-* 'to make (somebody) drunk', elsewhere *mat-(j)ar-*; *mul'-ak'ir-* 'to kill', elsewhere *mud-ar-*.

The Early Romani stock included two additional transitivising affixes: *-ker-* and *-a(r)ker-*. The simple form goes back to a grammaticalised variant of the word-formation affix *-ker-*, while the complex form derives apparently from a combination of *-ar-*, which was still productive in Early Romani, and *-ker-*. Both appear to have emerged in Early Romani as a means of reinforcing the productivity of transitive derivations. Markers in *-(a)(r)ker-* (occasionally also *-avker-*) survive in several distinct regions. The first is the Northeastern group, where they succeed *-ar-/-yr-* as productive factitive (denominal and deadjectival) and departicipial markers. The second is a Slavic-Hungarian contact zone in central Europe comprising the Northern Central dialects (Bohemian, Western and Eastern Slovak). Here, and in Romungro, the simple marker *-ker-*, and in the eastern regions also the complex forms *-avker-* and *-kerker-*, survive in an iterative function, modelled on the system of Slavic aspect. They lose their transitivising function, allowing aspectual modification of intransitive roots as well: *gil'av-ker-* 'to sing frequently'. In the southern Balkans, both the simple marker *-ker-* (also *-čer-/-kjar-*) and the long forms in *-arker-/-avker-* survive, deriving causatives from intransitives and, in dialects under more recent heavy Turkish influence (Agia Varvara, Sepečides), also from transitives and first causatives. The fact that the various regions are disconnected is evidence of the presence of the markers in Early Romani.[1] The patterns of productivity and the correlation with various degrees of contact intensity are a noteworthy example of language contact promoting structural archaism – rather than change – through functional adaptation.

We now turn to the historical development of **intransitive** derivations. The original OIA primary intransitives had been lost in Proto-Romani, a development which is quite common in NIA (while in Domari the original primary intransitive is preserved as *-y-*). To compensate for the lost primary intransitive, NIA languages tend to resort to periphrastic constructions involving participles of the verb, in conjunction with auxiliaries derived from the verbs 'to come' and 'to go'. Romani is exceptional, in two respects. First, the auxiliary verb is not one of movement, but the existential 'to become', OIA *bhav-* Proto-Romani **ov-*, which survives as the non-indicative existential *ov-* in present-day Balkan and Southern Central dialects (cf. Boretzky 1997), as well as in Latvian Romani. Second, this auxiliary has undergone full synthetisation with the verb stem, apparently already in the Proto-Romani period. Bubeník and Hübschmannová (1998: 42) have noted that the use of the auxiliary *bhav-* with the participle to form an analytic passive is attested in Apabhraṃśa. Among the NIA languages it is found in Awadhi in an active function, that is, it is amalgamated with the participle to form the active past tense. Deriving passives by cliticising the verb *ov-* 'to become' however has no counterpart in NIA. A passive auxiliary based on 'to become' is found in Persian, though, and a later Proto-Romani development calquing a Persian (or a similar Iranian) construction cannot be ruled out.

As is the case with the other passive auxiliaries in NIA, the Romani intransitive marker attaches to the participle (or perfective stem) of the transitive verb: *ker-* 'to do', participle/perfective stem *ker-d-* 'done', intransitive/passive *ker-d-(j)o(v)-* 'to be done/ to become'. In deadjectival intransitive formations (inchoatives), the marker attaches to the adjectival root: *baro* 'big' > *bar-(j)o(v)-* 'to grow'. With some verbs, intransitive derivations appear to attach directly to the root. A core group of those is shared, and appears to go back to Early Romani. They include *dik-(j)o(v)-* 'to appear' < *dikh-* 'to see', *phag-(j)o(v)-* 'to

[1] Possibly the earliest attestation of causatives in *-ker-* is *mar-ker-* 'to have somebody beaten', is the seventeenth-century text by Evliya Çelebi documenting Rumelian Romani (Friedman and Dankoff 1991). Traces of the transitivising function are also found in Zargari *ač̌h-ker-* 'to stand', from *ač̌h-* 'to stay'.

break (intr.)' < *phag-* 'to break' (tr.), *pek-(j)o(v)-* 'to be fried' < *pek-* 'to fry'. Bubeník and Hübschmannová (1998: 33) mention the possibility that some of these may be derived directly from plain MIA participles (*pakka* going back to OIA *pak-va*).

The intransitive derivational morph is *-(j)o(v)-*, preserving the OIA medial consonant while losing the initial one (often preserved in subcontinental NIA as an aspirated *h-*), and showing initial jotation, possibly a reflection of the loss of initial aspiration. A series of simplifications account for the variation that is found in present-day dialects. The vowel component sometimes alternates between *-o-* and *-u-*. The initial yod is usually reflected in the jotation (sometimes palatalisation or palatal mutation) of the preceding segment. The consonantal ending *-v-* of the original auxiliary root is often lost entirely (some Balkan and Southern Central dialects) or preserved in the first persons only (Vlax *sikhl-ov-av* 'I learn', but *sikhl-o-l* 's/he learns'). These contractions may result in the vowel component *-o-/-u-* being left on its own to mark out the stem as intransitive (*sikhljol* 'learns'). Some grammatical descriptions therefore postulate a second vocalic inflection class (*o*-class) for intransitive verbs (see discussion below, section 6.4.1). While this seems adequate for individual dialects, for Romani as a whole the fluctuation between the contracted stem and the full consonantal stem (*sikhljo-l* 'learns' alongside *sikhljov-el*) justifies the treatment of intransitive formations as derivational rather than inflectional. The past tense of intransitive derivations is the adjectival marker *-il-* (OIA *-ill-*), which attaches to the jotated perfective stem: *ker-d-j-il-o* 'was done'. As mentioned above, the adjectival past-tense marker is also extended to psych verbs and to a number of verbs of motion, forming an inflectional sub-class of past-tense intransitives.

The productivity of intransitive derivations varies among the dialects. They are lost completely only in Welsh Romani and in German Sinti, which represents a rather recent development that is likely to be contact-influenced; the Piedmontese Sinti and Finnish Romani dialects, both related to German Sinti, preserve intransitive derivations. In the Northern Central dialects, intransitive derivations from iteratives and psych verbs indicate non-durative aspect (see above). The Northeastern, most Balkan dialects, and the Central dialects have expanded the use of the intransitive marker *-(j)o(v)-* to productive deadjectival (and occasionally denominal) formations: *nasval-(j)o(v)-* 'to become ill', *rat-(j)o(v)-* 'to become night'.

There is however evidence of competition in Early Romani with another intransitive marker, *-áv-*, derived from the verb 'to come', also used as an existential and an analytic passive auxiliary in some dialects. Its development parallels that of the principal intransitive marker *-(j)o(v)-*, that is, it starts off as an auxiliary, later to become an integrated synthetic marker. Its past-tense formants are *-ájl-* < **-av-il-*, and *-a(n)d-il-*. In the present, it uses the older intransitive marker

-(j)o(v)- as an inflectional base, assuming a vocalic extension in *-o-* (Vlax *dil-áv-o-l* 'becomes crazy'); in the first person a repetition of similar segments is avoided: *dil-áv-av* 'I become crazy' < ***dil-áv-ov-av*. The new marker takes over all recent inchoative formations in Vlax: *kor-áv-* 'to become blind'. It is also responsible for the integration of intransitive loan verbs in Vlax, attaching to the Greek aorist in *-s-*: *xa-s-áv-* 'to be lost', past *xa-s-ájl-* < Greek *xa-*, aorist *xas-*; *slobod-is-áv-* 'to be freed', past *slobod-is-ájl-* < Slavic *slobod-*. Traces of *-áv-* in this past formation for loan intransitives (*-s-ajl-*) are retained in many different dialects, and it obviously was a productive auxiliary in Early Romani (see below).

In some dialects, such as Sepečides and Bosnian Gurbet, a secondary intransitive derivation marker emerges. The Sepečides form is *-(a/in)divo-*. It appears in recent intransitive derivations from transitive verbal roots (*bistar-divo-la* 'is forgotten'), with loans (*jazd-indivo-la* 'is written', Turkish *yazdı* 'wrote', followed by the loan-adaptation marker *-in-*), and in recent inchoatives (*breš-andivo-la* 'matures' < *breš* 'year'). In Bosnian Gurbet (Uhlik 1941), the complex formant is*-dinájvo-* (*bičhal-dinajvo-l* 'is sent'), and it appears alongside the older formant of the type *bičhaldol* <**bičhal-d-jov-el*. The basic Sepečides marker *-divo-* could have emerged through metathesis from *-d-jov-*, with vocalisation of the jotated component. The new marker ends in a vowel, and so it enters the conjugation of vocalic present stems (**-d-jov-ela* >*-d-ivo-la*). With loan verbs, the same marker follows the loan-verb adaptation marker *-in-* (see below; cf. Cech and Heinschink 1999: 129). In the inchoative formation in *-andivo-* the nominal stem is followed by a past-tense marker that is reserved for intransitives and especially for unaccusatives and verbs expressing change of state, namely *-and-(il)-* (**brešándilo* 'matured'). In the present tense this formation is partly assimilated into the existing intransitive derivation, giving *brešandivola*. In the Bosnian Gurbet form, the point of departure resembles the common Vlax development **-áv-ov-el* > *-ávo-l*, the difference being that it is based, like the Sepečides inchoative, on an extended past tense: *bičhal-d-in-o* 'sent', followed by *-áj-(l)-*, which is the intransitive marker *-áv-* in past tense, and integrated into the present-tense intransitive inflection pattern in *-vo-* (hence *bičhaldinájvol*).

Intransitive derivation in Romani undergoes yet another phase of renewal through the introduction of two **analytic** constructions. The first is the analytic reflexive/reciprocal, which involves the attachment of the oblique pronoun, or in the third person of the reflexive pronoun *pe(s),* to the transitive verb (*dikhas amen* 'we see one another'). In some dialects, contaminations with synthetic intransitives appear, which tend to be lexicalised: Northern Vlax *dičhol pe* 'appears', *bušol pe* 'is called', *kerdžol pe* 'happens'. The second development is the emergence of an analytic passive. The Early Romani base for this construction appears to have been a stative construction, involving a copula auxiliary and a past participle. This construction was employed both with transitive and with intransitive verbs, as can be seen from its continuation in various dialects: *si kerdo* 'is done', *si bešto/bešlo* 'is seated'. The expansion of the analytic passive sees the development of a full tense paradigm of the copula auxiliary in this function. Since the copula is suppletive (see below), non-indicative forms of the passive construction (present subjunctive and future) take *ov-* in the Balkan and Southern Central dialects, and *av-* in the other dialects. In German Sinti and in Burgenland Roman, German influence (the regularity of *werden* 'to become' as a passive auxiliary) has led to the generalisation of *av-* and *ov-*, respectively, throughout the paradigm: Sinti *vjas kerdo* 'was done', Roman *kerdo ulo*.

6.3 Loan-verb adaptation

Romani employs a set of morphological markers that attach to loan roots, mediating between them and the inflectional marking of aspect, person, and tense. The phenomenon resembles the split in nominal morphology referred to in chapter 4, in that it marks out European loans, thereby maintaining a structural dichotomy between inherited and borrowed vocabulary (cf. Boretzky 1989). This split in morphological patterns has been referred to as 'thematic vs. athematic grammar' (cf. Kaufman 1979, Hancock 1995a, Bakker 1997b). Both the inflection of European nouns and the adaptation of European verbs is shaped by elements of Greek morphology that are adopted in the Early Romani period and remain productive thereafter.

The origin of loan-verb adaptation markers in Greek inflectional endings was illustrated by Miklosich (1872–80, II:5–6). Their inventory differs however considerably among the dialects. The most common markers in the Balkan dialects of Romani are *-in-/-an-/-on-* and *-iz-/-az-/-oz-*, which go back to the Greek present-tense inflectional endings in (1SG) *-íno/-ízo/-ázo/-ózo* etc. (*ir-iz-* 'to return', Greek *jir-íz-o*). A further Greek present-tense marker, *-évo*, though missing from most Romani dialects, is cited by Boretzky (1999b:103) from Paspati's (1870) Rumelian material (*pandr-ev-* 'to marry', Greek *pandr-év-o*), though its distribution is limited and it could represent later loans. The original affiliation to a Greek inflection class is seldom retained however. This is due firstly to the reduction of the inventory of Greek-derived markers to usually just one or two forms in each individual dialect, but also to the rather small number of surviving Greek verbs in most dialects. Thus Greek *jir-íz-o* 'I return' may appear as *ir-iz-* (Bugurdži), *ir-in-* (Prilep), or *ir-an-* (Arli). Alongside the forms deriving from present-tense Greek inflection markers, we also find Greek aorist forms in *-ís-/-ás-/-ós-*. They usually appear in the past, especially of intransitives: *ir-is-ajl-* 'returned', Greek *jir-ís-a*. In Vlax in particular, they are also extended to other tenses.

Bakker (1997b) explains the adoption of the Greek markers in Romani as a replication of the pattern of loan-verb adaptation that is applied in contact varieties of Greek: Cappadocian Greek *anla-di-zo* 'I understand', aorist *anla-di-sa/anla-sa* < Turkish *anla-*, past *anla-dı*. Both Igla (1996: 210) and Bakker (1997b: 18) have interpreted the variation in the use of Greek-derived loan-adaptation formants among Romani dialects as an indication of a possible dialectal split within Early Romani. A comparison of the distribution in Romani dialects of the various loan-verb adaptation markers reveals a somewhat more complex picture, however. It does not support a dialectal split within Early Romani, but suggests instead that initially all Greek inflectional markers were adopted into Romani on a wholesale basis, with subsequent levelling in the individual dialects and selective retention of forms from among the original options. Moreover, it appears that Romani did not, at least initially, rely entirely on the adopted Greek-derived morphology for loan-verb adaptation, but that a pattern of native adaptation of loans was in use. This resembled the strategy of loan-verb adaptation found in Indo-Iranian and in Turkic, where loan verbs are accommodated by means of a transitive and an intransitive native carrier verb (Kurdish *-kirin/-bûn*, Hindi *-karnā/-honā*, Persian *-kardan/-šodan*, Turkish *-etmek/-olmak* < 'to do/to become'). Loan-verb adaptation in these languages is a derivational strategy which mirrors verb argument structure. The same strategy is also followed in Domari, where Arabic transitive loan verbs are followed by *-k(ar)-* < *kar-* 'to do', intransitives by *-ho-* 'to become': *š(t)rī-k(ar)-* 'to buy' < Arabic *-štrī-*, *skun-ho-* 'to live' < Arabic *-skun-*.

Although the use of native carriers with loan verbs is simplified in Romani to a considerable extent, there is sufficient evidence to be able to reconstruct two Early Romani transitive-adaptation markers, *-ker-* and *-ar-* (past *-ker-d-*, *-ar-d-*), which draw on the two productive transitive derivation affixes of Early Romani (see above), and an intransitive-adaptation marker *-áv-* (past *-á-jl-/-á-ndil-*). The similarities with Asian loan-verb adaptation strategies suggest a Proto-Romani origin of the carrier verbs, and their continuation and subsequent partial retreat in Early Romani. The outstanding feature of loan-verb adaptation in Early Romani is the productiveness of the Greek verbal inflection, with tense distinctions from Greek being carried over into the Romani paradigm. Table 6.2 illustrates the original loan-verb adaptation patterns as reconstructed for Early Romani. The first component is derived from Greek. Greek aorist forms appear in the past tense as well as in the present tense of the intransitive. Greek present endings are used with transitive verbs; they are diverse, and match presumably in the early stage the Greek inflection markers of the respective verbs. The second component is the indigenous derivational marker that serves as a 'carrier'. This is followed by Romani perfective markers in the past tense.

Judging by the diversity of Greek-derived markers in the present-day dialects, it appears that in Early Romani, Greek verbs retained their Greek tense

Table 6.2 *Reconstructed loan-verb adaptation markers in Early Romani*

	Present	Past
Transitives	**-(V)z-,-(V)n- + -ker-/-ar-*	**-(V)s- + -ker-d-/-ar-d-*
Intransitives	**-(V)s- + -áv-*	**-(V)s- + -á-jl-/-á-(n)dil-*

inflection. This was followed by a Romani derivational marker which distinguished valency. To this, Romani affixes marking aspect, person concord, and tense/modality were attached. Thus for a possible Greek transitive loan verb such as *gráf-o* 'I write', past/aorist *gráp-s-a*, one might reconstruct an Early Romani form **graf-ker-av/*graf-ar-av* 'I write', past **grap-s-ker-d-(j)om/ *grap-s-ar-d-(j)om*. The latter form is actually attested as *agrapsardom* 'I wrote' in the dialect of the Zargari of Iran (Windfuhr 1970). For Greek intransitive verbs such as *jir-íz-o* 'I return', past/aorist *jir-ís-a* we can reconstruct the pattern **jir-is-áv-(ov)-av*, 'I return', past **jir-is-á-jl-(j)om/*jir-is-á-ndil-(j)om*. The intransitive formation mirrors intransitive derivation in the inherited component. In the inherited component, the intransitive derivation marker attaches to the past participle: *ker-d-(j)o(v)-*. In the loan component, the intransitive derivation marker attaches to the Greek aorist (past) marker: *jir-is-áv-*.

Since few Greek verbs are inherited into Common Romani, it is difficult to trace the development of specific Greek verbs in the individual dialects. In fact, some of the verbs that do constitute Common Romani forms tend to be exceptions to the pattern: early borrowings from Greek – *troma-* 'to dare' – do not follow the pattern for loan-verb adaptation at all, but are accommodated directly into the inherited (thematic) inflection. The verb *xas-* 'to lose' (Greek *xán-o* 'I lose', past/aorist *xás-a*) is often cited as evidence that the Greek aorist formed the basis for the adoption of Greek loan verbs into Romani. In fact, *xas-* appears to be the only transitive verb whose present-tense form is based on the aorist in all dialects. We might interpret this as an indication that it was initially borrowed into Romani in an intransitive meaning (*xa-s-áv-o-* 'to be lost', past *xa-s-á-jl-*), from which a secondary transitive *xa-s-ar-/xa-s-ker-* 'to cause to be lost > to lose' then emerged; all forms are attested in present-day dialects.

Despite the small number of Greek verbs that are shared by present-day dialects, we must assume that the pattern of adaptation outlined above was available in the Early Romani period for the spontaneous incorporation of any Greek verbal root. Romani varieties then moved away from the Greek-speaking area, coming into contact with other languages that supplied loan verbs. The first generation of Romani emigrants from the Greek-speaking areas will have maintained competence in Greek; in fact it is quite possible that contact with South Slavic, Turkish, Albanian, and Balkan Romance emerged in a multilingual

Table 6.3 *Loan-verb adaptation markers in Romani dialects*

	Transitive present	Transitive past	Intransitive present	Intransitive past
Ursari/Crimean	*-(V)z-*	*-(V)s- + -ker-d-*	*-(V)s- + -áv-*	*-(V)s- + -á-jl-*
Ipeiros	*-(V)z-, -(V)s-*	*-(V)n- + -d-*		*-(V)s- + -á-jl-*
Serres	*-(V)s- + -ker-*	*-(V)s- + -ker-d/j-*	*-(V)s- + -ov-*	*-(V)s- + -á-jl-*
Vlax	*-(V)s- + -ar-*	*-(V)s- + -ar-d-*	*-(V)s- + -áv-*	*-(V)s- + -á-jl*
Bugurdži–Drindari	*-(V)z-*	*-(V)z- + -d-*		*-(V)s- + -á-jl*
Southern Balkan	*-(V)n-*	*-(V)n- + -d-*	*-(V)n-d- + -jov-*	*-(V)s- + -á-jl/-á-ndil-*
Central	*-in-*	*-in- + -d-*	*-in-d- + -jov-*	*-is- + -á-jl-*
Northeastern	*-in-*	*-in- + -d-*	*-is- + -jov-*	*-is- + -ij-/-á-dij-*
Northwestern	*-av-/-ar-*	*-av-/-ar- + -d-*	(*-juv-*	*-dil-*)
Welsh	*-(V)s-/* *-in-/* *-(V)s- + -ar-*	*-(V)s- + -d-*		

setting where Greek continued to play a role. The established patterns for the adaptation of Greek loan verbs continued to be productive. These patterns were ultimately fully integrated into the Romani morphological system, and, having undergone considerable simplifications and levelling in the individual dialects, they remained productive even after active command of Greek was lost.

The weakest formant in the Early Romani loan-verb adaptation pattern appears to have been the native carrier verb for transitives, especially in the present tense. Most Romani dialects have lost it, which indicates that the transitive, and especially the present transitive, came to be regarded as a default or unmarked form. On the other hand the most conservative and persistent formant is that of the past tense of intransitives, which survives in most dialects. The principal simplifications in the dialects involve (a) the reduction of the inventory of Greek inflection markers in the present tense to just one form, (b) the loss of the distinction between present and past/aorist in the replicated Greek morphemes, and (c) the loss of transitive/intransitive distinction in the present tense. On the whole, simplifications form geographical patterns, indicating that the development followed the dispersion, and that it is contained within recent patterns of settlement (see table 6.3; see also figure 9.11, p. 233).

A conservative system is maintained in the Ursari and Crimean dialect (cf. Boretzky 1999b: 103–5). The distinction between transitives and intransitives is retained. Within transitives, a distinction is also made between present, for which Greek *-(V)z-* is generalised, and past, which uses the Greek aorist marker *-(V)s-*. Vocalic variants are preserved for all Greek markers (cf. Greek *-ízo/-ázo/-ózo*). In addition, native carrier verbs are preserved in the past for both transitives (*-ker-*) and intransitives (*-av-*).[2] Conservative formations are also found in the dialects of Ipeiros and Serres, both in Greece and in continuing contact with Greek. In the Ipeiros dialects, the tendency is to generalise *-Vz-* in the present and *-Vn-* in the past tense: *xori-z-ava*/*xori-n-dom* 'I separate/separated' (Greek *xoríz-o* 'I separate'). In the Serres dialect, the inherited markers *-ker-* and *-jov-*, which attach to Greek-derived *-(V)s-*, continue to carry the valency distinction: *aravonja-s-ker-* 'to engage', *aravonja-s-ov-* 'to become engaged' (Greek *arravonjáz-*). With Turkish-derived verbs, the distinction is retained in the past tense: *beendi-s-ker-jom* 'I liked' (Turkish intransitive with dative-subject *beğendi*), *jasa-ndi-s-ajl-o* 'he lived' (Turkish *yaşa-*). As in other languages of the Balkans, Turkish verbs are usually adopted into Romani on the basis of their past tense in the source language.

The Vlax formation is also rather conservative. Vlax retains native carriers in both transitive (*-ar-*) and intransitive (*-áv-*) formations. The striking simplification is the loss of all Greek-derived present-tense markers and the use of the aorist marker with present-tense transitives instead: *ažut-is-ar-* 'to help' (Romanian *ajut-*).

The Balkan, Central and Northeastern groups form a geographical continuum, sharing some general simplification patterns. Throughout this continuum, native carriers are lost completely with transitive verbs. Greek-derived present-tense markers are extended to the past formation of transitive verbs. In the eastern Balkans (Bugurdži, Drindari, Kalajdži and Rumelian) the formant is *-(V)z-*. In the Southern Balkan and Central groups, the present-tense transitive markers are also used with present-tense intransitives, while for the Bugurdži–Drindari dialects no present-tense intransitive derivations are attested with loan verbs. Throughout this geographical continuum, the older intransitive derivation marker *-jov-* is generalised as a native carrier with present-tense intransitives. In the Sepečides dialect, loan intransitives are formed through a combination of the present-tense adaptation marker and the younger intransitive marker: *-in-divo-*. The native carrier **-áv-* only survives in the past-tense formation in *-ájl-/-á(n)dil-*. The carrier *-ker-* appears attached to the Greek aorist marker in *-is-ker-*, in the formation of causatives and of loan roots (*bekleti-s-ker-* 'to make somebody wait', Turkish *bekledi*). In the Northeastern group, it competes with the adjectival past-tense marker *-ij-* < *-il-* of inherited intransitive derivations. A geographical development contained in part of the continuum is the

[2] Boretzky (1999b: 103–5) interprets the past formations in these dialects as an innovation. But this must be rejected for three main reasons. First, due to the evidence of transitive-derivation markers in this position in other dialects as well. Second, due to the symmetry within the system, which distinguishes transitive and intransitives. And finally on the basis of the comparison with the Asian model of loan-verb adaptation, from which the formants under consideration appear to derive.

generalisation of the formant in *-(V)n-* as a present-tense marker in the Southern Balkan, Central, and Northeastern groups; in yet a further zone, comprising the latter two groups, the variant *-in-* is generalised: Burgenland Roman *roas-in-* 'to travel', Latvian Romani *mišl-in-* 'to think'.

The Northwesten group (Sinti-Manuš and Finnish Romani) stands out in having replaced all Greek-derived loan-adaptation markers by the available productive transitive markers. Eastern and southern dialects of Sinti preserve *-ar-/-er-*: Piedmontese Sinti *tink-ar-*, Bohemian Sinti *denk-er-* 'to think'. Elsewhere, *-av-/-ev-* is employed: German Sinti *denk-ev-* 'to think', Finnish Romani *heng-av-* 'to hang'. In the Sinti group there is also a tendency to allow direct incorporation of loan verbs with no adaptation. Intransitive loans are similarly assimilated into inherited intransitive derivation patterns: Piedmontese Sinti *komens-ov-* 'to begin'. Synthetic intransitives are reduced in the Northwestern group, however, disappearing completely in German Sinti.

Welsh Romani, finally, retains a unique selection of Greek-derived markers. An original aorist formant is used in the present tense: *snōr-as-* 'to snore'. For some verbs, it alternates with *-in-* for the third-person present only: *balanz-in-ela* 'weighs'. In the imperative, *-(V)s-ar-* appears. The affix *-isar-* is also found sporadically in Spanish Para-Romani or Caló (see chapter 10), as in *ayun-isar-ar* 'to fast' (Quindalé 1867: 75). The presence of *-(V)s-ar-* in Welsh Romani and Caló suggests that the form is not a Vlax innovation, but an archaism. This is further supported by the Zargari form *agrap-s-ar-d-om* 'I wrote'.

There are some additional regional developments in the loan-verb component. In the Southern Central dialects, the marker *-in-ker-*, a combination of the loan-verb adaptation marker *-in-* with the original transitive carrier verb *-ker-*, provides yet another iterative marker, like plain *-ker-*, and is diffused into the inherited component in this function: *dikh-inker-* 'to see often' < *dikh-* 'to see'. In the Central dialects, an intransitive derivation marker *-(V)sal-jo(v)-*, apparently from the Early Romani past-tense loan intransitive formation **-(V)s-ajl-*, to which the older intransitive marker *-jov-* is added, is employed as an inchoative marker with loan nouns and adjectives, and is diffused into the inherited component to form inchoatives from indeclinable adjectives: *šukar-isal-jo(v)-* 'to become beautiful' < *šukar* 'beautiful'. This in turn serves as the basis for factitive formations, even with declinable inherited adjectives: *kor-isa-(j)ar-* 'to blind' < *koro* 'blind'. In the Sepečides dialect, the past inflection of intransitive loans in *-s-aj-l-* is extended to inherited intransitive stems in *-a*, original past **-a-jl-*, which are evidently assimilated into the class of Early Romani intransitive loans with the carrier *-á(v)-*: *dara-* 'to fear' past *dara-sajl-*, *pakja-* 'to believe' past *pakja-sajl-*.

Finally, some dialects show a layer of borrowed loan-verb adaptation morphology that follows the Greek components. In the Romungro dialects and in

Table 6.4 *Inflection of Turkish loan verbs in Agia Varvara Vlax: 'to work' < Turkish çalış- (from Igla 1989:74)*

	Present	Past
1SG	*calusurum*	*calustum*
2SG	*calusursun*	*calustun*
3SG	*calusur*	*calustu*
1PL	*calusurus*	*calustumus/calustuk*
2PL	*calusursunus*	*calustunus*
3PL	*calusur(lar)*	*calustu(lar)*

Hungarian Lovari (Vlax), the Hungarian denominal affix *-az-* may be combined with the Greek-derived marker *-in-*: *buč-az-in-* 'to work' < *buči* 'work' (see also Elšík et al. 1999: 364–5). The most striking pattern of loan-verb adaptation, and one that is cross-linguistically rare, is the wholesale adoption of Turkish verb inflection with Turkish verb roots in some dialects spoken in the Balkans that have been under heavy Turkish influence. This results in the co-existence of two alternative sets of person concord and tense/aspect marking in the language. As Igla (1989, 1996) describes, the pattern survives even in communities that have lost active command of Turkish during the past three generations (see table 6.4).

There is evidence however of restructuring taking place in the speech of communities that have moved from Turkey to Greece in the first part of the twentieth century. In Dendropotamos Southern Vlax of Thessaloniki, a dialect that is closely related to the Agia Varvara variety described by Igla (1996), Turkish verb inflection is being replaced by Greek inflection, thereby maintaining the overall dichotomy through other means: *me jasar-o* 'I live' < Turkish *yaşar-*, with the Greek 1SG present ending *-o*. Possible insights into the emergence of split verb inflection are provided by the data presented in Eloeva and Rusakov (1990) and in Rusakov and Abramenko (1998) from North Russian Romani. Here, there is an overwhelming tendency for Russian verbs to take Russian inflection (Rusakov and Abramenko 1998: 110):

(8) me tas'a *pojed-u* de foro
I tomorrow will.go-1SG in town
'Tomorrow I shall go to town'

Although absolute constraints on the borrowability of verbs (as suggested by Moravcsik 1978) cannot be upheld, it does seem that inflected verbs are often less readily integrated into bilingual speech, and many languages show a special device or adaptation pattern for borrowed loan verbs. The reason for this can be sought in the significance of the finite verb for the initiation of the predication. For active bilinguals who have full access to the finite-verb inflection systems of both languages, the switch at the point at which the predication is initiated creates ambiguity as to the matrix language (cf. Myers-Scotton 1993) of the clause, disturbing the overall grammatical plan of the utterance. The ambiguity can be resolved by delegating the task of initiating the predication to a native carrier verb, thereby stripping the foreign verb of its grammatical or INFL-carrying role. This may have been the strategy employed in (Asian) Proto-Romani, in the context of a west-central Asian linguistic area.

The fact that some of the present-day dialects behave differently might be related to the particular sociolinguistic situation of Romani, in particular to the acceptance of full and prolonged bilingualism in the Romani-speaking community. Early Romani had already replicated Greek verb inflection, while still employing native carrier verbs inherited from Proto-Romani. The adoption of Turkish verb inflection is most common in dialects that have had continuous contact with Turkish, where it is comparable to the code mixing documented for North Russian Romani. In these dialects the constraint to harmonise the overall grammatical plan of the utterance with the grammatical initiation of the predication is relaxed. In Para-Romani varieties (see chapter 10), the constraint is reintroduced as finite verb inflection is adopted entirely from the contact language. Some attestations of nineteenth-century English Para-Romani (Smart 1862–3) show an intermediate stage, with the finite verb deriving either from Romani or from English. One can possibly identify the generalisation of the non-Romani finite verb as the point at which language shift has actually occurred.

6.4 Stem formation and inflection class

Romani, like other NIA languages, distinguishes two verbal stems. The present stem is the default, unmodified lexical root of the verb, or alternatively the product of valency alteration and loan-verb adaptation procedures. The perfective stem is based on the historical OIA/MIA past participle. In most cases it is marked by an extension to the lexical root (or its derivations and adaptations) by means of a perfective marker, which continues one of the OIA/MIA participial or adjectival markers (*-ita/-ina/-illa*). The key to the classification of Romani verb inflection is the final phonological segment of the verb stem. In addition, a number of archaic stem alternations are preserved. Verb inflection classes can be distinguished for both present and perfective stem formations: with present stems, inflection classes are distinguished through the vowel component by which subject concord markers are attached to the stem. With perfective stems, inflection classes are distinguished by the form of the perfective markers. Inflection classes may, but need not overlap, since the form of the perfective marker is only partly predictable from the structure of the present stem. Dialects show considerable variation especially with regard to the assignment of perfective stems to the individual classes. In addition, the effects of jotation on the perfective marker vary, contributing to the diversity of actual class forms.

6.4.1 *Present stems*

With present verb stems, Romani has a consonantal inflection class, and a vocalic inflection class, as well as a somewhat varied class of contracted forms. Recent German-language scholarship in Romani linguistics (Boretzky 1993a: 64–6, Holzinger 1993: 99–103, Igla 1996: 52, Halwachs 1998: 132–8, Cech and Heinschink 1999: 45–6) posits two conjugations for Romani, referred to as *e*-verbs, which represent the consonantal class, and *a*-verbs, which represent the vocalic class. They are named after the vowel that binds the personal concord markers in the second and third persons (*ker-el* 'does', *ker-es* 'you.SG do', but *xa-l* 'eats', *xa-s* 'you eat'). This vowel, however, although representative of the inflection class, is not constitutive of class affiliation. Rather, the vowel is merely conditioned by the form of the verb stem. The default personal concord markers of the consonantal class show the vowel components *-a-* in the first person, and *-e-* in the second and third persons: 1SG *ker-av* 'I do', 1PL *ker-as*, 2SG *ker-es*, 3SG *ker-el*, 2+3PL *ker-en*. Transitive derivations in *-av-/-ar-* and compounds in *-ker-/-kir-* and *-d-* belong to the consonantal class, as do the monoconsonantal stems *d-* 'to give' and *l-* 'to take'. The class of vocalic stems is much smaller, and contains mainly verbs in *-a* . The vowel component of the personal concord affix is assimilated to the *-a* vowel of the stem: *xa-l* 'eats', *xa-s* 'you eat'. As a result, distinctions among concord markers which are based on the vocalic component of the marker are levelled: *tu ker-es* 'you.SG do', *ame(n) ker-as* 'we do', but *tu xa-s* 'you.SG eat', *ame(n) xa-s* 'we eat'.

Stems ending in *-i* (*pi-* 'to drink') may have a glide insertion and pattern with the consonantal class in the present stem forms (*pijav* 'I drink', *pijel* alongside *pil* 'drinks'). In Vlax, there is an optional reduction of loan-verb adaptation affixes in *-(V)sar-* to their vocalic component *-i/-o*, which creates in effect additional vocalic stems (*tra-i-v* alongside *tra-isar-av* 'I live', *ram-o-l* alongside *ram-osar-el* 'writes'). The vocalic class of present stems is further extended through contractions of transitive and intransitive derivations, leading to a reassignment of the forms from the consonantal into individual vocalic groups. Roman, for instance, shows a class of contracted transitive derivations: *kera-l* 'causes, instigates' < **ker-av-el*. More widespread and quite clearly of Early Romani origin are the contractions of intransitive derivations in *-ov-e-* > *-o-*: *kerd-(j)o-l* 'becomes', alongside *kerd-(j)ov-el*.

The contraction of the consonant component in the marker*-ov-* and the subsequent assimilation of the concord vowel component (first-person *-a-*, third- and

Table 6.5 *Inflection formants of intransitive derivations*

	3 SG/PL	2PL	2SG	1SG/PL
Arli, Erli, Rumelian, Romungro, Kalderaš (*ov*>*uv*)	*-ov-e-/-o-*	*-ov-e-/-o-*	*-ov-e-/-o-*	*-ov-a-*
Piedmontese Sinti	*-o-*	*-ov-e-*	*-ov-e-*	*-ov-a-*
West Slovak	*-o-*	*-o-*	*-ov-e-*	*-ov-a-*
Roman	*-o-*	*-o-*	*-oj-*	*-oj-a-*
Bohemian, East Slovak, Lovari (*ov*>*uv*), Northeastern	*-o-*	*-o-*	*-o-*	*-ov-a-*
Sepečides, Bugurdži Agia Varvara	*-o-*	*-o-*	*-o-*	*-a-*

second-persons *-e-*) to the vowel of the intransitive marker *-o-*, tends to follow a person hierarchy: 3SG/PL>2PL>2SG>1SG/PL (table 6.5).

Early Romani thus seems likely to have had a contracted 3SG/PL in *-o-* as an optional form. The option is extended to the second persons in some dialects, represented by the top group in the figure. Elsewhere, the contracted form prevails in the third person. There is a tendency to preserve conservative consonantal forms for the second person in a number of dialects (second group in the figure), and an overwhelming tendency to do so for the first person (all but the bottom group in the figure). Even in those dialects that reduce the consonantal form in the first person (bottom group in the figure), the original vowel insertion *-a-* connecting the consonantal component of the concord markers (1SG *-v*, 1PL *-s*) overrides the *-o-* component of the intransitive marker: Sepečides *siklj-o-la* 'learns', but *siklj-a-va* 'I learn', *siklj-a-sa* 'we learn'. The same hierarchy in the assignment to vocalic versus consonantal inflection may be found in the treatment of other volatile verb stems; consider Roman *pi-l* 'drinks', *pi-s* 'you.SG drink', but *pi-j-av* 'I drink' and *pi-j-as* 'we drink', and the causative forms *ker-a-l* 'makes (somebody) do', but *ker-av-av* 'I make (somebody) do', and in an intermediary position *ker-aj-s* 'you make (somebody) do'. This hierarchical development creates a split within the paradigms, as a result of which there is no convenient way to assign contracted verbs to an inflectional class, and they are best regarded as a residual class (see Halwachs 1998: 139–42).

The Romani copula in *s-/h-* represents a distinct class: it has, strictly speaking, no present stem, but derives present-tense meanings from the historical perfective stems. The formation of the copula stems is therefore dealt with under the heading of perfective stems below (section 6.4.2). Noteworthy however is the suppletion in the copula: non-indicative forms (subjunctive and future) draw either on the older verb *ov-* 'to become' < OIA *bhav-*, or on the verb *av-* 'to come' (cf. discussion in Boretzky 1997). Both appear to have been possible options in Early Romani, *ov-* being the older and more established form, *av-* an innovation. As discussed above, both *ov-* and *av-* give rise to intransitive auxiliaries which then become synthetic intransitive derivation markers, though *av-* in this function is only productive in Vlax and the Sepečides dialect, being confined elsewhere to the adaptation of intransitive loan verbs, primarily in the past tense. For the non-indicative copula, dialects clearly tend to generalise just one of the two options. Here, *av-* is on the whole the more widespread variant; *ov-* is confined to an area comprising the Balkan and Southern Central groups, although it also appears in the Latvian dialect. As Boretzky (1997: 126) notes, *ov-/av-* are also the only forms available to express the subjunctive and future of *kerdjo(v)-* 'to become' (from *ker-* 'to do').

6.4.2 *Perfective stems*

Proto-Romani, though conservative in preserving the OIA/MIA present-tense inflection of verbs, evidently participated in the process that resulted in a complete collapse of the older past inflection. The latter was substituted for, as elsewhere in Indo-Iranian, through the generalisation of the past participle. The participle with adjectival concord still forms the unspecified past tense in languages like Hindi. In Eastern and Northwestern NIA, as well as in Iranian, person markers attach to the participle to form a new past-tense inflection, and this is also the path taken in Proto-Romani (as in Domari). The result is a perfective stem with synthetic morphology. As a result of phonological processes and class reassignments, the class affiliation of perfective stems is more complicated than that of present stems, both within individual dialects and in cross-dialectal comparison. Factors involved in the inflection class affiliation of perfective stems are: the final phonological segment of the stem (vowels versus consonants, and the position of the consonant), the overall phonological structure of the stem (monoconsonantal stems being a volatile category), grammatical valency (intransitive derivations and verbs of motion and change of state constituting a separate inflection class), structure and semantics (psych verbs in *-a* constituting a volatile category), as well as person (3PL and partly 3SG continuing adjectival participles, other persons showing person markers that are attached to the perfective stem via jotation).

The principal perfective marker derives from the OIA past-participle marker *-it-*. Romani (like Domari) is conservative among the NIA languages in retaining the consonantal value of the marker, which is often reduced to a glide or just a vowel in the subcontinental languages. In addition to the principal perfective marker we find forms deriving from the historical adjectival participle markers OIA *-in-* and *-ill-*, which contribute to the class differentiation in perfective stems.

Already during the Proto-Romani stage the principal perfective marker **-it-* > **-t-* underwent phonological differentiation. Following the voiced dental sonorants – *r, l, n* – as well as *v*, it shows voice assimilation, giving *-d-*: *ker-d-o* 'done'. Following vowels, the dental stop shifts to a dental lateral, giving *-l-*: *xa-l-o* 'eaten'. Elsewhere, one can assume continuation in Proto-Romani of **-t-*: **dikh-t-o* 'seen'. The outcome was an early differentiation into three distinct morphological classes of perfective markers – in *-d-*, *-l-*, and *-t-*. In the later Early Romani period, however, a tendency appears to have emerged to avoid certain consonant clusters resulting from the attachment of the old perfective marker *-t-* to consonantal verb stems. The cases which demanded earlier solutions were those where the clash resulting from dissimilar articulations was most extreme: the combinations **mt*, **gt*, **kt*, more so than **čt*, or the even more permissible **št*. The solution to the articulatory tension that the clusters create is to reassign the relevant verb stems to a different morphological class, namely to the class in *-l-*, which originally had included only vocalic stems. This class reassignment, a morphological solution to an articulatory problem, follows a regular hierarchical progression. On a phonetic hierarchy of obstruents vs. fricatives, the historical participial marker in an obstruent **-t-* tends to be avoided in positions next to other obstruents:

(9) The hierarchical progression of class re-assignment (**-t-* > *-l-*) in perfective markers (by stem consonant):
-t > *-m* > *-g, -k, -kh* > *-č, -čh* > *-š, -s*

Stems in *-t* are rare in the language. Those that can be found belong exclusively to the perfective inflection class in *-l-*: *xut-l-* for *xut-* 'to jump'. Only the most conservative dialects still show traces of the *-t*-marker with stems in *-m-*: Welsh Romani *kam-d-om* 'I wanted', with late voicing, Latvian Romani *kam-dž-om* alongside *kam-j-om* < **kam-lj-om*. By contrast, forms in *-t-* have the highest survival rate in positions following sibilants (see table 6.6). Owing to the regularity with which the change progresses in the various dialects, one can assume that the trigger for the development was shared. On the other hand, the diversity of outcomes among the individual dialects points to a recent development, one that followed the dispersion. We can therefore place the roots of the development in the Early Romani period.

The overall picture of the actual perfective forms and classes is further complicated by the effects of jotation. Jotation generally accompanies the attachment to perfective stems of person concord affixes deriving from oblique pronominal clitics (on the possible origins of jotation see below, and see chapter 4): *ker-d-j-om* 'I did'. There is no jotation in the adjectival past participle, which serves both as a passive participle (*ker-d-o* 'done'), and as the active perfective form of the 3PL (*ker-d-e* 'they did'). Adjectival participles also serve in the

Table 6.6 *Perfective markers: 1sg (jotated) and 3pl (non-jotated) forms*

	voiced dentals *ker-* 'to do'	vowels *xa-* 'to eat'	other consonants *dikh-* 'to see'	 *phuč-* 'to ask'	 *(a)res-* 'to meet'[3]	 *beš-* 'to sit'
Early Romani	*-*d/dj-*	*-*l/lj-*	*-*tj/t-*	*-*tj/t-*	*-*tj/t-*	*-*tj/t-*
Vlax	*-d-*	*-l-*	*-l-*	*-l-*	*-l-*	*-l-*
Sepečides	*-d-*	*-l-*	*-l-*	*-l-*	*(-l-)*	*-l-*
Arli	*-gj/d-*	*-lj/l-*	*-lj/l-*	*-lj/l-*	*-l-*	*-lj/l-*
Roman	*-č/d-*	*-j/l-*	*-l-*	*-l-*	*-l-*	*-l-*
Bugurdži	*-dz/d-*	*-j/l-*	*-j/l-*	*-j/l-*	*-j/l, t-*	*-j,ć/l, t-*
Ipeiros/Serres	*-d-*	*-lj/l-*	*-lj/l-*		*(-tj/t-)*	*-tj/t-*
Xaladitka	*-d'/d-*	*-j/l,n-*	*-j/l,n-*	*-j/l,n-*	*-t'/l,n-*	*-t'/l,n-*
Latvian	*-dž/n-*	*-j/n-*	*-j/n-*	*-j/n-*	*-č/n-*	*-č,dl/n-*
Bohemian	*-d'/d-*	*-l'/l-*	*-l'/l-*	*-l'/l-*	*-t'/t-*	*-t'/t-*
E. Slovak	*-d'/d-*	*-l'/l-*	*-l'/l-*	*-t',l'/t,l-*	*-t',l'/t,l-*	*-t',l'/t,l-*
Rumelian	*-g'/d-*	*-l'/l-*	*-l'-*		*-g'/t-*	*-g'/t-*
Erli	*-g'/d-*	*-l'/l-*	*-l'/l-*	*-l'/?-*	*-t'/t-*	*-t'/t-*
Sinti	*-d-*	*-j-*	*-j/t-*	*-j/t-*	*-j/t-*	*-j/t-*
Welsh	*-d-*	*-j/l-*	*-j/d-*	*-d-*	*-d-*	*-t/d-*
Polska Roma	*-dž/d-*	*-j/n-*	*-č/n-*	*-č/n-*	*-č/n-*	*-č/n-*

southern dialects as active perfective forms of the 3sg of intransitive verbs (see below): *(a)res-l-o* 'he arrived', *(a)res-l-i* 'she arrived'. The passive participle and the 3pl perfective form often show reinforced participial markers in *-in-*, *-n-* or *-dl-*, which are likewise unaffected by jotation.

In all persons except the 3pl (and intransitive active participles in the 3sg), where the adjectival participle form is preserved, the markers are jotated to the Early Romani forms **-dj-*, **-lj-*, **-tj-*. The effects of this Early Romani jotation are recent and particular to individual dialects (see chapter 4): the yod can either disappear, rendering *-d-*, *-l-*, *-t-*, or result in palatalisation to *-d'-*, *-l'-*, *-t'-/-ć-*, or in affrication of *-dj->* *-dž-/-dz-* and *-tj-* > *-č-*, or in substitution of the jotated voiced dental stop through a jotated or palatalised velar *-dj-* > *-gj-/-g'-*,[4] or in assimilation of the jotated lateral to the palatal glide *-lj-* > *-j-*. Jotation also adds a further dimension to the hierarchy depicted in (9), in that jotated forms are more likely to be reassigned to the *-l(j)-* class: German Sinti *dikh-j-om* 'I saw' < **dikh-lj-om*, but *dikh-t-e* 'they saw'. The combination

[3] There are few verb stems in *-s-* in Romani, and few that are shared by all or even most dialects. The verb *res-* has various meanings, including 'to arrive' (Vlax), 'to meet' (Roman), 'to satisfy' (Xaladikta), 'to achieve' (Polska Roma), 'to suffice' (Sepečides), some of which are impersonal and so lack a complete conjugation.

[4] In some Romani dialects of Turkey (Bakker 2001), substitution of the dental by a velar is found also in the voiceless perfective marker: *beš-k'-* < **beš-tj-* 'sat', as well as *garav-g'-* < **garav-dj-* 'hid (tr.)'.

of inflection class reassignment and jotation effects renders a highly diverse cross-dialectal inventory of perfective stem inflection classes, as illustrated in table 6.6.

For Early Romani it seems possible to reconstruct **ker-dj-/ker-d-* and **xa-lj-/xa-l-*, **dikh-tj-/dikh-t-*, **phuč-tj-/phuč-t*, **res-tj-/res-t-* and **beš-tj-/beš-t-*, the 3PL perfective markers possibly alternating with *-n-*.[5] In the present-day dialects, class reassignment from **-t-* to *-l-* encompasses all relevant consonantal stems in Vlax, Sepečides, Arli, and Roman. In the Bugurdži–Drindari dialects there are still traces of the original dental stop following sibilants. This also holds for other dialects of the Balkans (Serres *bestjom*, Ipeiros *beštjom*, Erli *bešt'om* 'I sat').

The northern dialects within the Northeastern group (Xaladitka and Latvian) have also retained the dental-stop marker following sibilants, though in the 3PL this is partly obscured by the alternation of the perfective markers *-l-/-n-*. Conservative forms are widespread in the Northern Central dialects, where the shifts appear to have taken place within the last century, and in the southeasternmost Balkan dialects. Sinti shows class reassignment only of the jotated forms. Welsh Romani represents an even more conservative stage, keeping the dental (which is subsequently voiced) also in positions following the affricate *-č* and selectively in some verbs following the velar stop. The Polska Roma dialect is the most conservative in retaining a reflection of the original dental stop throughout (affricated or strongly palatalised).

Apart from the principal inflection classes which continue the Early Romani classes in *-d(j)-*, *-l(j)-* and *-t(j)-*, there are additional classes and particular cases of perfective stems. Stems in *-n* generally belong to the *-d-* class, but individual verbs, such as *džan-* 'to know', may show full or partial reassignment to the *-l-* class: East Slovak Romani and Prilep *džan-l-*, Xaladitka *džan-dl-*, Vlax *džan-gl-*, elsewhere *džan-d-* 'knew'. In the Prilep dialect, it seems that class reassignment has begun to affect even prototypical *-d-* class items, namely verb stems in voiced dentals, beginning with stems in *-in*: *kinlum* 'I bought' alongside *kindum*, *čhinlum/čhindum* 'I cut'. Stems in *-v* also belong to the *-d-* class, but transitive derivations in *-av-* frequently show contractions of the consonant, resulting in atypical perfective *-d-* forms that follow a vowel: *gara-d-* 'hid' to *garav-* 'to hide (something)'.

Intransitive derivations form their perfective stems not from the historical participial ending in *-it-*, but from the adjectival ending in *-ill-* (see Bubeník 2000): *bar-il-* 'grew old' to *bar-(j)o(v)-* 'to grow old', *ker-d-il-* 'was done' to *ker-d-(j)o(v)-* 'to be done'. The perfective marker here overrides the auxiliary turned synthetic intransitive marker, *-(j)o(v)-*. The *-il-* class is subjected to

[5] The generalisation of *-n-* in the 3PL is a Northeastern innovation. But the choice of a participle form in the 3PL is Proto-Romani (see below, section 6.5), hence it seems possible that both variants of the participle – in *-t-* and in *-(i)n-* – continued into Early Romani.

the normal effects of jotation: Vlax *bijan-d-il-em* 'I was born', Northeastern *bijan-d-yj-om*; Bugurdži *bijan-dz-om* 'I was born' (with jotation assimilating to the affricate), but *bijan-dz-il-o* (adjectival agreement) 'he was born'. Adopted into this intransitive inflection class are a number of intransitive primary roots, mainly those denoting motion or change of state: *av-il-/av-(i)j-/a-l-/a-j-* 'came', *ačh-il-/ačh-(i)j-* 'stayed', *ušt-il-/ušt-(i)j-* 'stood'.[6] The existential verb *ov-* 'to become' has a contracted perfective stem in *u-l-*. Loan intransitives are included in the *-il-* class: Xaladitka *mraz-yj-* 'froze'. Typically, with loan intransitives the perfective marker attaches to the adaptation marker consisting of the Greek aorist affix followed by the carrier verb *-á(v)-* (see discussion above): Arli *žen-is-a-jl-o* 'he married', Bugurdži *živ-is-a-j-om* 'I lived', Xaladitka *xol'-as-yj-om* 'I became angry'; all deriving from the Early Romani format 'lexical root + Greek aorist + **-áv-* + *-il-*'. A further extension of the class in *-il-* are psych verbs in *-a*, where *-il-* may be the last element in a chain of participial affixes: *dara-jl-/dara-n-il-* 'feared', *asa-n-il-/asa-n-d-il-* 'laughed', *troma-jl-* 'dared' (an early Greek loan).

The historical participle marker OIA *-in-* has, on the whole, the status of a kind of perfective reinforcement in late Proto-Romani, as can be seen from the distribution of the perfective forms *-in-/-n-* in the dialects. The affix is most common in the 3PL, which is a direct continuation of the adjectival participle. In the Northeastern dialects, there are strong tendencies to generalise *-n-e* as the 3PL perfective marker, while elsewhere it is a frequent perfective marker of the 3PL in the more volatile perfective classes, notably psych verbs in *-a*, and monoconsonantal stems: Vlax *d-ij-as* 'he gave', but *d-in-e* 'they gave'. Markers in *-in-* also appear sporadically with intransitive derivations, e.g. Bugurdži *sić-in-i* 'she learned' (but *sić-il-o* 'he learned'), and with existentials, as in Rumelian *u-n-il-o* 'became'.

With psych verbs in *-a* and with monoconsonantal stems, there are tendencies to generalise *-in-* throughout the perfective paradigm. Psych verbs in *-a* may take plain *-n-*, as in Rumelian and Romungro *dara-n-* 'feared', or a combination with *-il-*, as in Erli *dara-n-il-*. A further option available for this group, as well as for adapted intransitive loans in **-áv-* > *-á-*, is the complex perfective marker *-n-d-il-* (*dara-ndil-* 'feared'). It is found in the Balkans, the Central dialects and the Northeastern group, and so it too seems to go back to an Early Romani variant. The form appears to be based on an extension in *-(i)n-*, reanalysed as an *-n-* stem which is assigned to the *-d-* class, then marked out as an intransitive through *-il-*. Psych verbs may however also show loss of the historical perfective marker and its replacement through

[6] Igla (1996: 55) points to the extension in *-i* to the root in the imperative forms *ušti!* 'stand!' (rarely also *ačhi!* 'stay'), suggesting an original stem in *-i*. This would imply a vocalic stem with a perfective marker deriving from *-ita* > *-l-*. It seems more likely that the present stem in *-i* is an innovation, reanalysed by analogy to the perfective stem (see also Boretzky 1999b: 97).

a glide which connects the vocalic stem to the concord ending: Vlax *asa-j-* 'laughed'.

Monoconsonantal stems include the verbs *d-* 'to give', *l-* 'to take', and *s-/h-* 'to be'. The latter employs the perfective stem in a present-tense meaning, though traces of a past-tense function are still found in some dialects (see below). In addition, compounds involving *-d-* (e.g. *trad-* 'to drive') are also treated as monoconsonantal stems. The original, Proto-Romani options here appear to have been to attach the person marker via jotation either to the participle in *-in-* (MIA *d-ina*), giving the type *d-in-(j)om* 'I gave', *s-in-(j)om* 'I am', or to attach it directly to the stem, giving *d-(ij)om*, *s-(ij)om* (cf. Domari *ṭ-om* 'I gave'). In the 3PL the adjectival plural participle is usually continued in the lexical verbs, thus *d-in-e* 'they gave', while in the copula the 3PL usually adapts to the 3SG in *si/hi* (but Arli 3PL and 3SG variant *s-in-e*). The *-in-* marker in the lexical stems may occasionally copy the *-l-* class, giving *l-il-* 'took' and *d-il-* 'gave', or be reanalysed as *-n-* stems, giving *d-in-d-* 'gave'. The copula in *s-* preserves a perfective marker in *-t-*, alternatively reassigned to the *-l-* class, in some dialects (Ukrainian Vlax and Southern Central *s-t-*, *s-l-*).

Irregularities in the formation of perfective stems are those that continue OIA/MIA irregular past participles, such as *pel-* to *per-* 'to fall', *mul-* to *mer-* 'to die', *sut-* to *sov-* 'to sleep', *runl-/rundl-* < **run-* to *rov-* 'to sleep', *-klist-* to *-kal-* 'to raise, to remove', or *gel-* to *dža-* 'to go'. The latter is the only case of historical suppletion among the perfective stems. Perfective markers in originally jotated positions have been recently lost altogether in dialects of Sinti, as a result of the weakening of the jotated segment: **beš-tj-om* > **beš-j-om* > *beš-om* 'I sat'. Phonological reduction also leads to the frequent disappearance of the perfective marker in Bugurdži.

6.5 Person concord

There are three types of concord markers in Romani. The primary dichotomy is between two sets of personal concord markers, which accompany present and perfective stems respectively. The third type, adjectival agreement, accompanies non-finite verb forms of the past and present participles, but it also infiltrates the paradigm of perfective concord markers with finite verbs, where it is subjected to a valency split (intransitives>transitives) and to a person split (third persons>other persons).

The present concord set is a direct continuation of the OIA set of present concord markers 1SG *-āmi* > Romani *-av*, 2SG *-asi* > Romani *-es*, 3SG *-ati* > Romani *-el*, 1PL *-āmas* > Romani *-as*, 2PL *-atha* (assimilated in Romani into the 3PL), 3PL *-anti* > Romani *-en*. Romani, like Domari, is remarkably archaic in preserving this old concord set, standing out in particular through the continuation of OIA *-t-* in the 3SG as *-l-* (Domari *-r-*), which elsewhere in NIA is generally lost, but also in the retention of consonantal forms for the other persons. The consonantal endings along with their thematic vowels constitute the core of the personal concord markers. The older present indicative forms are succeeded in Romani by 'long' forms in *-a*, with 'short' forms serving as subjunctive markers (see below). The OIA long vowels of the first persons are represented in Romani by *-a-*, the short vowels of other persons by *-e-*: 1SG *-av*, 1PL *-as*; 2SG *-es*, 3SG *-el*, 2PL/3PL *-en*. The only old form that is lost is that of the 2PL, which assimilates to the 3PL in *-en*. The two conspicuous phonological reductions of Proto-Romani involve the 1PL *-as* < *-āmas* and the 3PL *-en* < *-ant(i)*. We can thus assume a uniform system of present concord markers in Early Romani.

Later modifications involve shifts in the labial component of the 1SG, giving *-av/-aw/-ao/-af/-ap*, reduction of the sibilant, giving 2SG *-es/-eh/-e* and 1PL *-as/-ah/-a*, and more rarely modification of the vowel in the 3SG, giving *-el/-ol*. Sporadically, one encounters first-person forms in *-m* which can probably be interpreted as analogies to personal pronouns 1SG *me* and 1PL *ame(n)*. In the Balkans, we find 1SG *-am* with modals such as *trom-am-a* 'I dare', *kam-am-a* 'I want', Xaladitka has similarly *kam-am* (alongside *kam-av-a* 'I want'), as well as *džin-om* 'I know' (alongside *džin-av-a*), the latter possibly copying the perfective personal concord marker *-om*. Some Northeastern dialects add *-m* to the 1PL future: *ker-as-a-m* 'we shall do' < present/future **ker-as-a*. An aberrant marker for the 3SG is *-i*, which is normally confined to loan verbs. It is optional with loan verbs in Latvian and Welsh Romani, while in Gilan Arli (Kosovo; Boretzky 1996a) it is generalised for loans (*pomožin-i* 'helps'), and infiltrates in addition also inherited verbs (*mothav-i* 'speaks'). The Dolenjski dialect has even generalised *-i* as a 3SG present concord marker. The predominance of *-i* with loans, and the dialectal distribution which points to an Early Romani rather than to a recent development, suggest an origin in Greek 3SG *-i*.

More complex, and controversial as far as the early historical development is concerned, is the set of perfective personal concord markers (table 6.7). A series of modifications to the paradigms is clearly of recent date, and geographically contained. Typical of the Vlax dialects is the change in the vowel component in the 1SG *-em* < **-om*, a result of umlaut accompanying the loss of jotation.

In the 2SG, the form *-al* is generalised in a central European zone. Its spread in this region as an innovation is confirmed by its recent infiltration of central European Vlax dialects (Lovari). Nonetheless, there is reason to assume that we are dealing with an archaic form representing the original Proto-Romani 2SG marker (see below). The wide geographical distribution of *-an* on the other hand suggests that it too continues an Early Romani form, albeit one that emerged by analogy to the 2PL *-an*. It is likely then that Early Romani contained two 2SG variants, the older of the two, *-al*, having been retained and redistributed in a cluster of geographically contiguous dialects.

Table 6.7 *Perfective personal concord markers*

	1SG	2SG	3SG trans.	intrans.	1PL	2PL	3PL
Balkan	-om/-um	-an	-a(s)	-o,i	-am	-en	-e
Vlax	-em	-an/-al	-a(s)	-a(s)/-o,i	-am	-an/-en	-e
S. Central	-om	-al	-a	-a/-o,i	-am	-an	-e
N. Central	-om	-al	-a(s)	-a(s)	-am	-an	-e
Sinti	-om/-um	-al	-as		-am	-an	-an
Finnish	-om	-al	-as	-as/-o,i	-am	-an/-en	-e
Northeastern	-om	-an	-a		-am	-e	-e
Welsh	-om	-an	-as		-am	-an/-e	-e

In the 3SG, the reduction of *-s* is partly confined to this particular form and partly conditioned by the general reduction of final *-s* in the Southern Central and some of the Balkan dialects, including Vlax dialects of the Balkans. The retention of adjectival concord in the 3SG with certain types of intransitive verbs (intransitive derivations and unaccusatives) is an archaism, encountered especially in the Balkans: *bijandil-o* 'he was born', *bijandil-i* 'she was born', *gel-o* 'he went', *gel-i* 'she went'. In a transitional zone of southeastern Europe, as well as in Finnish Romani, adjectival inflection co-occurs with personal concord, while elsewhere it gives way to the personal concord of other verbs.

In the Balkans, the 2PL perfective concord marker has been replaced by *-en* by analogy to the 2PL present concord marker. This change is also found in Vlax dialects of the southern Balkan region, including Northern Vlax dialects such as Serbian Kalderaš. The same analogical change is under way in Finnish Romani. The Northeastern dialects, and in part also Welsh Romani, show an analogy of the 2PL to the 3PL,[7] while in Sinti the reverse change occurs, with the 3PL adopting the 2PL form. For Early Romani we can thus postulate the following series of perfective personal concord markers: 1SG *-om*, 2SG *-al/-an*, 3SG *-as/o,i* (with intransitives), 1PL *-am*, 2PL *-an*, and 3PL*-e* (alternating with *-n-e*).

In principle the same set is also used as personal concord markers for the present-tense copula, based on the stems *s-/h-/s-in-/h-in-* etc. The exception are the third persons, which usually continue a 3SG form in *si/hi/isi* etc., rarely a 3PL form in *s-in-e/h-in-e*. The traditional view in Romani linguistics has been to regard the perfective formation of lexical verbs as an amalgamation of the past participle with the copula auxiliary. This is indeed the path that is followed in various NIA languages as well as in Iranian, though in the latter it often figures in the renewal of both present- and past-tense concord sets.

[7] Modern Welsh Romani as documented by Tipler (1957) also shows occasional shift of the 2SG to *-as* (*tu gijas* 'you went'), motivated possibly by analogies both to the 3SG in *-as* and to the 2SG present marker in *-s*.

There are however several problems with the copula-turned-past-concord theory. First, it fails to account for the origin of the copula markers themselves, which are distinct from those of the present-tense concord set of lexical verbs, and which do not fit in with the older sound changes that are represented by the set of present concord markers: thus the 1SG present marker is *-av* < OIA *-āmi*, but the perfective/copula 1SG marker is *-om*. Second, it does not explain the forms of the third persons: the choice of the adjectival participle in the 3PL, and especially the split within the 3SG between person-inflected transitives and adjectival inflection with intransitives. Finally, it does not take into account the appearance of perfective markers in present-tense copula forms, the sporadic tense alteration of some copula forms (e.g. *s-t'-om* for 'I am' and 'I was' in Southern Ukrainian Romani), and the overall similarities between the present-tense copula and the perfective stems of other monoconsonantal verbs: *s-in-(j)om-/s-(ij)-om* 'I am', *d-in-(j)om/d-(ij)-om* 'I gave'.

A new direction in the historical reconstruction of the copula concord set was proposed by Bloch (1932a). Bloch derived the person markers from a combination of original verbal concord markers and pronominal elements.[8] Furthermore, he suggested that this mixed set of markers was attached not to the present stem of the copula, but to its past participle. His inspiration came from Pott's (1846) and Macalister's (1914) discussion of the Domari copula form in *ašt-*, where the participle affix is more clearly visible than in the Romani forms. Bloch's reconstruction goes as follows. For the 1SG he allows both an historical inflection ending from MIA *-ahmi* or a pronominal form in *me*. For the 2SG he suggests pronominal *tu*, basing his reconstruction on Domari 2SG perfective concord marker *-ur*, the cognate form having been lost in Romani according to him. For the 1PL Bloch proposes the concord marker in MIA *-mha* . The 2PL according to Bloch was the original present 2PL concord marker in *-tha* > *-l*.[9] The idea is that in Romani this 2PL form assimilated the 2SG, leading initially to a merger in the second person of singular and plural. The second person in *-l* is still preserved in the 2SG of the dialects of central Europe (Northwestern and Central dialects). According to Bloch the 2PL later shifted to *-an*, by analogy to the 3PL present concord marker of lexical verbs. The third-person markers are continuations of the plain participial markers. Bloch interprets the regularity of singular *-o-* (*-om, -or, os*) versus PL *-e-* (*-en, -es, -e*) in the Domari concord markers as support of his argument that the pronominal/person endings were attached to the participle.

Bloch's intuitive argument makes much more sense when pursued more consistently, however. What Bloch leaves entirely unanswered is the motivation

[8] A pronominal origin of the Domari 1SG copula concord marker had already been suggested by Turner (1926).

[9] Bloch (1928) relates this form to the Domari 2PL in *-s*, basing the sound shift on OIA *godhūma* Romani *giv* Domari *gesu* 'wheat'.

for the attachment of clitics to the participle, a necessary clue to their original identity. In Domari, the set of singular past-tense and concord markers 1SG *-o-m*, 2SG *-o-r*, 3SG *-o-s* is identical to the set of oblique pronominal clitics that serve as possessives (with nouns: *kury-om* 'my house', *kury-or* 'your house', *kury-os* 'his/her house'), while the identical consonantal forms also serve as object pronominal clitics (*lakedos-im* 'he saw me', *lakedos-ir* 'he saw you', *lakedos-is* 'he saw him'). This strengthens the argument in favour of their pronominal origin; in fact, it ought to trigger the search for their origin in oblique rather than nominative pronouns. The past-tense concord markers in both Romani and Domari are likely to have emerged as **possessives**, which followed the past participle in the construction **kerd-(j)o-me* 'done-by-me' leading to **kerdjom* 'I did'. Marking the agent through the possessive construction, following the generalisation of the past/passive participle in the past tense, led the way toward reanalysis of the past participle as an active personal construction, and to the emergence of ergativity in NIA; there is evidence that Proto-Romani participated in this development: the form of the 1SG pronoun *me* is based on an original oblique, and past participles are used actively, albeit only with intransitives (see Bubeník 2000).

The emergence of perfective personal concord in Proto-Romani seems to have taken the following path (table 6.8). The first stage (Proto-Romani I) saw the loss of the old past conjugation and the generalisation of past participles in its place. We may assume forms like **gata* plural **gate* 'gone' with subject agreement for intransitives, and **karda* 'done' with object agreement for transitives. In the second stage (Proto-Romani II), the transitive formation is adjusted to allow for the overt expression of the agent through an oblique enclitic pronoun (here: MIA oblique 3SG *se*), which is attached to the past participle by means of a jotated ezafe-type possessive particle:[10] **karda-jo-se* 'done-which-by-him = his doing', **karda-jo-me* 'done-which-by-me = my doing'. The transitive participle continues to agree with the object. (For the first two stages, close connections with the Northwestern NIA languages can still be assumed, hence the postulated phonological forms, which precede the developments medial *t* > *l*, grammatical final *a* > *o*, and internal *a* > *e*.)

The third stage (Proto-Romani III) involves the loss of ergativity and the generalisation of subject agreement. Once subject agreement is introduced into the transitive paradigm, the plural participle **kerd-e* can take over as the 3PL form. The original agentive marker in the transitive verb is incorporated into

[10] Ezafe (also: izafe) is the term employed in Near Eastern linguistics for three very distinct genitive-attributive constructions in Semitic, Turkic, and Iranian languages, respectively. The Proto-Romani construction alluded to here represents a structure that is akin to the Iranian ezafe, whereby a possessive particle, derived from a relative particle, appears between a noun and its postposed modifier: Persian *xune-ye man* 'my house'. In the more conservative Iranian languages, such as Kurmanji-Kurdish, the ezafe-particle still shows agreement with the head in gender and number: *mal-a min* 'my house', *mal-ên min* 'my houses'.

Table 6.8 *The renewal of perfective personal concord in Proto-Romani*

	Proto-Romani I
intransitive	**gata, -e* 'gone'
agreement:	subj
transitive	**karda* 'done'
agreement:	obj
	Proto-Romani II
intransitive	**gata, -e* 'gone'
agreement:	subj
transitive	**karda* 'done' / **karda-jo-se* 'done by him/her', **karda-jo-me* 'done by me', etc.
agreement:	obj
	Proto-Romani III
intransitive	**gelo, -e,* 'gone' **geljom* 'I went'
agreement:	subj
transitive	**kerdo, -e* 'done' **kerdjas* 's/he did', **kerdjom* 'I did', etc.
agreement:	subj
	Early Romani
intransitive	**gelo, -e,* 'he/they went', **geljom* 'I went'
agreement:	subj
transitive	**kerdjas* 's/he did', **kerdjom* 'I did', etc.
agreement:	subj

the perfective stem to form a new set of personal concord markers, which is gradually also copied into the intransitive paradigm, with the exception of the third persons. With transitives, the 3SG person-inflected form (original agentive) still co-exists with the transitive active participle. This stage continues in present-day Domari: *kard-a* 'he did', *kard-i* 'she did', but *kard-os-is* 's/he did it'. In Romani, traces of the active transitive participle are attested, alongside person-inflected forms, in the Prilep and Rumelian dialects: *hal-o* 'he ate', Rumelian *čind-o* 'he cut'. The transition to Early Romani sees the decline of the active participle with transitives, and the emergence of the original agentive form as the default 3SG, which is gradually extended to the intransitive verbs (the southeastern European dialects remaining more conservative).

As for the identity of the individual personal concord markers, we can account for all singular forms in Romani as well as Domari by deriving them from MIA oblique pronominal clitics: 1SG *-om*, 2SG *-al* (Domari *-or*), 3SG *-as* (Domari-*os*), from MIA *-me*, *-te* and *-se* respectively. The 3PL in both languages is a continuation of the adjectival past participle, which replaced an earlier agentive form

Table 6.9 *The development of perfective personal concord markers (*kard- > kerd- 'done') (arrow denotes sources and analogies)*

	Stage 1	Stage 2	
1SG	**karda-jo-me*	*kerdjom* (Domari *kardom*)	
2SG	**karda-jo-te*	*kerdjal* (Domari *kardor*)	
3SG	**karda-jo-se*	*kerdjas* (Domari *kardos-*)	
1PL	**karda-jo-ṇe*	**kerdjan* (Domari *karden*)	
2PL	**karda-jo-(pe/ve?)*	? (Domari *kardes* →*3PL)	
3PL	**karda-jo-(se)*	**kerdjas* (Domari **kardes*)	
	Stage 3	Stage 4	Stage 5 (partial)
1SG	*kerdjom*	*kerdjom*	*kerdjom*
2SG	*kerdjal*	*kerdjal*	*kerdjan* →2PL
3SG	*kerdjas*	*kerdjas*	*kerdjas*
1PL	**kerdjan*	*kerdjam* (→pronoun *amen*)	*kerdjam*
2PL	**kerdjan* →1PL	*kerdjan*	*kerdjan*
3PL	→participle *kerde* (Domari *karde*)	*kerde*	*kerde*

following the transition from object to subject agreement in transitives. The picture in the 1PL and 2PL remains somewhat more complicated. The Domari 1PL form *-en* can easily be traced back to the late MIA 1PL oblique pronominal clitic *ṇe*. It is possible that **-an* may have been the original Romani form too, which then underwent a change to *-am* under the influence of the 1PL pronoun *amen*. The original 1PL form **-an* could have infiltrated the 2PL, giving rise to what we now find as 2PL *-an*, which in Early Romani then began to spread to the 2SG (table 6.9).

This pattern bears similarities to the past-tense concord set of Kashmiri, where at least 1SG *-m*, 2SG *-th*, and 2PL *-wi* clearly originate in the respective late MIA oblique clitics *me*, *te*, and *bhe*. The similarities with the Kashmiri pattern (and that of other Dardic languages; cf. Grierson 1906: 60) provide perhaps the most outstanding innovation that Proto-Romani shares with the Dardic languages.[11] It is also the most conspicuous structural innovation shared by Romani and Domari. It is evident, then, that the renewal of the perfective conjugation in Romani is an areal feature dating back to its late subcontinental, or northwestern period, and that it is this areal development during the northwestern period, rather than a prolonged shared development in central India or after the emigration out of the subcontinent, that is responsible for the similarities between Romani and Domari.

There remains the question of the way by which oblique pronominal clitics were attached to the past participle. As hinted above, there is evidence to suggest a linking particle, a kind of possessive relativiser or ezafe attachment. An

[11] Domari is more conservative in retaining the clitics in their oblique function as well. Thus *ēr-os* 'it came to him', cf. Kashmiri *ā-s* (Masica 1991: 298).

important clue is provided by the pattern of number agreement represented by the vowels in the Domari set of personal concord markers (see above), pointed out by Bloch (1932a). Here too there are parallels with some of the Dardic languages described by Grierson (1906). In Shina the singular forms have a mediating vowel in *a/o* while the plural forms have *e*. In Gawar-Bati the singular forms have *e* and plurals have *a*. Kashmiri has preserved singular forms in *u* with variable plural forms.

Bloch's only source on Domari was Macalister's (1914) rather fragmented discussion, and so he was unable to detect that the set of oblique person clitics and personal concord markers is also case-sensitive. Thus we find, in their use as possessives, nominative *kury-os* 'his house', but oblique *kury-is-ma* 'in his house'; subject *lahed-or* 'you saw', object *lahedos-ir* 's/he saw you' (see Matras 1999c). This case sensitivity is independent of the case inflection of the noun to which the possessive marker attaches (nominative *kuri*, oblique *kurya-*, locative *kurya-ma*), and so it must derive from a nominal or pronominal entity that mediated between the noun and the possessive person marker.

It appears therefore that the oblique pronominal clitics that became the new set of perfective concord markers were linked to the past participle via a set of mediating possessive relativisers which inflected for number and case: **karda-(j)o-me* lit. 'done-which.NOM.SG-by.me' > *kerdjom* 'I did'. The same pattern will have applied to the linking of enclitic pronominal possessors in Domari: *kuri-o-me* lit. 'house-which.NOM.SG-of.me' > *kuryom* 'my house'. In the post-ergative stage, these mediating particles switched from object agreement to subject agreement, leading to the pattern now found in Domari.

The ezafe particle also allows a possible explanation for the origin of jotation in the Romani perfective forms. Jotation is always linked to the presence of a person marker, while adjectival participles remain unaffected by it. Its origin is therefore clearly connected to that of the person markers. Whether the yod component of the mediating particle can be related to the OIA relativiser in *y-* or not (in initial position the glide would have rendered *dž*), must be left unresolved; quite possibly we are dealing with a local jotation process, of which we find several in Proto-Romani morpheme boundaries. While jotation was lost, or never emerged, in Domari, its effect in Proto-Romani may have been to alter the quality of the vowel of the ezafe-like mediating particle to *-a-* in all positions except the salient 1SG (hence Romani *kerdjom* 'I did' but *kerdjal* 'you did', Domari *kardom* and *kardor*).

The internal consistency in the appearance of the 3SG person marker suggests that we are not dealing at all with the attachment to the past participle of the copula, but of oblique enclitic pronouns. From this, one must conclude that the present copula concord set and the past lexical concord set emerged together, as part of the same development by which the past participle was generalised and supplemented by endings of pronominal origin. The origin of both lexical past-tense verbs and the present copula in original participles explains the insertions in *-in-* which the two classes share. The Romani present copula is in fact a past copula, later turned present. It has lost its original past-tense function, which was compensated for at a later stage through the attachment of the remoteness marker *-as* to form an imperfective past (see below). A similar development is currently in progress in Domari, where the perfect form of the existential verb *h-* (OIA *bhav-*), *hromi* 'I have become', is gradually taking the place of the present-tense enclitic copula *homi* 'I am' (see Matras 1999c). But even in Romani there are still traces of the original function of the set in some dialects, namely in Southern Central and Southern Ukrainian varieties, where forms in *sjom/sl'om* may take either past-tense or present-tense meaning (cf. Boretzky 1999a: 238, Barannikov 1934: 99).

6.6 Tense–aspect–modality categories

6.6.1 *Inherited categories*

The basic or 'common' Romani system of TAM categories inherited from Early Romani consists of three dimensions: an aspectual dimension specifies the verb features for the category 'perfective:non-perfective', a temporal dimension distinguishes the categories 'remote:non-remote', and a modal dimension consists of the category of 'intentionality' (table 6.10).

Aspect is expressed as an extension to the verb stem. The extended stem, to which a marker deriving from the OIA participle in *-ta* is added, functions as a **perfective**: *ker-d-om* 'do-PFV-1SG = I did'. The function of the perfective is to denote a completed action or event. In actual distribution it usually refers to events in past time. As Masica (1991: 272) points out, perfective can be linked to past time even without tense specifications. Nonetheless, past time is not inherent in the perfective, which may also be used to indicate anticipated completion with future-time reference (*ži kaj ker-d-am* 'until where do-PFV-1PL = until we complete', lit. 'until we did'). I refer to the marker of participial origin that is added to the verb root in order to form the perfective aspect as a **perfective marker**. Most descriptions of Romani refer to the perfective as 'Preterite' (Sampson 1926, Boretzky 1993a, Igla 1996, Halwachs 1998) or "Aorist" (Paspati 1870, Hancock 1995a). Only Holzinger (1993, 1996) uses 'Perfective' and classifies the dimension that is expressed by the marker as an aspectual one.[12]

[12] My earlier use of 'resultative' (Matras 1994a: ch. 4) was intended to capture the same aspectual dimension. The term 'resultative' however is often interpreted as implying a resulting state that is observable, a meaning that is not contained in the Romani perfective. Johanson (1994: 260) indirectly even takes issue with the use of this label in connection with aspect, as does Friedman (1977). Furthermore, for the sake of consistency it appears beneficial to employ

Table 6.10 *Functional arrangement of TAM categories in Early Romani*

	non-perfective	perfective	intentional
non-remote	Present/Future	Past (Preterite, Aorist)	Subjunctive
remote	Imperfect	Pluperfect/Counterfactual	

It is important to note that the event encoded by the Romani perfective is viewed as one that has been completed prior to or at the contextual point of reference that is provided. The Romani perfective thus lacks the deictic anchoring function that characterises tenses. What is encoded by the perfective is rather a subjective perspective on the event as completed, in Johanson's (1971, 1994) terms a 'post-terminal' perspective. The fact that the event portrayed by the perfective is presented as a single whole, with no reference to its internal phases, seems to satisfy the criteria for perfective aspect as discussed and defined by Comrie (1976), Dahl (1985), Thieroff (1994, 1995) and others.

The absence of perfectivity renders an ongoing or 'intra-terminal' perspective (Johanson 1971, 1994) on events, which is characteristic of the Present and Imperfect. While Holzinger's (1993, 1996) functional interpretation of 'imperfective' as a non-completed event can be upheld, it seems more useful to simply regard 'imperfectivity' as the absence of 'perfectivity' (cf. discussion in Thieroff 1995).[13]

Actual **tense** in Romani is expressed by the agglutinative **remoteness** marker *-as/-a/-e/-s/-ys/-ahi*, through which an event is contextualised relative to 'O' (= the 'origo'; cf. Reichenbach 1947, Bühler 1934). More precisely, remoteness places the event outside the reach of 'O' by excluding overlap between 'R' (= the contextual point of reference) and 'O'. Recall that the perfective does not contextualise the event and includes no statement about the possible overlap or non-overlap between 'R' (the point of reference at which an event is regarded as completed, or as post-terminal) and 'O'. Conversely, remoteness makes no statement about the terminality of the event as far as its internal structure is concerned; in other words, it is aspectually neutral. But remoteness does not by necessity locate an event in time at a point of reference prior to 'O', either. Consider on the one hand the habitual-past reading of the Imperfect in *dža-v-as sako džes*

the term 'perfective' as used by Masica (1991: 262–79) in connection with aspect in other NIA languages, where it serves similar functions and draws historically on the same OIA structural resources, namely the participle affix in OIA *-ta*.

13 Here I must revise my earlier label 'progressive' (Matras 1994), on the grounds that the term is normally reserved for categories that add the feature of ongoing involved-ness into the various tenses (e.g. present-progressive, past-progressive, future-progressive). In Romani the only aspectual sibling of the Imperfect is the Present. The affinity between the two is sufficiently captured by the absence of 'perfectivity' in both. Since there is no non-perfective form that lacks progressivity, there is no point in introducing 'progressivity' as an additional category.

'go-1SG-REM every day = I used to go every day', the imperfective-past reading of the Imperfect in *džan-el-as* 'know-3SG-REM = s/he knew', the anterior-past reading of the Pluperfect in *phen-d-as-as aba* 'say-PFV-3SG-REM already = s/he had already said' (i.e. prior to a specified point of reference, which is located in the past); but on the other hand the conditional Imperfect in *te džan-av-as* 'COMP know-1SG-REM = if I knew', and the requestative reading of the Pluperfect in *mang-l-em-as* 'ask-PFV-1SG-REM = I should like to ask'. In the latter, remoteness only has indirect temporal significance – perhaps a future-oriented one – relative to 'O'. Its principal meaning of distance relates to the interactional context rather than to time. Distance here has the effect of neutralising the potentially manipulative significance of the request within the speech context. This effect is exploited for the purpose of politeness of expression. Contextual distance to real-world events is similarly achieved through the use of the conditional Imperfect in the preceding example, 'if I knew'. The combination of perfectivity and remoteness in the conditional renders the counterfactual or irrealis meaning in *te ker-d-om-as* 'COMP do-PFV-1SG-REM = if I had done'.

While some of these meanings of the remote category – in particular the polite-requestative meaning – are pragmatically derived, they share features that are semantically inherent to the category of remoteness. What remoteness generally achieves amounts to blocking the accessibility or contextual presence of an event, which satisfies the feature of 'distance' (Thieroff 1995; cf. also Johanson's (1971) 'tunc-idea'). The factual or non-conditional Imperfect in *džavas* 'I used to go' can be regarded as a non-perfective aspectual perspective on an event that is contextually inaccessible because its point of reference is located prior to 'O'. The conditional Imperfect in *te džanavas* 'if I knew' portrays a state that is likewise contextually inaccessible as it is purposefully detached from real-world factuality. The Pluperfect *phendasas* 'he had said' is a perfective perspective on an event whose outcome or result was relevant at a point 'R' prior to 'O', while the structurally related counterfactual (irrealis conditional or polite form) is a perfective whose validity is intentionally cancelled for reasons of factual non-achievability (irrealis conditional *te kerdomas* 'if I had done'), or as part of a discourse strategy (polite-requestative *manglemas* 'I should like to ask'). What all these usages have in common is the contextual neutralisation of the event – whether completed (perfective) or non-completed (non-perfective). It is the contextual cancellation of factual validity, and so contextual 'distance', that is the inherent meaning of the category 'remoteness'. Although not necessarily related to time, remoteness is a temporal rather than aspectual category since the statement it makes pertains not to the internal structure of the event, but to the placement of an event relative to the immediate context of speech.

While aspectual distinctions are carried out at the level of the verb stem, tense marking through *-as* is external to the stem, and is a comparatively late

Proto-Romani development. Bloch (1932b: 59) postulates **-asi* as the ancestral (Proto-Romani) form, from which present-day dialects of Romani derived both *-as/-ys/-s* and *-ahi* (the latter in the Southern Central dialects). The form suggests itself as a copula form, < OIA *asi-* (see Bloch 1932b). The addition of a copula as a remote tense marker is found elsewhere in Indo-Iranian, though usually the forms inflect for person and number. Romani agrees here too with Domari, which has a marker *-a* in identical function (Matras 1999c). While there is no evidence to support Hancock's (1995b: 33) impression that *-as(i)* was directly borrowed from the (literary) Persian 3SG enclitic copula *-ast*, Iranian does offer a possible model for imitation. Let us first establish that the Romani remoteness marker must have emerged in Proto-Romani after the complete restructuring of the perfective or past paradigm, since it appears in a position external to it. It is therefore quite possible that we are dealing with a development that arose in contact with Iranian, in-between the late Indian (Dardic) and European periods of Romani. A pattern that seems to match the requirements of a model for the Romani remoteness marker is found in Kurdish. Here, the perfect is formed through attachment of a uniform 3SG present copula form to the inflected (perfective) past tense: *ket-im-e* 'I have fallen', *ket-iy-e* 'you have fallen', *ket-in-e* 'we have fallen'. There is in addition a counterpart form *-a* which appears in conjunction with a subjunctive marker to form the irrealis, and which (depending on dialect) may be either internal or external to the person marker: *bi-ket-am-a* 'that I should fall' (cf. realis *bi-ket-im* 'that I fall'). The isolated function of the *-a* affix is related to semantic distance or remoteness. The Kurdish model is especially close to Domari: in addition to the remoteness marker in *-a*, Domari also has a contextualising affix in *-i* that attaches to the plain (non-perfective) stem to form the present tense, and to the perfective stem to form the perfect (*kardom* 'I did', *kardomi* 'I have done').

Much discussion has been devoted to the historical development of the Romani remoteness marker *-as(i)* (for a summary see Bubeník 1995: 6–10). Most attempts to explain the choice of the copula examined the Pluperfect/ Conditional and Imperfect separately, and failed to recognise remoteness as the semantic feature that unites the two. Neither the conditional meaning of the Pluperfect/ Counterfactual nor the progressive aspectual meaning conveyed by the Imperfect are inherent to *-as(i)*. The function of the Proto-Romani copula that attached to the person-inflected finite verb was to highlight a contextual point of reference against which the event encoded by the verb appeared as remote. It is likely to have been the past copula that was chosen for this purpose.

It does not seem justified to postulate an actual category of **modality** in Romani since there is, prototypically at least, only one form that is inherently non-indicative. Non-indicative uses of tense–aspect categories are achieved by placing them within the scope of a non-factual/conditional complementiser *te* (e.g. irrealis *te sikli-j-om-as* 'COMP learn-PFV-1SG-REM = if I had learned'). The only form that is inherently non-indicative is the Subjunctive (zero-marked in

Table 6.11 *Early Romani TAM categories and markers*

Past	Present/Future
(adjectival agreement with 3SG intransitives)	*-a*
Remote: Imperfect, Pluperfect/ Counterfactual	Subjunctive
-as(i)	*-ø*

the Early Romani system, as opposed to the indicative Present/Future in *-a*), whose reading is that of **intentionality**. The Subjunctive typically figures in linked clauses with non-factual semantics (purpose clauses, modal and manipulative complements), as well as in optative constructions.

6.6.2 *Innovations and restructuring*

Five formal TAM categories are inherited from Early Romani (see table 6.11): Past, Imperfect, Pluperfect/Counterfactual, Present/Future, and Subjunctive (the imperative consisting of the present stem in the singular, and the person-inflected subjunctive form in the plural).

The present section is devoted to the later developments that affected the TAM system in individual dialects. Some principal, representative developments are summarised in table 6.12.

The past tenses remain on the whole conservative. The perfective is the most conservative of all categories, having undergone little significant restructuring (disregarding of course changes to inflectional forms) in any of the dialects since the Early Romani period. The only noteworthy change is the gradual retreat of the 3SG form with adjectival agreement, or 'active participle', as in *gelo* 'he went' *geli* 'she went', *kerdjilo* 'it (M) was done' *kerdjili* 'it (F) was done', which appears to have been confined to intransitives already in Early Romani. It is gradually substituted through the person-inflected forms of transitive verbs: *geljas* 'he/she went', *kerdjilas* 'it (M/F) was done'. The distribution of the active participle is geographical: it has disappeared completely in the Northern and Northern Central dialects, but survives in the Balkans, and is facultative in the transition regions between the Balkans and central Europe. Active participles co-exist with person-inflected forms in Vlax and in most Southern Central dialects.[14]

The group of intransitive verbs that take the active participle is open to variation among dialects. Most common are verbs of motion and change of state. In some Vlax dialects, the opposition between active participle and person-inflected form has been functionalised, with the active participle denoting a

[14] Roman and other varieties of the Vend sub-group. The loss of participles in the northern varieties of the Southern Central dialects appears to be a recent development (cf. Elšík et al. 1999: 356).

Table 6.12 *TAM categories and markers in present-day Romani dialects (pfv = perfective, rem = remoteness, pres = present, subj = subjunctive, fut = future, perf = analytical perfect, cond = conditional particle, aktionsart = the origin of borrowed aktionsart markers, calq = calqued). Sources in brackets indicate marginal borrowing.*

	pfv	rem	pres	subj	fut	perf	cond	aktionsart
Arli	+	*s/h-ine*	*-a*	*-ø*	*ka-*		*bi*	(Slavic)
Sepečides	+	*-as*	*-a*	*-ø*	*ka-*	*ther-*		
Bugurdži	+	*-as*	*-a*	*-ø*	*ka-*		*bi*	(Slavic)
Prilep	+	*-as*	*-a/-ø*	*-ø*	*ka-*	*s-*		
Sofia Erli	+	*-as*	*-ø*		*ka-/-a*		(*bi*)	(Slavic)
Gurbet	+	*-ah*	*-ø*		*ka-*			
Keld/Lovari	+	*-as*	*-ø*		*-a*			
Romungro	+	*-ahi*	*-ø*		*-a*			calq/(Hungarian)
Roman	+	*-ahi*	*-ø*		*-a*			calq/German
Finnish	+	*-as*	*-ø*		*-a*			
N. Central	+	*-as*	*-ø*		*-a*		*bi*	Slavic
Polska Roma	+	*-ys*	*-ø*		*-a*		*by*	Slavic
Xaladitka	+	*-as*	*-a/-ø*	*-ø*	*l-*		*by*	Slavic
Latvian	+	*-as*	*-a/-ø*	*-ø*				Latv/Lith/Slavic
Welsh	+	*-as*	*-a/-ø*	*-ø*				
Sinti	+	*-s*	*-a/-ø*	*-ø*				calq/German

kind of evidentiality (see Matras 1995): *avilas* 'he arrived' (unmarked person-inflected form), *avilo* 'he arrived suddenly/unexpectedly/surprisingly' (evidential active participle). The primary function of these evidentials is to indicate surprise or unexpectedness at the discourse level, rather than to mark out the actual source of information as secondary (as is the case with prototypical inferentials, e.g. in Turkish). The use of Romani evidentials may however overlap with reported speech or inference (non-eyewitness) if the speaker wishes to disclaim responsibility for the possible effect that the presentation of information may have on the hearer, such as non-acceptance or disbelief by the hearer and subsequent weakening of the speaker's discursive authority.[15]

Structural stability is also characteristic of the remote tenses, the Imperfect and the Pluperfect/Counterfactual. Renewal of the remote tenses is found in Arli of Kosovo and Macedonia, as well as in the Croatian dialect, where the synthetic agglutinative markers are replaced by an analytic marker (these dialects lose final *-s* so that the long Present and Imperfect would be identical). This marker is *sine/hine*, the 3SG past tense of the copula, which follows the person-inflected tense form of the present for the imperfect – Arli *kerava sine* 'I was doing' – and

[15] There are similarities with the Balkan non-confirmative and inferential (cf. Friedman 1986, Aksu-Koç and Slobin 1986, Johanson 1971).

of the perfective for the pluperfect – Arli *kergjum sine* 'I had done'. A contact-induced innovation is the development of an analytic Perfect. In the dialect of the Sepečides, older speakers maintain a Perfect based on the possessive verb *ther-* 'to have' followed by the past participle, copying Greek perfect formation: *therava les dikhlo* 'I have seen him' (Cech and Heinschink 1999: 49). The construction is also common in the Ipeiros dialect: *therav kheldo* 'I have played', *teravas kheldo* 'I had played'. In some Arli varieties, a similar Perfect has emerged under Macedonian influence, linking the past participle with the auxiliary 'to be': *sinum tumenge vakerdo* 'I have told you'. For a small number of situative verbs, comparable constructions may denote the Present: Polska Roma and West Slovak Romani *me som bešto* 'I sit/am seated'.

By contrast to the past-tense categories, the original setup of the Present/Future/Subjunctive complex involving a long Present/Future form (i.e. no morphological marking of the future) and a short Subjunctive form has apparently not been preserved fully intact in any Romani variety. In the Balkan dialects Sepeči, Arli, and Bugurdži the morphological opposition between Present and Subjunctive is maintained, but here a further differentiation is introduced into the system through the emergence of an analytic future in *ka*. A transitional system is found in a number of dialects (Welsh, Latvian, Xaladitka, Prilep, some Sinti varieties). Here the short, Subjunctive forms infiltrate the Present indicative, leading to a gradual collapse of the subjunctive/indicative opposition. In some dialects a similar development has led to the specialisation of the original Present/Future long form in *-a* for modal/future use, while the short forms are generalised for the Present indicative. This is most obvious in a geographical cluster of central-eastern European dialects, comprising the Vlax and Central dialects as well as the adjoining Polska Roma variety. In Welsh Romani the long forms are optional in the Present, but obligatory in the Future. In Erli, the long forms appear sporadically in a confirmative-declarative function (Boretzky 1998a: 141). Likewise the long forms in Northern Vlax, which generally denote the future, may have present-tense declarative-confirmative meaning (*kamasa* 'we do indeed want!'). Hancock (1995a: 142) has referred to this as an 'oratorical present', due to its association with ceremonial speech.

The emergence of an analytic Future adds a further dimension to the changes in the Present/Future/Subjunctive setup. The feature is most conspicuous in the Balkans, where it is best represented by the particle *ka/kam*, a contracted form of *kam-* 'to want', and more marginally by *ma-* from *mang-* 'to want, demand'. Both are calques on a pan-Balkan future particle derived from the verb 'to want' (Greek *tha*, Balkan Slavic **htjě*, Romanian *o*, etc.). In Romani this may be considered a late Balkanism, one that is not exhibited by varieties of the language that are spoken outside the southern Balkans, while on the other hand it is adopted by Vlax dialects that are by comparison recent arrivals in the region (Gurbet and Džambazi, Serbian Kalderaš, Agia Varvara).While in Kalderaš the Northern Vlax long future in *-a* alternates with the more recently adopted Balkan-type analytic *ka*, the special case of Agia Varvara shows the takeover of the future through *ka* but retention of *-a* in the conditional. An auxiliary-based analytical future is known from the North Russian (Xaladitka) and Ukrainian dialects, where the verb *l-* 'to take' and *av-* 'to come' act as auxiliaries followed by the subjunctive, introduced by the non-factual complementiser *te*. In most Balkan dialects, *ka* also combines with the imperfect to form a conditional mood.

The interplay between the formation of the categories Present, Subjunctive, Future and modal functions such as declarative and conditional, are an indication of the universal affinity between the Future and modal categories (cf. Comrie 1989). The future is a recent category in the language. If it is not left unexpressed altogether, it may draw on three possible resources: it can derive from a kind of 'super-indicative', i.e. a specialisation of the original Present indicative for statements that demand increased confirmation since their factual basis is weak. Closely related readings of the same structure are the declarative and prospective conditional. A second source for the future is modal intentionality, expressed by the modal verb 'to want', from which the future particle derives. The final option is a lexical-aspectual modification through the use of an auxiliary verb. The diversity in the formation of the future and the entire domain of modality might be expected on structural grounds once we assume that a Future category was missing from the Early Romani system. But it is at the same time indicative of the volatility of modal categories: where a solid factual basis for an assertion is missing, speakers are inclined to devise new strategies to reinforce their assertive authority. This is confirmed by the borrowability of the Slavic conditional markers *bi/by*, as well as the interrogative (in Sliven also quotative) *li* (see also section 8.2.2).

Contact developments are also responsible for aktionsart marking in Romani. There are two types of aktionsart marking: that typical of verbs in German and Hungarian, where verb stems can be combined with semi-bound so-called verbal particles, and the verb-derivational system of Slavic languages, Latvian, and Greek. The Slavic system is often termed 'aspect' though it seems more suitable to consider it as a category in its own right, termed 'Slavic aspect' following Dahl (1985; cf. also Thieroff 1994, 1995). The first type of aktionsart appears in Romani dialects in intensive contact with German and Hungarian, namely Sinti and Roman (German), and Romungro (Hungarian). Igla (1992) points out that although the replication of verbal aktionsart must be viewed in the context of overall grammatical and lexical borrowing (from German into Sinti), material borrowing of verb roots and of verbal particles as well as calquing of verbal particles may all occur independently of one another. Thus entire German aktionsart-marked verbs may be replicated (*me ruferau an* 'I call', German *ich rufe an*), the particle can be replicated with inherited verbs (*joj karas an* 'she called', German *sie rief an*), a replicated verb may be accompanied by a calqued particle (*štrajtaras tele* 'disputed', German *stritt [<streit-] ab*), or the entire verb may be calqued (*kerau pre* 'I open', German *[ich] mache auf*). In Roman, calqued or metatypised particles tend to be separable from the verb: *tel pisin-* 'to sign' (*tel* 'under'), German *unterschreiben*, *ar cid-* 'take off' (*ar* 'out'), German *ausziehen* (but also *aun asav* 'to laugh at', dialectal German *aun*, German *anlachen*). Aktionsart modifications that are inseparable from the verb are on the other hand all replications of German material: *cadža-* 'to dissolve (intr.)', German *zergehen* (*zer-*), *camper-* 'to merge', German *zusammenfallen* (dialectal *zsamma-*) (see Halwachs 1998). Calquing based on the Hungarian model characterises the overwhelming majority of verbal particles employed in Romungro, with only isolated occurrences of aktionsart prefixes of Hungarian origin (Elšík at al. 1999: 373).

In Latvian Romani, aktionsart marking is inherited from the forerunner dialect, which emerged in contact with Polish. But the system is further enriched through borrowings of Lithuanian and Latvian aktionsart prefixes: *iedža-* 'to go in', Latvian *ieiet*, *piedža-* 'to approach', Latvian *pieiet* (Mānušs 1997). In Agia Varvara Vlax there is some borrowing of Greek aktionsart prefixes into the language: *ksanadikh-* 'to see again' (Igla 1996). The wholesale borrowing of the Slavic aktionsart prefix system (or Slavic aspect) is characteristic of the Northern Central and Northeastern dialects of Romani, in contact with western and eastern Slavic languages: Xaladitka (North Russian Romani) *dava* 'I give', *dodava* 'I add', *obdava* 'I embrace', *otdava* 'I confiscate', *piridava* 'I hand over', *podava* 'I obtain', *rozdava* 'I hand out', *vydava* 'I give away', etc. But there is also some infiltration of Slavic aktionsart markers as derivational prefixes into Balkan dialects of Romani (see also section 8.2.2).

6.7 Non-finite forms

Non-finite verbal forms in Romani are forms that are not marked for tense or person concord. They can express either states (perfective participles), or actions and events that are linked to other actions and events (converbs). The class of converbs is clearly less prominent in Romani, as clause-linking devices in most dialects rely primarily on finite constructions.

The most dominant class of non-finite forms in Romani – in terms of functional distribution and frequency, diachronic stability, and distribution among the dialects – are the participles, which are marked for perfective:non-perfective aspect. The most frequently encountered is the **perfective participle** (usually referred to as the 'past participle', in German-language descriptions also as the 'passive participle'). The perfective participle consists of a perfective extension to the verb root, with adjectival inflection. The perfective extensions are generally those employed in the formation of the active, finite perfective verb form, namely the non-jotated form *-d-/-l-/-t-*: *ker-d-* 'done', with adjectival inflection *-o* (M), *-i* (F), *-e* (PL). Other perfective affixes tend to be specialised: *-il-* is used with intransitive derivations (*sikh-il-* 'learned') as well as occasionally with intransitive roots, *-nd-* with psych verbs in *-a* (*dara-nd-* 'feared'), *-in-* for monoconsonantal verbs and their compounds (*d-in-* 'given', *tra-d-in-* 'driven'). With European loans, perfective participle markers in *-ime(n)/-ome(n)/-ame(n)* are employed, deriving from the Greek past participle in *-Vmen-*. This athematic participle is often declinable, and is assigned to the class of athematic masculines in *-o*: *pis-ime/pis-im-o* 'written'. There are cases of extension of the athematic participle to inherited vocabulary: Finnish Romani *džān-imen* 'known'.

Perfective participles of transitive verbs usually express the state of the semantic patient, and show morphological agreement with the patient. Default agreement is found in the case of the participles employed in the formation of the analytic perfect tense in some of the Balkan dialects (see above). Intransitive participles with subject agreement appear especially with verbs denoting motion and change of state. A compound present tense involving the copula and the intransitive perfective participle with subject agreement (*ov si beš-t-o* 'he is sitting') is found in a variety of dialects and appears to represent an older formation, but it is restricted to a small number of verbs of motion and change of state. The perfective participle serves as the third-person perfective form for such verbs in the southeastern dialects (*av-il-o* 'he has arrived'; see above), where in effect it occupies a position within the paradigm of finite verbs.

The other participle in Romani is the **gerund**. There are two gerundial forms. The inflected form *-nd-/-ind-* continues an OIA/MIA present participle, and has a non-perfective meaning. The non-inflected gerund *-i* lacks the inherent non-perfective reading. The origin of the gerund in *-i* is not obvious, but it could be related to the 3SG finite ending in *-i* found with loan verbs, which in all likelihood derives from the Greek 3SG present-tense ending. The two are sometimes combined into an integrated form (Bugurdži-*indoj*, Northeastern *-induj*) or assimilated into the adverbial derivation (Vlax *-indes*). The inherited form *-and-/-ind-* is often assimilated into the athematic nominal inflection class for masculines in *-o(s)*, indicating in all likelihood adaptation to Greek gerunds. Gerunds in *-i* are preserved in the Northeastern dialects (North Russian, Latvian) and in the eastern Balkans (Sepeči, Rumelian); they co-exist with the inherited forms in *-indo(s)*. No gerunds at all are attested in Welsh Romani and Sinti.

The gerund is a converb and is used to link a background predication with a foreground predication. Its principal semantic meanings are simultaneity or cause: Bugurdži *gele natele bašal-indoj* 'they descended, playing music' (Boretzky 1993a: 82), Sepeči *phir-indos khere džasas* 'we went home on foot (lit. walking)' (Cech and Heinschink 1999: 130), North Russian Romani *na sov-i* 'not having slept' (Wentzel 1980: 130). In Sepeči and Rumelian, a reduplicated form of the later gerund *-i* appears, based on the Turkish model of reduplicated converbs in *-e*. It expresses intensity of background action, often with a reading of cause or means: *pučh-i pučh-i arakhlas amaro kher* 'having asked a lot, he found our house', *rov-i rov-i šuvlilom* 'having cried a lot, I am swollen' (Cech and Heinschink 1999: 131).

Romani does not have an inherited infinitive, although, as Boretzky (1996b: 9–10) points out, there is restricted use of **nominalisers** in functions that correspond to the nominal use of infinitives in other languages, most notably in the modal dative representing goal: Bugurdži *kada pani nane pimnaske* 'this water is not for drinking', Sinti *koles hi či phenepaske* 'he has nothing to say' (cf. colloquial German *zum Sagen*). It is noteworthy however that constructions of this kind are not frequent in Romani, and indeed, in the case of the more overt modality in the Sinti example, where predications are linked, other Romani dialects draw on finite constructions: Lovari *kodoles naj khanči te phenel* 'this one has nothing to say'.

The reduction of the infinitive in modal constructions may have begun already through contact with Iranian languages. Its complete loss would have resulted later from contact with Greek and the overall reduction of the infinitive in the Balkan languages (see also chapter 8). What has been referred to as the **'new infinitive'** in Romani (Boretzky 1996b) involves the reduction of person agreement in the finite complement clause of modal constructions, and the generalisation instead of just one single form, based on a form that is selected from the present paradigm. The actual solutions adopted by the individual dialects differ, and it is obvious that we are dealing with a recent development, one that has emerged in dialects outside the Balkans, through contact with languages that rely on infinitives in same-subject modal constructions. Thus, we are dealing with a de-balkanisation effect (see Matras 2000b) on the western-central European dialects.

The so-called new infinitival form is usually introduced by the non-factual complementiser *te*: *me kam-av te šun-el*. The most common form on which the new infinitive is based is the 3SG short (subjunctive) present marker *-el*, which is used as a non-finite form in a region comprising Sinti, Bohemian Romani, Polska Roma, Bergitka Roma, Roman, Dolenjski, West Slovak Romani, and the western dialects of East Slovak Romani. The boundaries of this isogloss are defined by the neighbouring dialects of the North Russian Roma to the north, Welsh Romani to the west, and Piedmontese Sinti to the south, which do not show new infinitives. Bordering on the 3SG-infinitive region we find the generalisation of the 2PL/3PL as an infinitive: the eastern dialects of East Slovak Romani, Romungro, and partly Hungarian Lovari. An exclusively infinitival form appears in the Southeast Ukrainian variety, based on the 2SG/3SG short present or subjunctive without the consonantal ending (*sove* 'to sleep').

An outstanding case of a new infinitive is found in the Dolenjski dialect of Slovenia and Istria (Cech and Heinschink 2001). Here too, the form selected for the infinitive is that of the 3SG, which in this dialect is normally the Greek-derived *-i*, but in modal constructions it is not generally introduced by the complementiser *te*: *me ladžu vaker-i* 'I am ashamed to say'. There are however traces in the Dolenjski dialect of both the older 3SG in *-el* (*morinave lake del love* 'I had to give her money') and of the complementiser in same-subject modal constructions (*na tromi te šuni* 'he may not hear'), indicating that the form in *-i* without a complementiser is a recent innovation, one that is possibly reinforced by the form of the infinitive in *-iti* in the contact languages Croatian and Slovene. Sinti dialects also show a tendency to use infinitives without the complementiser: *ko haievas gar bašavel* 'he didn't know how to play music', alongside *kamau gar te pharel* 'I don't want to swap' (Holzinger 1993: 169). A further extreme case of an infinitive is the use of the plain stem of the verb in modern Welsh Romani as documented by Tipler (1957): *drumišadas man te pi* 'he dared me to drink'.

There is some indication that the spread of the new infinitive within individual dialects follows certain functional constraints. Holzinger (1993: 169) notes that the complementiser *te* is missing with topicalised complements and serialisation: *pharel kamau gar!* 'I don't want to swap (lit. to swap I don't want)', *miri daj džal mangel* 'my mother goes begging'. In older sources of Sinti, a person split appears, with third persons more likely to show infinitives than first persons: *akaja čai na džanel džala komi* 'this girl cannot yet walk', but *kamava te hunava* 'I want to hear' (from Rüdiger 1782; see Matras 1999a: 99). Bohemian Romani as described by Puchmayer (1821) appears to favour infinitives in less integrated clauses, such as serialisation (*džava te sovel* 'I am going to sleep') or manipulation (*de mange te pijel!* 'give me (something) to drink!'), while straightforward modality does not always trigger infinitives (*me les kamav te mukav te terd'ol* 'I want to leave it standing').

Further uses of the new infinitive include quasi-nominalisation of the verb – Northern Central *te vakerel hi rup, te na vakerel somnakaj* 'to talk is silver, not to talk is gold' (Boretzky 1996b: 19), Roman *lačho nana, ham te hal sina* 'it was not good, but it was food (=something to eat)' (Wogg and Halwachs 1998: 49) – and its use as a converb of simultaneity: West Slovak Romani *pale dikhle oda moxtore te džal tele pan'eha* 'again they saw those chests drifting down the river' (von Sowa 1887: 165).

6.8 Modal expressions

Basic modals of ability, necessity and volition are prone to renewal through both internal grammaticalisation processes and contact. Fluctuation is found between person-inflected and impersonal forms (cf. Boretzky 1996c). For Early Romani it is possible to reconstruct a system of modals that relied primarily on impersonal forms. For ability, the impersonal form **ašti* 'can', in all likelihood a conservative copula form, can be reconstructed on the basis of the forms *ašti* in Sofia Erli, *šti* in Italian Xoraxane, *aešte* in Zargari, and *astis* in Welsh Romani, and the negative form *našti* 'cannot' from **na-ašti*, which is continued in most dialects. An Early Romani variant of *našti* is *naštik/naštig*, preserved in Sinti and various Central and Vlax dialects. Alongside **ašti*, Early Romani must have had another impersonal form **šaj* 'can', which appears to be a Persian borrowing into later stages of Proto-Romani (*šāje/šājad*). This became the more widespread form in most present-day dialects. There is no trace of a person-inflected Indic form expressing ability (cf. Domari *sak-* 'to be able to'). For volition, Early Romani possibly used *kam-* 'to want < to love', the only person-inflected form among the basic modal expressions. The Early Romani form for necessity must have been based on the copula *si* followed by the non-factual complementiser *te*, a construction that is continued in many of the dialects (*si-te*). Most forms that continue the construction are impersonal, but North-western *humte/hunte* and Iberian *chomte* suggest that personal forms may have been used in some dialects (cf. *hum* 'I am'; cf. Welsh Romani *som te* 'I must', Polska Roma *sam te* 'we must').

The most stable of the modal expressions is *kam-* 'to want', which is continued in most dialects, while in the Balkans it is often replaced by another person-inflected form *mang-* 'to want' < 'to demand'. Volition thus constitutes a conservative category, showing consistent use of person-inflected forms and little borrowing. Also relatively stable is the expression of negative ability *našti*. Since ability itself is more volatile, individual dialects often show suppletion in the negation of ability, a state which already existed in Early Romani *šaj* 'can' vs. *našti* 'cannot'. In German Sinti and French Manuš, *našti* is reinterpreted as an affirmative marker of ability 'can'. The negative form is then renewed on the basis of the general negator: *našti gar* (but Piedmontese Sinti *stik/natik*). Negative ability usually remains uninflected, an exception being Welsh Romani *našti-v* 'I cannot'.

Positive ability is more prone to renewal. New person-inflected modal verbs of ability that are based on inherited verbs include Sinti *hajev-* 'to be able to' < 'to know (how to)' < 'to understand', and Sepeči, some Central as well as some Lovari varieties *džan-/žan-* 'to be able to' < 'to know'. Boretzky (1996c) notes a tendency toward a functional differentiation between an immediate ability, usually expressed by *šaj*, and potential ability, for which renewed or borrowed categories are used. Borrowings in the domain of ability include Slavic *možin-/mogin-* and impersonal *može* in Northeastern and Balkan dialects, Hungarian *bir-* in Central dialects and Lovari, and Greek *bor-* in Vlax and Arli dialects of Greece (see also section 8.2.2). The greatest extent of renewal and variation among the dialects is found in the domain of necessity. The original Early Romani *si te* is grammaticalised as a particle *iste* in Roman, and *hunte/humte* in Northwestern dialects (German Sinti, Finnish) also appearing as an interdialectal borrowing in neighbouring Bohemian Romani. Central dialects show grammaticalisation of an impersonal, reflexive form of *kam-* 'to want' to *kampel/pekamel*. There is, alongside these developments, extensive borrowing of both person-inflected and impersonal modals, such as *trob-/treb-*, *mora* (Slavic), *mus-/musa-/mušin-* (German; also Hungarian impersonal *musaj*), *mus-* (English), *prep-* (Greek), *lazim-*, *medžbur-* (Turkish), and more (see section 8.2.2). Impersonal modals are often followed by *-i* (*lazim-i*, *mus-i*, *madžbur-i*), which could represent the Greek-derived 3SG present person concord marker, borrowed into Early Romani with some loans and generalised in some dialects with loan verbs.

7 Syntactic typology

7.1 The noun phrase

The two most outstanding features of the Romani noun phrase from an Indo-Aryan viewpoint are the prepositioning of adpositions, and the presence of a definite article. The few exceptions are late and selective developments: some dialects have some postpositions, and some dialects have lost definite and indefinite articles. The first slot within the noun phrase is reserved for prepositions (table 7.1). Prepositions are not always kept distinct morphologically from location adverbs (cf. Sepeči *opral* 'up, over, above'; but Lovari preposition *opral* 'above, over' and adverb *opre* 'up'), but their position leaves no room for ambiguity between the two (*opral o phuv* 'above the ground' but *gelom opral* 'I went up'). A series of prepositions incorporate the definite article: *ande jekh them* 'in a country', *and-o them* 'in the country'. There is, as a result, some potential for referential ambiguity: *ande thema* 'in countries', and *and-e thema* 'in the countries'.

The next slot in the noun phrase layout is reserved for determiners, which constitute a more complicated class. The more straightforward determiners assign definiteness and are incompatible with one another: demonstratives, interrogatives, possessive adjectives, and usually also definite articles. In Greek Vlax, however, it is possible for demonstratives to precede and combine with a definite article, under Greek influence: *kadava o rom* 'this man' (cf. Igla 1996). The genitive adnominal essentially also belongs to the same slot, as it tends to precede the noun, acts as a determiner, and is incompatible with the other determiners such as definite articles or demonstratives (see Koptjevskaja-Tamm 2000: 130–2).

Problematic is the status of the indefinite article. It is not compatible with either the demonstrative, the possessive, or the interrogative. But Koptjevskaja-Tamm (2000: 132–3) refers to examples from various dialects of compatibility of the genitive adnominal with the indefinite article:

(1) jek Petritesko čavo
INDEF Peter.M.GEN son
'a son of Peter's'

Table 7.1 *Linear layout of the noun phrase: principal slots*

[preposition] + [determiner] + [quantifier] + [adjective] + noun + [options]

The natural functional explanation which Koptjevskaja-Tamm offers is that, when there are several referents belonging to the category described by the genitive adnominal, then the anchoring genitive is not sufficient for identifying a unique referent for the head noun. As Koptjevskaja-Tamm points out, there are also examples of compatibility of the definite and indefinite article:

(2) o jekh phral (Lovari; Gjerde 1994: 24)
ART INDEF brother
'one of the brothers'

The genitive adnominal is perhaps the most prominent morphosyntactic representative of the Indo-Aryan legacy in Romani. The preposed genitive is retained despite the shift to VO order in the verb phrase, making Romani a typological hybrid in Greenbergian terms (cf. Greenberg 1966). There are, however, tendencies in the language to achieve consistency, and the genitive appears to enjoy considerable freedom in occupying the 'option' slot that is postposed to the noun. There are some varieties in which this is the preferred order for compounds (Lovari *kher le dilengo* lit. 'house-of-the-crazy = mental institute') in 'non-anchoring' function (cf. Koptjevskaja-Tamm 2000). These kinds of genitive adnominals are compatible with definite articles (*o kher le dilengo* 'the mental institute').

The postnominal 'option' slot deserves this designation due to the fact that adnominals that are accommodated here are often exempt from the constraints that apply to them in their usual, prenominal slot. Demonstratives are generally incompatible with definite articles. But when a demonstrative is postposed, then the noun it follows must be accompanied by a definite article: Kalderaš Vlax *o rom kadava* 'this man'. Moreover, postposed demonstratives as well as postposed adjectives quite often carry nominal, rather than attributive, case agreement, reinforcing the impression that they serve as appositions: Kalderaš *e gažeskə kodoleskə* 'for that man' (Boretzky 1994: 55). Igla (1996: 166) cites, from Agia Varvara Vlax, reduplication of the definite article with postposed adjectives, but not with postposed possessives: *i čhej i bari* 'the big girl', *o dad tumaro* 'your father'.

While in some varieties such usages may be frequent, it seems that on the whole they are by far outnumbered by the conventional prenominal positioning of all attributes. Discourse data provide some insights into the communicative triggers behind the placement of attributive elements in the postnominal 'option' slot:

(3) muj i phuri, ačhile kadla rakle čore
died.F ART old.FEM remained.PL these boys poor.PL
(Bugurdži; Boretzky 1993: 87)
'the old woman died, these poor boys remained'

(4) ande jekh kesave cikno kheroro, žanes, kheroro
in INDEF such little house know.2SG house
cikno polski, tu žanes sar (Lovari)
small Polish you know.2SG how
'in such a small house, you know, a small Polish house, you know what kind'

In (3) the adjective *čore* 'poor' is exposed as an afterthought, evaluating the state of affairs referred to in the actual statement, i.e. the fact that the boys remained after the death of the old woman makes them qualify as 'poor'. In (4), the noun and its adjective *cikno* are repeated in order to add a further characterisation, *polski* 'Polish', which here too can be argued to be evaluative, as it is expected to trigger an association on the part of the listener (since the listener is familiar with Polish houses, he will now understand the speaker's initial attempt to describe the house). The postnominal 'option' position is therefore a pragmatic position for most attributives, and a lexicalised position for genitives in some dialects. Individual dialects also show formal postnominal positions within the noun phrase, which are occupied either by calques (postposed demonstratives and adpositions) or by direct borrowings (postposed focus particles, such as Turkish-derived *da*).

7.2 Constituent order in the verb phrase

There is a dominant pattern of word order in Romani which may be regarded as the 'conservative type' (cf. Boretzky 1996d). Exceptions to the pattern are usually confined to individual dialects or regions, and are rather recent innovations, which usually co-exist with the older conservative formations. In the conservative word-order type, the verb precedes the object (VO). Object fronting is a pragmatic option that is used to focus the object, usually in contrastive constructions. This also holds for pronominal objects. Pronominal direct objects precede pronominal indirect objects, exceptions being again contrastive constructions. The copula is more likely than lexical verbs to appear in final position. The position of the subject alternates between SV and VS. Word-order rules are essentially the same in main and subordinate clauses. In clauses that are introduced by *te* (non-factual subordinations, such as purpose clauses, modal complements, and conditional clauses), the verb immediately follows the conjunction *te*. There is no distinctive word order in interrogative clauses.

This 'conservative' word-order pattern is retained in the southeastern European dialects, as well as in Welsh Romani, while in other regions dialects may undergo partial changes. Under Slavic influence, some dialects show a tendency to place the object, and especially the pronominal object, before the verb. In *te*-clauses, the verb often occupies the final sentence position. Sinti varieties show various degrees of convergence with German word-order rules. In the most extreme cases, the German distinction between main clause (verb in second position), subordinate clause (verb in final position), and interogative clause (verb in initial position) is adopted consistently. An oddity is the Vend dialect group, where, presumably under the influence of dialectal Hungarian, the verb and especially the copula frequently appear in final position. According to Wogg and Halwachs (1998: 60), postposed subjects are rare in Roman, exceptions being right-dislocated subjects.[1] Verb-final order also appears in the Romani dialects of Azerbaijan (Windfuhr 1970),[2] and there is some evidence of tendencies toward verb-final order in Romani dialects of Turkey (Bakker 2001).

There is general agreement that, at least in regard to frequency of occurrence, Romani does not have a dominant order of either SV or VS (see Grumet 1986: 147, Holzinger 1993: 262).[3] Flexible word-order rules pose a theoretical challenge to descriptive work in linguistics. The tendency in modern studies on Romani is to interpret word-order alternation in discourse-pragmatic terms, such as topic accessibility, theme/rheme structure, propositional cohesion and mapping of speaker–hearer processing tasks (cf. Holzinger 1992, 1993: 259ff., Matras 1994a: 115ff., 1995b, Boretzky 1996a, 1998a, Igla 1996: 147ff., Wogg and Halwachs 1998).

SV order is usually interpreted as focused or topicalised, expressing contrast or surprise:

(5) murš hine (Arli; Boretzky 1996a: 26)
man was
'it was a boy' (about a new-born baby)

(6) vov avilo, ala in avili mi dej
he came.M but NEG came.F my.F mother
(Agia Varvara Vlax; Igla 1996: 149)
'he arrived, but my mother did not arrive'

For Sepeči, Cech and Heinschink (1999: 144) suggest that tendencies towards VS in temporal adverbial clauses, as in (7), may be overridden when S is focused, resulting in SV, as in (8):

1 *na džanlahi smirom te del, oda* 'he couldn't give peace, him'.

2 For Romano in Iran as described by Djonedi (1996), however, sentential data are scarce, and contradictory. Thus we find *čilālo mániš si* 'he is a bad man', *pāro si* 'it is heavy', but *tevro si del* 'God is mighty'.

3 Boretzky (1998a:150) on the other hand reports that SV is almost twice as common in Erli texts as VS, but he derives this from the frequent occurrence of quoted speech (*A says:* ..) in the corpus.

(7) kana isine o roma ko balanipe
when was ART Rom.PL in Greece
'when the Rom were in Greece'

(8) kana čhaj isinomas
when girl was.1SG
'when I was a young girl . . . '

More problematic is the function of VS. Holzinger (1993: 259–88) argues for an overall dichotomy in the Sinti dialect between VS order as an expression of **continuity**, and SV as an expression of **discontinuity**. Discontinuity may pertain either to the sequencing of actions, or to the introduction of a new subject/topic. Consider the following Sinti excerpt (Holzinger 1993: 274):

(9) a. čivel i romni i matrele dre, mas dre und kova dre
put.3SG ART woman ART potatoes in meat in and that in
'the woman puts in the potatoes, meat and that'
b. čiveli pre te gerel
put.3SG.F up COMP cook.3SG
'she places it to cook'
c. I romni lures, lures
ART woman slowly slowly
'the woman waits, waits'
d. vajas o rom khere
came.3SG ART man home
'the man came home'

Sinti has several means of expressing the postverbal subject. Apart from demonstratives, pronouns, full NPs, and zero-anaphora, which are present in all Romani dialects, it also has subject clitics as well as subject affixes that attach directly to the verb. The VS constructions in (9a–b) indicate that the events are embedded into a closely integrated sequence. The 'downgrading' of S between segments (a) and (b) from a full noun to a gender affix correlates with the increase in topic continuity. Holzinger interprets the foregrounding of S in (c) as an 'artificial thematic break', intended to trigger a dramatic effect towards a turning point in the story. Here, then, discontinuity pertains to the discourse-presentational level rather than to the identity of subject topics.

Holzinger does not comment on the VS construction in (9d), which accompanies, in fact, the introduction of a new subject. One way to account for VS here is to interpret it as a **connective** device, which serves to integrate the new proposition into the immediately preceding, established context (see Matras 1994a, 1995b). The use of connective VS order in (d) results in a consecutive interpretation of the relation between the preceding event and the one that follows, i.e. the arrival of the man is portrayed as a conclusion to the woman's waiting.

Consecutive word order might be viewed as one of the principal functions of VS order in Romani. Consider the following Lovari excerpt (Matras 1994a: 117):

(10) a. Vi mure papos avile line anda o
also my.OBL grandfather.OBL came.3PL took.3PL from ART
kher, marde les.
house beat.3PL him.OBL
'They came and picked up my grandfather too, they beat him.'

b. Taj gelas lesko káko taj počindas vareso bare
and went.3SG his uncle and paid.3SG something big.PL
bare love taj kindas les avri.
big.PL money and bought him out
'And (so) his uncle went and paid a lot of money and bought him free.'

c. Taj muri mami garádžulas ande veša mure
and my grandmother hid.3SG.REM in woods my.OBL
dadesa.
father. INSTR
'And my grandmother was hiding in the woods with my father.'

In (10b) we have a switch of subjects, which is accompanied nonetheless by 'connective' VS. The event portrayed in (b) is presented as the outcome of the preceding state of affairs. Again we see that connective VS at the level of proposition integration may outweigh discontinuity at the level of individual subject topics. Note that in (c), once again with a switch of subjects, the order is SV. Here, a new perspective is being established: the event portrayed in (c) coincides with that of the preceding segment in time, and is not a result or outcome. On this basis it is possible to define VS as connective-integrative, and SV as perspective-establishing (see Matras 1995b).

These discourse-pragmatic functions allow us to make some general predictions about the occurrences of SV and VS, which relativise the impression of free or extremely flexible word-order rules. Arguably, there are also additional factors that play a role in the choice of word order, most notably the choice of particular **types of predicates and subjects**. Igla (1996: 153) understands predictability in regard to word order as constraints on variation, pertaining especially to types of subjects. She suggests that VS is the unmarked word order when the subject is inanimate, non-determined, and a non-agent, the variant SV being restricted with such subjects to a (contrastive) emphasis of S. On the other hand, maximum variation is found with subjects that are animate, determined, and which figure as agents. The constraints on variability are thus understood as a continuum (non-agentive animate subjects figuring in between, and so on). Predicates that are more likely to trigger VS are those involved in presentative constructions, such as existentials and some verbs of motion, particularly those expressing arrival. Igla (1996: 151) lists in this connection statements about time and nature (*nakhlas ekh berš* 'a year passed', *del buršun* 'it is raining').

There are also some **formal constraints** on the order of S and V. Non-factual complement clauses and conditional clauses, both introduced by *te*, show an overwhelming, if not absolute, tendency toward VS order. Functional considerations are not out of place here either, however. The rule might be regarded as a formalisation of the principle of contextual embedding of the predication through VS. This rule is applied to non-indicative predications which have no independent truth-value of their own, and so are dependent on their context – here, on the truth-value of the main-clause predicate. The non-separability of the *te* conjunction from the subordinate verb is an iconic, structural representation of this dependency on the main predicate:

(11) amende akana te merel varekon . . . (Lovari; Matras 1994a: 225)
us.LOC now COMP die.3SG somebody
'with us, now, if somebody dies . . . '

(12) me kamoms te vals tu (Sinti; Holzinger 1993: 163)
I wanted.1SG COMP came.2SG.PLUP you
'I would have liked you to have come'

(13) te krel miri čaj kova, dan lel-i daba
COMP do.3SG my daughter this then get.3SG.F blows
(Sinti; Holzinger 1993: 156)
'if my daughter does this, she will get blows'

This rule is not compromised even in those varieties of German Sinti which have adopted German word order and which have the verb in final position in all other subordinate clauses (see Matras 1999e). Isolated exceptions to the rule are found however in some of the Central dialects (cf. Boretzky 1996d: 107), and most systematically in Roman (Wogg and Halwachs 1998: 53):

(14) te me valakaj gejom
COMP I somewhere went.1SG
'if I went somewhere'

As a result of convergence with German word-order rules, some German Sinti varieties have obligatory VS when the sentence shows a first constituent that is not the subject (so-called verb–subject inversion; see Matras 1999e). A tendency toward VS is found in interrogative clauses and yes/no questions, though they too are open to variation (cf. Holzinger 1993: 188).

The normal position of the object in Romani is postverbal, exceptions being contrastive constructions:

(15) xan pien, (e) rikones kokalós na den
eat.3PL drink.3PL ART dog.OBL bone NEG give.3PL
(Erli; Boretzky 1998a: 148)
'they eat and drink, (but) they don't give the dog a bone'

Roman stands out as an exception. Wogg and Halwachs (1998: 59–64) calculate for Roman discourse the same percentage of SVO and SOV sentences, while in sentences that do not include an overt S, OV is twice as frequent as VO. The conservative VO type is prevalent in serialisation and with negated verbs (Wogg and Halwachs 1998: 64):

(16) lija o kereko taj ladlahi peske
took.3SG ART bicycle and ride.3SG.REM REFL.DAT
'he took the bicycle and rode off'

(17) ov na džanlahi o čačipe
he NEG know.3SG.REM ART truth
'he didn't know the truth'.

Not typically for a Balkan language, Romani also has the pronominal object in postverbal position (cf. Boretzky 1996d: 98). As alluded to in section 5.5.5, this could reflect the rather late grammaticalisation of anaphoric pronouns from deictics (*dikhav oles* 'I see this one' > *dikhav les* 'I see him/it'). This rule is retained even in Roman, though Wogg and Halwachs (1998: 62) describe a tendency to place pronominal objects between the aktionsart modifier and lexical verb in complex verbs:

(18) tel le mukle
down him let.3PL
'they lowered him'

Some central European dialects show tendencies towards what Boretzky (1996d: 104–5) defines as a 'split verb frame'. This involves the fronting of constituents of the modal quasi-infinitive verb in *te*-clauses:

(19) ada berš kezdinčom andi iškola te džal
this year began.1SG in school COMP go.3SG
(Roman; Wogg and Halwachs 1998: 48)
'that year I began to go to school'

(20) taša džasam sare dro veš kašta te čhineł
tomorrow go.1PL all in forest wood.PL COMP cut.3SG
(Polska Roma; Matras 1999b: 19)
'tomorrow we will all go to the forest to cut wood'

The Northeastern dialects in turn show tendencies to place non-topical objects before the verb, though this is not observed consistently (see also Boretzky 1996d: 102):

(21) me tuke raspxenava pal paskiro d'ectvo
I you.DAT tell.1SG about REFL.GEN childhood
(North Russian Romani; Rusakov and Abramenko 1998: 128)
'I will tell you about my childhood'

(22) kon miro kher phagirel? (Polska Roma; Matras 1999b: 21)
who my house break.3SG
'who is breaking my house?'

In constructions with two objects, the pronominal object generally precedes the nominal object:

(23) kergjas lake jek moxton (Erli; Boretzky 1998a: 147)
made.3SG her.DAT INDEF box
'he made her a box'

In VS constructions, the pronominal object follows immediately after the verb, separating V and S, and so retaining its postverbal position:

(24) pale dikhel la o thagar (Erli; Boretzky 1998a: 147)
again see.3SG her ART king
'the king saw her again'

(25) kamdias les ī raklī (Welsh Romani; Sampson 1926: 226)
loved.3SG him ART girl
'the girl loved him'

Even the Balkan dialects of Romani resist convergence in regard to the position of the pronominal object in the sentence. One feature which they do share with their co-territorial languages is **pronominal object doubling**. The construction is found in the Balkan and Vlax branches, and involves exposition of a topical patient, with a co-referent resumptive pronoun in the position following the verb (cf. Bubeník 1997: 100; see also Friedman 2000):

(26) adaja gili da but gilavelas la
this song too much sing.3SG.REM her
(Sepeči; Cech and Heinschink 1999: 142)
'she used to sing often too'

(27) patózel les o divi e romes
squeeze.3SG him ART giant ART man.OBL
(Bugurdži; Boretzky 1993a: 95)
'the giant squeezes the man'

Oblique case may be, but need not be reduplicated in the exposed position. A favourite candidate for doubling is the possessor, which in Romani is expressed by the independent oblique or direct object case:

(28) phenas akana, ma naj ma love (Lovari; Matras 1994a:118)
say.1PL now me NEG.is me money
'let's now say, I don't have any money'

(29) voj si la ek čhavo (Sepeči; Cech and Heinschink 1999: 141)
she is her one son
'she has one son'

While object doubling in Romani is clearly influenced by a similar phenomenon in the neighbouring Balkan languages, there is agreement that it is not grammaticalised in Romani, but represents rather a facultative structure triggered at the discourse level (see Boretzky 1993a: 94–6, Bubeník 1997: 102, Friedman 2000: 197). Friedman (2000) points out that unlike the other Balkan languages, Romani preserves a rather complex case declension, and does not have a clear opposition between clitic and non-clitic object pronouns. Both the motivation for object doubling and the structural resources employed in the construction therefore differ. Significantly, the most formalised object doubling in Romani occurs at the interclausal level, namely in relative clauses in which the head noun assumes an object role, which Friedman lists as one of the types of object doubling:

(30) me kingjum o lil so dikhljam ole solduj ki dukjana
I bought.1SG ART book REL saw.1PL this both at shop
(Arli; Jusuf and Kepeski 1980: 177, in Friedman 2000: 193)
'I bought the book that we both saw in the shop'

7.3 Possession and external possession

The possessive construction with the verb 'to be' and oblique possessor was already alluded to above. The oblique possessor appears to be an archaism, in all likelihood a relic of the genitive origin of the oblique case in MIA. The discrepancy between the semantic prominence of the possessor and its non-nominative case marking triggers exposition of the possessor to preverbal, topical position, where it is often assigned nominative marking. The oblique case is then carried by the resumptive pronoun in postverbal position.

Dative-subject constructions are limited in Romani. In most cases they come about through omission of the actual nominative subject: *mange dukhal* 'I am in pain', Roman *pekal tuke* 'you need'. Crevels and Bakker (2000) discuss the basis for such verbs in external possession constructions. The notion of external possession captures possessors that are external to the constituent of which the possessum is part, and which are instead expressed as a core grammatical relation of the verb (cf. Payne and Barshi 1999, in Crevels and Bakker 2000: 151). Crevels and Bakker (2000: 165–76) note several types of external possessor marking in Romani dialects, involving accusative, dative, locative, as well as double possessor marking:

(31) Accusative (Independent Oblique):
dukhal ma(n) o šero (Vlax)
hurt.3SG me ART head
'my head hurts'

(32) Dative:
mange dukhala šero (Latvian Romani)
me.DAT hurt.3SG head
'my head hurts'

(33) Locative:
odmarde mandi parora (South Russian Romani)
injured.3PL me.LOC liver
'they injured my liver'

(34) Double:
mo šoro dukhal man (Erli)
my head hurt.3SG me
'my head hurts'

Crevels and Bakker conclude that the distribution of the individual types among Romani dialects does not correspond to the principal division into dialect groups. Moreover, they suggest that the patterns of external possessor marking cannot be attributed to recent contact phenomena either, since they do not generally match the external possessor constructions found in the co-territorial European languages. The question whether Romani may have had an inherited external possessor construction, and the question why the construction may have been lost – or acquired – in particular dialects, are both left open in Crevels and Bakker's discussion.

Of the twenty-eight dialects in the sample considered by Crevels and Bakker, the most coherent group consists of those dialects that show accusative – or rather, independent oblique – marking of the external possessor, some of them in a so-called 'double' construction involving a possessive pronoun. This group includes Erli, Arli, Sepeči, Kalderaš, Slovak Romani, and Piedmontese Sinti. Thus, independent oblique marking of the external possessor is found in considerable density in the Balkans, the historical centre of diffusion, as well as in other dialect branches. This is consistent with the independent oblique marking of the possessor 'proper' in existential possessive constructions, as well as with the exploitation of the independent oblique possessor for the semantic experiencer, as in Sinti *man hi rōpaske* 'I feel like crying' (Holzinger 1995: 11). It appears therefore that both constructions, the plain and external possessor, are Early Romani and in all likelihood Proto-Romani archaisms, which draw on the original genitive function of the oblique in MIA (see above).

In this light, deviations from the independent oblique marking of the external possessor must be regarded as later developments. Some are simply cases where the construction may have been lost and is therefore unattested, as in nine of the twenty-eight sample dialects considered by Crevels and Bakker. In other instances, where a different case is employed to mark the external possessor, there appears indeed to be an areal correlation: the three Romani dialects that show locative marking – Russian Romani, but arguably also Ukrainian Romani, and Harbin Romani (the latter a migrant dialect from Russia) – are influenced by Russian, which likewise has locative marking in external possession. All sample dialects that show dative marking – Latvian Romani, Bohemian Romani, Roman, Bugurdži, and Drindari – are spoken in the zone in which European languages show dative marking for external possessors (cf. König and Haspelmath 1997).

From this it appears that Proto-Romani did have an external possessor construction, and that it employed the independent oblique (or 'accusative') as its case marking. This construction has been preserved in various Romani dialects, while individual dialects have either lost it completely, or have rearranged it, copying the case-marking used for external possession in the co-territorial languages.

7.4 Complex clauses

7.4.1 *General features of clause linking*

The principal feature of clause-linking devices in Romani is the predominance of finiteness. Converbs are employed only marginally. The morphological inventory of genuine converbal constructions is essentially limited to the two gerunds; the 'new infinitive' is a case of recent loss of concord agreement on what was originally a finite form (see section 6.7). Moreover, the productive use of gerunds is limited to a number of dialects. Paratactic chaining is achieved almost entirely by means of clause-initial conjunctions, which are often borrowed; some borrowed conjunctions follow the first constituent (Turkish *da*, Hungarian *iš*). Marginally, serialisation appears, involving mainly verbs of motion:

(35) vi mure papos avile line anda o kher
alo my.OBL grandfather.OBL came.3PL took.3PL from ART house
(Lovari; Matras 1994a: 117)
'they also came and took my grandfather from the house'

There is some evidence that serialisation is employed in dialects in contact with Turkish, as a means of imitating Turkish converbal constructions (e.g. Turkish *alıp götürdüm* 'I took it and brought it'):

(36) ljem andem les khere (Agia Varvara Vlax; Igla 1996: 173)
took.1SG brought.1SG him home
'I took (it) and brought it home'

7.4.2 *Relative clauses*

On the one hand, Romani follows the European type of relative clause. No expression is used exclusively as a relativiser, and no trace is found of the Indo-Aryan relativiser in *y-/j-*. Rather, relativisers (and the embedding conjunctions) are recruited from the inventory of interrogatives. On the other hand, Romani has obligatory resumptive pronouns when the head noun assumes a role other than the subject role within the relative clause. This is a relatively stable feature of Romani and one that is not usually compromised as a result of contact. The origins of the obligatory resumptive pronoun in Romani could be in convergence with Iranian, or, more likely if one considers the rather young grammaticalisation of resumptive pronouns, with Greek (or other Balkan languages).

Resumptive pronouns typically accompany relativisers that are not inflected for case. The most common relativiser in Romani is *kaj*, from *kaj* 'where'. The etymology corresponds to that of the general relativisers of several Balkan languages, most notably Greek. Most Romani dialects also employ *so/hoj* 'what', which usually follows inanimates, generic expressions, or determiners:

(37) sas kothe bajora so či čálonas ma
was there things REL NEG appeal.3PL.REM me
(Lovari; Matras 1994a: 203)
'there were things there that I didn't like'

(38) saro so pesa lija kherestyr sys maro
all REL REFL.INSTR took.3SG home.ABL was bread
(Polska Roma; Matras 1999b: 17)
'all he took with him from home was bread'

(39) ham andar odola so adaj sam, o džuvla, me som
but from those REL here are.1PL ART women, I am.1SG
i lek phuraneder (Roman; Wogg and Halwachs 1998: 57)
ART SUPER old.COMP
'but from among those who are here, the women, I am the eldest'

There are two relativisers which do carry inflection: *savo* 'which', which agrees in gender and number with its head also in the nominative form, and *kon* 'who'. Both inflect for case (*savo* also for gender/number) and are used mainly with animate heads, and usually as a form of disambiguating head nouns. They are particularly common in possessive constructions, which occupy the lowest position on the noun accessibility hierarchy (Keenan and Comrie 1977) and so are most likely in universal terms to show case marking:

(40) o gažo kasko si kado sa (Lovari; Matras 1994a: 35)
ART man REL.GEN is this all
'the man to whom all this belongs'

(41) panč džene andi cili sidlung, saven khera sin upre
five persons in whole settlement REL.OBL houses is up
pumengere thana (Roman; Wogg and Halwachs 1998: 58)
REF.GEN.PL places
'five persons in the whole estate, who had houses on their lots'

The use of resumptive pronouns is conditioned by hierarchies of animacy and thematic role, and more generally by the predictability of the semantic case role of the particular head noun in the relative clause (cf. Matras 1994a: 206–10). Dendropotamos Vlax for example requires a resumptive pronoun with the animate benefactive, but it is optional with the animate direct object, although the formal case marking of both roles is identical (oblique):

(42) kaa si o čhaoro kaj dijem les iraki pares
this is ART boy REL gave.1SG him yesterday money
'this is the boy to whom I gave money yesterday'

(43) o rom kaj dikhlem (les) iraki avilas kaj mo ćher
ART man REL saw.1SG him.OBL yesterday came.3SG to my house
'the man whom I saw yesterday came to my house'

According to Holzinger (1993: 173–8), the resumptive pronoun in Sinti is optional with animate head nouns in both direct object and benefactive roles.

Most locative head nouns appear to be treated as non-ambiguous in regard to their case roles in the relative clause, and tend not to show a resumptive pronoun:

(44) o foro, kaj dživē (Sinti; Holzinger 1993: 174)
ART town REL live.2SG
'the town in which you live'

With inanimate heads in object roles, however, there is variation, depending on the extent to which the head and the verb allow a predictable association with particular thematic roles:

(45) koi čuri kaj čindom i matrele (Sinti; Holzinger 1993: 174)
this knife REL cut.1SG ART potatoes
'the knife with which I cut the potatoes'

(46) e bučja so keras (Lovari)
ART things REL do.1PL
'the things we do'

(47) jek torba kaj ikeravas la katro dumo
INDEF bag REL carry.1SG.REM it from.ART back
(Bugurdži; Boretzky 1993a: 101)
'a bag which I carried on my back'

Cleft constructions rely on the same devices as relative clauses, employing the relativiser in exposed position:

(48) kon lija lija, kon na, na
who took.3SG took.3SG who NEG NEG
(Roman; Wogg and Halwachs 1998: 58)
'whoever took, took, whoever did not, did not'

Much like relative clauses, embeddings are constituents of the complex sentence. They are introduced by any one of a range of semantically specified interrogatives:

(49) na džanla so te vakerel mange
NEG know.3SG.REM what COMP say.3SG me.DAT
(Bugurdži; Boretzky 1993a: 101)
'she didn't know what to say to me'

(50) me na džanav, sar bučonahi
I NEG know.1SG how call.3PL.REM
(Roman; Wogg and Halwachs 1998: 55)
'I don't know what [how] they were called'

7.4.3 *Complementation and purpose clauses*

Perhaps the most obvious morphosyntactic Balkanism that characterises Romani as a whole, not just its Balkan dialects, is the dichotomy in the representation of integrated/subordinated events as factual or real vs. non-factual or non-real. In the absence of an infinitive in modal constructions, the contrast is most clearly maintained in 'classic' complement constructions. Complements of epistemic verbs, which represent events that are potentially independent and real, are introduced by what might be called the *KAJ*-type complementiser:

(51) mislizla mečka kaj si (Bugurdži; Boretzky 1993a: 99)
think.3SG bear COMP is
'he thinks that it's a bear'

(52) jon phenen, kaj o rom romedinevela la
they say.3PL COMP ART man marry.3SG.FUT her
(Sinti; Holzinger 1993: 158)
'they say, that the man will marry her'

(53) dikhča kaj lakro pšal čhija bara
saw.3SG COMP her brother threw.3SG stones
(Polska Roma; Matras 1999b: 18)
'she saw that her brother threw stones'

The form *kaj* (< 'where') represents the conservative, inherited form of the *KAJ*-complementiser. The choice of the interrogative/conjunction 'where', which also serves as a relativiser, allows the alignment of epistemic complements with other factual extensions to the main proposition. The inherited conjunction is replaced by borrowings in three main zones (see also section 8.2.2). In Vlax, it is replaced entirely by *kə/ke* from Romanian, which is its functional equivalent. In the Arli and Southern Vlax varieties of Greece it is replaced by Greek *oti*, again a functional equivalent. This development appears to be of recent date, also affecting varieties such as Dendropotamos and Agia Varvara Vlax spoken by immigrant communities. It is likely then that the *KAJ*-type complementiser in these varieties underwent successive replacement, from **kaj* to **kə/ke* to *oti*. Finally, in the Central dialects, Hungarian-derived *hod/hodž/hod'/hot/hoj* is gaining ground. In some dialects, such as Roman, it still co-exists with *kaj*; in Hungarian Lovari it co-exists with *ke*.

Modal complements are introduced by *te* (in some varieties *ti*):

(54) job kamel te dšalo khere (Sinti; Holzinger 1993: 137)
he want.3SG COMP go.3SG.M home
'he wants to go home'

(55) jame moginas dava te zumaveł (Polska Roma; Matras 1999b: 18)
we can.1PL this COMP try.3SG
'we can try this'

(56) le hi jek parno gra te bikinel (Roman; Halwachs 1998: 196)
him is INDEF white horse COMP sell.3SG
'he has a white horse to sell'

(57) akana mangela o Gudis ti čumidel la
now want.3SG ART G. COMP kiss.3SG.SUBJ her
(Sepeči; Cech and Heinschink 1999: 187)
'now Gudis wants to kiss her'

The split corresponds to the two sets of complementisers in other Balkan languages (Romanian *că* vs. *să*; Greek *oti* vs. *na*, etc.). The etymology of *te* is unclear. It is not a cognate of Domari *ta* 'in order to', which is borrowed from Arabic. There are however other languages in the Near East that employ *ta* in purpose clauses, e.g. Kurdish and Neo-Aramaic, where it appears to originate in the Iranian preposition *tā* 'until'. A deictic etymology for *te* has been considered by various authors, linking it with the OIA pronoun *ta-* (Pobożniak 1964: 58), the Hindi correlative *to* (Pott 1845: 281), or OIA *iti* 'so' (Sampson 1926: 363). The correlative function is an attractive etymology as it can be related to the semantic dependency that characterises Romani *te* (see Matras 1994a: 231–3).

Friedman (1985) discusses *te* in the context of what he calls the 'Dental Modal Subordinator' of the Balkan languages (Balkan Slavic *da*, Albanian *të*, Romanian *să*, Greek *na*). The primary function of the modal subordinator in all Balkan languages is, according to Friedman, to denote ontologically non-real events. Four domains are typically covered by the modal subordinator: dependent modal (infinitive), dependent aspectual (such as 'to begin'), directive (optative), and conditional. Consider the (Common) Romani examples:

(58) astaren te keren buti
start.3PL COMP do.3PL work
'they are starting to work'

(59) so te phenav?
what COMP say.1SG
'what shall I say?'

(60) te sas ma love . . .
COMP was me money
'if I had money'

It is clear from the functional scope covered by *te* that its inherent meaning is semantic–pragmatic, namely to relativise the truth-value of a predication. The conditions for the actual realisation of the predication may be set either in the modal or aspectual verb, or in the conditional protasis, or pragmatically in the situational context of the directive-optative.

Unlike *KAJ*, which is often borrowed, *te* is stable.[4] There are only two dialects that have not retained the factuality dichotomy; both use *te* in factual/indicative (epistemic) complements as well:

(61) phendas peskē dakī 'kanå te wåntselas te
said.3SG REFL.GEN mother.DAT now COMP want.3SG.REM COMP
džal (Welsh Romani; Sampson 1926: 225)
go. 3SG
'he told his mother that he now wanted to go'

(62) dopo šuni ti hilo mulo
then hear.3SG COMP is.M dead.M
(Istrian/Slovene Romani; Dick Zatta 1996: 201)
'then she hears that he is dead'

Similar use of *te* in epistemic complements is also found in Rüdiger's sample from 1782 (see Matras 1999a: 100).

In linking two predications, *KAJ* and *te* can be taken to represent two extreme ends on a continuum of clause integration (in the sense of Givón 1990): *KAJ* links clauses with independent truth-value, *te* represents the higher degree of integration, marking out predications that have no independent truth-value. In between these two extremes, there is a continuum of clause-linking devices drawn upon to express more ambivalent relations, notably manipulation and various kinds of purpose clauses. The key to a typology of clause-linking devices in such constructions is the degree of semantic integration of the events, and more specifically the degree of semantic control that is attributed to the agent of the main clause. The cline of semantic control governs a choice between *te* for the highest degree of control (and so tightest integration), and a complex subordinator in which *te* participates alongside a 'reinforcer', for the lower degree of control (less tight integration of the clauses).

The use of a 'reinforcer' in combination with the Modal Subordinator is another typical Balkan feature (see Friedman 1985: 385). The reinforcer in Romani is either the *KAJ* subordinator itself, or a borrowed conjunction or preposition,

[4] An exception is the Dolenjski dialect of Slovenia (Cech and Heinschink 2001). See note in chapter 8, and see below.

which is modelled on the purpose clause structure in the contact language. Thus we find iconicity at two levels. First, tight integration is represented by the structurally simple subordinator, while loose integration is represented by the more complex form. This is in line with the universals of clause integration discussed by Givón (1990). Second, with tighter semantic integration inherited forms persist, while loose integration aligns itself with discourse-level operations in its susceptibility to external contact influences (see chapter 8 on grammatical borrowing).

We find tight integration when manipulative intent is attributed to the agent/manipulator. Here, control is less relevant, since the truth-value of the agent's intent stands, irrespective of whether or not the target action is actually realised by the manipulee:

(63) mangav te des ma o pares (Dendropotamos Vlax)
demand.1SG COMP give.2SG me.OBL ART money
'I would like you to give me the money'

(64) me kamaua te krel ko rom kova (Sinti; Holzinger 1993: 157)
I want.1SG COMP do.3SG this man that
'I want this man to do this'

Permission attributes control to the agent, equally allowing for tight integration. In Sinti, the *te* subordinator can even be omitted, calquing German (*machen lassen*):

(65) job mukel man an i virta te džal
he let.3SG me.OBL in ART pub COMP go.3SG
(Sinti; Holzinger 1993: 159)
'he let me go to the pub'

(66) tek nicht mukēs les an peskro kher sovel
nobody NEG let.3SG.REM him.OBL in REFL.GEN house sleep.3SG
(Sinti; Holzinger 1993: 169)
'nobody allowed him to sleep in their house'

(67) na dełys łake te xał (Polska Roma; Matras 1999b: 19)
NEG give.3SG.REM her.DAT COMP eat.3SG
'he gave her nothing to eat'

(68) le graste andi len paj meklom te pil
ART.OBL horse.OBL in river water allowed.1SG COMP drink.3SG
(Roman; Halwachs 1998: 198)
'I let the horse drink water in the river'

(69) na mukelas i rakles ti kerel phari buti
NEG let.3SG.REM ART.OBL boy.OBL COMP do.3SG hard work
(Sepeči; Cech and Heinschink 1999: 119)
'he didn't allow the boy to work hard'

Imperative directives on the other hand rank lower on the semantic integration continuum for manipulation. Here, the agent tries to force the manipulee into carrying out the target action, but lacks the kind of control that is attributed to the agent for instance with verbs that express permission. Individual dialects behave differently in this respect, and sometimes different solutions can be found within an individual dialect. In the Polska Roma variety in (71), the additive conjunction in the second part of the complement allows the downgrading of the complex subordinator *kaj te* to plain *te*. In Roman, the *KAJ*-type subordinator is Hungarian *hot*; in Bugurdži the complex subordinator is modelled on Albanian *që të*:

(70) phendem lake te anel amenge pai (Dendropotamos Vlax)
said.1SG her.DAT COMP bring.3SG us.DAT water
'I told her to fetch us water'

(71) phendža łake kaj te jandeł pani, i te kereł jag
told.3SG her.DAT COMP COMP bring.3SG water and COMP make.3SG fire
andry bov (Polska Roma; Matras 1999b: 19)
in stove
'she told her to fetch water, and to light a fire in the stove'

(72) phen tra dake, hot te mekel len mange
say your.OBL mother.DAT COMP COMP let.3SG them.OBL me.DAT
efkar te koštalinel . . . (Roman; Wogg and Halwachs 1998: 49)
once COMP taste.3SG
'tell your mother to let me taste them . . . '

(73) zapretizas lake o rom či te na tromal . . .
warned.3SG her.DAT ART man COMP COMP NEG dare.3SG
(Bugurdži; Boretzky 1993a: 99)
'her husband warned her that she should not dare . . . '

Like manipulation clauses, purpose clauses also show a continuum of semantic integration, marked out by the complexity of the subordinator. Here too, there is variation among the dialects. Rather tight semantic integration is given in predications that express movement of an agent toward achieving a target. In most dialects, plain *te* is used to link the clauses. However, some dialects employ, either optionally or regularly, a borrowed purpose expression as a 'reinforcer' in a position preceding *te*. This is the case with Sinti *um te* (German *um . . . zu*), and Dendropotamos *ja te* (Greek *gia . . . na*):

(74) me avilom ti dikhav tumen
I came.1SG COMP see.1SG you.PL
(Sepeči; Cech and Heinschink 1999: 19)
'I have come to see you'

(75) taša džasam sare dro veš kašta te čineł
tomorrow go.1PL all in forest wood.PL COMP cut.3SG
(Polska Roma; Matras 1999b: 19)
'tomorrow we will all go to the forest to cut wood'

(76) me ka džav ko drom kadle raćja te rodav
I FUT go.1SG to road this.OBL girl.OBL COMP search.1SG
(Bugurdži; Boretzky 1993a: 99)
'I will go to search for this girl'

(77) job džajas an i gačima (um) te piel-o lovina
he go.3SG.REM in ART pub COMP COMP drink.3SG.M beer
(Sinti; Holzinger 1993: 183)
'he went to the pub to drink beer'

(78) avilem ćhere ja te dikhav tut (Dendropotamos Vlax)
came.1SG home COMP COMP see.1SG you.OBL
'I came home in order to see you'

Note that Romani has no strict rule on linking purpose clauses that show subject agreement (Same Subject), as opposed to subject switch (Different Subject). If there is no overall preference for a complex subordinator in purpose clauses, then variation is likely to be sensitive to the degree of control in regard to the specific combination of predications, i.e. the likely outcome of the target event. Thus, both same-subject and different-subject constructions can be linked by plain *te* when the outcome is not contentious:

(79) bikinas colura te šaj traisaras (Lovari; Matras 1994a: 230)
sell.1PL carpets COMP can live.1PL
(Same Subject)
'we sell carpets to make a living'

(80) job džajas an i gačima te budevel naj leskri
he go.3SG.REM in ART pub COMP work.3SG can his
romni khere (Sinti; Holzinger 1993:183) (Different Subject)
wife home
'he went to the pub so that his wife could work at home'

(81) ánde thovav dúj sekviségi, ságošno t' ovel
in put.1SG two cloves fragrant COMP be.SUBJ.3SG
(Farkašda Romungro; Elšík et al. 1999: 379) (Different Subject)
'I put in two cloves to make it smell good'

Different-subject constructions take a complex subordinator when agent control is weaker and it is more difficult to achieve the target. Note in (84) the combination of both *kaj* and *te* in Farkašda Romungro (southern Slovakia) with the Croatian-derived purpose clause marker *nek*:

(82) phendas łokes ki peskry phen, kaj dada te na
said.3SG quietly to his sister COMP parents COMP NEG
šuneł (Polska Roma; Matras 1999b: 20)
hear.3SG
'he said quitely to his sister, so that their parents would not hear'

(83) mri baba dschálahi te schmuginel, kaj len
my grandmother go.3SG.REM COMP smuggle.3SG COMP them.OBL
te hal sina (Roman; Halwachs 1998: 192)
COMP eat.3SG was
'my grandmother went to smuggle, so that they will have (food) to eat'

(84) čino čiken thoves upro plého, kaj nek te na
small fat put.2SG on pan COMP COMP COMP NEG
thábol (Farkašda Romungro; Elšík et al. 1999: 379)
burn.3SG
'you put a little fat on the baking pan, so that it will not burn'

(85) kodo maj anglal kamavas te phenav ke
this COMP before want.1SG.REM COMP say.1SG COMP
te xačaras so kérdžolas pe ando Njamco
COMP understand.1PL what happen.3SG.REM REFL in.ART Germany
ando marimo (Lovari;Matras 1994a: 234)
in.ART war
'I wanted to say this earlier so that we may understand what happened in Germany during the war'

On the other hand, same-subject constructions can also show a complex subordinator if agent control is weak:

(86) Jankos na sys kana zor kaj pałe te ponaskendeł
J.OLB NEG was now strength COMP again COMP gather.3SG
bara (Polska Roma; Matras 1999b: 20)
stones
'Janko no longer had the strength to gather stones'

(87) sako dad kamlahi kaj nek t' ovel
every father want.3SG.REM COMP COMP COMP be.SUBJ.3SG
le but murša (Farkašda Romungro; Elšík et al. 1999: 379)
him.OBL many males
'every father wanted to have many sons'

7.4.4 *Adverbial subordination*

As indicated above, adverbial subordination in Romani relies almost entirely on semantically specified conjunctions that introduce subordinated clauses. The conjunctions themselves are often diverse, a result of renewal on the basis of inherited morphological material, and borrowing. The present section summarises just some of the typical features. We may divide conjunctions that participate in adverbial subordination into roughly three types. The first two correspond to the factuality dichotomy already encountered in complementation. There is a *te*-type and a KAJ-type linking of adverbial clauses. The first, with *te*, covers adverbial relations that are non-factual, unreal, or non-presupposed, the second, with KAJ, typically covers subordinations that are factual, real, or presupposed.[5] A further type includes subordinators that are based on interrogatives. The subordinators *te* and KAJ may combine with other elements, including interrogative-based conjunctions, prepositions and deictics. Borrowings may play a role in all types, although some adverbial constructions are more prone to the infiltration of borrowings (see chapter 8).

The *te*-type covers firstly conditional clauses. Unlike other kinds of adverbial subordinations, conditional clauses rely heavily on the interaction of tense, aspect, and modality categories in the two parts of the construction, the protasis and apodosis. Boretzky (1993b) notes that Romani dialects distinguish realis from irrealis (counterfactual), but do not show a fully developed potentialis conditional. The potential construction can pattern with either realis or irrealis. The usual pattern in the realis protasis is to have *te* with either the present, future or conditional future, subjunctive, or perfective, some dialects even allowing a choice among these categories, with flexibility in the choice of TAM category in the apodosis:

(88) te dela kana, vē sapno (Sinti; Holzinger 1993: 182)
COMP give.3SG now be.SUBJ.2SG wet
'if it rains now, you will get wet' (present:subjunctive)

(89) te na pjesa o drab, na ka lačhárdos
COMP NEG drink.2SG.CONDFUT ART medicine NEG FUT recover.2SG
(Agia Varvara; Igla 1996: 135)
'if you do not drink the medicine, you will not get better' (conditional future:future)

(90) ti manges, vurtinesa les xoraxanes
COMP want.2SG.SUBJ translate.FUT it Turkish.ADV
(Sepeči; Cech and Heinschink 1999: 121)
'if you wish, translate it into Turkish' (subjunctive:present)

(91) te adala adaj ale, me mange fuat džav
COMP these here came.3PL I me.DAT go.away.1SG
(Roman; Wogg and Halwachs 1998: 53)
'if they come here, I will go away' (perfective:present)

For irrealis or counterfactual, the stable distinctive category is *te* followed by the pluperfect (or remote perfective), but the imperfect may also appear here:

[5] See Hengeveld (1998) for the use of these dimensions in a typology of adverbial subordination in European languages.

(92) manglalahi, dijomahi tut
asked.2SG.REM gave.1SG.REM you.OBL
(Roman; Wogg and Halwachs 1998: 54)
'if you had asked, I would have given you'(pluperfect:pluperfect)

(93) ma ti khelavkerasas la, ka xalas amen
NEG COMP dance.CAUS.1PL.REM her.OBL FUT eat.3SG.REM us.OBL
sarimiz (Sepeči; Cech and Heinschink 1999: 123)
all.1PL(TURK)
'if we hadn't made her dance, she would have eaten us all' (pluperfect: *ka*+imperfect)

(94) aver romni t' avelas . . . (Agia Varvara; Igla 1996: 135)
other woman COMP be.SUBJ.3SG.REM
'if it had been/were another woman . . . ' (imperfect)

(95) te vals ko rom naslo, dan dalso
COMP be.SUBJ.3SG.REM this man ill, then pronounce.3SG.REM
o dramaskres gole (Sinti; Holzinger 1993: 182)
M. ART doctor.OBL call
'if this man had been/were ill, then he would have/would call the doctor' (imperfect:imperfect)

For the potential we find a variety of forms. Roman appears to use the imperfect only for the potential, thus codifying the potential as a separate category:

(96) te o grencn cuj ojanahi, feder ovlahi
COMP ART borders shut be.SUBJ.3PL.REM better is.SUBJ.3SG.REM
(Roman; Wogg and Halwachs 1998: 54)
'if the borders were closed, that would be better'

Although the conditional conjunction *te* is stable and there is no evidence that it has been lost in any of the dialects, there are nevertheless examples of variation, with *te* being extended by, or alternating with borrowed markers such as the Slavic particle *bi/by*, the South Slavic conjunction *ako*, the Turkish verbal suffix *-se*, or Greek *an* in *an te*, or else appearing alongside *kana* 'when' (e.g. in Sinti and Sepeči).

The subordinator *te* is employed in a number of other adverbial subordinations that relate to the non-epistemic or modal domain. Potential condition ('whether') is usually expressed by *te*, occasionally in combination with a borrowing (Sinti *ob te*), or else by a borrowed particle or conjunction (West Slavic *či/čy*, South Slavic *li* or *dali*, Turkish *mi*). Concessive conditionals ('even if') typically have a focus particle preceding *te* (Lovari *vi te*, Sinti *nina te*, Roman *kajk te*). Negative circumstance ('without doing X') is expressed by *bi te* (cf. *bi* 'without'), followed by the present or subjunctive.

Anteriority ('before') and the anterior-durative ('until') constitute an intermediate domain between non-factuality and factuality. Some dialects show

Table 7.2 *Adverbial subordinators in Romani*

epistemic compl	*kaj, hot/hodž/hod', kə/ke, oti*
modal compl	*te/ti*
purpose	*te/ti, kaj te, hot te, kə te, ja te, či te*
relative	*kaj, so/hoj, savo/havo, kon*
condition	*te, bi/by, ako, -se, kana, kada, an te*
potential condition	*te, ob te, či/čy, dali, li, mi*
concessive condition	*vi te, nina te, kajk te*
unreal concession	*har/sar te, hata kaj*
negative circumstance	*bi te, oni te*
anterior-durative	*dži kaj, dži te, bis te, džikim, bisko, medig*
anteriority	*sar/syr/har, angla sar, angla kodo ke, bi te na, prin te*
cause, reason, explanation	*kaj, kə/ke, vajl, anda kodo ke, sostar, soske, sar, adake sar, sebepi kaj, afu, jati, zere, bo, mer, jer, lebo, pošto*
concession	*xoč, hjaba kaj, trocdem kaj, sa jekh ke, jeva*
simultaneity	*kana, kada/keda, sar/har/syr, kaj, so, afu*
posteriority	*kana, kada/keda, sar/har/syr, kaj, so, posle, čim, pala kodo ke, akana, jekh kaj, jekh ta*

two separate conjunctions for anteriority, corresponding to the degree of presupposition: Lovari *angla kodo ke avilo* 'before he arrived', and *angla kodo te avel* 'before he arrives'. Other dialects assign anteriority and anterior-durative to one of the two groups (i.e. either *dži kaj* or *dži te* for 'until'). Both domains show heavy infiltration of borrowings. Also in intermediate position is unreal concession ('as if'), with *sar te/har te* (cf. *sar/har* 'how') in some dialects, but in the Balkans also *hata kaj* (Turkish *hatta* 'just').

Constructions that are dominated by the KAJ-type involve location ('where' and 'wherever'), usually with plain *kaj*, and cause (Roman *kaj*), though many dialects have borrowings for cause (cf. Northern Vlax *kə/ke* from Romanian, which is both the general non-factual complementiser and the causal conjunction in Romanian). Cause, reason, and explanation may also be expressed by case-marked interrogatives, usually in the dative or ablative (*soske* 'because'). Outcome ('such . . . that') normally involves a deixis and a straightforward factual complementiser (Central *afka . . . hot/kaj*, Vlax *kade . . . ke*). Few dialects appear to have inherited markers of concession, but borrowings employed for presupposed concession are often followed by KAJ (Sinti *trocdem kaj* 'although').

Remaining is the type of adverbial subordinators that are based on plain interrogatives. These cover almost exclusively the domain of temporality, in particular simultaneity and posteriority ('when', 'as', 'after'). The basic inventory of conjunctions is *sar/har/syr* (< 'how'), *so* ('what'), and *kana/kada* (< 'when'). The actual distribution of the forms varies. Many dialects make a distinction between general simultaneity ('when', Vlax *kana*, Polska Roma *so*) and specific simultaneity ('just as', Vlax *sar*, Polska Roma *syr*). The tendency is also to distinguish simultaneity from posteriority. In Sinti, however, *har* can be used for all three functions. The general temporal subordinators 'when'/'as' are also used for more precise temporal relations such as immediate anteriority ('as soon as') or parallel duration ('while', 'as long as'). The temporal domain too shows rather extensive borrowing of conjunctions.

7.5 Negation

Negation in Romani is expressed in two ways: through verb negators that are attached to the verb, and through negative indefinites. Verb negators are clearly the more conservative and more established of the two. Negative indefinites on the other hand are generally prone to renewal processes through internal grammaticalisation and borrowing (see section 5.5.6). Their specialisation as negatives, though part of a general trend to advance along a negative cline (cf. Elšík 2000c), is recent and dialect-specific.

The most distinctive feature of verb negators in Romani is the fact they are sensitive to the mood of the verb. All Romani dialects have separate negators for indicative and non-indicative; some show a three-way distinction between indicative, subjunctive, and imperative negators. The inherited negators are *na* (indicative; *na džanava* 'I don't know') and *ma* (non-indicative, i.e subjunctive and imperative; *ma dža!* 'don't go!', *ma te džal* 'may he not go'). In the Northeastern dialects, *na* takes over the function of the imperative negator as well. Elsewhere, the original state of affairs is preserved in most dialects except for Vlax. In Vlax, *ma* is reserved for imperatives, while *na* is preserved in the subjunctive, though it retains its position immediately before the verb (*ma dža!* 'don't go!', *te na džal* 'so that he may not go'). The indicative negator in Vlax shows several different forms. Southeastern Vlax varieties have *in*; its origin is not clear, and could be a reduced form of the original negator, later modified through an initial vowel (cf. Domari *in-/n-*). Southwestern Vlax varieties have *ni*, perhaps an original Southern Vlax innovation, which may have merged with the Slavic negators of the surrounding languages (*ne/nie*). In Northern Vlax, the indicative negator is *či*. Elšík (2000c) interprets it as an original negative scalar focus particle 'neither, nor, not even' deriving from the indefinite *či*, which, in all likelihood under the influence of Romanian *nici ... nici* became a marker of negative clause coordination (*či xal či pel* 'he neither eats nor drinks') and finally an independent negator.

The indicative negator undergoes changes in several other dialects, too. Here too, they are connected to the grammaticalisation of indefinites and focus markers, and to contact influences. The indefinite marker *kek* 'nothing' (<**ka-jekh*) is occasionally used as an independent, postposed negator in Welsh Romani and in some Sinti/Manuš varieties, having gone through the stage of a negative indefinite: *na kamelas kek* 'he didn't want anything/at all' > *kamelas kek* 'he wanted nothing' > *kamelas kek* 'he didn't want' (cf. Elšík 2000c). In German Sinti, the borrowed particle German *gar* undergoes a similar development, and in some varieties it serves as the principal indicative negator: *na kamom gar*

'I didn't want anything' > *kamom gar* 'I didn't want'. Other Sinti varieties borrow the German postposed negator *nicht/nit*. Several dialects have a unique negator for the third-person copula: non-Vlax *nani/nane*, Vlax *naj* 'is-not'.

Negative indefinite expressions in Romani are generally related to indefinites with a positive meaning, though in some cases the traces of positive readings appear only marginally (cf. generalVlax *khanči* 'nothing', but Agia Varvara Vlax *kajši* 'something'). One can therefore assume that clause negation relied originally primarily on the verb negator, rather than on an indefinite negative. This state of affairs is generally continued in Romani, irrespective of the subsequent specialisation of some of the indefinite expressions as negative indefinites: Lovari *varekon* 'somebody', *khonik* 'nobody', but *khonik či avilas* 'nobody arrived'; Polska Roma *varyso* 'something', *čhi* 'nothing', but *čhi na šundžol* 'nothing is heard'; Sinti *jek/komoni* 'somebody', *tek* 'nobody', but *tek nicht kamel man* 'nobody likes me' (Holzinger 1993: 77).[6]

7.6 The areal position of Romani

In the noun phrase, the characteristic syntactic features of Romani from an NIA perspective are the emergence of prepositions and a definite article, the continuation of prenominal position of determiners and adjectives, the retention of oblique possession, and the late emergence of an optional, pragmatically marked postnominal position for modifiers. Significantly, all features that might be assumed to have been retained from a subcontinental form of Proto-Romani are not incongruent with the Balkan model. The only exception is the oblique possessor, essentially a morphological phenomenon with syntactic implications. Romani has also retained a differentiated case system, contrasting with the morphological case declension pattern of the Balkan languages. While we have no clear indication of the initial trigger for the emergence of prepositions (see above), it is obvious that the postnominal 'option' position is a late contact development.

There are three principal features of Romani syntactic typology that must be considered as Early Romani innovations. The first is the relative clause construction with resumptive pronouns. Even if there was an Iranian trigger for this development, the use of interrogatives as relativisers supports convergence with Greek. The second is the factuality distinction in the use of subordinators. The third is the pattern of word order, with predominant VO with the option of object fronting for focusing, VS as connective-narrative order, and SV as predominantly contrastive-thematic order. These features are retained in most Romani dialects; changes are recent, restricted to individual dialects, and in most cases they modify the pattern, but do not replace it completely.

6 But also Sinti *ko nutsas la či* 'this was of no use to her' (Holzinger 1993: 143), a borrowing and semi-calque on German *das nutzte ihr nichts*.

8 Grammatical borrowing

8.1 General considerations

'Contact languages' is a term normally reserved for languages that arose in situations of multilingualism and which can be said to lack a single 'parent language' in the sense of an ancestral language that is transmitted with no interruption across generations of speakers. The term is usually employed in connection with pidgins, creoles, and 'mixed languages' (see Thomason and Kaufman 1988, Bakker and Mous 1994, Thomason 1997, Sebba 1997). Although there is no direct attestation of the forerunner of Romani, the continuation of OIA/MIA inflection paradigms and core vocabulary rule out that the language arose in a way that is similar to the emergence of pidgins, creoles, or mixed languages (but see discussion of Para-Romani varieties in chapter 10). Nonetheless, Romani is a language in contact. With the exception of very young children, there are no monolingual speakers of Romani. The preservation of the language outside India in the absence of a territory where Romani speakers constituted a majority population suggests that multilingualism has been the reality in Romani-speaking communities for many centuries, and most certainly since the Early Romani period. We might therefore designate Romani as a language that is 'permanently in contact'.

In many ways, the sociolinguistic situation of Romani is unique: Romani is used on the one hand as a token of ethnic distinctness and often as a secret language (see Hancock 1976, Boretzky 1989), while on the other hand there have been, until the twentieth century, no organised or conscious attempts to safeguard the language or to expand its usages. While Romani shows remarkable preservation of a core of conservative structures and basic vocabulary, there is at the same time full acceptance of bilingualism and of the intrusion of vocabulary and grammatical structures from the various contact languages. Grammatical and lexical borrowing into Romani has consequently been described as 'massive' and in some respects 'exceptional' (cf. Kostov 1973, Haarmann 1986: 155ff, Boretzky 1989).[1]

However defined, it is clear that the extent of structural borrowing in Romani offers a test-case for the regularities and the constraints involved in contact-induced change. The dispersion of Romani dialects offers an opportunity to compare the impact of diverse contact languages on a rather homogeneous stock of inherited structures. Moreover, migrations of Romani popluations have led to changing contact constellations, resulting in successive layers of contact influences within individual dialects. This allows us to correlate the historical depth of contact (both the time and intensity factor) with the system-internal position and functions of the categories that are affected by contact-induced change (cf. Matras 1996a).

8.1.1 *Structural borrowing*

I use the term 'structural borrowing' to denote the productive replication of actual (phonological) forms – or structural 'material' – within the grammatical system of Romani. Defining what constitutes 'borrowed' material entails several difficulties. First, there is the question of whether and how to differentiate borrowing as a diachronic process through which the structural composition of the system changes, from ongoing language mixing, where components of a current contact language (L2) are inserted synchronically at the utterance level without any obvious long-term implications for the structural system of Romani as a whole.

A clear case for borrowing are **lasting replications** of material from an earlier L2; consider the Greek-derived elements in Romani dialects outside the Greek-speaking area. But equally of interest are **consistent** patterns of mixing involving elements of a currently 'active' L2. The most obvious case is when inherited material is substituted by elements from the current L2, as in the case of discourse markers and adversative conjunctions in numerous dialects (see below). A different kind of example of consistent borrowing from an active L2 is the replication of Russian and Turkish verb inflection to accompany verbal lexical insertions from these languages in Romani dialects of Russia and the southern Balkans, respectively. Insertions of an option might also be considered borrowings if they are representative of an overall typological drift; consider the use of the German preposition *mit* 'with' in German Sinti and German Lovari *mit tumensa* 'with YOU.PL.INSTR.' alongside *tumensa*, which mirrors the expansion of prepositions with full nouns at the expense of synthetic case markers.

[1] For a partial overview of structural borrowing in Romani dialects see Boretzky and Igla (1991); chapters devoted to grammatical borrowing are included in the descriptions by Boretzky (1993a, 1994), Igla (1996), and Cech and Heinschink (1999).

A further consideration when defining grammatical borrowing is the extent of **diffusion** of replicated grammatical material into the inherited or native component of the language. There is a universal tendency for borrowed morphology to appear first with borrowed lexical items before spreading to inherited vocabulary (see Thomason and Kaufman 1988, Moravcsik 1978). The intermediate stage results in a compartmentalisation of structures, where different sets of grammatical markers are employed with different parts of the vocabulary. One of the most obvious examples for the diffusion of borrowed bound morphology into the inherited component of Romani is the productive use of Slavic aktionsart prefixes or Slavic aspect with all verb stems, in the Northeastern and Northern Central dialects (see chapter 6). On the other hand, a characteristic trait of Romani is the relative stability of split morphology or morphological **compartmentalisation**, where the diffusion of borrowed material remains selective. All Romani dialects maintain productive use of Greek-derived nominal and verbal markers, but this is largely restricted to the European loan component, and diffusion into the pre-European component remains on the whole marginal. The consistent employment of the original verb inflection with Russian- and Turkish-derived verbs, referred to above, is a further case of stable grammatical compartmentalisation.

Borrowed grammar, specifically borrowed morphology in Romani, then, can satisfy any one of three criteria: (a) it can be adopted as a regular structure and become diffused 'backwards' into the inherited component; (b) it can be adopted and used productively, its diffusion stretching 'forwards' to all subsequently acquired lexicon, but not 'backwards'; or (c) it can remain restricted to a particular layer or inventory of elements, which in turn can constitute either a closed class (as in the case of Turkish loan verbs in Vlax dialects in Greece that have lost contact with Turkish), or an open class (as in the case of Russian and Turkish in dialects that are still in contact with these languages).

8.1.2 *Borrowing hierarchies*

As language contact acquires a more prominent position in approaches to language change, the rich amount of evidence of contact-induced change has prompted scepticism with regard to the formulation of any absolute constraints on structural borrowing (Thomason and Kaufman 1988, Campbell 1993). Nonetheless, tentative generalisations about the relative likelihood of borrowing have been made in the literature. It is generally accepted that lexical items are more frequently borrowed than grammatical items, that nouns are more frequently borrowed than verbs or adjectives, that unbound elements are more easily borrowed than bound elements, and that derivational morphology is more easily borrowed than inflectional morphology (cf. Haugen 1950, Weinreich 1953, Moravcsik 1978, Thomason and Kaufman 1988, Campbell

1993). The overall picture from a structural perspective thus points to the relative autonomy of the word (compared with the tightly integrated status of the inflectional morph) as a factor that facilitates borrowing (on 'paradigmaticity' as an inhibiting factor, cf. van Hout and Muysken 1994).

Thomason and Kaufman's (1988) borrowability scale is probably the most widely cited attempt to date to provide a predictive hierarchy which matches structural properties with length and intensity of cultural contacts. The scale predicts a progression from the lexical borrowing of content words, through function words with minor phonological, syntactic, and lexical semantic features, to adpositions, derivational suffixes, and phonemes, on to word-order patterns, distinctive features in phonology, and inflectional morphology, and finally to what is called 'significant typological disruption' and phonetic changes. The successive layers of L2 influences in Romani dialects may often be taken to represent different degrees of intensity and length of contact; to some extent they provide us with a formal tool to examine the predictions on the borrowability of individual grammatical categories.

8.1.3 *L2 stratification*

The layered structure of borrowings in Romani dialects, reflecting different historical phases of contact, was alluded to with respect to the lexical component in the earliest comprehensive descriptions of the language (Pott 1844, Miklosich 1872–80). After ongoing contact with a particular L2 is broken (as a result of migration), retention of borrowed lexicon from this L2 often becomes selective. Boretzky (1989) argues that the loan component in the lexicon is recognised as foreign as long as speakers still possess active knowledge of the respective donor L2. The loan component is consequently detached from the inherited core lexicon and can be replaced through a new layer of lexical borrowings from the new L2 once a group has migrated. The decline of competence in the earlier L2 correlates with a retreat in the functions and domains of usage of this L2, and with the growing importance of the new L2 to the younger generation of immigrants (Halwachs 1993, Halwachs and Heinschink 2000).

However, some basic degree of familiarity with earlier L2s often remains for a certain period after emigration, as a result of interaction of younger and older generations. At least the L2 used by the parent generation immediately prior to migration may still be used at home, and so the generation born after migration is still exposed to it (cf. Matras 1994a: 22, Halwachs and Heinschink 2000). The kind of social and cultural networks maintained by Romani communities dictate that migration is only very seldom a migration of individuals or core families. Usually, it involves extended families and several generations. In this context, even the L2s of the grandparent generation may still play a limited role in family communication. The diachronic effect of these circumstances on migratory dialects is the successive replacement of large parts of the borrowed lexicon from a particular L2 over time, but the prevalence nonetheless of stable lexical as well as grammatical borrowings that continue to represent the historical contact phases.[2]

Taking into consideration the sociolinguistic distribution of multiple L2s across the various generations in a migratory community, it appears useful to define up to three potential layers of contact influences in individual dialects (cf. Matras 1998d). The Byzantine Greek component, along with some southern Slavic and isolated Balkan Romance influences on Early Romani, can be taken for granted as they are shared by the present-day dialects to a considerable extent. Beyond this shared component, it is possible to identify an **older L2** which has had considerable, prolonged impact on the forerunner of a particular dialect. Speakers, especially older speakers, are often aware of this impact, even if the L2 is no longer spoken by members of the community and has been succeeded by a new L2. The **recent L2** by contrast is the contact language which is no longer used by the entire community of speakers of a particular Romani dialect as their everyday language outside the home, but which may still be used by the parent or grandparent generation (or by the first generation of immigrants, in migrating communities), and to which the younger generation may still be exposed, at least occasionally. The **current L2** finally is the principal contact language used by the community for everyday interaction with the non-Romani majority, and often as a family language alongside Romani.

Vlax dialects, in many ways the classic migratory Romani dialects, have Romanian as an older L2. Communities of Serbian Gurbet or Kalderaš Vlax who have immigrated to Germany or Austria have Serbian as a recent L2, and German as their current L2, while Agia Varvara Vlax has Turkish as a recent L2 and Greek as the current L2. For Italian Sinti and French Manuš dialects, German can be defined as the older L2, and Italian and French respectively as the current L2s. For the Istrian Hravati dialect, Croatian is the older L2, Slovene possibly the recent L2, and Italian the current L2; and so forth. One must keep in mind however that L2 stratification profiles vary. In some communities, such as the Arli of Kosovo, there are multiple current L2s (Albanian, Turkish, Serbian). Some dialects may show overlap between the older and recent, or between the recent and current L2. Various older L2s may have played a secondary role in the history of individual dialects; thus there are German lexical items in the Northeastern dialects, but no traces of any German grammatical influence. Also noteworthy is the fact that the succession of contact languages is not always the outcome of Romani migration, but can also result from changing geopolitical circumstances; thus, competence in Hungarian among the Roman-speaking

[2] Observations among American Kelderaš suggest that speakers are often aware of these layers, and encourage each other to use 'old words' when conversing with members of other Romani communities, in order to increase comprehensibility (E. Casella, p.c.).

community of the Austrian Burgenland declined during the twentieth century, and German has become the only current contact language. Similarly, Turkish is retreating as a current L2 among the Muslim Rom of northeastern Bulgaria, and is gradually acquiring the status of a recent L2.

8.2 Historical layers of grammatical borrowings

8.2.1 *The pre-European and Greek component*

It is difficult to reconstruct the inventory of grammatical borrowings which Early Romani may have inherited from its pre-European forerunner. Possibly the oldest borrowing is the transitivising suffix *-ar-* which is likely to have been acquired during the northwestern Indic period of Proto-Romani, and so constitutes a case of interdialectal borrowing. Evidence for an areal interdialectal development was cited in chapter 6 in connection with the emergence of the past-tense conjugation. Somewhat ambiguous cases are the adjectival comparative marker *-eder* and the adjectival prefix *bi-* 'without', as well as the indefinite *či*, all of which have been discussed in connection with the Iranian component (cf. Boretzky and Igla 1994b, Hancock 1995b; but see chapter 3), though Indo-Aryan cognates cannot be excluded. Possible function words of Iranian origin are *šaj* 'can' (Persian), *orde* 'there' (argued to be Ossetian; but cf. Turkish *orada*; see Matras 1996b), *inća* 'here' (possibly Persian), and the additive conjunction *-u-* in numerals above 'ten' (in some dialects, such as Welsh Romani and the Central group, also between verb phrases). The nominal derivational marker *-ik* is shared with Armenian and Iranian, as are other lexical items, which might indicate overall areal convergence which late Proto-Romani underwent, prior to the Byzantine period, in western Asia. Syntactic-typological properties of Romani that could derive from areal convergence tendencies in western Asia are the prepositioning of local relation adverbs (i.e. the development of basic prepositions), the emergence of external tense markers, the reduction of the infinitive in modal constructions, the use of obligatory resumptive pronouns with head nouns in non-subject roles in relative clauses, and the loss of MIA relativisers in *y-/j-* and reliance instead on conjunctions derived from interrogatives. For many of these features, early triggers in the northwestern NIA languages cannot be ruled out.

Greek grammatical borrowing into Early Romani has had a lasting, dominating impact on the language. However, the retention rate of Greek-derived borrowings after the Early Romani period is higher for elements that form part of grammatical paradigms, than for free-standing lexical morphemes. Significantly, at the lexical level present-day Romani dialects outside the Balkans retain only up to three or four dozen nouns of Greek origin, and few verbs or adjectives. Grammatical adverbs with a high retention rate include those expressing reversal and repetition (*pale* 'again', *palpale/parpale/papale* 'back'), the word for 'tomorrow' (*tasja/tajsa/taha-*), and in some dialects also the phasal adverbs *komi* 'still' (attested in earlier sources of Sinti) and *panda* 'still' < 'always' (Balkan dialects). The most stable free morphemes of Greek origin are the numerals *efta* 'seven', *oxto* 'eight', *enja* 'nine', and *trijanda* 'thirty', in some dialects also *saranda* 'forty' and *pinda* 'fifty', while higher Greek-derived numerals are retained mostly in the Balkans.

Bound derivational morphemes from Greek that are diffused into the inherited pre-European vocabulary include the suffix for ordinal numerals *-to* (as in *duj-to* 'second'), which has completely replaced any pre-European equivalent. The abstract nominal marker *-imo(s)* PL *-imata* is retained in Vlax, in the Ukrainian and North Russian dialects, in Welsh Romani and in Iberian Romani, usually in competition with inherited *-ipen/-iben* (see chapter 5). Elšík (2000c) proposes a Greek etymology for the indefinite marker *-moni* (< Greek *monos* 'only') found in the western dialects of Romani (Welsh, Iberian, Sinti, Finnish, Abruzzian), which attaches to inherited semantic specifiers (*či-moni* 'something', *ko-moni* 'somebody'). In other domains, diffusion of Greek-derived morphology into the pre-European inherited component is more limited, while on the other hand Greek morphemes remain the dominant productive pattern for the adaptation of European loans. In derivation, all Romani dialects retain the adjectival suffixes *-itik-/-itk-/-ick-/-ik-* (Greek *-itikos*, *-ikos*, possibly also Slavic *-ick-*). The Slavic diminutive marker *-ica/-ici* and the feminine marker *-ica* are shared with other Balkan languages, which seems to reinforce their continuing productivity.

One of the most outstanding contact features of Romani is the adoption of productive Greek inflectional patterns. With nouns, Early Romani adopts the nominative markers singular *-o(s)*, *-i(s)* and *-a*, plural *-i* as markers of new inflectional classes (see chapter 5). While the plural markers are often replaced through later European borrowings, the singular markers are retained. Similarly, Greek-derived adjectival (neuter) inflection endings in singular *-o*, plural *-a* are used with European loan adjectives as well as with new adjectival derivations. With verbs, Early Romani maintained Greek tense/aspect endings, present *-iz-/-az-/-in-* etc. and aorist *-s-*, with Greek loan verbs; the present-day dialects continue to employ these endings, in a simplified and adjusted format, for the adaptation of European loan verbs (see chapter 6). It seems likely that the motivation to preserve the Greek markers for loan adaptation derived from the use of such indigenous tense/aspect markers in Greek itself to adapt loans from other languages (see Bakker 1997b). Also productive with loan verbs is the Greek-derived participle marker *-ime(n)* (< Greek *-imenos*). The 3SG concord marker *-i*, in all likelihood of Greek origin, appears with loan verbs in Welsh Romani, Latvian Romani, and Gilan Arli of Kosovo (*pomož-in-i* 'helps'; see Boretzky 1996a), and with all verbs in Dolenjski/Hravati.

There is limited diffusion of Greek-derived verb inflection into the inherited component, usually with some functional and structural transformation. The participle ending *-imen* attaches to inherited roots in a number of dialects as a means of adjectival derivation (Welsh *baxtimen* 'lucky', Finnish *džānimen* 'knowledgeable'). In Romungro and Lovari, Greek *-in-*, combined with the Hungarian-derived verb-derivation marker *-az-*, may attach to inherited roots (Lovari *buč-az-in-* 'to work'). Combinations with inherited morphemes that are diffused into the inherited component are *-is-ar-* > *-isal-* (Slovak Romani *šukar-isal-jo(v)-* 'to become beautiful'), *-is-ajl-* (Sepeči *dara-sajl-* 'feared'), and *-in-ker-*/*-inger-* (Romungro *dikh-inger-* 'to see often'). The 3SG concord marker *-i* appears facultatively in Arli with inherited bi- and polysyllabic verbs (*arakhi* 'finds', alongside *arakhel*), while in the Dolenjski dialect it has even replaced the inherited 3SG concord marker with all verbs.

A series of syntactic-typological properties are shared with Greek, though it is sometimes less obvious that they result directly or exclusively from Greek influence on Early Romani. The development of a definite article in Romani is the outcome of the internal grammaticalisation of anaphoric elements. It is unlikely that any language other than Greek could have served as a model for this development, since the NIA and Near Eastern languages lack a definite article, while the other Balkan languages have postposed articles. Likewise, the shift to VO word order is likely to have resulted from contact with Greek. Most Romani prepositions appear to be Early Romani or even later developments, and so it is likely that the system of prepositions, if it had existed at all prior to contact with Greek, was expanded as a result of this contact. Romani and Greek (and other Balkan languages) share the obligatory use of a resumptive pronoun in relative clauses with head nouns in lower-ranking thematic roles, but this is also found in Persian. The employment of a general relativiser (Romani *kaj*) as a factual complementiser is in principle shared with Iranian (Persian *ke*, Kurdish *ku*), though in Romani there is a parallel employment of modal/conditional/final *te* in non-factual complements. The resulting complementation typology adheres strongly to the Balkan model (cf. Friedman 1985, Matras 1994b). Boretzky (1996d: 97–8) points out the contrast between the position of the pronominal direct object after the verb in Romani (the conservative word order), and its proclitic position in Greek and other Balkan languages. However, it is likely that the position of the Romani pronoun reflects the rather recent grammaticalisation of demonstratives as pronominal anaphora (**dikhav oles* 'I see this one' > *dikhav les* 'I see him'; see chapter 5). The position of the demonstrative object is in fact shared with Greek (*vlepo aftó*).

Arguably, the Europeanisation of Romani – especially the shift to VO word order, the development of the definite article, the emergence or at least expansion of the system of prepositions, and the typology of complements and adverbial clauses – is the result of Romani settlement first in the Asia Minor periphery, and later in the core of the Balkans, and the exposure of the language to the general convergent developments in this area. The effects of convergence on Romani will have been more radical in some respects than on other languages of the region, if we assume a point of departure in later Proto-Romani that adhered, if not to the Indo-Aryan type, then to the western Asian type: VO word order, no definite articles, some use of nominalised verb forms, a small and restricted inventory of prepositions. Thus, from the perspective of the historical development of Romani, Balkanisation in Early Romani also entails the Europeanisation of many of its features (cf. Matras 1994a: 13–14, 1994b). From the perspective of Balkan linguistics there is however a tendency to consider as 'Balkanisms' only those features that cluster in the Balkans and that are diagnostic of the Balkans as a linguistic area (see Boretzky and Igla 1999). In any event, 'Balkanisation' in Romani is dynamic and layered. Convergence with the Balkan languages has only a marginal effect on the system of synthetic case marking in Romani, for instance. On the other hand, Balkanisation is gradual and continues after the Early Romani period, affecting those dialects that remain in the Balkan area (see below).

8.2.2 *Widespread patterns of borrowing following the Early Romani period*

For the period that follows Early Romani and the decline of Greek as the principal contact language, it is necessary to distinguish **prolonged and intense impact** of respective contact languages on individual dialects from **short-term impact**. With the dispersion of the dialects in the fourteenth to fifteenth centuries, migrant communities became exposed to additional contact languages and in many cases to successive contact influences. Long-term and intense contacts emerged during the period of settlement that followed in the sixteenth to seventeenth centuries. Typical for this period is the formation of group-specific identities in individual Romani communities. These are often reflected through the religious affiliation, the pattern of occupations, and the identification with a particular territory or nation, all of which may be flagged through the individual group names. The principal languages that influenced Romani dialect groups during this period are Turkish (on Muslim dialects of the Balkans, later also Southern Vlax), Romanian (on Early Vlax), Southern Slavic (on dialects of the Balkans, later also Southern Vlax), Hungarian (on the Central dialects and Northwestern Vlax), German (on the Sinti group), and Western Slavic (on the Northern Central and the Northeastern dialects), as well as other languages in individual regions.

Changes triggered by prolonged and intense contact following the settlement period affect indeclinable unbound function words, bound and semi-bound derivational morphology, some inflectional morphology, phonology, and certain word-order features. Particularly outstanding among the unbound function words are phasal adverbs ('still', 'already', 'no longer'), focus particles

Table 8.1 *Frequently attested Romani indeclinables by source language (in the column 'Pre-European',* atoska *is of unknown origin,* komi *and* panda *are Greek, and* vi *is Indic or Indo-Iranian)*

	Slavic (S/W)	Romanian	Hungarian	Turkish	German	Pre-Eur/Greek
'then'	posle	atunči	akkor	son(r)a	dan	atoska
'still'	još/ješče	inke	meg	da(h)a	nox	komi, panda
'already'	još/uže	aba	(i)ma(r)	–	šon	–
'only'	samo/tylko	numa/feri	čak	sade	nur, blos	moni, monsi
'also'	i/tyš, též	–	iš	da, hem	–	vi, nina
'always'	zavše		mindig	hep	imer	panda

('even', 'only', 'every', 'also/too'), sequential discourse markers (of the type 'and then', 'and so'), and the temporal deixis 'then' and adverb 'always', which are overwhelmingly European borrowings. These categories are usually acquired through contacts that can be assumed to have lasted at least a century. In migrant dialects, they remain on the whole stable for the duration of at least several generations after contact with the older L2 has been broken. Consider for instance the retention of Hungarian-derived items in these classes in most of the Central dialects. By contrast, the Southern Vlax dialects do not typically show Romanianisms in these classes; instead, Gurbet-type varieties have South Slavic borrowings, while eastern Balkan Southern Vlax varieties such as the Agia Varvara dialects have Turkish inventories, an indication of the early breakup of the Vlax group and the emigration of the Southern Vlax dialects from Romanian territory probably before the nineteenth century.

Most susceptible to borrowing at a very early stage of contact are discourse particles that are low on the content-lexical or syntactic scale, but high on the interactional scale, such as fillers and tags. These are often adopted within just one generation of contact with a new L2, i.e. at the level of the current L2 (see Matras 1998d). Consider in (1)-(2) examples from the first generation of migrants who moved from Poland to Germany as young children in the 1950s; the older L2 in this Vlax dialect is Romanian, the recent L2 Polish (which is still spoken by the younger generation), and the current L2 is German, from which the fillers and tags derive:

(1) Laki familija sas *also* kesave sar te phenav, artisturi, *nə*?
'Her family were *like* such how shall I say, showpeople, *right*?'

(2) Taj žasas ande veša taj rodasas, taj dikhasas, khelasas
and we-went in woods and we-searched and we-saw played
ame *halt*, *nə*.
we like right
'And we used to go into the woods and search, and look around, we *like* used to play, *right*.'

Table 8.2 *Coordinating conjunctions in some dialects*

	'and'	'or'	'but'
Roman	taj	vaj	ham
Lovari (Polish, in Germany)	taj, aj	vaj	ale
Lovari (French, in Norway)	taj, aj	vaj	me
German Lovari	taj, aj	vaj	aber
Agia Varvara	ta	ja, i	alá
Romungro (Hungary)	taj	vadj	de
Romungro (Slovakia)	taj	vadj	ale
Serbian Gurbet	taj, a, i	ili	ali
Bugurdži	i, a, ta	ili	ali, po
Manuš	un, te	otar	aver, me
Sinti	und	oder	aber
Polska Roma	i	čy	ale
North Russian	i	ili	no

The early adoption of discourse particles of this kind in bilingual settings is well attested. It has been attributed both to the sentence-peripheral position of these elements, which makes them easily adaptable and so convenient for occasional flagging of bilingual competence (see Poplack 1980, Stolz and Stolz 1996), but also to the overall merger of communicative strategies (cf. Salmons 1990) with the 'pragmatically dominant language' (Matras 1998d).

Particularly prone to early replacement, within two or three generations, through elements of a current L2 are contrastive conjunctions. No Romani dialect shows a pre-European or early Greek adversative. Indo-Aryan forms are preserved for the other coordinating conjunctions (*ta/taj/thaj/te* 'and', *vaj* 'or'), though here too there are tendencies toward replacement. The three conjunctions form a consistent implicational hierarchy – 'and' < 'or' < 'but' – with respect to their borrowing likelihood, i.e. if no pre-European form exists for 'and', then none exists for 'or' either. All dialects borrow 'but' from a current or recent L2, while borrowings of 'or' may be from an older or recent L2, and borrowings for 'and' are likely to continue to coexist with an inherited form (table 8.2).

In table 8.2, 'but' may derive from the immediately recent L2 in communities where the current L2 has only recently gained ground, as in the case of Hungarian *ham* in the Roman dialect of the Austrian Burgenland, currently with German as a principal L2, or Polish *ale* in the Lovari variety described in Matras (1994b), spoken by first-generation immigrants from Poland in Germany and Sweden. In most cases, however, 'but' corresponds to the current L2: French-derived *me* in French/Norwegian Lovari (Gjerde 1994), German *aber* in German Lovari and in Sinti, Greek *alá* in the Southern Vlax varieties of Agia Varvara in Greece, Hungarian *de* in Hungarian Romungro, Slovak *ale* in Slovak Romungro, Serbian *ali/po* in Gurbet and Bugurdži, Alsatian German *aver* for varieties of

Manuš in Alsace (Rao 1976) alongside French-derived *me* (Valet 1991), and so on. In the 'or' column, both Roman and Lovari retain Indic *vaj*. Agia Varvara has forms from both older L2 (Turkish) and current L2 (Greek), Manuš retains German-derived *otar*, while the other dialects represented here show current L2 forms. For 'and', retention of Indic *ta/taj/te* is quite extensive; in Lovari *aj* is added, perhaps under earlier Slavic influence, and is integrated into the structural pattern of the language, probably by analogy to *taj* and *vaj*. In Gurbet, Serbian *a* and *i* appear alongside *taj*, while in Bugurdži the Serbian forms are more frequent. The older conjunction *te* is cited for Manuš by Valet (1991), and appears in earlier sources for Sinti as well. The other dialects have borrowed all three forms from the current L2, with which they have been in prolonged contact for many generations.

Among the subordinating conjunctions, borrowings of European origin include those expressing cause and reason: Vlax *ke* (Romanian), Sinti *vajl* (German), Southern Central *mint/mer* (Hungarian), Northern Central and Polska Roma *bo/lébo* (Western Slavic), Southern Vlax and Arli-type dialects in Greece *jati* (Greek) or *zere* (Turkish). The factual complementiser is also frequently borrowed: *ke* (Romanian) in Vlax, *hoj/hod/hodž* (Hungarian) in the Central dialects, *oti* (Greek) in dialects in Greece, *da* (Slovene) in the Dolenjski dialect (see p. 210). Borrowings are also attested for conditional conjunctions (Slavic *ako/jesli*), potential/optional conjunctions (Western Slavic *čy*, German *op*), and temporal conjunctions (Russian *kogda*, Turkish *zaman*).

Generally prone to borrowing is the domain of modality. Sentence-level and clitic modality particles include the conditional particles *bi/by* (Slavic) and *(i)se* (Turkish), the interrogative *mi* (Turkish) and interrogative/quotative *čy/li* (Slavic), interjectional-imperative particles *haj/hade* (Turkish and general Balkan), *nek/neka* (Slavic), *davaj* (Russian). Borrowing also affects the lexico-grammatical domain of modal expressions, both personal (inflected) and impersonal. Expressions of necessity figure at the top of the borrowability hierarchy for modals, and it is here that one finds the greatest diversity among the dialects: *treba/trebuie/trjabva* (various Balkan languages), *mora-*, *valja-* (South Slavic), *lazimi*, *madžburi* (Turkish) and *prepi* (Greek) in the Balkans, *mus-/mos-musaj/musin-* (English, Hungarian, Romanian, West Slavic) in Welsh Romani, Vlax, Central, and Northeastern dialects (cf. Boretzky 1996c). Also attested are borrowings in *mogin-/možin-* (Slavic) for 'can' in the Balkan, Central and Northeastern groups, and *bor-* 'can' (Greek) in Agia Varvara Vlax. Frequently borrowed are also 'to think/believe' – widespread is *misl-* (Slavic), Vlax *gind-* (Romanian), Sinti *denk-* (German), Roman *muan-* (Austrian German) – and 'begin' – Central and Lovari *kezd-* (Hungarian), Italian Sinti *komens-* (Italian).

The verbal system of several dialects and dialect groups has been significantly influenced through borrowings in the domain of aktionsart modification. The Northeastern and Northern Central dialects have adopted the full system of

Slavic aspect prefixes (*po-*, *-za-*, *od-* etc.). In Latvian Romani, Slavic prefixes deriving from the older L2 Polish coexist with more recently acquired Latvian prefixes (*ie-*, *uz-*). Occasional use of borrowed Slavic aspect prefixes with inherited verb stems is also found in Balkan dialects in contact with South Slavic languages. Borrowed particles from German marking aktionsart (*an*, *hin*) appear in the Sinti group and in Burgenland Roman. Elšík et al. (1999: 373) also report on the borrowing of *sît/síja* from Hungarian into Romungro dialects of Slovakia, and individual Greek-derived aktionsart markers are attested for Southern Vlax in Greece (Igla 1996).

Overt expression of the superlative in Romani relies predominantly on borrowed preposed particles such as *naj* (Slavic) in the Balkan, Northeastern and Northern Central groups, *maj* (Romanian) in Vlax, *lek* (Hungarian) in the Southern Central group, *am* (German) in Sinti, and *en* (Turkish) in the Balkans. This often combines with the Romani synthetic comparative in *-eder*. In some dialects, borrowed comparatives – Vlax *maj* (Romanian), Northern Central and Balkan *po* (Slavic), Balkan *da(h)a* (Turkish), Ipeiros *pio* (Greek) – replace the inherited synthetic comparative. The excessive-superlative ('too much') is also borrowed: Vlax *pre* (Slavic, via Romanian), Sinti *cu* (German). European adjectival derivational markers include the widespread Slavic *-n-*, as well as *-ičos-* (Romanian) in Vlax, and *-oš-n-* (Hungarian-based) in Central dialects, all of which are mainly confined to the loan component. In Burgenland Roman, the dialectal German adjectival ending *-i* (*brauni* 'brown') is generalised as an inflectional ending for recently borrowed adjectives.

Borrowing dominates the inventory of bound indefinite markers, which attach to inherited semantic specifiers of time, manner, person, etc.. The most widely distributed of those is *vare-*, for which a Romanian etymology in *oare-* is usually assumed. The unique feature of *vare-* is its diffusion beyond Vlax, and its presence also in the Northern Central and Northeastern dialect as well as in Welsh and Iberian Romani (see section 5.5.6). This widescale diffusion suggests a borrowing that had entered the language in the Early Romani period (see footnote and discussion on p. 115). Other bound indefinite markers include *-godi*, *i-*, *bilo-*, *de-*, *se-* (South Slavic), *-far* (Albanian), *xoč-* (Polish), *malo-* (Slovak), *vala-*, *akar-* (Hungarian), *nibud'-* (Russian), and the negative indefinite *ni-* of general Slavic origin (cf. Boretzky and Igla 1991: 21–3). Renewal of the inventory of indefinites is generally more widespread in the dialects of the Balkans and central Europe, while dialects in northern and western Europe retain the Greek-derived indefinite marker *-moni* (Elšík 2000c). Some dialects also borrow entire indefinite expressions: Vlax *uni* 'some' (Romanian), Central and Balkan *nič/ništa* (Slavic) and Balkan *hič* (Turkish) 'none, nothing', Central *šoha* 'never' (Hungarian), Dendropotamos Vlax *kapios* 'somebody', *kati* 'something' and *tipota* 'nothing' (Greek) (cf. Elšík 2001). Exclusively of European origin are the focal quantifiers 'every' (*svako/sako* from Slavic, *her/er* from Turkish), 'entire/whole' (*celo* from Slavic, *intrego* from Romanian, *-lauter* from German, *kre(j)t* from Albanian), 'same' (*isto* from South Slavic), and frequently also the ordinal 'first' (*pervo* from Slavic, *eršto* from German). In Balkan dialects in direct contact with Turkish, the Turkish general quantifier *tane* is frequently replicated. In the numeral system, 'thousand' is usually a European loan: Sinti and Central dialects *ezero(s)* (Hungarian), Northeastern *tisač* (Slavic), Vlax *mija* (Romanian), Balkan *hilja* (Greek).

Prone to renewal through borrowing in the nominal domain is the inventory of nominal derivational markers expressing abstract nominalisation, agentives, diminutives and feminine derivations (cf. Boretzky and Igla 1991: 13–21). The overwhelming tendency here is for additional markers to enrich the inventory of pre-European and Greek-derived affixes, rather than replace them. Borrowed abstract nominal markers in individual dialects include *-išag-* (Hungarian), *-luk-* (Turkish, possibly via South Slavic), and *-um-* (Lithuanian) in dialects in recent contact with the respective languages. A widespread agentive marker is *-ar-*, found in the Northern, Central and Vlax branches, possibly of diverse origins (Romanian, Slavic). Vlax also shows Romanian-derived *-aš-* and *-tor-* and in the Balkans we find Turkish-derived *-dži-* (also present in other Balkan languages). Abstract nominal derivations and agentives are widely diffused into the inherited pre-European component. On the other hand, borrowed feminine and diminutive markers tend to be restricted to European loans. Feminine derivations are formed with *-ica* (Greek, Slavic, Romanian) in most dialects, alongside *-ka* and *-inka* (Slavic). Diminutive markers include *-ičko*, *-inka* (Slavic), and *-uca* (Romanian).

The borrowing of nominal inflection markers after the Early Romani period is restricted to the nominative plural markers *-urj-/uri* of Romanian origin in Vlax, *-e* of Southern Slavic origin in the (predominently western) Balkan dialects, and *-ides* of Greek origin in the eastern Balkan dialects (Erli, Bugurdži, Sepeči, Drindari).[3] The latter appears to be the result of continuing contact with Greek following the breakup of the dialects. All three markers spread within the European loan component; Vlax *-urj-* even attaches to some Greek loans which entered the language prior to the Romanian period at which the suffix itself was acquired (*for-uri* 'towns'). In addition, plurals in *-i* continue to be widespread in most dialect branches, in all likelihood as a result of a merger of the Early Romani Greek-derived suffix with Slavic plurals in *-i*.

In the nominal complex we find primarily prepositions that express abstract rather than concrete spatial relations: *protiv/proci/prečiv* 'against' (Slavic), Vlax *de* 'since' (Romanian), Balkan *sebepi* 'because of' (from Turkish, also Albanian and other Balkan languages). Other borrowed prepositions include Sinti *oni*

[3] Romani translators rendered the plural of 'planets' as *planeturi* (Vlax), *planete* (Serbian Gurbet), *planeti* (Polska Roma) (cf. Matras 1997b). In the eastern Balkan dialects, *-ides* attaches to Turkish loans, cf. *sepečides* 'basket weavers' (Turkish *sepetçi*).

'without' and *durx* 'through' (German), the latter also found in the Northeastern dialects, *bez* 'without' (and *bizo*, contaminated by inherited *bi*) and *mesto* 'instead of' (Slavic) in Northeastern and Balkan dialects, and *priko/preko* 'beyond' (Slavic) in Central and Balkan dialects. In addition, there is a preference in some dialects to employ prepositions expressing sociative/instrumental/comitative relations ('with') from the current contact language with loan nouns, rather than draw on the synthetic instrumental case. Diffusion of the borrowed preposition into the inherited component is attested for Sinti, German Lovari, and Roman (*mit*), Vlax and non-Vlax dialects of Greece (*me*), Italian Sinti, Argentinian Kalderaš, and Istrian Hravati (*kon/kun*).

Structural domains that generally tend to derive from the current L2 are, apart from the discourse markers dealt with above, sentential adverbs, numerals expressing dates, names of the months, and usually also days of the week (though most dialects retain *kurko* 'Sunday', from Greek *kyriakí*, and *paraštuj* 'Friday', from Greek *paraskeví*). Many of these may be regarded as institutional terminology used to negotiate administrative affairs outside the Romani community.

In phonology, perhaps the most noticeable contact-induced changes that affect the system as a whole are the shift in stress patterns toward pre-final or initial stress in dialects of western and central Europe as well as under Albanian influence in the Prizren dialect, the adoption of vowel-length distinction in dialects in western and central Europe, and the phonemic status of palatalisation in the Northeastern dialects. Individual dialects show diffusion into the inherited component of loan phonemes, such as English /ɔ/ in British Romani, Hungarian /ɒː/ in Romungro, Romanian /ə/ and /ɨ/ in Kalderaš, Polish, and Russian /ɨ/ in the Northeastern dialects, the Turkish (or Albanian) rounded vowel /y/ in some Arli varieties, and consonant gemination in Italian Romani dialects. Inherited phonemic distinctions may in addition be reduced based on the model of contact languages, as in the case of the simplification of /h:x/ in (some) Balkan and Southern Central dialects, or the loss of postalveolar sibilants in Vlax dialects of Greece. Somewhat controversial is the status of intonation, partly due to the lack of any comprehensive experimental phonetic study on Romani. The tendency towards convergence with intonation patterns of the principal contact language within two to three generations is overwhelming. On the other hand, Romani speakers often have recognisable intonation patterns in their current L2s. It has even been argued that some Romani dialects might preserve intonation patterns of pre-European origin (Grigorova 1998).

Some phonetic features are likely to be diffused into the Romani component within two to three generations of contact. For the phoneme /r/ the uvular articulation [ʀ] is prevalent in German and French Sinti–Manuš, but is also found among the first generation of Lovari migrants from Norway born in France (Gjerde 1994) and of Lovari migrants from Poland born in Germany.

Syntactic convergence with European contact languages following the dispersal and settlement period can be said to affect three principal domains: word-order rules, agreement patterns, and the status of categories. With word order, there is a tendency in dialects in contact with western and eastern Slavic languages for the pronominal object in interrogative and modal complement clauses to appear in pre-verbal or second enclitic position (*kana les dikhlan?* 'when did you see him?'). In the dialects of the Balkans, there is a tendency toward pronominal object doubling, mirroring constructions found in other Balkan languages (see Friedman 2000). In Burgenland Roman, the resumptive pronoun appears in a position adjoined to the relativiser (*so leske* 'for whom') and preceding the verb, a construction that is modelled on dialectal (Austrian) German (*dem wos*) (Halwachs 1998: 95). Similar forms are found in the Central dialects, through Czech/Slovak influence.

Rearrangement of the position of the finite verb also appears. There is a loose tendency in dialects in contact with western Slavic languages for the verb to occupy the final position in adverbial subordinations and especially in modal complements. The position of the finite verb is formalised in some Sinti varieties, replicating German word-order rules: the finite verb appears in final position in relative clauses and adverbial subordinations (cf. Boretzky 1996d), though not in modal complements with *te* (cf. Matras 1999e). In declarative clauses, the finite verb is in the second position, triggering verb–subject inversion when the first position is occupied by another element (deictic or adverb). There is some evidence of a shift toward OV word order in Romani dialects of Turkey (Bakker 2001). Recent contact phenomena affecting word order in the noun phrase are the optional placement of demonstratives after the definite noun in some Vlax dialects under Romanian and recent Greek influence, and the emergence of postpositions under Turkish influence in Sepeči, and under Finnish influence in Finnish Romani. Borrowed grammatical markers in Romani follow a universal tendency to be replicated together with the rules on their position (cf. Moravcsik 1978). Examples are the postpositioning in Balkan dialects of *da* (Turkish) and in Central dialects of *iš* (Hungarian), both meaning 'too, also', the postpositioning of the Sinti verb negators *ni(ch)t* and *gar* (German), and the postpositioning of the Turkish temporal adverbial subordinator *zaman* in non-Vlax dialects of Turkey (*dikhlas zaman* 'when she saw'; Bakker 2001).[4]

A widespread contact-induced change in agreement patterns is the loss of agreement between the subjects of modal constructions and the embedded verb in the complement, and the generalisation instead of just one single form, often the 3SG, sometimes the 2SG or 3PL. This tendency toward syntactic de-Balkanisation has been referred to as the 'new infinitive' in Romani (Boretzky

[4] But cf. on the other hand the Turkish-derived conditional *ise* in Erli (Boretzky 1998: 142, from Gilliat-Smith): *ise me džavas* 'if I could go'.

1996b). It is particularly strong in central Europe, encompassing the Central dialects, Sinti, Hravati/Dolenjski, and the Polska Roma dialect, and to a lesser extent in other Northeastern varieties. Under Slavic influence in North Russian Romani and in Dolenjski, adjectival agreement copies the full set of nominal case endings. In some Vlax dialects, under the recent influence of Romanian and Greek, the definite article and demonstrative determination become compatible (*kava o rom* 'this man').

Finally, the status of some categories is modified as a result of contact with European languages. Dialects in continuing contact with the Balkan languages have developed an analytic future in *ka* or *ma* based on the verbs *kam-* and *mang-* 'to want', mirroring the analytic future of the contact languages. An analytic future also emerges in Russian Romani dialects, drawing either on the (suppletive) subjunctive copula in *av-* (copying Russian *bud-*), or on a reanalysis of the modal *l-* 'to begin' (< 'to take', calquing Ukrainian). More rarely we find analytic past tenses, drawing on the copula *sin-* or on the verb *ter-* 'to have', modelled on the analytic perfect of Greek and Macedonian. A drift towards category compatibility leads to the loss of the definite (and partly also indefinite) article through contact with Slavic languages in the Northeastern group and in Dolenjski, and to the reduction and loss of the synthetic intransitive in German Sinti and in Welsh Romani. Perhaps the most radical case of category-reduction is the loss of nominal case inflection markers in the Abruzzian dialect. On the other hand, the productivity of some categories increases through contact; consider the productivity transitive/causative derivations in dialects in contact with Hungarian and Turkish, and the anaphoric and sequential use of the deictic *koi* in Sinti, modelled on German *da* (*koi pre* 'on that', German *da-rauf*).

8.2.3 *Rare instances of borrowing*

As 'rarely attested' instances of borrowing I understand phenomena that are exceptional among the dialects of Romani, as well as instances of borrowing that are not typically attested in situations of language contact elsewhere. As an illustrative example consider the recent borrowing in the Dolenjski dialect of the numerals 'six' to 'nine' from Slavic, replacing inherited 'six' and Greek-derived 'seven' to 'nine'.

Borrowing on the scale of the adoption of the full set of Greek tense/aspect markers is not attested after the Early Romani period. However, morphological compartmentalisation is encountered in dialects in prolonged contact with Turkish in the Balkans, and in North Russian Romani. In both cases, the entire verb inflection of the source language is replicated with verbs deriving from these languages (see chapter 6). In some dialects of the Balkans, borrowed modals retain the person inflection of the source language: Bugurdži *mora-m* 'I must' (South Slavic), Agia Varvara *bor-ó* 'I can' (Greek) (cf. Boretzky 1996c).

Southern Central varieties and Lovari have borrowed the Hungarian-derived verb derivational marker *-az-*, which can be diffused into the inherited component (*buč-az-in-* 'to work'). Kosovo Gurbet employs the Albanian-derived particle *tuj* for the progressive aspect. English tense/aspect inflection is used occasionally in the specimen of modern Welsh Romani published by Tipler (1957), though it coincides with the overall inconsistent use of Romani inflection at an advanced stage of language decline. Thus we find *muler'd šī-lī* 'she is dead', but also *man'l dža* 'I'll go', where the oblique form of the pronoun appears instead of the nominative. Note also the use of the plain verb stem for the infinitive.

Person inflection that is diffused into the inherited component is found in the Dolenjski dialect of Slovenia, which has adopted the Slavic (most likely Croatian) present-tense endings of the 1SG, 1PL, and 2PL *-u*, *-ame*, and *-ate*, and which uses Greek-derived *-i* consistently in the 3SG. Although 3SG. *-i* from Greek is attested elsewhere, and must have entered the language in the Early Romani period, it rarely diffuses into the inherited component, and it is not attested in any other dialect as having completely replaced the inherited 3SG suffix *-el*. The generalisation of *-i* in the Hravati/Dolenjski dialect possibly licensed the adoption of further person markers. At least for the 1PL *-ame*, reinforcement through the inherited *-am* of the past-tense paradigm is likely. The form of the Slavic infinitive in *-i* has without doubt also promoted the generalisation of the 3SG *-i* in the Dolenjski dialect as an infinitive form which, unlike in other dialects that have developed a 'new infinitive', is not introduced by the conjunction *te*.

The most widespread negative focus marker ('neither . . . nor') in Romani is *ni . . . ni* borrowed from Slavic. Balkan dialects under Turkish influence have Turkish *ne . . . ne*, while Northern Vlax has *či . . . či*, likely to be reinforced by Romanian *nici . . . nici* (Elšík 2000c), alongside the actual Romanian-derived form *niči . . . niči*. Direct borrowing of a finite-verb negation marker is Sinti *ni(ch)t* (German), while other Sinti varieties employ *gar*, from the German focus particle in *gar nicht* 'not at all'.

Extensive borrowing of prepositions is found in Sinti, which has adopted even the basic prepositions *für* 'for', and *fon* 'from' from German. Istrian Hravati and the Abruzzian dialect employ *di* 'of', from Italian. Although definite articles are not borrowed and diffused freely into the inherited component, Romani dialects of Greece show regular use of the Greek-inflected definite article with the Greek-derived preposition *me* 'with', attaching to inherited elements: *e rakli me to parno gad* 'the girl with the white shirt' (see Matras 1997a: 81). Frequent use of the English indefinite article *a* is documented for modern Welsh Romani (Tipler 1957), and the indefinite article of the Abruzzi dialect *ni* could derive from dialectal Italian *na*. A marker of definiteness *-to* from the Bulgarian relativiser *koj-to* is adopted in the Erli dialect, and attached to inherited relativisers *kon-to*, *kova-to* as well as to the temporal adverbial subordinator *kana-to* (Boretzy and Igla 1991: 23). A parallel case is reported for some Romungro varieties, where the preposed Hungarian relativiser *a-* is attached to inherited conjunctions (Elšík et al. 1999).

Further instances of rare grammatical borrowing involve the apparent convergence of inherited forms with counterparts that are formally and functionally similar. The only attested borrowing of a deictic element is the place deixis *ore* in Roman, of Hungarian origin, which figures in the dialect alongside the older *orde* 'there'. Cases of merger in personal pronouns are Hravati/Dolenjski 3PL *oni* modelled on Slavic, but drawing on inherited *on*; Zargari 1SG *min* from Azerbaijanian, drawing on inherited *me*, oblique *man*. In Nógrád Romungro, the 3PL pronoun is *ōnk*, combining inherited *on* with a Hungarian plural suffix *-k*, reinforced in all likelihood by the Hungarian 3SG pronoun *ő*, PL *ő*-k (cf. Elšík 2000b). The interrogative for 'when' is borrowed from Slavic in the Prilep dialect (*koga*) and in Burgenland Roman (*kada*), showing similarities with the inherited Romani form *kana*. Some Arli varieties borrow Macedonian *koj* 'who', which resembles the inherited interrogative *kon*. Finally, the productivity in Zargari of the directive case marker in *-e* is triggered by the Azerbaijanian dative *-e/-a*, but draws on the inherited, nearly obsolete directive in *-e* (*kher-e* 'home', *angl-e* 'forwards', etc.).

8.3 An assessment of grammatical borrowing

There are some instances of grammatical borrowing in Romani that might be considered as rather exceptional, or perhaps better as indicators of particularly 'heavy' borrowing. Most outstanding is the borrowing into Early Romani of bound inflectional class markers (of nouns, verbs, and adjectives) from Greek, allowing the language to copy the Greek pattern for adapting loans by drawing on exactly the same resources as the model language Greek itself (see Bakker 1997b). More peripheral even within Romani is the borrowing of bound person markers on the verb, of entire indefinite expressions, of basic prepositions, and of the finite verb negator, and the restructuring of personal pronouns. Taken as a sample of dialects in contact, Romani also presents us with a number of constraints on borrowing: there is no borrowing of demonstratives, of bound tense markers (except as adaptation markers, followed by indigenous tense markers), of productive definite articles (except when attached to borrowed prepositions), of entire forms of personal or reflexive pronouns (except when drawing on inherited forms, as above), of possessive pronouns, of bound case markers, of the locative preposition 'in', of the interrogative 'what', of individual numerals below 'five' or of the numerals 'ten' and 'twenty' (except in cases where the entire L2 system of numerals is employed, e.g. with dates), or of the copula (with the exception of the negative copula *niso* from Slovene, in the Dolensjki dialect). There is also no attestation of a replacement through borrowing of the Romani non-factual complementiser *te*.[5]

Despite extensive borrowing into individual dialects from the respective European contact languages, Greek impact during the Early Romani phase had been qualitatively unique in supplying the language with morphological material to construct new inflectional classes, with numerals, and marginally even with bound person markers. Especially the verbal, nominal, and adjectival inflection classes and inflectional endings are continued in the dialects. Among later (European) influences, it is possible to distinguish borrowings which typically replace earlier forms (that are attested or can be assumed to have existed), from those which typically enrich the existing means of structural representation of a category. Belonging to the items that tend to be **replacive borrowings** are phasal adverbs, conjunctions, focus particles, modal particles, modal verbs, superlative/comparative markers, indefinites and indefinite markers, and partly also class-identifying plural inflection of nouns. Borrowed nominal and adjectival derivational morphology on the other hand tends to enrich the inventory and continues to coexist with previously acquired or inherited morphology.

A number of tentative structural universals are confirmed by the Romani sample: derivational morphology is likely to be borrowed more easily and more frequently than inflectional morphology; nominal derivational morphology figures at the top of the borrowability hierarchy, followed by adjectival derivation and finally verbal derivation; unbound morphemes are borrowed sooner and more frequently than semi-bound morphemes, followed by bound morphemes. The generalisation that borrowed bound morphology is more likely to appear with borrowed lexicon before spreading to the inherited lexicon holds in general, and for verb inflection in particular. This is seen in the treatment of Russian and Turkish verbs, as well as the occasional retention of verb inflection with borrowed modals. The distribution of the Greek-derived 3SG marker *-i*, along with the retention in Welsh Romani of the Greek-derived loan-verb adaptation marker *-in-* only in the 3SG (the general marker being *-as-*), also suggest that borrowed verb morphology is more likely to appear in the 3SG than in other persons.

Despite the use of the term 'borrowing' to denote primarily replication of forms (see above), and partly of structural patterns, it is necessary to point out three additional and more specific types of contact-induced structural changes. The first is **morphological compartmentalisation**, which has already been alluded to in the introductory remarks to this chapter. The selective diffusion

[5] In the Dolenjski dialect of Novo Grad (Cech and Heinschink 2001), Slovene *da* is used as a non-factual complementiser. This however is preceded by the merger of the factual and non-factual complementisers in this dialect, as attested in the material published by Dick Zatta (1996), in which *ti* appears in both functions. This general subordinator is then replaced by a borrowing that carries out both functions.

of Greek-derived inflectional markers and of other, later borrowed morphology and its confinement to loan vocabulary is extensive in Romani. Perhaps more than any other contact development, compartmentalisation can be viewed as representative for the contact behaviour of Romani, specifically for the persistent preservation of a conservative core of inherited structures while allowing for massive structural intrusion from the contact languages.

A further type of contact development is **convergence**, by which structural adaptation draws on the rearrangement of inherited resources to match an external model (also 'calquing'). Ross (1996) has termed this process 'metatypy', and has argued convincingly that it is disconnected from the structural hierarchy involving replications of actual forms. In other words, the borrowing of morphological forms or even of lexicon need not be a precondition for the appearance of metatypy. Convergence of this kind is typical for the arrangement of clauses, e.g. word order and clause combining. It also allows some of the tentative constraints on borrowing to be bypassed, by generating indigenous counterparts to structural categories such as the definite article or semi-bound future tense marker.

Finally, there is room to consider as an additional process the phenomenon of **fusion** of categories (cf. Matras 1998d, 2000c). Fusion is the non-separation of languages for a particular category. It can also be seen as the structural 'devolution' of certain functions to the contact language, or alternatively as the wholesale adoption of markers belonging to a particular category. It is thus qualitatively and quantitatively different from 'borrowing' in the conventional or superordinate sense. Examples of fusion in Romani are the sets of phasal adverbs, focus particles, discourse markers, and sometimes also coordinating conjunctions, as well as, most outstanding of all, the wholesale adoption of Slavic aspect markers in the Northeastern and Northern Central dialects.

To some extent it is possible to associate different motivations with these individual processes. Compartmentalisation encourages the smooth adoption of loans and thus the maintenance of stable multilingualism without compromising significant portions of the inherited morphology. The adoption, but selective diffusion, of derivational morphology with nouns and adjectives, for instance, allows lexical loans to be accommodated rather easily. Convergence or metatypy allows for the syncretisation of the linear arrangement of the sentence or utterance with the structures of the contact language, and so also for a syncretisation of the mental planning operations that are applied at the utterance level in the two languages. The balance between the import of forms and calquing through internal elements is often a function of resource availability. Sinti, for example, calques the German aktionsart modifier *auf* in *aufmachen* 'to open' by using the local relations adverb *pre* (< 'up'), as in *ker-pre* 'to open'. There is however no unbound directional expression and so no available spatial metaphor in the inherited inventory that corresponds to the German aktionsart marker *hin*, as in *hingehen* 'to go (towards . . .)', and so *hin* is replicated: *dža- hin*. No such splits occur however in the replication of Slavic aspect markers, which, as bound morphemes, are apparently not open to interpretation and imitation through native resources.

Both the borrowing of individual forms, and fusion (wholesale borrowing of a category), can serve to develop new categories that did not exist previously in the language, as in the case of aktionsart markers, instrumental prepositions, loan-verb adaptation markers, and possibly superlatives. But borrowing and fusion can also lead to the replacement and even successive replacement of existing categories. One might explain this replacement at least in part as an overall tendency toward the merger of communication structures, and a cognitive motivation to avoid a double inventory of forms with elements that are high on the scale of interaction-related functions (see Matras 1998d). Evidence for this cognitive motivation is supplied by the semantic–pragmatic profile of categories that are more likely to be affected by structural borrowing, as opposed to those that remain conservative. Stable categories that tend to be resistant to borrowings are those that capture the **internal structure of meaning**: deictics, nominal case markers, markers of tense and largely also of aspect, or the non-factual complementiser *te* which directly qualifies the predication expressed by the verb which it introduces. On the other hand, prone to renewal through borrowing are elements that are reponsible for the **external arrangement of meaning**: discourse markers, fillers, tags, and interjections, focus particles and phasal adverbs, conjunctions and especially contrastive conjunctions, modality and aktionsart, word-order rules, and the factual complementiser, which links independent events.

Moreover, even within those categories that are prone to borrowing, hierarchies can be found that confirm the tendency for expressions of external evaluation, interactional and presuppositional attitudes, and contrast to be more susceptible to merger with the contact language. Thus, within the class of discourse markers, fillers and tags through which the speaker negotiates interaction with the hearer, are replaced earlier and more frequently than sequential markers, on which the speaker draws for the internal structuring of the discourse. Among the coordinating conjunctions, a higher degree of contrast (implying surprise and so potential interactional disharmony) correlates with higher borrowability. Within the class of subordinating conjunctions, reason and causality (i.e. interactional justification) figure at the top of the borrowability hierarchy, alongside potential ('whether', expressing options and so potential interactional uncertainty), followed by conditionality and only then by temporality. With complementisers, the split between borrowable factual (linking independent predications) and non-borrowable non-factual (qualifying a predication) was referred to above. In the domain of modals, highest on the borrowability hierarchy are expressions of necessity, which convey the involvement of an external dimension. Focus particles and phasal adverbs, all of which help convey attitudes towards the interactional relevance of the proposition, are higher on the borrowability scale than other grammatical adverbs such as those of reversal and repetition, for instance, which relate to the internal structure of the proposition. Even the domain of aktionsart, though derivational in its overall appearance and structure, involves the systematic application of spatial metaphors to events and so similarly an attitudinal perspective.

9 Dialect classification

9.1 Methodological considerations

Since Romani is a non-territorial language with discontinuous spread of population, it is not obvious that its dialects should form a geographical continuum. The mobility of Romani communities adds to the difficulty in assigning dialectal features to a particular area. As a result of migrations, it is not unusual for several different dialects to be spoken in one location, or for speakers of a particular dialect to maintain ties with one another, irrespective of their location. Boretzky (1998b) has therefore referred to the dialects of Romani, and to those of the southern Balkans in particular, as 'insular' dialects.

There is nevertheless evidence that, at least in some regions, speakers of Romani form social networks with Rom from neighbouring communities in stable settlement patterns, allowing innovations to spread over a geographical continuum in much the same way as is the case in 'territorial' languages. In line with the assumptions of the theory of geographical diffusion (based on the earlier 'wave-theory'), an innovation is introduced in one location, spreading gradually over time and space, creating transitional zones as it advances. Elšík et al.'s (1999) investigation of transitional zones between the Northern Central and Southern Central sub-groups in southern Slovakia illustrates how innovations can be variable in these zones. A typical feature of the Southern Central sub-group is the loss of final *-s*. In the Northern Central transitional dialects, final *-s* is lost in some lexemes (*dive* 'day') but not in others. Local dialects within the transitional zone often differ in their treatment of candidate lexemes: Prenčov and Revúca *d'ive*, Chyžné *d'ives*. For some grammatical morphemes containing final *-s*, there may be variation in individual local dialects: in Roštár, the accusative masculine singular varies between *-e* and*-es*; in Prenčov it is the reflexive *pe/pes* that varies. In some cases, the presence of final *-s* in the same morpheme is lexically determined, as in Prenčov adverbial endings in *láčh-e* 'well' but *bár-es* 'very' (Elšík et al. 1999: 298–9).

There have been attempts to postulate 'membership' of individual Romani dialects in 'genetic' branches (see discussion below). The idea of 'genetic' membership derives from the well-known *Stammbaum* or tree metaphor in traditional historical linguistics. How can we adapt the tree metaphor to Romani? We might assume that Early Romani was the uniform stem from which individual dialect branches descended. These branches are likely to have been formed after emigration from the southern Balkans. Sub-branching then followed when the individual groups broke away from a main wave of migrants and settled in a particular region. Fraser (1992b), using Lee's (extremely controversial) glottochronological method, dates the split between the major Romani dialects, including those of the southern Balkans, to around 1040 AD, and the split between the Vlax branch and Welsh Romani, both dialects that are spoken outside the southern Balkans, to around 1200 AD. Regardless of the (in)accuracy of the dates, the pattern is consistent with the idea of a large wave of Romani migrants leaving the southern Balkans, then splitting into several groups, with further splits resulting in linguistic diversification as migration continued.

Ideally, then, a comprehensive classification of Romani dialects should take into account both the branching of individual groups through migrations, as well as the geographical diffusion of innovations through neighbouring Romani communities. Both kinds of developments may give rise to isoglosses – the differentiating features that can be taken as a basis for dialect classification. Adding geographical diffusion into the equation complicates the picture inasmuch as 'genetic' group membership can no longer be considered to be absolute. Rather, dialects must be classified as more or less closely related, depending on the number (and perhaps also the importance, from a system point of view) of isoglosses that they share.

A further methodological difficulty is distinguishing innovations from archaisms. Although we are fortunate enough to have OIA/MIA etymologies for much of the core Romani lexicon, the lack of historical documentation on Early Romani often dictates that dialectology and historical reconstruction must go hand in hand: as the connections between the dialects are studied more carefully, a clearer and more nuanced picture of the language's diachrony gradually unfolds.

Consider the following example. Early Romani inherited the words **āṇḍa* > **andřo* 'egg' and **aṭṭa* > **ařo* 'flour' from OIA/MIA. In the subsequent development of the dialects, the two words were affected by a number of phonological and morpho-phonological changes: 1. for the historical MIA cluster **ṇḍ* we can postulate Early Romani **ndř*, with various subsequent simplifcations (*ndr*, *nd*, *nř*, *nl*, *rn*, *ř* etc.); 2. *ř* may merge with *r*; 3. the initial vowel *a-* may show prothesis of *j-* (phonological, or analogous); or 4. prothesis of *v-* (masculine definite article prefixing, or analogous). The distribution of the two forms in the dialects is shown in figure 9.1 (the display in this and in the other figures and tables in this chapter follows the representation of dialect locations as introduced in chapter 2, figure 2.2.).

		Fin 1.*jāro* 2.*vāro*			Pol 1.*jaro* 2.*jažo*		Lat 1.*jāro* 2.*jārlo*
					Brg 1. *jandro* 2.*jaro*		NR 1.*jaro* 2.*jaržo*
W 1.*jāro* 2.*vārō*		Sin 1.*jaro* 2.*jaro*	Boh 1.*jāro* 2.*jarro*	WS 1. *jāro* 2.*jarro*	ES 1.*jandro* 2.*(j)aro*		Ukr 1.*arno* 2.*varo*
				Rmg 1.*jāro* 2.*jāro*		Lov 1.*anro* 2.*aro*	
	M 1.*jaro* 2.*jaxo*		BR 1. (lost) 2.*jaro/čaro*			Kal 1.*anřo* 2.*ařo*	
PS 1.*jaro,ranjo*		LS 1.*jaro* 2. *jarxo*	Hrv 1.*jaro* 2.*varo*	Gur 1.*arno* 2.*aro*		Bug 1.*aro* 2.*aro*	
				Arl 1. *angřo, jaro, aro* 2.*jaro, varo*		Erl 1.*ařo*	Rum 1.*vanro* 2.*varo*
						Ser 1.*vanglo* 2.*valo*	
Basque Para-R. 1.*yandro*	Ib 1.*anro* 2. *aro*		Ab 1.*varo* 2. (lost)		Prl 1.*ando* 2.*varo*	Sep 1.*vandro* 2.*varo*	AV 1.*anro/ arno* 2.*aro*

Figure 9.1 Forms for 1. 'egg' (**āṇḍa* > **andřo*) and 2. 'flour' (**aṭṭa* > *ařo*)

In the Balkans and in Vlax, the cluster *ndř* is often continued as a cluster – a common archaism in the area surrounding the historical centre of Romani population diffusion. This archaism is also preserved in the extreme periphery, in the Basque Romani vocabulary. In Vlax (represented here by Lovari, Kalderaš, Gurbet, and Agia Varvara), the successor is *nr*, metathesised in some Vlax varieties to *rn*. Migrant Vlax dialects (Gur, AV) preserve this in their new locations. This Vlax feature might therefore qualify as 'genetic', as it characterises branch membership irrespective of the present location of the dialect.

Consider now the distributional hierarchy for prothetic *v-* in the two words. If a dialect has *v-* in 'egg', then it also has *v-* in 'flour', but not vice versa. This generalisation is valid regardless of geographical location.[1] It appears that Early Romani had two variants for 'flour', with and without prothetic *v-*. The form carrying *v-* was originally a morphological variant, a result of the attachment of the definite article **ov-ařo*. The dialects inherited the variation, then selected one of the forms. Option selection in this case is common, and not diagnostic of genetic or geographical relations, though retention of *v-ařo* is more common in the geographical peripheries. In the dialects of northern Greece (Serres, Rumelian, Sepeči), however, **v-ařo* was consistently selected for 'flour'. This, and other selections of *v*-initial variants, then triggered analogous change in **andřo* > **v-andřo* 'egg'. This latter development is clearly geographical.[2]

In the western and northern regions we have a series of innovations whose geographical spread can be traced back to a centre of diffusion in western-central Europe. The first innovation involves jotation and gradual cluster reduction in **andřo* > **jandro* > *jaro* 'egg'. Jotation reaches maximal spread. The eastwards spread of cluster reduction on the other hand comes to a halt in Eastern Slovak Romani and the Bergitka Roma dialect of southern Poland, a transitional zone with variation: *jandro* 'egg', but **mandřo* > *maro* 'bread'. An archaism is also preserved in Piedmontese Sinti, which alongside *jaro* also has *ranjo* < **janro*.[3] For 'flour', the diffusion centre selects **ařo*, which undergoes jotation to *jařo*, while in its periphery we find selection of **ov-ařo* > *varo* (British Romani, Finnish Romani, Hravati/Dolenjski). The final innovation involves merger of *ř* with *r*. This occurs selectively in the centre, leaving archaisms within the zone (Manuš, Lombardian Sinti, Bohemian Romani). It does not spread to the northeast, where **jařo* > *jaržo* etc. prevails, and so it may have followed the separation and eastward migration of the Northeastern Baltic sub-branch.

Note that western Iberian Romani (Catalonian Romani and the Caló lexicon) does not participate in either initial jotation or cluster reduction. This can be explained through its remoteness from the diffusion centre in western-central Europe. On the other hand, the simplifications it shows – **ndř* > *nr* and merger of *ř* and *r* – are common, and although they resemble the Vlax pattern, there is no need to postulate a shared development with Vlax.

1 The southern Italian dialects of Romani in Abruzzia and Calabria have *varo* for 'egg', but have lost the inherited etymon for 'flour'.

2 A similar development might thus be postulated for the southern Italian dialects (see above), though data are lacking to confirm this.

3 Vulcanius' vocabulary from 1597, collected in all likelihood in France (Anon. 1930), has *yanre* for 'eggs' and *manron* for 'bread'; Ewsum's list, collected in northern Germany or the Netherlands before 1570, has *maro* for 'bread' (Kluyver 1910).

When due consideration is given to the history of migration, dialect comparison thus allows us to postulate several kinds of processes. There is **geographical diffusion** of innovations. Some innovations however are **common**, i.e. they are not part of a **shared** process, and so they are not diagnostic of any **isogloss**-based relations among the dialects. Some innovations involve **simplification**, others are cases of **option selection** from inherited variation. The geographical distribution of forms can provide valuable clues as to the **relative chronology** of some of the historical changes. Finally, there are limits to the diagnostic value of so-called **genetic** features. These are only relevant inasmuch as they can represent innovations shared by what were once contiguous dialects which are now separated as a result of migration.

9.2 A history of classification schemes

The pioneer of dialect classification in Romani was Franz Miklosich, whose reconstruction of migration routes and the splits between the groups has had a significant impact on dialect classification in Romani. Miklosich (1872–80, III) based his classification not on internal developments (internal isoglosses), but on contact features, specifically on the layers of European lexical borrowings found in his sample dialects. Miklosich recognised that migration had been a phase in the history of the Rom. Despite the persistance of itinerant traditions, migration had become exceptional by the late nineteenth century, most groups having acquired roots in their regions of settlement. He thus postulated thirteen groups, based on the linguistic groups (rather than state boundaries) among whom the Rom live (see figure 9.2).

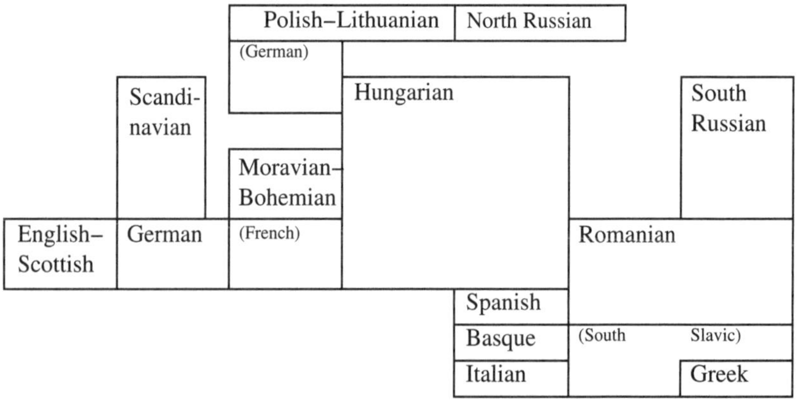

Figure 9.2 Historical connections among the thirteen Romani dialects according to Miklosich (1872–1880, III). (Contact influences without group status in brackets)

The historical point of departure is what Miklosich called the 'Greek' group, situated in what had been the Ottoman Empire. Miklosich was aware of the dialectal diversity among the Rom of this region, pointing out among other things differences between the speech forms of settled and itinerant Rom. The formation of subsequent groups corresponds to their breaking away from the main wave of migration. Thus, the Italian dialects of Romani have Greek and South Slavic loan vocabulary, but no Romanian-derived vocabulary, an indication that they did not spend time in Romanian territory. By contrast, the North Russian group shows traces of Polish, German, Hungarian, Romanian, South Slavic, and Greek loan vocabulary. Its migration route must therefore have included these areas. Moreover, one can assume that they participated in a major migration wave, from which they eventually broke away.[4]

The next classification attempt, and one that was to become no less influential, was Gilliat-Smith's (1915) distinction between Vlax and Non-Vlax dialects. Gilliat-Smith observed that distinctive, diagnostic features can be found in the speech of the various groups of Rom in northeastern Bulgaria, irrespective of their exact location. These features partly correlate with religion (Vlax are mainly Christians or recently converted Muslims, Non-Vlax are Muslims), as well as with the use of the self-designation *vlax*, which Gilliat-Smith adopted as the distinctive term. The value of Gilliat-Smith's classification is twofold: it attempts to capture the 'genetic' nature of dialect differentiation in the southern Balkans by assigning features to branches, rather than to locations, and it is the first classification attempt to actually define groups based on internal linguistic features, in various domains of grammar and vocabulary (see table 9.1).

Gilliat-Smith's terminology has remained central in Romani dialect classification. It was taken up again by Kochanowski (1963–4), who attempted a synthesis between the classifications offered by Gilliat-Smith (1915) and by Miklosich (1872–80, III). With the Vlax and Non-Vlax distinction as a basis, Kochanowski proceeded to divide the Non-Vlax branch into four subbranches: Balkan, Carpathian (Hungary, Czechoslovakia, southern Poland), German (France and Germany), and Northern (the Baltic area, northern Poland, Russian). Though no diagnostic features are given by Kochanowski, his division of the Non-Vlax dialects laid the foundation for a division of the dialects of central, western, and northern Europe. Peripheral dialects – South Russian (and Ukrainian), British (Welsh), Italian, Iberian, and Scandinavian – are left out of Kochanowski's classification. Ventcel' and Čerenkov's (1976) comparative

[4] An elaboration on the model of migration waves is found in Cortiade (1991; also Courthiade 1998), who distinguishes three so-called historical 'strata': the Balkan–Carpathian–Baltic wave (Miklosich's migrations), and within it the subsequent spread, from German territory, of the Sinti dialects into neighbouring territories; the Gurbet–Čergar (or Southern Vlax) migrations from Romania into the southern Balkans; and the Kelderaš–Lovari (or Northern Vlax) migrations from Romania into central, eastern, and western Europe as well as overseas.

Table 9.1 *Classification criteria of the Romani dialects of northeastern Bulgaria according to Gilliat-Smith (1915)*

	Non-Vlax	Vlax
opposition *r:ř*	cerebral *ř* retained	merger in *r*, or *r:R*
negation	*na*	*in*
loan-verb adaptation	*-iz-*, *-in-*; past tense occasionally *-(i)sar-*	*-isar-*
ṇḍ in 'bread'	*mařo*	*manro, marno*
aj in 'mother', 'daughter'	*daj, čhaj*	*dej, čhej/šej*
initial *a-*	*biav* 'wedding', *lav* 'word', *nav* 'name', *šun-* 'to hear'	*abiav* 'wedding', *alav* 'word', *anav* 'name', *ašun-* 'to hear'
1SG perfective	*-(j)om*	*-em*
inherited lexicon:		
'finger'	*angušt*	*naj*
'to call'	*čand-*	*akhar-*
'tomorrow'	*javina, tasja*	*tehara*
'month'	*masek*	*čhon*
'tree'	*ruk*	*kašt*
'arm'	*musi*	*vast*
'wet'	*suslo*	*kingo*
'to burn (intr.)'	*thabjov-*	*phabjov-*
'to open'	*phiřav-*	*phuter-*
'to understand'	*axaljov-*	*xakjar-*
lexical replacement through loans in Vlax:		
'to lose'	*našal-*	*xasar-*
'dust, ashes'	*čhar*	*praxos*
'alive'	*dživdo*	*traime*
'brother-in-law'	*salo*	*kumnáto*
'to speak'	*vaker-*	*orbisar-*
'to bury'	*paron-*	*praxosar-*

outline of Romani divides the dialects into eight numbered groups (see table 9.2). The purpose of this classification was to provide a grid for reference, rather than to postulate geographical or genetic isoglosses. Accordingly, the list of group-typical features provided by Ventcel' and Čerenkov is selective and not systematic.

Kaufman (1979), in a rather brief note on dialect classification, suggested a three-way division of the main dialects: 1. Balkan, which also includes South Italian and Hungarian, presumably the Southern Central group; 2. Northern, including Sinti, Nordic, Baltic, British, and Central, the latter referring to Northern Central; and 3. Vlax (which includes Ukrainian). Thus in addition to Gilliat-Smith's term 'Vlax' and to Kochanowski's 'Northern', Kaufman introduced the terms 'Balkan' as well as, though not as an independent branch,

Table 9.2 *Dialect classification according to Ventcel' and Čerenkov (1976)*

Group	Dialects (region and group names)	Characteristic features
I	north Russia (*ruska roma, xeladitka roma*; Latvia, Lithuania and Estonia (*lotfika roma*); central Poland (*polska roma, felditka roma*)	*a* > *i* in *džin-* 'to know', *sir* 'how', ablative ending *-tir*, *-isis* 'was'; prothetic *v-* in *vangar* 'coal', *vavir* 'other'; raised central vowel /ɨ/; genitive in *-kir-*; Slavic aspectual prefixes, Polish and German lexical influences; demonstratives *adava/odova/da/odo*
II	*sinti* (Germany, France, Austria, northern Italy, Poland, USSR, Yugoslavia)	vowel reduction to /ə/; *h*-forms in grammatical paradigms; German influences; demonstratives *dova/kova*
III	northern and eastern Slovakia (*servika roma*); southern Slovakia and northern hungary (*ungrike roma*)	forward shift of stress (*báro* 'big); 2SG copula and perfective in *-l*; instrumental SG in *-ha*; borrowing of Hungarian function words and derivational morphology; oblique definite articles in *(o)l-*; demonstratives *ada/oda*
IV	Bulgaria, Macedonia, Southern Serbia (*erlides*); Romania, Moldavia (*ursari*); Crimea; central Bulgaria (*drindari*)	central vowel /ă/; analytic future; productive use of case suffixes without prepositions; plurals in *-ides*; demonstratives *adavka/odovka/akava/okova*
V	Romania, Moldavia; *kelderari, lovari* (outmigrants in various countries); southern Yugoslavia (*gurbet*)	presence of /R/; central vowels /ă, î/; 1SG perfective in *-em*; plurals in *-uri/-urja/-urja*; loan verbs in *-isar-*; oblique definite articles in *l-*; demonstratives *kado/kako/kodo/kuko*
VI	Ukraine	raised central vowel /ɨ/; *k', g'* > *t', d'* e.g. in dative case endings; oblique definite articles in *l-*; demonstratives *kadava/kada/kava* etc.
VII	Finland	*š, čh* > *x* in *berx* 'year', *puxáa* 'I ask'; instrumental SG in *-ha*
VIII	Wales	vowel /ɔ/

'Central'. Unaligned according to Kaufman are Zargari and Iberian, as well as Greek (though it is unclear which dialects the latter refers to). A similar division is followed by Boretzky and Igla (1991), who, like Kochanowski (1963–4), depart from a Vlax vs. Non-Vlax division, then divide the latter into 'Southern' and 'Northern'. Noteworthy is the fact that they include Caló in the Northern division (but see arguments to the contrary in Boretzky 1998c: 121–6). 'Northern' had thus become a reference to shared features, rather than to a geographical location.

In the discussion context of the 1990s, the primacy of the Vlax/Non-Vlax dichotomy – which Gilliat-Smith had applied with specific reference to northeastern Bulgaria – was dropped in favour of four branches with a hierarchically equal status: Balkan, Vlax, Northern, Central. This division appears to have been mentioned in print for the first time by Bakker and Matras (1997), who attribute branch 'status' to the Central group, while at the same time emphasising the diversity of the Northern branch. The four-way classification has since been referred to as the 'consensus' grouping by Bakker (1999: 178), and has been applied, primarily as a reference grid, in a number of works that cite comparative data from different dialects (e.g. Elšík 2000b), including the present book.

Recently, there have been attempts to connect specific features to this rather intuitive division. Bakker (1999) lists a series of features which he argues are genetic characteristics of the Northern branch: jotated third-person pronoun *jov* etc.; indefinites *či* 'nothing', *čimoni* 'something', *kuti* 'a little'; place deictics *adaj/odoj/akaj* and demonstratives that differ from Vlax; long genitives and possessives; negator *kek* in some of the dialects; lexical retentions such as *stariben* 'prison', *kaliko* 'tomorrow, yesterday', *bolipen* 'sky', *bero* 'ship', and shared lexical borrowings such as *vodros* 'bed', *stanja* 'stable', *škorni* 'boot', from Slavic, or *filicin* 'castle' from Greek; prothetic *v-* in *vaver* 'other', loss of *a-* in *amal* > *mal* 'friend', and cluster simplification in *vraker-* > *raker-* 'to speak'.

The diagnostic 'genetic' value of many of these features is questionable, however. The shared indefinites, deictics, long genitives, lexical items, and lexical borrowings from Greek and South Slavic are all archaisms, some of them found in isolated Romani dialects outside the Northern branch (e.g. Florina Arli *čumuni* 'something'; Southern Central *vodro* 'bed'). Prothetic *v-* in *vaver* 'other' is a case of option selection (cf. Florina Arli *vaver*, Prilep *ovaver*). Of the innovations, *kek* < **kajekh* and *amal* > *mal* 'friend' are regional and are not diagnostic of the branch as a whole, while prothetic *j-* is geographical and spreads beyond the Northern branch into neighbouring branches (Northern Central, and variably Hravati/Dolenjski). Boretzky (1998c: 121–6) points out a series of features that separate Sinti from Caló,[5] both classified by Bakker as Northern. This adds to the overall impression that branch membership is relative, not absolute, and must rather be described in terms of shared individual isoglosses.

[5] Caló has a cluster *nr* for **ṇḍ* (Sinti *r*) and initial *a-* in *akhar-* 'to call' etc. (Sinti *khar-*), it shows palatalisation of dentals in *buči* 'work', *kliči* 'key' (Sinti *buti*, *klidin*), and no prothetic *v-* in *aver* 'other' nor *j-* in *anro* 'egg' (Sinti *vaver*, *jaro*).

Bakker lists further Northern features which I have elsewhere (Matras 1998b, 1999b; see also footnote in Bakker 1999: 198) characterised as sociolinguistic strategies that are typical of the dialects of the western geographical periphery. They include the loss of *rom* as an ethnic designation and its replacement through group-specific ethnonyms (*kale*, *manuš*, *sinti*, *romaničal*), the formation of cryptic place names, the productive use of nominalised genitives for internal word formation (as an alternative to borrowing), and finally the fact that 'Northern' dialects are frequently replaced by Para-Romani special vocabularies. These features can be explained by the social and geographical isolation of the groups and their dependency on Romani as a secret language.

In a series of works on the Central, Balkan, and Vlax branches of Romani, Boretzky (1999a, 1999b, 2000b, 2000c) takes an inventory of features that are shared by the respective branches (see table 9.3). Boretzky postulates two separate groups within the Balkan branch, which he refers to as Southern Balkan I and II; 'southern', since, technically, Vlax too is spoken in the Balkans. South Balkan I includes Arli, Erli, Sepeči, Rumelian, Zargari, Romano, Crimean, and Ursari (all spoken originally in the southernmost regions of the Balkans), while South Balkan II comprises Drindari, Bugurdži, and Kalajdži (all formed in northeastern Bulgaria, with some outmigrants in other areas).

Sub-branching is also postulated for the Central branch (table 9.4). Southern Central shares a number of features with the Balkan group: simplification of *ṇḍ* to *r/ř* (in Arli, Erli), loss of final *-s* in grammatical endings (Arli), loss of final *-n* in *-ipen, -imen* (Balkan and Vlax), lack of jotation in the third-person pronouns *ov* etc., subjunctive and future copula in *ov-*, past copula in *sin-*. Boretzky (1999a) explains this through later immigration of the Southern Central speakers from the Balkans into their present location. Arguably, though, this cluster of shared innovations and archaisms could just as well be the outcome of geographical diffusion and coherence. Significantly, all these features are also shared by Hravati/Dolenjski, originally spoken in Croatia, thus constituting the geographical link between Arli in the southeast, and Romungro and the Vend dialects in the northwest.

For Vlax, Boretzky (2000c) proposes a division between Southern Vlax and Northern Vlax. Southern Vlax shows palatalisation of velars before *e* and the emergence of short possessives *mo* etc., Northern Vlax retains the nominaliser *-imo(s)* and the oblique feminine definite article in *la* and shows demonstratives in *kak-* and a negator *či*.

From the inventories of shared features it appears that, when the intuitive division into dialect branches is taken for granted, the relation between diagnostic isoglosses turns out inevitably to be asymmetrical: isoglosses that are diagnostic of one branch may be irrelevant to the definition of another. The challenge still facing dialect classification in Romani is to approach diversification from

Table 9.3 *Diagnostic features of the Central, Balkans, Vlax branches (based on Boretzky)*

Central (following Boretzky 1999a)	lexical jotation, penultimate stress, short forms for the present tense and long forms for future, 2SG perfective concord *-al* and 2PL *-an*, *s>h* in intervocalic positions in grammatical endings, genitive in *-ker-*, oblique definite article in *(o)l-*, loan-verb adaptation marker *-in-*, 'new infinitive' based on 3SG or 3PL(also 2PL), necessitive modal in *kampel/pekal.*
Southern Balkan I (following Boretzky 1999b) (some features shared with Southern Balkan II)	reflexive in *pumen*, perfective *-in-* of verbs in *d-* and in *-n-il* of verbs in *-a*, causatives in *-ker*, *asavka* for 'such', loss of *-n* in *-ipe*, no Greek-derived *-imo(s)*, future in *ka(m)*, presence of short posessives *mo to po*, plural definite article *o*, verbs of motion have 3SG adjectival endings (*gelo, geli*), traces of perfective formations in *-t-*.
Exclusive Southern Balkan II (following Boretzky 2000c)	palatalisation of velars leading to affricates (*kin* > *cin* 'to buy', *vogi* > *vozi* 'soul'), palatalisation of dentals to affricates or sibilants (*buti* > *buci* 'work', *dives* > *zis* 'day', *phendjom* > *phendzom* 'I said), palatalisation and loss of *l* (*lil* > *il* 'letter'), partly (Bugurdži only) palatalisation of clusters of velar + *l* (*dikhljom* > *dičhom* 'I saw', *kangli* > *kandži* 'comb'), in Kalajdži and Drindari loss of intervocalic *n* (*kuni* > *kui* 'elbow'), plurals in *-oja* for loan nouns in *-os*, demonstratives *kada, kaka, kava*, vowel *i* in *kidiso/kikesu* etc. 'such', copula present *sjom, sjan*, optional loss of perfective marker, loan-verb adaptation in *-iz-*, plurals in *-ides* with nouns in *-is* (also in SBI).
Vlax (following Boretzky 2000c)	centralisation of *i* > *î* and of *e* > ə in the environment of *s, š, x, ř.* (later decentralised in Lovari), loss of intervocalic *n* in *pani* > *pai, paj,* plurals in *-uri/-urja*, third-person pronouns in *v-*, *kesavo* for 'such', negative indefinites *khanči* 'nothing' and *khonik* 'nobody', negators *či/ni/in*, 1SG perfective concord *-em*, perfective *-j-* of verbs in *-a* (*asa-j-a(s)* 'he laughed'), perfective *-j-/ø* of verbs in *-d-* (*d(j)as* 'gave'), loan verbs in *-isar-* (short form *-i-*), productive use of *-áv-* for intransitive derivations, *tehara* for 'tomorrow'

Table 9.4 *Principal differences between Northern Central and Southern Central dialects (based on Boretzky 1999a)*

	Northern Central	Southern Central
ṇḍ	*ndr, r*	*r (ř)*
final *-s* in grammatical endings	*-s* is retained	*-s* is lost
final *-n* in *-ipen, -imen*	*-n* is retained	*-n* is lost
third-person pronouns	*jov, joj, jon*	*ov, oj, on*
reflexive pronoun	*pes*	*pumen*
demonstratives in *akada*	present	missing
remoteness marker	*-as*	*-ahi*
subjunctive/future copula	*av-*	*ov-*
'how much'	*kit'i*	*keci*
3SG perfective in verbs of motion	only *-a(s)*	*-a(s)*, partly also *-o/-i*
subject clitics	loss or reduction to *o,i,e*	retention of *lo,li,le*
third-person copula past	*sas, ehas*	*sine, sja, sl'a, st'a*

the perspective of the historical emergence of isoglosses and their geographical diffusion; this is my agenda in the next section.

9.3 Diagnostic isoglosses

9.3.1 *Innovations*

It is possible to distinguish three **centres of diffusion** for internal innovations. The first centre is in southeastern Europe, with innovations spreading toward the northwest. One of the features that follows this direction of diffusion is the loss of the final consonant in the inherited abstract nominal marker *-ipen* > *-ipe* (see figure 9.3). (The same line overlaps to a considerable degree with an innovation in the opposite direction, namely from the northwest eastwards, by which the 3SG perfective form of intransitive verbs of motion is assimilated into the regular person concord, and the older active participle forms are lost: *gelo, geli* > *geljas* 'he/she went').

Another innovation spreading from the southeast centre is the assimilation of stems with historical perfective markers in -**tj-* to the inflection class in *-lj-* (*-j-*). In the southeast, conservative forms in *-t-* are retained sporadically only with stems in *-s/-š* (Arli, Erli), but not for stems in *-k* or *-č*. In a transitional zone comprising the Central dialects, *-t'-* appears with stems in *-s/-š* as well as *-č*, while dialects to the west and north are most conservative, some showing *-tj-* even with stems in *-k* (see chapter 6).

The second centre of diffusion is in western-central Europe, with innovations typically spreading to the east or southeast, but also in other directions to include

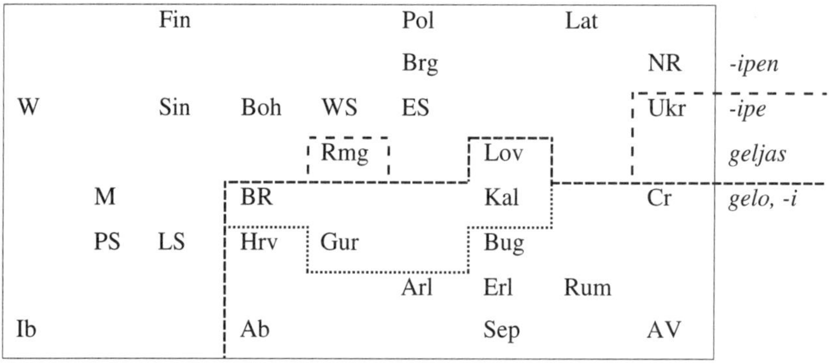

Figure 9.3 Southeast–northwest division line: *-ipen/-ipe* and *geljas/gelo*

British Romani, Finnish Romani, and the Northeastern dialects. It is possible that some of the innovations from this centre even predated the break-away of the latter three groups from the western-central area itself. The decline of active participles was already mentioned (figure 9.3). The innovation leaves a transitional zone comprising Vlax and some of the Southern Central dialects, in which both the active participle and person-inflected 3SG perfective are found. Initial jotation in third-personal pronouns (*jov, joj, jon*) and in the word for 'egg' (*jaro*; see figure 9.1) is predominant throughout the west and north, its diffusion pattern resembling that of the decline of active participles. Some dialects continue the jotation yet further. Especially noticeable are positions preceding *a-* where phonetic palatalisation is not expected (thus unlike *jiv* 'snow'), and words that are not feminine nouns, where jotation might have morphological reasons (as in **oj-asvi* > *jasvi* 'tear'). *jav-* 'to come' and *jaro* 'egg' are therefore diagnostic.

The truncation of *a-* in *amal* > *mal* 'friend' and *akana* > *kana* 'now' as well as the regularisation of the oblique inflection of the interrogative *kon* to *kones-* (from **kas*) are western and northern features, shared by the Sinti group, Hravati/Dolenjski, Welsh and Finnish Romani, Polska Roma, the Baltic dialects and partly North Russian Romani. The centre of the *a*-truncation isogloss is clearly Sinti, where the process progresses to include most lexical items in *a-* (*avri* > *vri* 'out', *akhar-* > *khar-* 'to call', etc.).

Two further innovations from northwest to southeast are the full affrication of the dental in the interrogative *keti* > *keci/kici* 'how much', and the reduction of the cluster **ṇḍ* > **ndř* to *r* in **mandřo* > *maro* 'bread', **mindřo* > *miro* 'my', **pindřo* > *piro* 'foot', and **andřo* > *(j)aro* 'egg' (figure 9.4; see also figure 9.1). The latter development spreads as far as the Balkans, encompassing the westernmost dialects in the region, with a transitional zone in the eastern Northern Central dialects. From the fact that Gurbet shares the

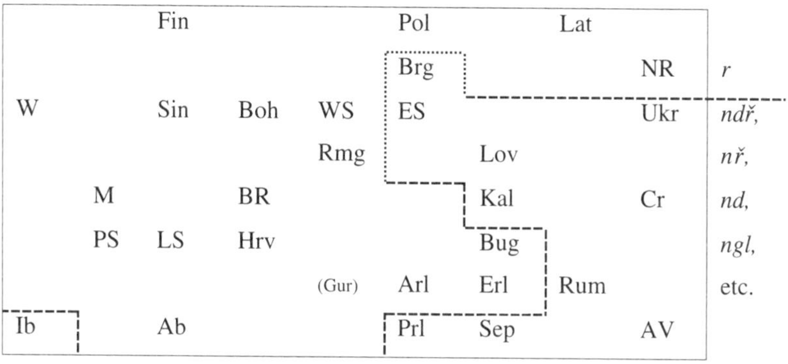

Figure 9.4 Northwest to southeast cluster reduction

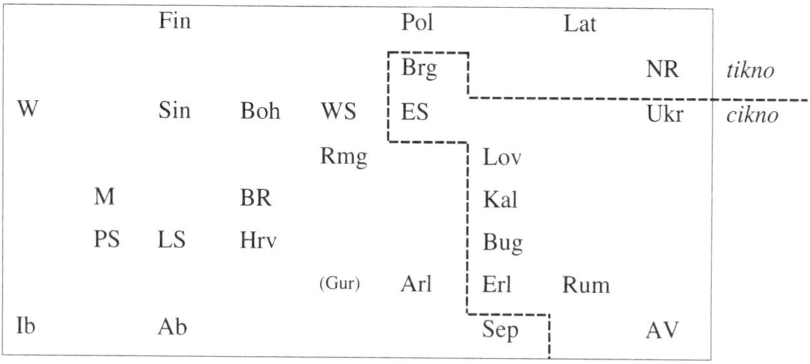

Figure 9.5 Vlax outwards: affrication in *tikno* > *cikno* 'small'

Vlax cluster (*marno* etc.) it seems that the innovation could have predated the immigration of Southern Vlax groups into the southwestern Balkans. Finally, the extension of *s>h* selection in grammatical paradigms to interrogatives has its centre in the Sinti group of central Europe, affecting only partly the southern dialects of Sinti, and spreading selectively eastwards to the Northern Central dialects.

The third and final geographical diffusion centre is Vlax, with innovations spreading to the south, north, and especially westwards. Rather extensive is the diffusion of affrication (through palatalisation) of the initial dental in *tikno* > **t'ikno* > *cikno* (figure 9.5). For the corresponding voiced dental in *dives* 'day', the change is structurally much more contained: Northern Central has *d'i-*, Northern Vlax has *d'i-*, *dži-*, *dźi-*, or *g'i-*, Southern Vlax has *g'i-* or *dži-*, and the Bugurdži group has, through a later development, *dzi-*. In all likelihood,

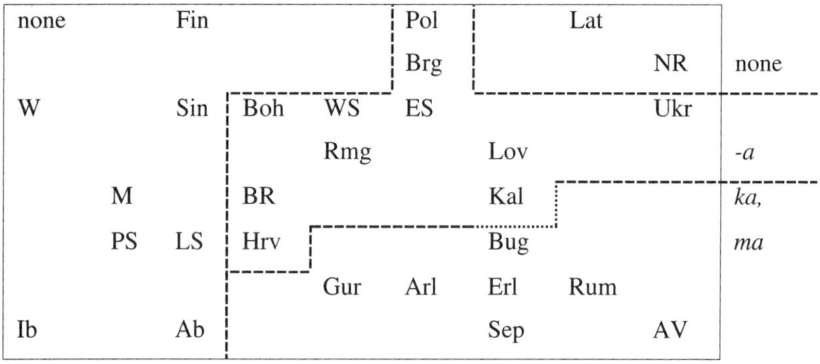

Figure 9.6 Future-tense marking

palatalisation of initial dentals in selected lexemes was an Early Romani feature (cf. Catalonian Romani *dzives* 'day'). In Vlax itself, the development is more extensive (*tiro > t'iro/čiro* 'your', *pativ>pat'iv/pak'iv/pačiv* 'honour'), allowing us to identify Vlax as its diffusion centre. (Noteworthy is a parallel development, namely *kiral > ciral* 'cheese', which is confined to the eastern Northern Central dialects). Another instance of westwards diffusion from Vlax is the prothesis of *a-* in *nav > anav* 'name'. The pattern bears some similarities with that depicted in figure 9.5 for *tikno > cikno*, but is located farther to the south, excluding the Northern Central dialects (Bergitka Roma and Eastern Slovak Romani) but including Sepeči, and it extends farther to the east to include all Southern Central dialects (Roman and Romungro). Vlax continues the process to include other lexemes as well (*šun- > ašun-* 'to hear', *bijav > abijav* 'wedding', *lav > alav* 'word').

Another innovation spreading from Vlax is the specialisation of long forms of the present conjugation in *-a* for future tense (figure 9.6). Occasional modal uses of the long forms are also found outside the area (for instance the declarative and conditional future in Welsh Romani, Erli, Agia Varvara), while in the southern Balkans, the analytic future in *ka* (or *ma*) prevails. (Analytic future tenses may also be found in the North Russian and Ukrainian dialects). Apart from a series of innovations that remain confined to the Vlax group itself (see table 9.3), Vlax is also the diffusion centre for reduplicated demonstrative stems *k_d-* (in Vlax as well as West and East Slovak Romani, the Bugurdži group, Southern Ukrainian Romani)[6] and *k_k-* (Northern Vlax and the Bugurdži group). A lexical innovation shared by Vlax and the Bugurdži group is the semantic shift of *naj* from 'nail' to 'finger', substituting for **angušt*.

[6] A similar development also occurs in Rumelian.

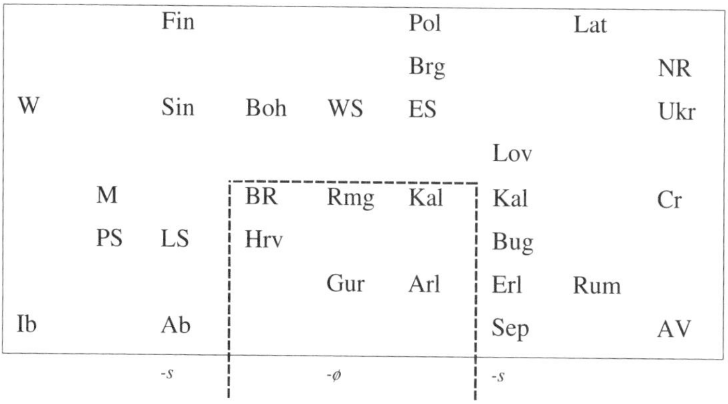

Figure 9.7 Phonological loss of final *-s*

A number of innovations have regional character, and do not spread from any of the three dominant diffusion centres. Some of these are **areal** phenomena, triggered through contact with the surrounding languages, rather than internal innovations with a geographical spread. One such phenomenon is the evolution of an analytic future particle in *ka* or *ma* (figure 9.6), triggered by recent contact with the Balkan languages. Others include the emergence of the 'new infinitive' in an area roughly corresponding to the western-central diffusion zone, triggered by recent contact with infinitival languages, and the productive use of transitivising derivational morphology to form causatives (Central dialects and the Balkans; see chapter 6).

The loss of final *-s* as a phonological development that is not confined to individual morphemes (such as 3SG perfective concord marker *-as* or Greek-derived masculine inflection markers) encompasses Western Balkan, Southwestern Vlax and Southern Central dialects, and some of the Transylvanian Kalderaš varieties (figure 9.7). A more restricted regional innovation in part of the same zone is the palatal mutation of velars before front vowels (*kin-* > *čin-* 'to buy'), shared by some Arli varieties and some Gurbet varieties.

9.3.2 *Option selection*

One of the most intriguing classificatory features in Romani is the alternation of *s* and *h* in grammatical paradigms. In chapter 4, I suggested that the *s/h* alternation is a case of inherited variation. The dialects show a rather atypical central zone, comprising Finnish Romani in the north and Arli and the Serres dialect in the southeast (figure 9.8). Throughout this zone, *h* is selected in the third-person form of the copula (present > past) and in intervocalic position

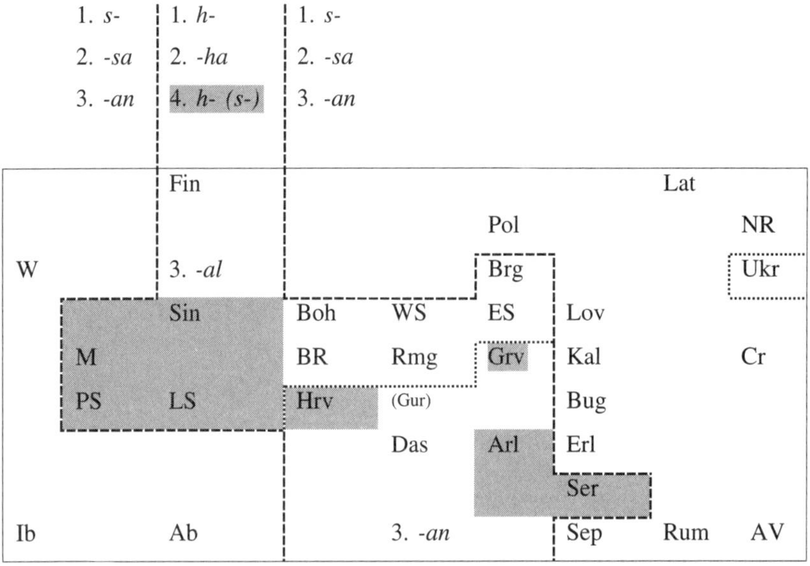

Figure 9.8 Option selection: *s>h* and 2SG concord (1. copula third person, 2. intervocalic grammatical endings, 3. 2SG perfective concord, 4. full copula set)

in grammatical endings (1PL and 2SG long present conjugation markers, and instrumental singular case endings, *-aha/-eha*). Some of the Southern Vlax varieties spoken within the zone, such as the dialect of the Montenegrin Das, participate in the development. In addition, full *h*-paradigms for the copula are retained in two cores in the west (Sinti) and southeast (Arli, Serres), and in isolation in Gurvari (Hungary). These *h*-paradigms are either used exclusively (German Sinti, Manuš), or, continuing the Early Romani state of affairs, in variation with *s*-paradigms (Piedmontese Sinti, Arli, Serres, and possibly also Gurvari). In the north of this central area we also find selection of *-al* for the 2SG perfective concord marker.

Another case of option selection involves the 'intrusion' of a perfective stem extension *-in-* in the copula: *s-in-(j)-/h-in-(j)-* (figure 9.9). We might assume variation in the perfective extensions used with mono-consonantal stems already in Proto-Romani. The retention patterns are typical of option selection, in that the feature is not confined to one area, but shows other isolated occurrences. Functionally, the distribution of *-in-* in the copula differs. In some varieties (Bugurdži, some Arli varieties, Roman), it remains a marker of the past tense. In others (Finnish Romani, Southern Central, East Slovak Romani), it is restricted to the third person. In partial overlap we also find selection of

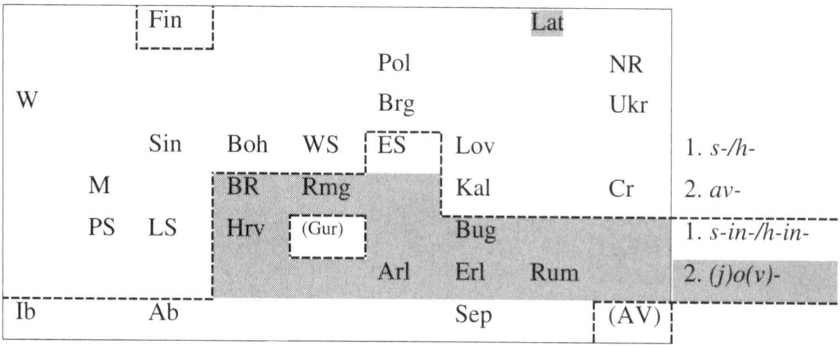

Figure 9.9 Selection of 1. stem extension *-in-* and 2. subjunctive *-av-/-ov-* in the copula

the subjunctive copula in *(j)o(v)-* (figure 9.9; see also Boretzky 1997: 127). Its competitor, the verb *av-*, was an Early Romani option, as testified by the use of *-áv-* as an adaptation marker with intransitive loans, especially in the past tense. In Latvian Romani the variation continues, and *jov-* occurs alongside *jav-*. Vlax on the other hand is even more consistent in selecting *-áv-*, generalising it also as the productive intransitive derivation marker at the expense of *-(j)o(v)-*.

Other instances of option selection include morphological prothetic *v-* and *j-*, as discussed above for **ov-ařo* 'flour' and **ov-aver* 'other', and especially the selection of competing lexical and morpholexical items. We are dealing here with individual selections, at the level of local dialects, among numerous words, developments which rarely form consistent patterns. The overall tendency favours greater diversity in the Balkans, and greater uniformity within the Vlax group as well as in the northern and western European periphery. Salient examples are 'neck' (*kоř* in Vlax, Rumelian, Sepeči; *men* elsewhere), 'arm' (*vast* in Vlax and the Northeastern group; *musi* elsewhere), 'burn' (*phabar-* in Vlax and Sepeči, *thabar-* in the Balkan and Central branches, *labar-* in some Northern Central dialects, *hačar-* in northern and western Europe), and the interrogative 'how much' (*keci/kici* in the Northern and Central dialects, *keti* alongside *kazom*, *kabor* and *sode* in the Balkan and Vlax dialects).

9.3.3 *Simplification*

Like option selection, simplification is often an interplay of continuity and discontinuity of forms, and so a priori less diagnostic of shared developments. There are, however, simplifications that cause major disruption to the system and require rearrangement of entire categories or paradigms. Such processes involve long-term systemic developments. Plain simplifications of lesser diagnostic value are the reduction of the genitive marker *-ker-* > *-k-* (primarily Vlax, but also Finnish Romani and partly Welsh and Latvian Romani, and sporadically in the Balkans), the reduction of the masculine inflection marker *-va* in demonstratives (Central dialects, partly Vlax, Southern Ukrainian, and Bugurdži), neutralisation of the opposition *-iben/-ipen* in the (deverbal and deadjectival) nominaliser to just *-ipen* (Vlax, Roman, Sepeči, Prilep, Piedmontese Sinti) and the reduction of its oblique form *-pnas/-bnas* to *-mas* (Vlax, Welsh Romani, some Sinti varieties, Sepeči), *-pas/-bas* (Arli), or other forms.

More dramatic in terms of their paradigmatic functionality are the simplifications in the set of demonstratives and in the morphological adaptation of loan verbs. The original Early Romani demonstrative sets survive intact in the extreme eastern (southern Balkans), western (Welsh Romani), and southern (Abruzzian Romani) peripheries (figure 9.10). As discussed in chapter 5, other dialects may lose one of the consonantal stems (Vlax, Northeastern), or the initial (carrier) vowel as an opposition feature (Sinti-Finnish, Central, Vlax). In the case of Vlax and surrounding dialects, the losses are compensated for through innovations (see above).

Although not a perfect match, there are some similarities between the diffusion pattern of demonstrative simplification, and that of the reduction of Greek-derived markers of loan verbs (figure 9.11). Here too, there are resemblances

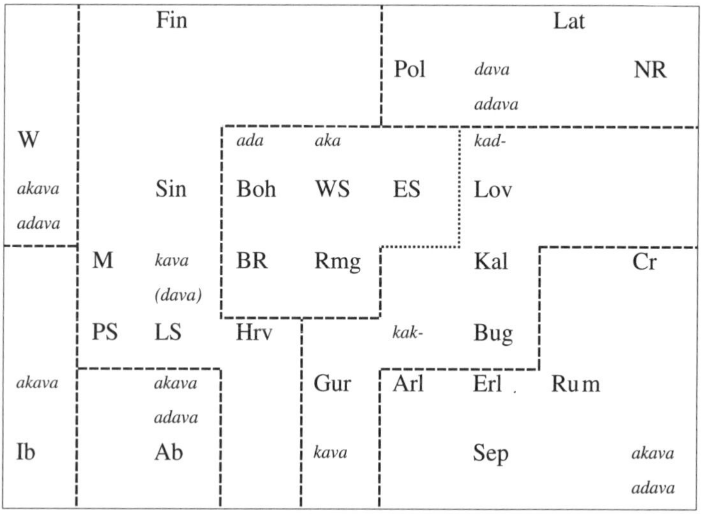

Figure 9.10 Simplification of demonstratives (the dotted line indicates a transitional zone)

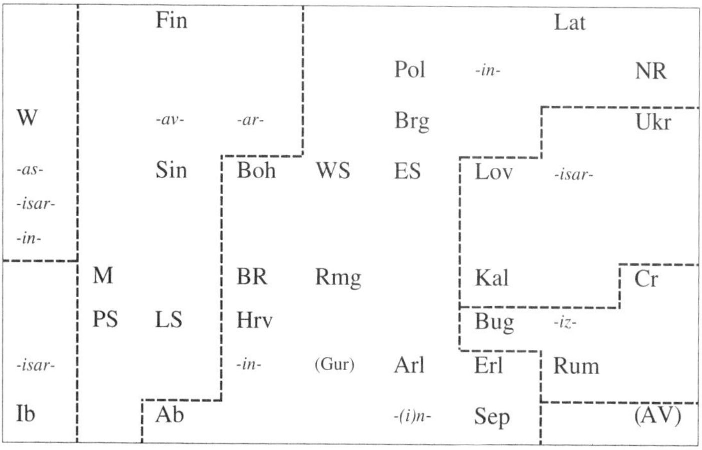

Figure 9.11 Simplification of loan-verb adaptation markers (transitives)

among the peripheries, in this case Vlax, Iberian, and Welsh Romani. Both phenomena show rather clear boundaries between the Sinti–Finnish group and the Central dialects, with Hravati/Dolenjski occupying an intermediate position, patterning with Sinti for demonstratives and with the Central group for loan verbs. Vlax patterns independently for loan verbs, but shares features with surrounding dialects for demonstratives, where innovations are involved (cf. above). Both developments point to a close affinity between Sinti and Finnish Romani.

A further case of paradigm simplification is the assimilation of the 2PL/3PL perfective concord markers (figure 9.12). In the Balkans, including some of the Vlax varieties, assimilation is partial, influencing the vowel of the 2PL. In two separate zones, the Sinti group and the Baltic–Ukrainian area, forms merge. Elsewhere the conservative pattern is retained. This development is apparently more recent than the former two, relying on Sinti as a consolidated group (with variable patterns), while on the other hand the Northeastern group is not coherent.

It is interesting to note that with paradigm simplifications, the patterns conform more closely to the so-called consensus classification, which itself is based on some historical evidence of migration patterns and contact developments as well as on shared features. Paradigm simplification and restructuring constitutes a more complex process than the simple adoption vs. rejection of an innovation, or the selection of one option rather than another. The choices and direction of merger processes are less predictable. Paradigm simplification therefore turns out to be a more reliable, diagnostic indicator for the internal coherence of a group of dialects.

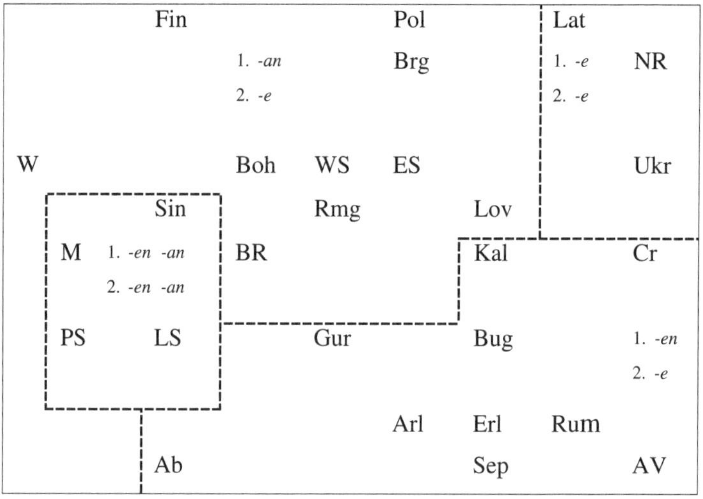

Figure 9.12 Simplification of perfective concord markers: 1. 2PL, 2. 3PL

9.3.4 *Archaisms*

We finally turn to the retention of archaisms. Classifying a form as an archaism (rather than classifying its absence as a case of simplification) simply means that the rule tends toward simplification, that simplification may have already begun in Early Romani, and that the retention of the archaic trait is therefore more outstanding. Salient archaisms include the inherited synthetic comparative in *-eder* in the Northern and Central branches, the indefinites *či* and *-moni* and quantifier *kuti* 'a little' in the northern and western European dialects (with a transitional zone comprising Bohemian Romani and Polska Roma with *či* but not *-moni*), the adjectival oblique feminine marker *-a* in Vlax, Central, and some Sinti varieties, the Greek-derived abstract nominal ending *-imo(s)* in Vlax, Welsh and Iberian Romani, subject clitics with lexical verbs in Sinti, some Romungro varieties, and Roman, and the form of the remoteness marker in **-asi* > *-ahi* in the Southern Central group (and *-aj* in Prizren).

With archaisms, relations among the dialects are often circumstantial. The peripheries are often conservative. Innovation through borrowing appears to be more extensive in the southeast, leaving the northwest with more conservative features (such as the synthetic comparative marker and inherited indefinites; see also chapter 8). The case of the definite article (figure 9.13) shows however that there are also retention zones for specific archaisms. The original definite

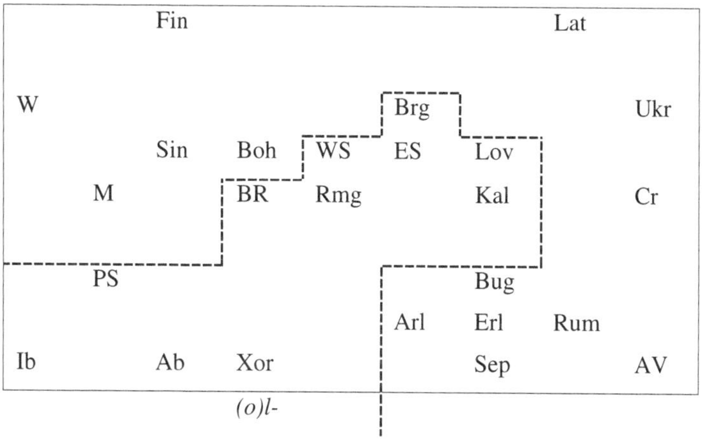

Figure 9.13 Retention of definite articles in *-l-*

article in *-l-* has been reduced throughout for the nominative singular forms. But forms in *-l-* survive in Northern Vlax and Central dialects for the oblique feminine and for the plural. Conservative nominative plural forms also survive in the southern periphery: Piedmontese Sinti, Italian Xoraxane, Abruzzian Romani, and Catalonian Romani (*ol*).

9.4 Implications of the geographical diffusion model

Although the direction of geographical diffusion of changes is not uniform in Romani, it is possible to draw a number of conclusions. There is a general northwest–southeast division, which serves as a boundary for innovations spreading in either direction. Vlax appears as an innovative and dynamic dialect group, whose influence extends into neighbouring dialects and beyond. Another influential centre, in the northwest, has the Sinti group at its core; this centre projects a number of innovations, but it appears particularly effective in blocking innovations from the southeast. In addition, the Sinti core stands out in its patterns of option selection, which it partly projects eastwards. In a sense, the dynamics of dialect evolution in Romani might be viewed as a competition between two cores, each pulling in its own direction. The Central dialects are caught in the middle, alternating their orientation between the two centres to the west and east of them.

The fact that many of the salient isoglosses separating Romani dialects show clear geographical diffusion relativises the importance of genetic group affiliation somewhat. On the other hand, it strengthens some of the intuitive notions on dialect groupings, and it helps integrate the realisation that individual preconceived groups share inventories of features, into a broader framework of feature differentiation in Romani.

The essential criterion for classification, based on this background, is participation in a cluster of isoglosses. From the above discussion, the Sinti group emerges as extremely coherent (with some archaisms in the Piedmontese variety). It also tends to pattern together with Finnish Romani, allowing us to postulate a Northwestern or Sinti–Finnish group. The Northeastern (Polish–Baltic–North Russian) dialects find themselves on the same side of the dividing line for most forms, the Polska Roma dialect differing on a number of items, as might be expected from a frontier dialect. Northern Vlax is a coherent group in almost all items, but it patterns in different ways in relation to Southern Vlax. The impression is, therefore, that many of the isoglosses that are constitutive of the Vlax group tend to be of a more specific nature, rather than developments that are relevant for Romani as a whole. (Consider as an example the umlaut in the 1SG concord marker **-jom* > *-em*, which is rarely encountered outside Vlax.)

The Central branch seems at first glance to be divided by a large number of isoglosses. However, at closer scrutiny the Central dialects appear remarkably consistent in their morphological patterns, sharing future-tense marking, person concord, case markers, demonstratives, and loan-verb adaptation. The dialects of the southern Balkans are diverse, but their diversity in respect of many of the isoglosses considered here is not atomised. Instead, we witness different orientation targets. Some dialects, like Bugurdži or Sepeči, are prone to Vlax influence (partly through later contacts with migrant Vlax communities), while Arli (and to a lesser extent Erli) is susceptible to northwestern influence (via Hravati, from the Southern Central dialects, and ultimately from the Northwestern or Sinti–Finnish diffusion centre).

An advantage of the geographical-diffusion approach is that aberrant dialects that do not pattern smoothly with any of the established groups do not in any way present a theoretical problem. Conservativism, and in some cases deviant selection of options and simplification patterns, are predictable for dialects in peripheral locations. The profiles of Welsh Romani, Iberian Romani, and southern Italian Romani are therefore rather helpful in reconstructing the relative chronology of some of the changes. Most of the features that these three dialects share with the so-called Northern branch are conservativisms. The fact that they also resist some of the innovations triggered within the western-central (Sinti) diffusion centre creates the impression of isolated or non-classifiable varieties.

Another dialect that is often considered isolated is Hravati/Dolenjski or Croatian (also Slovene, Istrian) Romani (cf. Soravia 1977, Bakker 1999, Cech and Heinschink 2001). The position of Hravati/Dolenjski, however, like that of the peripheral dialects, makes perfect sense from the viewpoint of a geographical diffusion model: it is situated precisely at the crossroads of developments between all three diffusion centres, and close to the dialects of the south, which maintain some archaisms but also undergo a number of regional innovations of their own. It is to be expected, purely on the basis of its location, that Hravati/Dolenjski should pattern differently in regard to different isoglosses, and that it would therefore resist accommodation on a simplified genetic tree-diagram.

10 Romani sociolinguistics

10.1 Aspects of language use

There are no genuinely reliable census figures confirming the number of Romani speakers.[1] Numbers cited in the literature are usually based on informal estimates by multilateral organisations and by non-governmental organisations that specialise in advocacy work on behalf of Romani communities (cf. e.g. Bakker et al. 2000: 40). Perhaps the most accurate picture is therefore obtained from relative, rather than from absolute estimates, for the countries with the largest Romani-speaking populations (table 10.1). The actual figures may be considerably higher; for Romania for instance, it is assumed that there are around one million speakers of the language. There are numerous other countries with smaller Romani-speaking minorities, including most European countries, Canada, Argentina, Brazil, and Australia. Even the most conservative estimates agree that Romani is spoken by a population of more than 3.5 million people worldwide.

Romani is primarily an oral language. It is acquired almost exclusively as a first language (or as one of two first languages) by children in the context of the family home, with no institutional or normative reinforcement through schools or media. All adult speakers of Romani are fully bilingual or even multilingual. Romani always stands in a diglossic relation to the majority language, and in many cases also to other surrounding minority languages. Patterns of language use in Romani communities are usually seen as a continuum between the private and public spheres (see especially Halwachs 1993; also Hübschmannová 1979, Réger 1979). The public (or acrolectal) domain of communication – interaction with government officials, schools, or media – is almost always reserved exclusively for the majority language. Intermediate (mesolectal) points on the continuum are semi-public activities such as work, shopping, leisure, and interaction with friends outside the family circle. In the Balkans, it is common for Romani

[1] Some central and eastern European countries have included 'Rom' as an ethnicity category in census questionnaires for many years now. However, non-governmental organisations estimate that many Rom, perhaps even the majority, do not identify as Rom for official purposes for fear of discrimination. In addition, only some census questionnaires, such as that of Macedonia (Friedman 1999: 322), have separate entries for 'Rom' nationality, and 'Romani' mother tongue.

Table 10.1 *Possible numbers of Romani speakers for some countries*

Over 250,000	Romania, Bulgaria, Slovakia, Russia, Yugoslavia (Serbia, Montenegro and Kosovo), Turkey
100,000–250,000	Macedonia, Czech Republic, Greece, United States
50,000–100,000	Albania, Germany, Italy, Poland, Ukraine, Hungary

to assume extensive mesolectal functions, often alongside other minority languages (such as Turkish, Macedonian, or Albanian). In western communities, mesolectal functions are typically covered by the majority language. Immigrant Rom in western Europe however often continue to use the majority language of their countries of origin (such as Serbian among the Yugoslav Kalderaš, Macedonian among the Arli) in interaction with other, non-Romani immigrants from these countries (cf. Halwachs 1999).

Romani is clearly strongest in its basilectal function as a language of the extended family. Some communities rely exclusively on Romani for communication within the family domain (see Réger 1979: 61, on the Lovara in Hungary). In other communities, basilectal multilingualism is common (cf. Hancock 1976 on American Vlax, Halwachs 1993, 1999 on Sinti and Burgenland Rom in Austria). Hancock (1976: 87) describes Romani as a symbol for the separation of Romani and Gadžo (i.e. non-Romani) worlds, and as a central criterion for group membership. Romani is often used in the presence of Gadže as a means of secret communication, and Rom in many western communities tend to give a false answer when questioned about their language.[2] For some groups, this secretive function of Romani appears to be both a practical tool and a cultural-ideological attitude (see Tong 1983). This can have structural implications: in dialects that were traditionally spoken by isolated communities of peripatetic Rom in western Europe, euphemistic and cryptolalic formations are especially widespread (see chapters 5, 9).

Although Romani has primarily basilectal functions in traditional communities, use of the language in public domains has been expanding dramatically in recent years, especially since the political transition in central and eastern Europe in 1989–90. Romani-language theatre companies were established in Moscow already in 1931, in Czechoslovakia in 1948, and in Macedonia in 1971, and several more emerged during the 1990s. There are a number of films in Romani (mostly by non-Romani directors and producers), the most famous of them is probably Emir Kusturica's *Time of the Gypsies* (1989). Romani song lyrics are perhaps the most traditional public use of Romani,

[2] Identifying it as 'Greek' in the United States. The first time I heard Romani spoken in Germany by Serbian Gurbet, the speakers identified it to me as 'American Bulgarian'.

and the close of the twentieth century saw an expansion of the commercial distribution of popular music in Romani in all parts of Europe, in many different dialects (see Bakker et al. 2000: 39–56). Noteworthy is the growth of Romani-language evangelical missionary activities, with public rallies and productions of tapes containing sermons and popular music and even international radio broadcasts. Romani-language broadcasting (both radio and television) is reported at the national level from Hungary, Serbia, and Macedonia, and at local level from Austria, Kosovo, and the Czech Republic. The increased availability of modern descriptive grammars of the language, and interaction with a growing number of Romani intellectuals engaged in cultural and political activities, has triggered interest in the language on the part of many non-Rom, and there is a modest but growing number of non-Romani learners of the language.

Diglossia within Romani is limited. Hübschmannová (1979) has argued that the Romani-speaking community is socially homogeneous, the principal divisions being between families and clans. Nonetheless, in interdialectal contact situations, certain varieties may carry more prestige due to the relative social and economic standing of their speakers (cf. Lípa 1979: 56). Individual speakers in mixed communities may be multidialectal, switching with different interlocutors. Strategies of accommodation to other dialects are common, and may result in long-term interdialectal interference and structural change (cf. Boretzky 1995c). With the expansion of semi-public use of the language in international cultural and political events, interdialectal communication among speakers from different countries is becoming more frequent and more intense. The challenge facing speakers is to 'switch off' code switching into their respective majority languages, and maintain a monolingual Romani discourse.

There is growing interest in the study of discourse styles in Romani. Hancock (1995a: 142) mentions an 'oratorical register' used in Vlax ceremonial speech, which is characterised by the conservative use of the long present conjugation (*-a*) for present (rather than future) tense (cf. also Matras 1994a: 89–90). The emergence of institutional discourse and of lectures in the context of Romani political activities carries with it an extension of situational deictic functions to the text as an object of analysis, triggering the evolution of text deixis (Matras 1998a: 413–14). Traditional narratives (*paramiči* 'folk tale') often have institutional status in Romani; they are told by professional narrators to an assembled audience, and tend to follow strict sequences, which include formulae for greeting and asking permission (of the audience), as well as songs (Kovalcsik 1999). Playful-manipulative language use appears to be deeply embedded in Romani culture. Language riddles have been documented for a number of dialects (cf. Bakker et al. 2000: 54–56), as have been proverbs (e.g. Hübschmannová 1981), and teasing has been shown to have a salient function in adult–child interaction (Réger 1999).

Surprisingly few studies have been devoted in detail to the issue of **bilingualism** in Romani communities. Romani children usually acquire the majority language either at infancy, parallel to their acquisition of Romani, or else at childhood, with the beginning of school attendance. There is however evidence from different countries that separate socialisation and isolation from majority-group peers prevents Romani children from attaining the same level of communicative competence before entering school, and especially from acquiring the ability to form independent discourse (cf. Hancock 1975 on the United States, Réger 1979 on Hungary, Kyuchukov 1994 on Bulgaria).

Even in the most traditional communities, Romani-language conversation contains extensive code mixing. Hübschmannová (1979: 37) sees the integration of the majority language into Romani discourse as a representation of the various cultural sectors of Romani life, with loanwords (majority-language insertions) used for referents that are considered 'property of the Gadžos'. With growing integration of the Rom into urban society, mixing patterns are no longer limited to single referents, but are often exploited for stylistic and conversation-strategic purposes as well. Consider the following Romani–German excerpt from a speaker of Lovari in Hamburg, Germany:

(1) Aj akana, *obwohl* kadka meres ke muljas tuke varekon, hačares, *du bist total fertig*, tu si te žas inke te des tu gindo kaj te praxov les, kudka si te žav, *Bestattungsinstitut*, ehm/ pa/ pa/ pa *Meldeamt*, eh *Geb/ Sterbeurkunde*, hačares, *es ist weg*. *Beispiel* akana feri phendem tuke. *Es sind so alles, alles verschiedene Sachen.*

'And now, *although* you are dying (=grieving) here because one of your relations has died, you understand, *you are totally devastated*, you still have to go and think where shall I bury him, I have to go here, *funeral parlour*, uhm/ to/ to/ to the *registration office*, uh *birth/ death certificate*, you understand, *it's gone*. I only gave you an *example* now. *It's all, all these different things*.'

The speaker is addressing changing social patterns within the community and the loss of extended family support. The first switch is grammatical, and can be explained as a fusion of clause-combining expressions, which typically occurs around discourse markers and contrastive expressions (cf. Matras 1998d; see also chapter 8). Other individual lexical insertions are designations for institutions, all of which represent activities that are negotiated outside the Romani community. The word *Beispiel* 'example' can be viewed as a case of a lexical gap, or alternatively it can also be related to an attempt to bridge Romani-language family discourse with analytical discourse. The remaining brief alternations of codes in the excerpt all involve evaluative statements. Language alternation is used as a contextualisaion cue (Gumperz 1982) in order to mark out positions in the discourse where highlighted evaluative points are paraphrased and summarised, or where consensus is being sought with the listener. Bilingualism is thus not just reflected in the domain-specific use of two or more languages, but it is also functional within Romani discourse itself.

Apart from maintaining Romani as an ethnic language, the majority language as spoken by the Rom in most countries tends to show ethnolectal features. For American English as spoken by Vlax Rom, Hancock (1975, 1980) mentions phonological features such as the lack of contrast between /w/ and /v/, /t/ and /θ/, /d/ and /ð/, and malapropisms, especially confusion of formal vocabulary, such as the use of *knowlogy* for *knowledge* or *junction* for *injunction*. Ethnolectal German as spoken by Rom (and Sinti) usually shows de-rounding of *ü, ö* (*gerist* < *Gerüst* 'scaffold', *bēse* < *böse* 'angry'), neutralisation of dative and accusative cases (*mit den Bruder* < *mit dem Bruder* 'with the brother', *bei die Leute* < *bei den Leuten* 'at those people's'), and use of auxiliaries in subordinate clauses (*er versteht mehr als er zugeben tut* 'he understands more than he [does] admit'). All these individual features can be found in dialectal German, though not in the combination in which they occur in the ethnolectal German spoken by the Rom.

Shifting patterns of bilingual behaviour have an effect on **language maintenance** in many communities. While the historical decline of Romani in Britain and Scandinavia is probably due to the isolation of very small communities of speakers, persecution of Romani by the state in seventeenth-century Spain and in the eighteenth-century Habsburg Monarchy are believed to have been responsible for the decline of Romani in Spain and in large parts of Hungary. For the past two to three generations, changes in language attitudes have followed changes in the interaction with majority society. The move to regular paid employment, and urbanisation and the move away from 'Gypsy colonies' at the outskirts of towns and villages in central, eastern, and southeastern Europe have opened, in theory at least, the prospect of integration, triggering changes in the self-image of the Rom. Speaking Romani is often seen as a hindrance to upward social mobility, while abandoning the language is regarded as a token of integration (cf. Hübschmannová 1979, Haarmann 1980, Tong 1985, Halwachs 1999). Some Romani communities however abandoned the use of Romani centuries ago, but continue to maintain ethnic distinctness.[3]

10.2 Para-Romani

In some communities of Rom, the Romani language is no longer in use, but a Romani-derived special vocabulary is retained, which may be inserted into

[3] Some groups of Muslim Roms in the Balkans have Turkish as their first language. Some groups of Christian Rom in all the Balkan countries identify as Rom but have the country's national language as their mother tongue. Ethnically distinct settled communities speaking Albanian, Macedonian, and Greek with ethnonyms cognate with English *Gypsy* live in Albania, Greece, Macedonia, and Kosovo. The *Beaş* of Hungary are an ethnically distinct group and speak an Aromanian dialect, but are often discussed in connection with the Rom due to their socio-economic profile.

discourse in the respective majority language. 'Para-Romani' is now the established term for this phenomenon (see Cortiade 1991, Bakker and van der Voort 1991; Matras 1998b). In older descriptions, mixtures involving Romani words and non-Romani grammar were referred to implicitly as dialects of Romani, more precisely as the languages of the Gypsies of Spain, Scandinavia, and so on (cf. Miklosich 1872–80). Boretzky and Igla (1994a; cf. also Boretzky 1998c) have called them 'Romani mixed dialects'. Para-Romani varieties are best documented for the western European periphery regions, where they have completely replaced inflected dialects of Romani: so-called Angloromani in Britain, Caló in Spain, so-called Basque Romani in the Basque Country, and so-called Scandoromani in Scandinavia. Speakers however generally continue to refer to the use of Romani-derived lexicon as 'Romani': e.g. *romani jib* < *řomani čhib* in England,[4] *caló* < *kalo* in Spain, *errumantxela* < *romaničel* in the Basque Country, *romano* in Scandinavia.

Other known Para-Romani varieties are Dortika in Greece (Triandaphyllidis 1923), the secret language of the Geygelli Yürüks in Turkey (Lewis 1950–55, Bakker 2001), the German-based Romnisch in Denmark (Miskow and Brøndal 1923), and the recently discovered Finikas Romani in Greece (Sechidou 2000). In some cases there is partial overlap between the use of Romani vocabulary and local argots used by native peripatetic populations, such as Norwegian *Rodi*, German *Jenisch*, or Spanish *Germanía*. The Jenisch variety used in Giessen in Germany, for instance, has been enriched by a lexical layer of Romani origin which now makes up the bulk of the vocabulary (Lerch 1976). It is referred to by other peripatetics as *Manisch*, from *manuš* 'Rom, Gypsy' (Romani *manuš* 'person', and name of a Romani tribe of France and formerly also southern Germany). In Bosnia, the secret language *Šatrovački* or 'tent-dwellers' speech' has a strong Romani-derived component (Uhlik 1954).

Most sources on Para-Romani varieties consist of wordlists and small numbers of sample sentences collected among Rom in the respective countries. Sources on Caló are the oldest, going back to the seventeenth century. Arguably, a wordlist and a few sentences included in the *Winchester Confessions* (MacGowan 1996) document the insertion of Romani words into English discourse as early as 1616 (cf. Bakker 2000). The bulk of the documentation on Para-Romani in England, Spain, and the Basque Country dates from the nineteenth century,[5] while the principal sources on Para-Romani in Sweden and Norway are from the first half of the twentieth century.[6]

[4] Also *pogadi jib* 'broken language'.

[5] E.g. Bright (1818), A.R.S.A. (1888), Jiménez (1853), Quindalé (1867), Baudrimont (1862). Much of the material on English Para-Romani was collected in the nineteenth century but edited and published in the early twentieth century in the *Journal of the Gypsy Lore Society*. For discussions of the sources see Bakker (1998), Boretzky (1985, 1992b, 1998c), Leigh (1998), Torrione (1989).

[6] E.g. Ehrenborg (1928), Etzler (1944), Iversen (1944); for a discussion see Ladefoged (1998).

Text material documenting actual usage of Para-Romani is rare. Authentic narratives in English Para-Romani are recorded by Smart and Crofton (1875), who refer to it as the 'new dialect' to distinguish it from the conservative (non-mixed) form of Romani still known to their informants. The novelists George Borrow (1841, 1851, 1874) and Charles Leland (1874) included texts in Spanish Para-Romani and English Para-Romani in their books, and Borrow even translated a gospel into Caló; but the reliability of this material as authentic samples of Para-Romani text composition is questionable (see Hancock 1997, Bakker 1998: 84–7). De Luna (1951) cites a small number of songs collected from Andalusian Gitanos which include Caló vocabulary.

The fact that speakers have maintained active knowledge of a special Romani-derived vocabulary is thus well-documented. What is not clear, however, is the extent and frequency of employment of this vocabulary in actual conversation. Modern elicitations suggest that active knowledge of Para-Romani vocabulary still exists, though its usage appears to be in decline (McLane 1977, Román 1995, Leigh 1998 on Caló; Johansson 1977 on Scandoromani; Hancock 1969 and 1986, Wood 1973, Acton and Kenrick 1984 on Angloromani). The following excerpt from a conversation with a Romani horse-dealer from County Durham, northern England, tape-recorded in February 2000, is perhaps closest to an authentic documentation of Para-Romani – i.e. of active and spontaneous (non-elicited) use of special Romani-derived vocabulary in a non-Romani grammatical and discourse framework. The speaker has no active knowledge of inflected Romani. His knowledge of special vocabulary was acquired in the family. Although he admits to not having used his Romani vocabulary for many years, during a two-hour conversation (part of it natural conversation, as documented here, part of it elicitation) he was able to use or recall some 250 different lexical items. The excerpt documents the beginning of the conversation. The speaker had not been asked to use Romani words at this stage; rather, it was the context – my visit, as a researcher with an interest in Romani – that triggered the choice:

(1) RJ Yes *bish ta pansh besha* twenty-five years I've never really *rokkered* in *Romani jibb.*

YM No.

RJ My mind works in English/these last *do trin divvis* I've been trying to *pench* in Romani because I knew you were . . .

YM Oh right.

RJ And all the time it just comes slowly, what's that *lav*? Ah right yes and it comes back to me. And if you don't/ if you went abroad and you could speak French and you'd never spoken to anybody in French for twenty-five years, you wouldn't just be able to switch if you hadn't been using it. I just *adge* here *kokkero*, stay here

> alone right, so other than when I go away *lena*, summer, and meet a few people and *sash in* you know, and exchange one or two words with them, never really get into conversation. [. . .] A lot of them don't have a *vardo* to pull but they still/ they just like to have a *grai* or two, put them on the tether and go to the fairs with them, flash them up and down the road, down the *drom*, there's still a lot of travelling people in this country but there's not many *tatchi Romani* round here, mostly sort of *posh* and *posh*.

The origin and translation of the special vocabulary items in the excerpt: *biš ta pandž berša* 'twenty-five years', *råker-* 'to speak', *romani čhib* 'Romani language', *duj trin dives* 'two three days', *pench* 'to think' (French *pense-*), *lav* 'word', *ačh-* 'to stay', *ko(r)koro* 'alone', *lena* 'summers', *sar-šan* 'how are you', *vordo* 'wagon, caravan', *graj* 'horse', *drom* 'road', *čače/čači* 'true', *paš* 'half'. There is some selective retention of Romani grammatical inflection and of conjunctions, but it is restricted to stereotypical expressions such as 'X year-s', 'how are you'.

The only other recent, tape-recorded documentations of Para-Romani conversation stem from Leigh (1998) and Sechidou (2000). Both are staged interviews, in which speakers were explicitly asked to provide examples of Romani vocabulary and its use. Leigh (1998: 272–8) presents the following from two Andalusian Gitanos:

(2) A *acobá* el *quer* de José, el *quer* es la casa, estamos aquí, la casa de José
'this [*akava* 'this'] is the house of José, *quer* [< *kher* 'house'] is 'house', we are here, the house of José.'

(3) B *changaripen.*
[< *čingaripen* 'quarrel']
A O *chingaripen.* Se ha ido a la guerra. Mi *chaborí* ha *najado* a la guerra.
'Or *chingaripen.* He has gone to war. My boy [*čavoro* 'boy'] has gone [*naš-* 'to run'] to war'

Sechidou (2000) reports on the mixed variety of Finikas in Thessaloniki, originally spoken in the Peloponnese. This Para-Romani is used in a number of families in which the men are speakers of Greek with knowledge of some Romani-derived vocabulary, while the women are Romani-Greek bilinguals:

(4) O *dais* mu ta *aveljazi sare* ta *love*. I *dai* mu dhe *dzalizi* puthena.
'My father [*dad* 'father'] brings [*avel* 'he comes'; *anel* 'he brings'?] all [*sare* 'all'] the money [*love* 'money']. My mother [*daj* 'mother'] is not going [*džal* 'she goes'] anywhere.'

The sporadic insertion of lexical items is not a case of code mixing, since the speakers have – except for the women in the Finikas case – no competence in Romani beyond a limited lexical inventory. Rather, it resembles the use of special vocabularies in argots such as Cant or *Rotwelsch* among other peripatetic communities. In the case of Para-Romani, the need for a means of secret communication in the presence of Gadžos after the abandonment of inflected Romani contributed to the motivation to preserve a separate lexical reservoir. However, secret communication is not the only function. The Romani special lexical reservoir also serves as a symbol which helps consolidate and flag separate ethnic identity. Modern uses of Para-Romani on websites and in evangelical missionary pamphlets confirm this identity-related function. It seems therefore justified to regard Para-Romani varieties as styles or registers. The insertion of special vocabulary is subject to considerable variation and contextual choices, some of which are addressee-oriented (the creation of solidarity), others are bystander-oriented (the exclusion of outsiders; cf. Rijkhof 1998) (see also Kenrick 1979, Hancock 1986: 215–18).

It is difficult to estimate the size of Romani vocabulary at the disposal of individual speakers. Dictionaries of Para-Romani may show up to ca. 600 Romani etymologies. Typically, the rate of retention from Romani of basic vocabulary, measured on the basis of the Swadesh-lists, is around 70–80 per cent (Boretzky 1998c: 100–14). One of the features of Para-Romani is extensive in-coining of vocabulary, which testifies to the playful-manipulative character of its use. Hancock (1984: 377–8) notes Angloromani expressions such as *sasti-čeriklə* 'aeroplane' (lit. 'iron bird', *saster* 'iron', *čirikli* 'bird'); our Angloromani consultant from Durham, RJ, used *dikinevs* for 'window' (*dikh-* to see'), as well as *muttremengri* for 'tea' (*mutr-* 'to urinate', with a genitive derivation suffix). There is also borrowing from local secret languages and from languages of other minorities. The relative proportion is difficult to estimate for the varieties as a whole. Iversen (1944) notes up to 30 per cent non-Romani vocabulary in the special lexicon of the Norwegian travellers. In some of the Caló dictionaries, the proportion is even higher. RJ used Cant *skreeves* for 'cars', as well as French-derived *pench* 'to think', also a Cant borrowing. Such borrowings are a further indication of the functional overlap between Para-Romani and the in-group vocabularies of other peripatetic groups.

Although there are differences, a number of generalisations can be made about the **structural profile** of Para-Romani varieties. The sound system of Romani generally collapses, and the Romani-derived vocabulary is integrated into the phonologies of the 'host' or grammar language. Apart from lexical content-words, a number of grammatical categories are retained in Para-Romani, though inflection agreement is generally lost. These include numerals, demonstratives, and negators (Angloromani *kek*, Caló *nati*, Scandoromani and Manisch *či*, Errumantxela or Basque Para-Romani *na*). Personal pronouns are usually a mixture of Romani nominative or non-nominative pronouns or demonstratives for the third person (*kava, dova, lo, yov/yoy, lester*, etc.), and non-nominative pronouns for the first and second persons. There is some variation among individual Para-Romani varieties. Angloromani tends to select locative forms (*mandi* 'I', *tuti* 'you'), Caló has dative or instrumental forms (*mange, mansa* 'I', *tuke, tusa* 'you'), while Scandoromani selects the genitive-possessive form (*miro* 'I', *diro* 'you' < Romani *tiro* 'your' contaminated with Scandinavian *din* 'your'). Singular pronouns are most prominent; plural pronouns are either not documented at all within the special vocabulary, or else they are based on a camouflaged form of the host language pronoun (Scandoromani *vårsnus* 'we' < Scandinavian *vår* 'our', possibly Romance *-nus* 'us' via other secret languages). Possessives draw on the possessive inflection of the host language (Angloromani *mandi's* 'my', Scandoromani *miros*, Finikas *o mindos mu*).

Other grammatical categories retained from Romani include place deictics, indefinites, and quantifiers such as 'all', 'every', and 'other', and more rarely expressions of local relations and interrogatives. Caló has the Romani-derived copula *sinelar* (*s -in-* 'to be'), while in Scandoromani sources one finds grammaticalisation of Romani verbs of location – *asja* (*ačh-* 'to stay') and *besja* (*beš-* 'to sit') – alongside *honka* (of obscure origin, possibly Romani *hom-te* 'must'). Speakers often have some awareness of Romani grammatical inflections, though these are only retained in fossilised form: Caló *gachó* 'non-Gypsy man', *gachí* 'non-Gypsy woman' (*gadžo, -i*), *lacró* 'boy', *lacrí* 'girl' (*raklo, -i*); Angloromani *besh* 'year', *besha* 'years' (*berš, -a*), *dzuckel* 'dog', *dzuckle* 'dogs' (*džukel, džukle*). The nominaliser *-ipen* is usually also retained in semi-productive function: Angloromani *nafli* 'sick', *naflipen* 'sickness' (*nasvali/-o, nasvalipen*), Caló *jalar* 'to eat', *jalipe* 'food' (*xa-* 'to eat'; the nominal form is a Caló composition, cf. Romani *xal* 'eats', *xaben* 'food').

The use of verbs is based on either the lexical stem, or the 3SG present form. Romani roots in *-a* generally appear in the 3SG: Caló *jalar*, Angloromani *hal* 'to eat' (< *xa-l* 'eats'). With other verbs, Angloromani and Scandoromani usually select the Romani stem. Caló alternates, showing a preference for the 3SG with verbs ending in nasals: *camelar* 'to like' (< *kam-el* 'likes'), *chanelar* 'to know' (< *džan-el* 'knows'). Finikas generally adopts the 3SG form, to which Greek loan-verb adaptation markers are added: *rovel-jaz-o* 'I cry' (< *rov-el* 'cries'). Romani loan-verb adaptation markers are retained as part of the Romani stem: *psoniserel-jaz-o* 'I buy' (*pson-is-er-* 'to buy').

There has been much debate in Romani linguistics concerning the emergence of Para-Romani varieties. Since they replace inflected varieties of Romani, the evolution of Para-Romani has been seen as a result of gradual language attrition (Kenrick 1979) or increasing grammatical borrowing from the host language (cf. Thomason and Kaufman 1988). Alternatively, it has been suggested that Para-Romani arose through population mixture of Rom with native marginalised groups. These mixed communities developed an in-group and emblematic code of their own. Once formed, this mixed variety replaced Romani as a symbol of identity, and Romani was abandoned (Hancock 1970, 1984, 1992). Such a process would resemble the formation of mixed languages in communities with mixed households, such as the Michif of Saskatchewan and North Dakota, a process that is rapid rather than gradual (cf. Bakker 1998, 2000; also Bakker 1997a). Boretzky (1985) has pointed out that the retention of lexicon does not match the normal progress of language attrition, and has suggested instead that Para-Romani arose through language shift to the host language. The shifting generation then held on to the lexicon of the 'old' language, possibly reinforced through interaction with immigrant Rom who continued to speak Romani (Boretzky 1998c; Boretzky and Igla 1994a).

It certainly seems justified to regard Para-Romani as a case of language shift. The language that provides the grammatical blueprint for the utterance – the 'matrix language' (Myers-Scotton 1993) – and especially the language that provides finite-verb inflection, which serves as a basis for the anchoring of the predication – or 'INFL-language' (Matras 2000e) – is consistently the host language. The question is therefore, what motivates the retention of Romani vocabulary. Haugen (1949: 390), commenting on Iversen's (1944) work on Norwegian Para-Romani, described the introduction of special vocabulary as an act against assimilation. It is possible that mixing was once the unmarked choice in the respective communities (see Bakker 1998c), although there is no concrete evidence to support such an assumption. But it is fairly clear that the historical background for the formation of special vocabularies is the loss of Romani as an everyday language which had also served as a symbol of identity. This loss – or language shift – occurred as Romani lost even its basilectal functions. The only function it retained was that of identity-flagging and secret communication. Consequently, only those structures that were functional for these purposes were replicated – notably referential expressions. Other structures, those responsible for processing and organising the utterance – such as inflection or conjunctions – were abandoned. Para-Romani thus evolved through a turnover of functions carrying with it selective structural replication from Romani (cf. Matras 1998b, 2000d).

The Para-Romani debate has so far been mainly a debate among specialists in Romani linguistics. But it has theoretical implications in a number of fields. From the viewpoint of the ethnography and pragmatics of communication, Para-Romani can be seen as a case of euphemistic language use (cf. Burridge 1998) and as a system with bystander-oriented functions (Rijkhof 1998). It is also a challenge to theories of language death and language shift, exemplifying partial, selective maintenance (cf. Thomason and Kaufman 1988). From the perspective of language contact theory, there is the question of the position of Para-Romani between structural borrowing, code mixing, and the emergence of mixed languages as all-purpose languages (Bakker 1997a, 2000). Finally, explaining the choice of grammatical morphemes (such as indefinites, deictics, quantifiers) that stand a chance of survival through selective replication is a challenge to grammatical theory (Matras 2000d, 2000e).

10.3 Romani influence on other languages

Romani is often cited as a recipient language for borrowings, and rightly so. But it has also been a donor language. The influence of Romani on other languages is best observed in those domains of interaction with mainstream society in which the Rom had prestige: activities that questioned or challenged the norms of the establishment. The Rom have often been regarded by other marginalised groups in society as successful conspirators against social order, and as ideologically self-sufficient in the sense that they are consistent in maintaining their own internal system of loyalties, resisting external pressure to accommodate. A conspicuous point of interface between Romani and other languages are the special vocabularies of other peripatetic communities. Romani influence has been considerable on secret languages such as German Jenisch (Matras 1998c), Czech Hantýrka (Treimer 1937), or Hungarian secret lexicons (Sulán 1963), where up to one hundred different lexical items of Romani origin may be found. Romani is also present in the in-group slang of other marginalised and anti-establishment groups: gay communities (Petropoulos 1971, Kyuchukov and Bakker 1999), the urban lower class (Kotsinas 1996), and adolescents (Leschber 1995, Pistor 1998).

Miklosich (1874–8, III) was the first to compile a comprehensive list of Romani-derived items in European argots. Several compilations have followed, devoted to Romani elements in the slangs of individual languages: for Dutch Kluyver (1934); for Italian Pasquali (1935) and Soravia (1977); for French Esnault (1935), Sandry and Carrère (1953), and Max (1972); for Hungarian Kakuk (1994); for Romanian Graur (1934), Juilland (1952), and Leschber (1995); for Bulgarian Kostov (1956); for German Wolf (1985) and Matras (1998c); for Turkish Kostov (1970); for Swedish Ward (1936) and van den Eijnde (1991); for English Ward (1947) and Grant (1998). The recurring Romani-derived items give a vague indication of the domains associated with Romani. The most frequently encountered Romani item in European slangs is *čor-* 'to steal', closely followed by *mang-* 'to beg', *ma(n)ro* 'bread, food', *gadžo, gadži* 'non-Romani man, woman = outsider, foreigner', *love* 'money'. Other items are typically terms of reference to economic resources – food, drink, and animals –, to persons, and to sex.

There are two principal triggers for the recruitment of Romani items. The first is the image of the Rom. Precisely those activities that mainstream society brings in connection with a negative image – stealing food and money, begging for food and money, and mistrust of outsiders – are for the anti-establishment minority groups positive, survival-oriented domains, where the Rom consitute a prestigious model for imitation. Perhaps the most obvious expression of this is the adoption of *gadžo, gadži* – a specific term used by the Rom regularly to refer to those who do not belong to the group. The second domain is unrelated to the specific role of the Rom, but rather to the inherent function of in-group slangs: to allow members of the group to by-pass the norms of communication – through direct reference to taboo domains or conspiracies – while avoiding the sanctions that such a breach of norms would normally entail. Kakuk (1994: 203) observes that the majority of Romani-derived words in Hungarian have a pejorative meaning, a fact he derives from the negative attitudes toward Gypsies. I would contend however that the meaning of the items is conditioned by the need to enrich both euphemistic and dysphemistic vocabulary in taboo-domains. The fact that Romani vocabulary is considered attractive for such purposes testifies, quite to the contrary of Kakuk's claim, to the high prestige of the Rom among the users of slang – those challenging established social order. Romani is perceived by them as a useful 'anti-language'.

The path of Romani-derived items follows a diffusion continuum from the specialised, secret vocabularies of non-Romani peripatetics, on to the in-group lexicons of the urban underworld and anti-establishment circles, on to the slang of more open and socially mobile groups such as adolescents, and finally into general colloquial usage (cf Matras 1998b). The end of the road usually correlates with a decrease in the number of Romani items. In regional and local slangs of northern England and the Scottish border areas, the words *gaji* 'man, woman' (*gadži*), *chavvy* 'boy' (*čhavo*), *nash* 'to go' (*naš-* 'to run'), and *peev* 'to drink' (*pijav* 'I drink') are common (see Pistor 1998), while general colloquial English has only few Romani items, the most widespread being *pal* (*phral* 'brother'). German secret languages show up to one hundred Romani items, but mainstream colloquial German appears to have adopted only *Zaster* 'money' (*saster* 'iron, metal') and *Bock* 'inclination' (*bokh* 'hunger, appetite'). As one would expect, the number is higher in colloquial Romanian and Hungarian, correlating with the number of Rom in the country.

11 Language planning and codification

11.1 Models of language planning

Romani is an oral language with only a recent, limited tradition of literacy. There is no education system in which Romani is the primary language; Romani-language literacy is always acquired, if at all, after literacy in the state language, and usually at individuals' own initiative, usually without institutional support. Norm selection in Romani is complicated through the fact that Romani is a contact language with considerable dialectal variation. There is no single dialect that enjoys either general prestige or power and which would make a natural candidate upon which to base a standard norm. Moreover, Romani is not spoken in a coherent territory, but spread among different countries with different state languages. Not only is there no centralised government or other institutional agency to assume responsibility for the implementation of a norm, there are also few internal resources – financial, logistic, or professional – that can be allocated by Romani communities themselves to help pursue codification attempts. As a result, standardisation, codification and implementation measures, and the allocation of resources in particular, are generally negotiated, decided upon, and evaluated in circles that are external to the community of speakers. Given the decentral character of codification efforts, a major theoretical question is the extent to which compatibility between various codification models can or should be achieved, and the prospects of successful implementation of any norm.

Suggestions for the selection of an individual dialect as the basis of a universal norm in Romani have had an abstract, rather than practical character. Kochanowski (1989, 1994, 1995) proposes to adopt his native Baltic Romani dialect as a basis for a standard on the grounds that it has preserved more of the original Romani morpho-phonology, while Hancock (1993) sees in mutual linguistic adaptation in oral usage among speakers of Vlax in North America an empirical justification for basing an international standard on Russian Kelderaš Vlax. Suggestions for a universal norm have been received with scepticism on the part of some linguists, who have challenged their practicability (Wolf 1960b, Igla 1991), as well as on the part of activists, who have questioned the moral justification for excluding non-normative varieties (Acton 1995).

A unification model was pursued by Cortiade/Courthiade (Courthiade 1989a, 1989b, 1990, 1992) during the 1980s and 1990s. It is based on the adoption of a meta-phonological alphabet that would allow dialectal variation to be accommodated at the phonological and morpho-phonological level. The archegraphemes (or graphemic abstractions) *θ*, *q*, *ç* are intended to capture the variation in Layer II case endings *-te, -ke, -sa* etc.: *manqe* representing *mange/mandže*, and *tuqe* for *tuke/tuće*; *tuça* representing *tusa/tuha*; the archegrapheme *ʒ* is used to represent different reflexes of historical /dž/: *ʒal* could be pronounced *džal* or *žal*. The proposal was put to the International Romani Union (IRU), a loose organisation representing Romani leaders, activists, and intellectuals from many different countries, at its congress in April 1990, where it was adopted as the 'official alphabet' (see Kenrick 1996, Hancock 1995a: 44–5).

The authority of the IRU gave the Cortiade alphabet the recognition it needed to qualify for support from the European Commission and its agencies, who agreed to fund publications using the alphabet. The EU also funded the work of a standardisation group devoted to implementing the alphabet and to enriching the standard by designing new, formal vocabulary to replace loanwords. Proposals included terms like *maśkarthemutno* 'international' (*maškar* 'between', *them* 'country'), *bi-raipno* 'non-governmental' (*bi-* 'without', *raj* 'official', *-ipen* nominaliser), *berśivaxta* 'seasons' (*berš* 'year', *vaxti* 'time' < Turkish), *paśkernavni* 'adverb' (*paš* 'next to', *ker-* 'to do', *nav* 'name'). Plans for a dictionary and an encyclopedia using the 'official' alphabet did not materialise, however. Nor could authors of Romani texts – with a couple of exceptions – be persuaded to accept the authority of the standardisation commission.

In the meantime, codification has continued to follow a decentral path, official government agencies taking only peripheral initiative in most cases. There is only one model of language planning in Romani that resembles the standardisation processes of national languages, namely that of the Republic of Macedonia (see Friedman 1999). Jusuf and Kepeski's (1980) bilingual Romani grammar (Romani–Macedonian) was the first attempt to create a regional normative grammar. The norm selected by Jusuf and Kepeski was based on the Arli and Džambazi (South Vlax) varieties spoken in Macedonia. The writing system was based on the Roman version of the South Slavic (Serbo-Croat) alphabet, rather than on Cyrillic, allowing compatibility in principle with Romani writing systems in most other European countries. Some suggestions were made for neologisms, including the adoption and adaptation of terms from Hindi, as an NIA sister language. Somewhat ironically, some of these terms are based on Arabo-Persian borrowings into Hindi: *zamani* 'tense', *šartijalo* 'conditional' (cf. Friedman 1989).

Following Macedonian independence, a Romani Standardisation Conference was organised by the Ministry of Education and the Philological Faculty at the

University of Skopje and attended by a number of Romani intellectuals as well as government representatives and linguists. The Conference produced a document with guidelines for orthographic and some grammatical rules, narrowing some of the variation in Jusuf and Kepeski's (1980) grammar (see Friedman 1995). Romani was later included as one of the official languages in the questionnaire documents and instructions to census takers produced in connection with the 1994 population census in Macedonia, and is the language of periodicals and school textbooks (Friedman 1996, 1997, 1999).

The more widespread model is for individual authors to select their own dialects, and use an orthography based on the writing system of the national language (see below). Text production and dissemination have benefited from occasional support from government agencies, multilateral organisations, and private foundations (the most active in recent years being the Soros Foundation and its Open Society Institute for central and eastern Europe). In the Czech Republic, a Romani orthography was drafted by Romani cultural associations in the 1970s, and has since been in use in publications in various dialects of the country, especially Eastern Slovak Romani. There is however no normative control over the productions, and Hübschmannová (1995) has described the process of gradual consolidation of a written norm as 'trial and error'. Hübschmannová and Neustupný (1996) go even further and propagate a concept of 'post-modern' and 'polycentric' standardisation, citing experimental findings that readers are able to accommodate to different dialects and comprehend and accept variation in writing.

A rather exceptional language-planning model is the creation of an artificial variety of Romani in Spain by one of the leaders of the Gitano political movement, Juan de Dios Ramirez-Heredia (1993). This designed variety, referred to as *Romanó-Kaló*, is based on a selection of basic vocabulary and grammatical features from a number of different Romani dialects, avoiding constructions that are strongly deviant from Spanish (such as case declension, which is abolished in favour of prepositions). The language is taught in courses offered by cultural associations, and is used occasionally in a periodical published in Spain. The orthography is original, based on the Roman alphabet and avoiding diacritics. The political vocabulary is calqued on Spanish, recruiting Romani roots. The main idea of this medium is to demonstrate the revival of Romani in Spain.

One of the most successful language-planning models is the codification project of Roman, an endangered variety of Romani spoken in the Austrian Burgenland district. The project, launched in the early 1990s, is led by a team of linguists at the University of Graz under the direction of Dieter Halwachs (1996, 1998), in close cooperation with the leadership of the Burgenland Romani community. A writing system was designed on the basis of German orthography, based on results of a survey in which speakers were questioned about their spelling preferences. The unique feature of the writing system is its consistency, adapting the same pronunciation-based rules of spelling also to German loans: *schpita* 'hospital' (German *Spital*), *dahea* 'hither', (German *daher*).

The project involved comprehensive documentation of the structures, lexicon, and oral narratives in the dialect. With support from the Austrian federal government, instruction materials were composed, including a series of school textbooks and collections of fables, as well as computer language games and an online internet dictionary. The community, with support from the University of Graz and government funding, continues to hold language courses for young adults, and to produce two bilingual periodicals, for two different age groups. The project has thus benefited from an active organisation at the community level, from regular collaboration with an academic institution, and from the recognition in 1993 of the Rom as a national minority in Austria and of Romani as a minority language.

11.2 Codification contexts and strategies

Descriptive linguistics by now has a long and established tradition of transliterating Romani. Despite some differences, on the whole the transliteration systems employed for Romani dialects in recent documentation work are compatible. Their principal distinctive features are the employment of the Roman alphabet with wedge accents for postalveolars (*č*, *š*, *ž*), with postposed *h* for aspiration (*ph*, *th*, *kh*, *čh*), and the use of *x* for the velar fricative. Different solutions are employed for palatalisation (for example *tj*, *ć*, *čj* for the palatal stop). There are two points of interface between descriptive linguistic documentation and the production of texts for a Romani audience of readers. The first is the production of dictionaries by linguists, which are used as reference works by speakers and writers. It is difficult to estimate the actual impact of academic lexicographic work on popular codification endeavours, however. The second is the personnel overlap, i.e. the involvement of linguists in popular codification work. The latter factor has been directly responsible for a number of choices made at the level of textbook production, where Romani codification at a local level was not oriented towards a modified version of the national language orthography, but toward the international conventions of descriptive linguistics. Examples are the production of multidialectal school textbooks in Bulgaria, Sweden, and Germany, in the first two cases with support of national education councils (see also Matras 1997b).

The overwhelming majority of texts produced in Romani do not form part of coordinated language planning efforts. Rather, they are the outcome of local and individual text-production initiatives. A large proportion of these texts can be regarded as 'emblematic' (cf. Matras 1999f): they are not intended to transmit information, nor are they expected to provide a leisure activity for an audience of readers. Rather, their purpose is to serve as a symbol and to trigger emotional identification. Emblematic texts include the Romani titles of many periodicals that are published in the national languages, titles of CDs, or single-line statements in Romani in leaflets or periodicals. But books may also have emblematic function. Bible translations, for instance, of which there are several dozen, are rarely read or studied, but demonstrate the wish to attribute to the language a particular status.

The importance of emblematic text production must not be underestimated: in a community with no tradition of native literacy, Romani song titles on CDs and even isolated Romani headlines in newsletters demonstrate the feasibility-in-principle of native language codification. Changing attitudes toward codification can be observed in recent years among the Sinti community in Germany, parts of which have been traditionally more reserved and even hostile to the idea of written Romani. Evangelical missionaries produced a series of religious texts for children as well as gospel translations in the Sinti dialect during the 1990s. Still, in 1997, the Association of German Sinti and Roma in Düsseldorf protested against an initiative to introduce a Romani-language reader for use in voluntary classes for immigrant Rom from Macedonia and Serbia, stating that Romani was an 'orally transmitted language that should not be codified'.[1]

Parallel to this, however, the Documentation Centre on German Sinti and Roma, run by the Central Council of German Sinti and Roma in Heidelberg, displayed a bilingual commemoration text at the exit to an exhibition on the Romani Holocaust.[2] A number of Sinti–Romani CD productions in Germany include Romani lyrics of songs on the sleeve (e.g. *Ab i Reisa* 1998, *Newo Ziro* 2000), and a publication by the Association of Sinti and Roma in Kiel was devoted in part to the prospects of Romani literacy (Wurr 2000). In the late 1990s, Sinti associations also urged the German federal government to list the Sinti dialect of Romani (but not the dialects of immigrant Rom living in Germany) among the regional languages entitled to protection under the European Charter for Regional and Minority Languages of 1992, and indeed succeeded in obtaining this recognition.

In other countries, there is a growing number of non-emblematic texts, including collections of short stories and bilingual periodicals. Although there are no precise statistics available, it is safe to say that between 1995 and 2000, several dozen publications in Romani appeared each year. They include collections of original short stories and poems, illustrated Romani-language and bilingual readers for children with traditional tales, and occasional translations into Romani of prose. Most of this material is produced by individuals or by

[1] Letter by Roman Franz, Chief Executive, from 14.02.1997 to the Ministry of Education of Upper-Rhine Westphalia.

[2] The Romani text (Sinti dialect) reads: *I Rikerpaske ap u Sinti de Roma, mare Mulenge, gei weian maschke 1933 de 1945 mardo an u Manuschengromarepen* 'In memory of the Sinti and Roma, our dead, who were murdered during the Holocaust between 1933 and 1945'.

local cultural associations and foundations, and not by commercial publishers, and the great majority of publications is distributed free of charge to interested readers and collectors. In addition, in 2000 there were at least forty bilingual current affairs periodicals appearing on a regular basis, most of them in Bulgaria, Czech Republic, Austria, Yugoslavia, Macedonia, Poland, Hungary, and Slovenia.

A recent informal report on Romani language publications (Acković 2000) notes that there is little exchange of publications among Rom in different countries. This lack of exchange is also represented in the choices of variety, formal vocabulary, and orthography. In most publications, the variety chosen is that spoken by the author. Since the publications are usually intended for local distribution, there is normally overlap between the author's dialect and the dialect of the target audience. There are examples of accommodation strategies employed in writing, with authors incorporating forms from other dialects, or occasionally inserting other dialectal forms in brackets. A small number of multidialectal readers for children have appeared in several countries (Sweden, Bulgaria, Germany, Czech Republic) in an attempt to cater for different groups living in the same location while at the same time promoting interest in other dialects among the readership.

Most text productions employ a writing system based on that of the respective national language, with moderate adjustments. The principal adjustment that is made fairly consistently in most texts, regardless of country, is the marking of aspirates through addition of *h* (*ph*, *th*, *kh*). In some cases, the velar fricative is represented by *x*, in others by *h*. Differences are also apparent in the treatment of the phoneme */ř/*, which in some texts is represented as *rr*. In some cases, additional adjustments are introduced. A bilingual periodical in Poland uses *š*, *č*, *ž* for Romani postalveolars, rather than the corresponding Polish graphemes. In Hungary, a convention has been adopted in a series of publications, using *sh*, *ch*, *zh* for the same sounds, instead of the Hungarian graphemes. (In the Czech Republic, Slokavia, and Slovenia wedge accents are used in the state language alphabets, and are also adopted when writing Romani.) These can be seen as compromises between the national alphabets, and the internationalised conventions used for Romani by linguists. They testify to the international orientation of many of the writers – despite their choice of a local variety, and despite the fact that their target audience is normally regional or national, rather than international.

The general trend in codification can therefore be characterised as a network of decentral activities, with no common denominator at the level of norm selection (choice of dialect), but with a tendency in the choice of orthography to aim at a compromise solution between the writing system of the respective national (state) language, and the international transliteration conventions used in Romani descriptive linguistics. With no institutionalised planning, there is little effort to introduce neologisms. However, in occasional publications and correspondence that is intended for international circulation, especially in the context of organised, European-level political activities, there are tendencies to restrict formal vocabulary to internationalisms (*televizija* 'television', *internacjonalno* 'international'), while substituting loans through 'soft neologisms' that are easily decoded: *akharipesko lil* 'letter of invitation' (*akhar-* 'to call', *lil* 'letter'), *forosko rig* 'neighbourhood' (*foro* 'town', *rig* 'side').

This formula for a **'common written Romani'** – dialectal flexibility, orthographic compatibility, and avoidance of language-particular loans – is best observed in email and internet communication. The establishment of Romani-language websites and email discussion lists from around 1995 onwards has changed the face of written communication in Romani completely. It is impossible to estimate the number of Romani-language email users; the figure is definitely rising rapidly. Email has given Rom from different countries, who do not necessarily share a second language, a medium for spontaneous written communication in Romani. Perhaps the most crucial feature of email is that it is free from the normative constraints that are normally imposed on text production: inconsistency is not a handicap and cannot be penalised. Romani email writers employ an orthography that is loosely oriented toward English, for lack of diacritics in the medium, using *sh* and *ch* (and often *zh*) for postalveolars, while usually indicating aspiration in the 'international' way (*ph*, *th*, *kh*). But the medium allows for swift mutual adaptation, with writers copying each other's writing conventions and experimenting with new spellings and often with new terminology, as well as alternating between dialectal variants. This reinforces the tendency toward a **decentral and pluralistic** codification movement, striving to maintain basic compatibility in the use of a writing system while allowing for variation in the selection of actual linguistic forms and structures.

11.3 Issues of status

Until recently, the Rom were not recognised as an ethnic minority, in any country. Politically, this had to do firstly with the fact that no state regarded them as its own cultural-linguistic diaspora community, and so they could not benefit from bilateral agreements among governments concerning the mutual protection of national minorities. In addition, the lobbying capacity of organised Rom at national levels has traditionally been very weak, and their position was made difficult through years and centuries of overt hostility toward them on the part of governments and society as a whole. Only in the Soviet Union and in Yugoslavia were Rom recognised officially as an ethnic group before the 1990s. In the Soviet Union, Romani was used as a language of instruction in some communities during the 1920s, and a number of Romani books and translations (including a Pushkin translation) appeared. Recognition was later withdrawn, however. In Yugoslavia a number of Romani-language publications appeared, but the language was not used regularly either in the media or in the education system (Puxon 1979).

Aware of the limited opportunities to trigger change at individual national levels, Romani associations such as the International Romani Union found **multilateral organisations** much more willing to take supportive action, at least at the level of declarations. The IRU's lobbying during the 1970s succeeded in obtaining recognition of the Rom by the Indian government as a nation with ties to India. This was followed by a study on behalf of the Commission on Human Rights of the United Nations Economic and Social Council, which in 1977 recognised that the Rom have 'cultural and linguistic ties of Indian origin', and called upon governments to grant them 'the rights to which they are entitled' (cf. Danbakli 1994). During the 1980s, the centre of initiative shifted to the Council of Europe. The Council had already been examining the situation of Travellers during the 1960s, making recommendations on caravan sites as well as special school provisions. There was therefore a basis on which to approach the Council, and interest in the Rom among Council officials.

In a series of resolutions adopted in the 1980s, the Council of Europe's various bodies[3] called on governments to make provisions for teaching Romani in schools, and for training teachers of the Romani language. In the most emphatic statement on Rom, the Council of Europe's Parliamentary Assembly Resolution 1203 from February 1993, the Council called for the establishment of a European programme for the study of Romani and a translation bureau specialising in the language. In the early 1990s, following the political transition in eastern and central Europe, the situation of the Rom was also taken up by the Conference/ Organisation on Security and Economic Cooperation in Europe (CSCE/OSCE) as well as by the European Parliament. There is however no binding legislation concerning Romani, and the resolutions adopted by multilateral organisations have recommendation status only. Nonetheless, they have made a decisive contribution to the political pressure put on national governments to recognise Romani.

Three European countries recognised Romani officially as a minority language in response to these recommendations: Finland, Austria, and Macedonia (which had already recognised Romani in its constitution of 1991). In all three countries, the government is involved in funding initiatives to teach, broadcast, and document Romani. Other European states – Germany, Sweden, and the Netherlands – have listed Romani as a minority language under the specific provisions of the Council of Europe's European Charter for Regional and Minority Languages of 1992. There are however other forms of official support

[3] E.g. the Standing Conference on Local and Regional Authorities in Europe (CLRAE), the Council for Cultural Co-operation (CDCC), the Council of Ministers; see Danbakli (1994).

by governments without specific legal provisions. Governments in Bulgaria, Romania, the Czech Republic, Norway, and Italy, in addition to Finland, Macedonia, Austria, Germany, and Sweden have supported the production of educational material in Romani, and have in most cases allocated, at the local level, school instruction time and funding and sometimes training for teachers to teach Romani children in Romani. So far, most of these initiatives have not been operating on a regular basis, however. Official use has been made of Romani in translation of census documents in Macedonia (1994) and in the United States (2000), as well as in OSCE publications devoted to Romani issues.

Recognition of Romani is also expressed in the status of academic research on the language. During the 1990s, classes on the Romani language and Romani linguistics were offered by at least sixteen different universities in Europe and the United States.[4] Many of these universities also hosted international research conferences, seminars, and workshops devoted to the Romani language. Research in Romani lexicography, historical linguistics, dialectology, and applied linguistics has been supported by a number of national research foundations as well as by the Commission of the European Union, the Open Society Institute, and other foundations. Perhaps the most conspicuous presence of Romani in the public domain is on the numerous websites devoted to the language (see partial list in Bakker et al. 2000: 133–5). Their emergence during the last few years of the past millennium has now changed forever the anonymous and enigmatic image that the Romani language has had for so many centuries.

[4] Austin, Chicago, Prague, Bochum, Hamburg, Amsterdam, Greenwich, Manchester, Liverpool, Aarhus, Graz, Paris, Thessaloniki, Sofia, Budapest, Pécs.

References

Abraham, Werner, and Theo Janssen, eds. 1989. *Tempus-Aspekt-Modus.* Tübingen: Niemeyer.

Ackerley, Frederick George. 1914. The Romani speech of Catalonia. *JGLS,* new series, 8: 99–140.

1929. Basque Romani. *JGLS*, third series, 8: 50–94.

1932. A Lovari vocabulary. *JGLS*, third series, 11: 124–87.

1941. Bosnian Romani: prolegomena. *JGLS*, third series, 20: 84–99.

Acković, Dragoljub. 2000. Report on Romany publishing. Ms.

Acton, Thomas. 1995. Chibiaki politika – politica linguistica. *Lacio Drom* 31(2): 6–17.

ed. 2000. *Scholarship and the Gypsy struggle. Commitment in Romani studies.* Hatfield: University of Hertfordshire Press.

Acton, Thomas, and Donald Kenrick, eds. 1984. *Romani rokkeripen to-divvus.* London: Romanestan.

Acton, Thomas, and Gary Mundy, eds. 1997. *Romani culture and Gypsy identity.* Hatfield: University of Hertfordshire Press.

Aertsen, Henk, and Robert Jeffers, eds. 1993. *Historical Linguistics 1989.* Amsterdam: Benjamins.

Akiner, Shirin, and Nicholas Sims-Williams, eds. 1997. *Languages and scripts of Central Asia.* London: School of Oriental and African Studies.

Aksu-Koç, Ayhan A., and Dan I. Slobin, 1986. A psychological account of the development and use of evidentials in Turkish. In: Chafe and Nichols, eds. 159–67.

Amanolahi, Sekandar, and Edward Norbeck, 1975. The Luti, an outcaste group of Iran. *Rice University Studies* 61(2): 1–12.

Anon. 1930. Vulcanius' Romani vocabulary. *JGLS*, third series, 9: 16–25.

Ariste, Paul. 1964. Supplementary review concerning the Baltic Gypsies and their dialect. *JGLS*, third series, 43: 58–61.

1978. On two intonations in a Romani dialect. *Estonian Papers in Phonetics* 1978: 5–7.

A.R.S.A. 1888. A Spanish Gypsy vocabulary. *JGLS* 1: 177–8.

Ascoli, G. J. 1865. *Zigeunerisches.* Halle: Heynemann.

Bakker, Peter. 1991. Basque Romani – a preliminary grammatical sketch of a mixed language. In: Bakker and Cortiade, eds. 56–90.

1995. Notes on the genesis of Caló and other Iberian Para-Romani varieties. In: Matras, ed. 125–50.

1997a. *A language of our own. The genesis of Michif – the mixed Cree–French language of the Canadian Métis.* New York: Oxford University Press.

1997b. Athematic morphology in Romani: the borrowing of a borrowing pattern. In: Matras, Bakker, and Kyuchukov, eds. 1–21.

1998. Para-Romani language versus secret languages: differences in origin, structure, and use. In: Matras, ed. 69–96.

1999. The Northern branch of Romani: mixed and non-mixed varieties. In: Halwachs and Menz, eds. 172–209.

2000. The genesis of Angloromani. In: Acton, ed. 14–31.

2001. Romani and Turkish. In: Igla and Stolz, eds. 303–27.

Bakker, Peter, and Marcel Cortiade, eds. 1991. *In the margin of Romani. Gypsy languages in contact.* Amsterdam: Institute for General Linguistics.

Bakker, Peter, and Yaron Matras, 1997. Introduction. In: Matras, Bakker, and Kyuchukov, eds. vii–xxx.

Bakker, Peter, and Maarten Mous, 1994. eds. *Mixed languages. 15 case studies in language intertwining.* Amsterdam: IFOTT.

Bakker, Peter, and Hein van der Voort, 1991. Para-Romani languages: an overview and some speculations on their genesis. In: Bakker and Cortiade, eds. 16–44.

Bakker, Peter, Milena Hübschmannová, Valdemar Kalinin, Donald Kenrick, Hristo Kyuchukov, Yaron Matras, and Giulio Soravia, 2000. *What is the Romani language?* Hatfield: University of Hertfordshire Press.

Balić, Sait et al. eds. 1989. *Jezik i kultura Roma.* Sarajevo: Institut za Proučavanje Nacionalnih Odnosa.

Barannikov, A. P. 1934. *The Ukrainian and South Russian Gypsy dialects.* Leningrad: Academy of Sciences of the USSR.

Bari, Karoly. 1990. *Le Vēšeski Dēj.* Budapest: Országos Közművelődési Központ.

1999. *Gypsy Folklore: Romania-Hungary.* Private publishing.

Bataillard, Paul. 1875. The affinities of the Gypsies with the Jats. *The Academy* 7: 583–5.

Baudrimont, Alexandre Edouard. 1862. Vocabulaire de la langue des bohémiens habitant le pays basque français. *Actes de l'Académie Impériale des Sciences, Belles-Lettres et Arts de Bordeaux*, series 3, 24: 81–112.

Beames, John. 1872–9 [reprint 1970]. I–III. *A comparative grammar of the modern Indo-Aryan languages of India.* Delhi: Munishiram Manoharlal.

Benninghaus, Rüdiger. 1991. Les Tsiganes de la Turquie orientale. *Etudes Tsiganes* 3–91: 47–60.

Berger, Hermann. 1959. Die Burušaski-Lehnwörter in der Zigeunersprache. *Indo-Iranian Journal* 3: 17–43.

Bloch, Jules. 1928. La désinence de 2e personne du pluriel en Nuri. *JGLS*, third series, 7: 111–13.

1932a. Le présent du verbe 'être' en tsigane. *Indian Linguistics* 2: 309–16.

1932b. Survivance de skr. āsīt en indien moderne. *Bulletin de la Société Linguistique* 33(1): 55–65.

1970. *The formation of the Marāṭhī language.* Delhi: Motilal Banarsidass.

Bódi, Zsuzsanna, ed. 1994. *Studies in Roma (Gypsy) ethnography.* Budapest: Mikszáth.

Boretzky, Norbert. 1985. Sind Zigeunersprachen Kreols? In: Boretzky, Enninger, and Stolz, eds. 43–70.

1986. Zur Sprache der Gurbet von Priština (Jugoslawien). *Giessener Hefte für Tsiganologie* 3: 195–216.

1989. Zum Interferenzverhalten des Romani. (Verbreitete und ungewöhnliche Phänomene.) *Zeitschrift für Phonetik, Sprachwissenschaft und Kommunikationsforschung* 42: 357–74.
1991. Contact induced sound change. *Diachronica* 8: 1–16.
1992a. Zum Erbwortschatz des Romani. *Zeitschrift für Phonetik, Sprachwissenschaft und Kommunikationsforschung* 45: 227–51.
1992b. Romanisch-zigeunerischen Interferenz (zum Caló). In: Erfurt, Jessing, and Perl, eds. 11–37.
1993a. *Bugurdži: deskriptiver und historischer Abriß eines Romani-Dialekts.* Wiesbaden: Harrassowitz.
1993b. Conditional sentences in Romani. *Sprachtypologie und Universalienforschung* 46: 83–99.
1994. *Romani. Grammatik des Kalderaš-Dialekts mit Texten und Glossar.* Wiesbaden: Harrassowitz.
1995a. Armenisches im Zigeunerischen (Romani und Lomavren). *Indogermanische Forschungen* 100: 137–55.
1995b. Die Entwicklung der Kopula im Romani. *Grazer Linguistische Studien* 43: 1–50.
1995c. Interdialectal interference in Romani. In: Matras, ed. 69–94.
1996a. Arli: Materialen zu einem sudbalkanischen Romani-Dialekt. *Grazer Linguistische Studien* 46: 1–30.
1996b. The 'new infinitive' in Romani. *JGLS*, fifth series, 6: 1–51.
1996c. Zu den Modalia in den Romani-Dialekten. *Zeitschrift für Balkanologie* 32: 1–27.
1996d. Entlehnte Wortstellungssyntax im Romani. In: Boretzky, Enninger, and Stolz, eds. 95–121.
1997. Suppletive forms of the Romani copula: *ovel/avel.* In: Matras, Bakker, and Kyuchukov, eds. 107–32.
1998a. Erli. Eine Bestandsaufnahme nach den Texte von Gilliat-Smith. *Studii Romani* 5–6: 122–60.
1998b. Areal and insular dialects and the case of Romani. *Grazer Linguistische Studien* 50: 1–27.
1998c. Der Romani-Wortschatz in den Romani-Misch-Dialekten (Pararomani). In: Matras, ed. 97–132.
1999a. Die Gliederung der Zentralen Dialekte und die Beziehungen zwischen Südlichen Zentralen Dialekten (Romungro) und Südbalkanischen Romani-Dialekten. In: Halwachs and Menz, eds. 210–76.
1999b. *Die Verwandtschaftsbeziehungen zwischen den Südbalkanischen Romani-Dialekten. Mit einem Kartenanhang.* Frankfurt am Main: Peter Lang.
2000a. The definite article in Romani dialects. In: Elšík and Matras, eds. 31–63.
2000b. South Balkan II as a Romani dialect branch: Bugurdži, Drindari, and Kalajdži. *Romani Studies*, fifth series, 10: 105–83.
2000c. The Vlach dialects of Romani. Characteristics and subclassification. Paper presented at the Fifth International Conference on Romani Linguistics, Sofia, 14–17 September 2000.
2001. Palatalization and depalatalization in Romani. *Sprachtypologie und Universalienforschung* 54(2): 108–25.

Boretzky, Norbert, and Birgit Igla. 1991. *Morphologische Entlehnung in den Romani-Dialekten.* (Arbeitspapiere des Projektes 'Prinzipien des Sprachwandels' 4.) Essen: Universität GH Essen. Fachbereich Sprach- und Literaturwissenschaften.

1993. *Lautwandel und Natürlichkeit. Kontaktbedingter und endogener Wandel im Romani.* (Arbeitspapiere des Projekts 'Prinzipien des Sprachwandels' 15.) Essen: Universität GH Essen, Fachbereich Sprach- und Literaturwissenschaften.

1994a. Romani mixed dialects. In: Bakker and Mous, eds. 35–68.

1994b. *Wörterbuch Romani-Deutsch-Englisch für den südosteuropäischen Raum: mit einer Grammatik der Dialektvarianten.* Wiesbaden: Harrassowitz.

1999. Balkanische (Südosteuropäische) Einflüsse im Romani. In: Hinrichs, ed. 709–31.

Boretzky, Norbert, Werner Enninger, and Thomas Stolz, eds. 1985. *Akten des 1. Essener Kolloquiums über Kreolsprachen und Sprachkontakt.* Bochum: Brockmeyer.

1989. *Vielfalt der Kontakte.* (Beiträge zum 5. Essener Kolloquium über 'Grammatikalisierung: Natürlichkeit und Systemökonomie'. 1. Band.) Bochum: Brockmeyer.

1996. *Areale, Kontakte, Dialekte. Sprache und ihre Dynamik in mehrsprachigen Situationen.* Bochum: Brockmeyer.

Borrow, George. 1841. *The Zincali, or, An account of the Gipsies of Spain.* London: John Murray.

1851. *Lavengro: The Scholar – The Gypsy – The Priest.* London: John Murray.

1874. *Romano Lavo-Lil.* London: John Murray.

Bourgeois, Henri. 1911. Esquisse d'une grammaire du romani finlandais. *Atti della Reale Academia delle Scienze di Torino* 46: 541–54.

Brekle, Herbert E., and Leonhard Lipka, eds. 1968. *Wortbildung. Syntax und Morphologie.* The Hague: Mouton.

Bright, Richard. 1818. *Travels from Vienna through Lower Hungary, with some remarks on the state of Vienna during the Congress, in the year 1814.* Edinburgh: Constable.

Bubeník, Vít. 1995. On typological changes and structural borrowing in the history of European Romani. In: Matras, ed. 1–23.

1996. *The structure and development of Middle Indo-Aryan dialects.* Delhi: Motilal Banarsidass.

1997. Object doubling in Romani and the Balkan languages. In: Matras, Bakker, and Kyuchukov, eds. 95–106.

1998. *A historical syntax of Late Middle Indo-Aryan (Apabhraṃśa).* Amsterdam: John Benjamins.

2000. Was Proto-Romani an ergative language? In: Elšik and Matras, eds. 205–27.

Bubeník, Vít, and Milena Hübschmannová. 1998. Deriving inchoatives and mediopassives in Slovak and Hungarian Romani. *Grazer Linguistische Studien* 50: 29–44.

Bühler, Karl. 1934 [reprint 1982]. *Sprachtheorie.* Stuttgart: Fischer.

Burridge, Kate (with Keith Allan). 1998. The X-phemistic value of Romani in non-standard speech. In: Matras, ed. 29–49.

Calvet, Georges. 1982. *Lexique tsigane. Dialecte des Erlides de Sofia.* Paris: Publications Orientalistes de France.

Campbell, Lyle. 1993. On proposed universals of grammatical borrowing. In: Aertsen and Jeffers, eds. 91–110.

Cech, Petra. 1995/1996. Inflection/derivation in Sepečides-Romani. *Acta Linguistica Hungarica* 43: 67–91.
Cech, Petra, and Mozes F. Heinschink. 1998. *Basisgrammatik.* (= Arbeitsbericht 1 des Projekts 'Kodifizierung der Romanes-Variante der Österreichischen Lovara'). Vienna: Romano Centro.
1999. *Sepečides-Romani: Grammatik, Texte und Glossar eines türkischen Romani-Dialekts.* Wiesbaden: Harrassowitz.
2001. A dialect with seven names. *Romani Studies*, fifth series, 11(2): 137–84.
Cech, Petra, Mozes Heinschink, and Christiane Fennesz-Juhasz, eds. 1998. *Lovarenge paramiči taj tekstura anda Österreich. Texte der österreichischen Lovara.* Vienna: Romano Centro.
Chafe, Wallace, and Johanna Nichols. eds. 1986. *Evidentiality: the linguistic coding of epistemology.* Norwood: Ablex.
Cohn, Wener. 1969. Some comparisons between Gypsy (North American *ṛom*) and American English kinship terms. *American Anthropologist* 71: 476–82.
Comrie, Bernard 1976. *Aspect.* Cambridge: Cambridge University Press.
1981. *Language universals and linguistic typology.* Chicago: University of Chicago Press.
On identifying future tenses. In: Abraham and Janssen, eds. 51–63.
Constantinescu, Barbu. 1878. *Probe de limba şi literatura Ţiganilor din România.* Bucureşti: Typografia Societăţii Academice Române.
Cortiade, Marcel. 1991. Romani versus Para-Romani. In: Bakker and Cortiade, eds. 1–15.
Courthiade, Marcel. 1989a. La langue Romani (Tsigane): évolution, standardisation, unification, réforme. In: Fodor and Hagège, eds. 79–109.
1989b. O kodifikaciji i normalizaciji romskog zajedničkog jezika. In: Balić et al. eds. 205–21.
1990. Les voies de l'émergence du romani commun. *Etudes Tsiganes* 36: 26–51.
1992. Research and action group on Romani linguistics. *Interface* 8: 4–11.
1998. The dialect structure of the Romani language. *Interface* 31: 9–14.
Crevels, Mily, and Peter Bakker. 2000. External possession in Romani. In: Elšík and Matras, eds. 151–85.
Crofton, Henry Thomas. 1907. Borde's Egipt speche. *JGLS*, new series, 1: 157–68.
Dahl, Östen. 1985. *Tense and aspect systems.* Oxford: Blackwell.
Danbakli, Marielle. ed. 1994. *On Gypsies: texts issued by international institutions.* Paris: Centre de Recherches Tsiganes.
De Goeje, M. J. 1903. *Mémoire sur les migrations des tsiganes à travers l'Asie.* Leiden: Brill.
De Luna, José Carlos. 1951. *Gitanos de la Bética.* Madrid: Efesa.
DeSilva, Cara, Joanne Grumet, and David J. Nemeth, eds. 1988. *Papers from the eighth and ninth annual meetings, Gypsy Lore Society, North American Chapter.* New York: Gypsy Lore Society, North American Chapter.
Dick Zatta, Jane. 1986. Narrative structure in the Rom Sloveni oral tradition. In: Grumet, ed. 123–34.
1996. Tradizione orale e contesto sociale: i Roma sloveni e la televisione. In: Piasere, ed. 179–203.
Diessel, Holger. 1999. The morphosyntax of demonstratives in synchrony and diachrony. *Linguistic Typology* 3: 1–49.
Dillard, J. L. ed. 1980. *Perspectives on American English.* The Hague: Mouton.

Djonedi, Fereydun. 1996. Romano-Glossar: gesammelt von Schir-ali Tehranizade. *Grazer Linguistische Studien* 46: 31–59.

Dow, James R., and Thomas Stolz, eds. 1991. *Akten des 7. Essener Kolloquiums über 'Minoritätensprachen/Sprachminoritäten'*. Bochum: Brockmeyer.

Durie, Mark, and Malcolm Ross, eds. 1996. *The comparative method reviewed.* Oxford: Oxford University Press.

Ehrenborg, Harald. 1928. Djôs Per Andersson's vocabulary. *JGLS*, third series, 7: 11–30.

Elšík, Viktor. 2000a. Romani nominal paradigms: their structure, diversity, and development. In: Elšík and Matras, eds. 9–30.

2000b. Dialect variation in Romani personal pronouns. In: Elšík, and Matras, eds. 65–94.

2000c. Inherited indefinites in Romani. Paper presented at the Fifth International Conference on Romani Linguistics, Sofia, 14–17 September 2000.

2001. Word-form borrowing in indefinites: Romani evidence. *Sprachtypologie und Universalienforschung* 54: 126–47.

Elšík, Viktor, and Yaron Matras, eds. 2000. *Grammatical relations in Romani: the noun phrase.* Amsterdam: Benjamins.

Elšík, Viktor, Milena Hübschmannová, and Hana Šebková. 1999. The Southern Central (ahi-imperfect) Romani dialects of Slovakia and northern Hungary. In: Halwachs and Menz, eds. 277–390.

Eloeva, Fatima Abisalovna, and Aleksandr Jurevič Rusakov. 1990. *Problemy jazykovoj interferencii (cyganskie dialekty Evropy): učebnoe posobie.* Leningrad: Leningradskij gosudarstvennyj universitet.

Erfurt, Jürgen, Benedikt Jessing, and Matthias Perl. eds. 1992. *Prinzipien des Sprachwandels, I. Vorbereitung. Beiträge zum Leipziger Symposion Prinzipien des Sprachwandels 1991 an der Universität Leipzig.* Bochum: Brockmeyer.

Esnault, G. 1935. Ciganismes en français et gallicismes des cigains. *JGLS*, third series, 14: 72–86, 127–48.

Etzler, Allan. 1994. *Zigenarna och deras avkomlingar i Sverige.* Uppsala: Almqvist och Wiksell.

Feuillet, J. ed. 1997. *Actance et valence dans les langues de l'Europe.* Berlin: Mouton de Gruyter.

Finck, Franz Nikolaus. 1903. *Lehrbuch des Dialekts der deutschen Zigeuner.* Marburg: Elwert.

1907. *Die Sprache der armenischen Zigeuner.* St Petersburg: Kaiserliche Akademie der Wissenschaften.

Fodor, István, and Claude Hagège. eds. 1989. *Language reform. History and future.* Vol. IV. Hamburg: Buske.

Formoso, Bernard, and Georges Calvet. 1987. *Lexique tsigane. Dialecte Sinto piémontais.* Paris: Publications Orientalistes de France.

Franzese, Sergio. 1985. *Il dialetto dei Sinti Piemontesi. Note grammaticali. Glossario.* Turin: Centro Studi Zingari.

1986. *Il dialetto dei Rom Xoraxané. Note grammaticali. Glossario.* Turin: Centro Studi Zingari.

Fraser, Angus. 1992a. *The Gypsies.* Oxford: Blackwell.

1992b. Looking into the seeds of time. *Tsiganologische Studien* 1: 135–66.

Friedman, Victor A. 1977. *The grammatical categories of the Macedonian indicative.* Columbus: Slavica.

1985. Balkan Romani modality and other Balkan languages. *Folia Slavica* 7: 381–9.
1986. Evidentiality in the Balkans: Bulgarian, Macedonian, and Albanian. In: Chafe and Nichols, eds. 168–87.
1988. A Caucasian loanword in Romani. In: DeSilva, Grumet, and Nemeth, eds. 18–20.
1989. Toward defining the position of Turkisms in Romani. In: Balić et al., eds. 251–67.
1991. Case in Romani: old grammar in new affixes. *JGLS*, fifth series, 1: 85–102.
1995. Romani standardization and status in the Republic of Macedonia. In: Matras, ed. 177–88.
1996. Romani and the census in the Republic of Macedonia. *JGLS*, fifth series, 6: 89–101.
1997. Linguistic form and content in the Romani-language press in the Republic of Macedonia. In: Matras, Bakker, and Kyuchukov, eds. 183–98.
1999. The Romani language in the Republic of Macedonia: status, usage, and sociolinguistic perspectives. *Acta Linguistica Hungarica* 46: 317–39.
2000. Proleptic and resumptive object pronouns in Romani: a Balkan noun phrase perspective. In: Elšík and Matras, eds. 187–204.
Friedman, Victor A., and Robert Dankoff. 1991. The earliest known text in Balkan (Rumelian) Romani: a passage from Evliya Celebis Seyāhat-nāme. *JGLS*, fifth series, 1: 1–20.
Gilliat-Smith, B. J. 1911. The sound Ŗ. *JGLS*, new series, 5: 139–40.
1914. The dialect of the Drindaris. *JGLS*, new series, 7: 260–98.
1915. A report on the Gypsy tribes of North East Bulgaria. *JGLS*, new series, 9: 1–54, 65–109.
1935. The dialect of the Moslem Kalajdžis (Tinners) of the Tatar Pazardžik district. *JGLS*, third series, 14: 25–43.
1944. A Bulgarian Gypsy tale: Ali the Master Craftsman. *JGLS*, third series, 23: 14–21.
1945. Two Erlides fairy-tales. *JGLS*, third series, 24: 17–26.
Givón, Talmy. 1990. *Syntax. A functional-typological introduction.* II. Amsterdam: John Benjamins.
Gjerde, Lars (with Knut Kristiansen). 1994. *'The Orange of Love' and other stories: The Rom-Gypsy language in Norway.* Oslo: Scandinavian University Press.
Gjerdman, Olof, and Ljungberg, Erik. 1963. *The language of the Swedish Coppersmith Gipsy Johan Dimitri Taikon: grammar, texts, vocabulary and English word-index.* Uppsala: Lundequist.
Gobineau, A. 1857. Persische Studien. *Zeitschrift der Deutschen Morgenländischen Gesellschaft* 11: 689–99.
Görög, Veronika, ed. 1985. *Tales of János Berki told in Gypsy and Hungarian.* Budapest: MTA Néprajzi Kutató Csoport.
Grant, Anthony P. 1998. Romani words in non-standard British English and the development of Angloromani. In: Matras, ed. 165–91.
Graur, Alexandru. 1934. Les mots tsiganes en roumain. *Bulletin Linguistique Romane* 2: 108–200.
Greenberg, Joseph H. 1966. Some universals of grammar with particular reference to the order of meaningful elements. In: Greenberg, ed. 73–113.

ed. 1966. *Universals of language.* Cambridge: MIT Press.
ed. 1978. *Universals of human language.* Stanford: Stanford University Press.
Grellmann, Heinrich M. 1783 [1787]. *Historischer Versuch über die Zigeuner, betreffend die Lebensart und Verfassung, Sitten und Schicksale dieses Volkes seit seiner Erscheinung in Europa und dessen Ursprung.* Göttingen: Dietrich.
Grierson, George A. 1887. Arabic and Persian references to Gypsies. *Indian Antiquary* 16: 257–8.
1888. Ḍoms, Jats, and the origin of the Gypsies. *JGLS* 1: 71–6.
1906. *The Piśāca languages of North-Western India.* London: Royal Asiatic Society.
1908. India and the Gypsies. *JGLS*, new series, 1: 400.
1922. *Linguistic survey of India. Vol XI: Gipsy languages.* Calcutta: Superintendent Government Printers.
Grigorova, Evelina. 1998. Interrogative intonation of two Bulgarian Romani dialects: Sofia Erli and Kalderaš. *Grazer Linguistische Studien* 50: 45–63.
Grumet, Joanne Sher. 1985. On the genitive in Romani. In: Grumet, ed. 84–90.
1986. Word order in Kelderash. In: Grumet, ed. 146–56.
ed. 1985. *Papers from the fourth and fifth annual meetings: Gypsy Lore Society, North American Chapter.* New York: Gypsy Lore Society.
ed. 1986. *Papers from the six and seventh annual meetings: Gypsy Lore Society, North American Chapter.* New York: Gypsy Lore Society.
Gumperz, John. 1982. *Discourse strategies.* Cambridge: Cambridge University Press.
Haarmann, Harald. 1980. *Spracherhaltung und Sprachwechsel als Probleme der interlingualen Soziolinguistik. Studien zur Mehrsprachigkeit der Zigeuner in der Sowjetunion.* Hamburg: Buske.
1985. Zur lexikalischen Charakteristik massiver Kontaksprachen: Entlehnte Körperteilbezeichnungen im Zigeunerischen. *Indogermanische Forschungen* 89: 66–88.
1986. *Language in ethnicity: a view of basic ecological relations.* Berlin: Mouton de Gruyter.
Halwachs, Dieter W. 1993. Polysystem, Repertoire und Identität. *Grazer Linguistische Studien* 39–40: 71–90.
1996. *Verschriftlichung des Roman.* (Arbeitsbericht 2 des Projekts Kodifizierung und Didaktisierung des Roman). Oberwart: Verein Roma.
1998. *Amaro vakeripe Roman hi – Unsere Sprache ist Roman: Texte, Glossar und Grammatik der burgenländischen Romani-Variante.* Klagenfurt: Drava.
1999. Romani in Österreich. In: Halwachs and Menz, eds. 112–46.
Halwachs, Dieter W., and Mozes Heinschink. 2000. Language change in progress. The case of Kalderash Romani in Vienna. Paper presented at the 5th International Conference on Romani Linguistics, Sofia, 14–17 September 2000.
Halwachs, Dieter W., and Florian Menz, eds. 1999. *Die Sprache der Roma: Perspektiven der Romani-Forschung in Österreich im interdisziplinären und internationalen Kontext.* Klagenfurt: Drava.
Hamp, Eric. 1987. On the sibilants of Romani. *Indo-Iranian Journal* 30: 103–6.
1990. The conservatism and exemplary order of Romani. In: Salo, Matt T. ed. 151–5.
Hancock, Ian F. 1969. Romanes numerals and innovation. *JGLS*, third series, 48: 19–24.

1970. Is Anglo-Romanes a creole? *JGLS*, third series, 49: 41–4.
1975. The acquisition of English by American Romani children. In: Raffler-Engel, ed. 353–62.
1976. Patterns of lexical adoption in an American Dialect of Řomanés. *Orbis* 25: 83–104.
1980. The ethnolectal English of American Gypsies. In: Dillard, ed. 257–64.
1984. Romani and Angloromani. In: Trudgill, ed. 367–83.
1986. The cryptolectal speech of the American roads: traveler Cant and American Angloromani. *American Speech* 61: 206–20.
1987. Il contributo armeno alla lingua romani. *Lacio Drom* 23: 4–10.
1988. The development of Romani linguistics. In: Jazayery and Winter, eds. 183–223.
1991. Romani foodways: the Indian roots of Gypsy culinary culture. *The World and I*, April 1991: 12–26.
1992. The social and linguistic development of Scandoromani. In: Jahr, ed. 37–52.
1993. The emergence of a union dialect of North American Vlax Romani, and its implications for an international standard. *International Journal of the Sociology of Language* 99: 91–104.
1995a. *A handbook of Vlax Romani.* Columbus: Slavica.
1995b. On the migration and affiliation of the Ḍōmba: Iranian words in Rom, Lom, and Dom Gypsy. In: Matras, ed. 25–51.
1997. George Borrow's Romani. In: Matras, Bakker, and Kyuchukov, eds. 99–214.
1998. The Indian origin and westward migration of the Romani people. Ms. University of Austin, Texas.
2000. The emergence of Romani as a Koïné outside of India. In: Acton, ed. 1–13.
Hanna, Nabil Sobhi. 1993. *Die Ghajar.* Munich: Trickster Verlag.
Haspelmath, Martin. 1997. *Indefinite pronouns.* Oxford: Clarendon Press.
Haugen, Einar. 1949. A note on the Romany 'language'. *Norsk Tidskrift for Sprogvidenskap* 7: 388–91.
1950. The analysis of linguistic borrowing. *Language* 26: 210–31.
Hengeveld, Kees. 1992. *Non-verbal predication. Theory, typology, diachrony.* Berlin: Mouton de Gruyter.
1998. Adverbial clauses in the languages of Europe. In: van der Auwera, ed. 335–419.
Hinrichs, Uwe, ed. 1999. *Handbuch der Südosteuropa-Linguistik.* Wiesbaden: Harrassowitz.
Holzinger, Daniel. 1992. Die Funktion des präverbalen Subjekts in narrativen Texten des Romanes (Sinte). *Papiere zur Linguistik* 46: 67–81.
1993. *Das Romanes: Grammatik und Diskursanalyse der Sprache der Sinte.* (= Innsbrucker Beiträge zur Kulturwissenschaft, 85.) Innsbruck: Verlag des Instituts für Sprachwissenschaft der Universität Innsbruck.
1995. *Romanes (Sinte).* Munich: Lincom Europa.
1996. Verbal aspect and thematic organisation of Sinte narrative discourse. *Grazer Linguistische Studien* 46: 111–26.
Hübschmannová, Milena. 1979. Bilingualism among the Slovak Rom. *International Journal of the Sociology of Language* 19: 33–49.
1981. Devinettes des Rom slovaques. *Etudes Tsiganes* 26: 13–19.
1995. Trial and error in written Romani on the pages of Romani periodicals. In: Matras, ed. 189–205.

Hübschmannová, Milena, and Vít Bubeník. 1997. Causatives in Slovak and Hungarian Romani. In: Matras, Bakker, and Kyuchukov, eds. 133–45.

Hübschmannová, Milena, and Jiří V. Neustupný. 1996. The Slovak-and-Czech dialect of Romani and its standardization. *International Journal of the Sociology of Language* 120: 85–109.

Hübschmannová, Milena, Hana Šebková, and Anna Žigová. 1991. *Kapesní slovník romsko český a česko romský*. Prague: Státní pedagogické nakladatelství.

Igla, Birgit. 1989. Kontakt-induzierte Sprachwandelphänomene im Romani von Ajia Varvara (Athen). In: Boretzky, Enninger, and Stolz, eds. 67–80.

1991. Probleme der Standardisierung des Romani. In: Dow and Stolz, eds. 75–90.

1992. Entlehnung und Lehnübersetzung deutscher Präfixverben im Sinti. In: Erfurt, Jeßing, and Perl, eds.

1996. *Das Romani von Ajia Varvara. Deskriptive und historisch-vergleichende Darstellung eines Zigeunerdialekts*. Wiesbaden: Harrassowitz.

1997. The Romani dialect of the Rhodopes. In: Matras, Bakker, and Kyuchukov, eds. 147–58.

Igla, Birgit, and Stolz, Thomas, eds. 2001. *Was ich noch sagen wollte . . . A multilingual Festschrift for Norbert Boretzky on the occasion of his 65th birthday*. Berlin: Akademische Verlag.

Iversen, Ragnvald. 1944. *Secret Languages in Norway*, vol. 1: *The Romany Language in Norway*. Norsk Videnskaps-Akademi, II Filosofisk-Historisk Klasse 1944, part 3. Oslo: Norsk Videnskaps-Akademi.

Jahr, Ernst Håkon, ed. 1992. *Language contact: theoretical and empirical studies*. Berlin: Mouton de Gruyter.

Jazayery, Mohammad Ali, and Werner Winter, eds. 1988. *Languages and cultures. Studies in honor of Edgar C. Polomé. Berlin:* Mouton der Gruyter.

Jean, Daniel. 1970. Glossaire Manouche. *Etudes tsiganes* 16: 1–69.

Jiménez, Augusto. 1853. *Vocabulario del dialecto Jitano*. Seville: Imprenta del Conciliador.

Johanson, Lars 1971. *Aspekt im Türkischen*. Uppsala: Uppsala University.

1994. Türkeitürkische Aspektotempora. In: Thieroff and Ballweg, eds. 247–66.

Johansson, Roger. 1977. *Svensk Rommani*. (Acta Academiae Regiae Gustavi Adolphi, 55.) Uppsala: Lundquist.

Juilland, Alphonse. 1952. Le vocabulaire argotique roumain d'origins tsigane. In: Juilland, ed. 151–81.

ed. 1952. *Cahiers Sextil Puşcariu I*. Roma: Dacia.

Jusuf, Šaip, and Kepeski, Krume. 1980. *Romani gramatika*. Skopje: Naša Kniga.

Kakuk, Mátyás. 1994. On the research of Gypsy loanwords in the Hungarian language. In: Bódi, ed. 200–3.

Kaufman, Terrence. 1979. Review of Weer Rajendra Rishi, Multilingual Romani Dictionary. *International Journal of the Sociology of Language* 19: 131–44.

Keenan, Edward, and Bernard Comrie. 1977. Noun phrase accessibility and universal grammar. *Linguistic Inquiry* 8: 63–99.

Kenrick, Donald. 1967. The Romani dialect of a musician from Razgrad. *Balkansko Ezikoznanie* 11: 71–8.

1979. Romani English. *International Journal of the Sociology of Language* 19: 79–88.

1993. *Gypsies from India to the Mediterranean*. Toulouse: CRDP Midi Pyrénées.

1996. Romani literacy at the crossroads. *International Journal of the Sociology of Language* 119: 109–23.

Kluge, Friedrich. 1901. *Rotwelsch. Quellen und Wortschatz der Gaunersprache und der verwandten Geheimsprachen.* Straßburg: Karl Trübner.

Kluyver, A. 1910. Un glossaire tsigane du seizième siècle. *JGLS*, new series, 4: 131–42.

1934. Romani words in Dutch slangs. *JGLS*, third series, 13, 1–8.

Kochanowski, Vania de Gila [Vanya]. 1946. Some notes on the Gypsies of Latvia. *JGLS*, third series, 25: 34–8.

1963–4. *Gypsy studies.* New Delhi: International Academy of Indian Culture.

1989. Problems of the Common Romany – problems of an international language. In: Balić et al., eds. 187–203.

1990. Migrations aryennes et indo-aryennes. *Diogènes* 149: 119–41.

1994. *Parlons tsigane. Histoire, culture et langue du peuple tsigane.* Paris: L'Harmattan.

1995. Romani language standardization. *JGLS*, fifth series 5: 97–107.

Koivisto, Viljo. 1994. *Romani-finitiko-angliko laavesko liin. Romani-suomi-englanti sanakirja. Romany-Finnish-English dictionary.* Helsinki: Panatuskeskus.

König, Ekkehard, and Haspelmath, Martin. 1997. Les constructions à possesseur externe dans les langues de l'Europe. In: Feuillet, ed. 525–606.

Kopernicki, Izydor. 1930. *Textes tsiganes. Contes et poésies avec traduction francaise.* (= Prace Komisji orjentalistycznej, 7.) Cracow: Polska akademja umiejętności.

Koptjevskaja-Tamm, Maria. 2000. Romani genitives in cross-linguistic perspective. In: Elšík, and Matras, eds. 123–49.

Kostov, Kiril. 1956. Ciganski dumi v bulgarskite tajni govori. *Izvestija na Instituta za Bulgarski Ezik* 4: 411–25.

1960. Zu den fallenden Diphthongen in einigen Mundarten der Zigeunersprache. *Zeitschrift für Phonetik, Sprachwissenschaft und Kommunikationsforschung* 13: 41–3.

1965. Noch einmal zum Abstraktensuffix -be/-pe im Zigeunerischen. *Münchener Studien zur Sprachwissenschaft* 18: 41–51.

1970. Lehnwörter zigeunerischen Ursprungs im türkischen Argot. *Balkansko Ezikoznanie* 14: 83–97.

1973. Zur Bedeutung des Zigeunerischen für die Erforschung grammatischer Interferenzerscheinungen. *Balkansko Ezikoznanie* 16: 99–113.

1989. Zur Determination der a-stämmigen entlehnten Maskulina in der Zigeunersprache Bulgariens. *Balkansko Ezikoznanie* 32: 119–22.

Kotsinas, Ulla-Brit. 1996. *Stockholm-slang. Folkligt språk från 80-tal till 80-tal.* Stockholm: Norstedts.

Kovalcsik, Katalin. 1999. Aspects of language ideology in a Transylvanian Vlach Gypsy community. *Acta Linguistica Hungarica* 46: 269–88.

Kyuchukov, Hristo. 1994. The communicative competence of Romani (Gypsy speaking) children in Bulgarian discourse, in a classroom situation. *International Journal of Psycholinguistics* 10: 59–82.

Kyuchukov, Hristo, and Peter Bakker. 1999. A note on Romani words in the Gay slang of Istanbul. *Grazer Linguistische Studien* 51: 95–8.

Ladefoged, Jakob. 1998. Romani elements in non-standard Scandinavian varieties. In: Matras, ed. 133–61.

Leigh, Kate. 1998. Romani elements in present-day Caló. In: Matras, ed. 243–82.

Leland, Charles Godfrey. 1874. *The English Gypsies and their language.* London: Trubner.

Lerch, Hans-Günter. 1976. *Das Manische in Giessen.* Giessen: Anabas.

Leschber, Corinna. 1995. Romani lexical items in colloquial Rumanian. In: Matras, ed. 151–76.

Lesný, V. 1916. Über die langen Vokale in den Zigeunerdialekten. *Zeitschrift der Deutschen Morgenländischen Gesellschaft* 70: 417–22.

1928. Die Vertretung des Ai. (Mi.) *a* und *ā* in den europäischen Zigeunersprachen. *JGLS*, third series, 7: 177–84.

1941. Die Zigeuner sind ursprünglich die indischen Dōms. *Archiv Orientálni* 12: 121–7.

Levinson, Stephen. 1983. *Pragmatics.* Cambridge: Cambridge University Press.

Lewis, Geoffrey. 1950–5. The secret language of the Geygeli Yürüks. In: Velidi, ed. 214–26.

Liebich, Richard. 1863. *Die Zigeuner in ihrem Wesen und ihrer Sprache.* Leipzig: Brockhaus.

Lípa, Jiři. 1979. Cases of coexistence of two varieties of Romani in the same territory in Slovakia. *International Journal of the Sociology of Language* 19: 51–7.

Lorimer, D. L. R. 1939. *The Ḍumāki language.* Nijmegen: Dekker and Van de Vegt.

Macalister, R. A. S. 1914. *The language of the Nawar of Zutt, the nomad smiths of Palestine.* (Gypsy Lore Society Monographs 3.) London: Edinburgh University Press.

MacGowan, Alan. 1996. *The Winchester confessions 1615–1616. Depositions of travellers, Gypsies, fraudsters and makers of counterfeit documents, including a vocabulary of the Romany language.* South Chailey (East Sussex): Romany and Traveller Family History Society.

Mann, S. E. 1933. Albanian Romani. *JGLS*, third series, 12: 1–14.

1935. South Albanian Romani. *JGLS*, third series, 14: 174–84.

Marsden, William. 1785. Observations on the language of the people commonly called Gypsies. *Archeologica* 7: 382–6.

Masica, Colin P. 1991. *The Indo-Aryan languages.* Cambridge: Cambridge University Press.

Matras, Yaron. 1994a. *Untersuchungen zu Grammatik und Diskurs des Romanes. Dialekt der Kelderaša/Lovara.* Wiesbaden: Harrassowitz.

1994b. Structural Balkanisms in Romani. In: Reiter, Hinrichs, and van Leeuwen-Turnocová, eds. 195–210.

1995a. Verb evidentials and their discourse function in Vlach Romani narratives. In: Matras, ed. 95–123.

1995b. Connective (VS) word order in Romani. *Sprachtypologie und Universalienforschung* 48: 189–203.

1996a. Prozedurale Fusion: grammatische Interferenzschichten im Romanes. *Sprachtypologie und Universalienforschung* 49: 60–78.

1996b. Review of Boretzky and Igla 1994b. *Zeitschrift für Balkanologie* 32: 214–24.

1997a. The typology of case relations and case layer distribution in Romani. In: Matras, Bakker, and Kyuchukov, eds. 61–93.

1997b. Schriftliche Lehrmittel in Romanes: ein Beispiel von Sprachplanung in einer Minderheitensprache. *Osnabrücker Beiträge zur Sprachtheorie* 54: 165–91.

1998a. Deixis and deictic opposition in discourse: evidence from Romani. *Journal of Pragmatics* 29: 393–428.

1998b. Para-Romani revisited. In: Matras, ed. 1–27.

1998c. The Romani element in German secret languages: Jenisch and Rotwelsch. In: Matras, ed. 193–230.

1998d. Utterance modifiers and universals of grammatical borrowing. *Linguistics* 36: 281–331.

1999a. Johann Rüdiger and the study of Romani in eighteenth-century Germany. *JGLS*, fifth series, 9: 89–106.

1999b. The speech of the Polska Roma: some highlighted features and their implications for Romani dialectology. *JGLS*, fifth series, 9(1): 1–28.

1999c. The state of present-day Domari in Jerusalem. *Mediterranean Language Review* 11: 1–58.

1999d. s/h alternation in Romani: an historical and functional interpretation. *Grazer Linguistische Studien* 51: 99–129.

1999e. Subject clitics in Sinti. *Acta Linguistica Academiae Scientiarum Hungaricae* 46: 147–69.

1999f. Writing Romani: the pragmatics of codification in a stateless language. *Applied Linguistics* 20: 481–502.

2000a. The structural and functional composition of Romani demonstratives. In: Elšík and Matras, eds. 95–122.

2000b. Migrations and replacive convergence as sources of diversity in the dialects of Romani. In: Mattheier, ed. 173–94.

2000c. Fusion and the cognitive basis for bilingual discourse markers. *International Journal of Bilingualism* 4: 505–28.

2000d. Mixed languages: a functional-communicative approach. *Bilingualism: Language and Cognition* 3: 79–99.

2000e. Mixed languages: re-examining the structural prototype. Paper presented at the International Workshop on Theoretical Advances in the Study of Mixed Languages, Manchester, 8–9 December 2000.

ed. 1995. *Romani in contact: the history and sociology of a language.* Amsterdam: Benjamins.

ed. 1998. *The Romani element in non-standard speech.* Wiesbaden: Harrassowitz.

Matras, Yaron, Peter Bakker, and Hristo Kyuchukov, eds. 1997. *The typology and dialectology of Romani.* Amsterdam: John Benjamins.

Mattheier, Klaus, ed. 2000. *Dialect and migration in a changing Europe.* Frankfurt: Peter Lang.

Max, Frédéric. 1972. Apports tsiganes dans l'argot français moderne. *Etudes Tsiganes* 10: 12–18.

McLane, Merrill. 1977. The Caló of Guadix: a surviving Romany lexicon. *Anthropological Linguistics* 19: 303–19.

Mānušs, Leksa (with Jānis Neilands and Kārlis Rudevičs). 1997. *Čigānu-latviešu-angļu etimoloģiskā vārdnīca un latviešu-čigānu vārdnīca.* Rigi: Zvaigzne ABC.

Mészáros, György. 1968. Lovāri-Texte aus Ungarn. *Acta Linguistica Hungarica* 18: 173–90.

1976. The Cerhāri Gipsy dialect. *Acta Orientalia Academiae Scientiarum Hungaricae* 30: 351–67.

Miklosich, Franz. 1872–80. *Über die Mundarten und Wanderungen der Zigeuner Europas X–XII.* Vienna: Karl Gerold's Sohn.
1874–8. *Beiträge zur Kenntnis der Zigeunermundarten. I–IV.* Vienna: Karl Gerold's Sohn.
Minkov, Michael. 1997. A concise grammar of West Bulgarian Romani. *JGLS*, fifth series, 7: 55–95.
Miskow, Johan, and Brøndal, Viggo. 1923. Sigøjnersprog i Danmark. *Danske studier* 1923: 97–145.
Moravcsik, Edith. 1978. Language contact. In: Greenberg, ed. 93–122.
Mori, Tiziana. 1999. Ergatività, passivo e causativo in un dialetto di Xoraxané Romá. In: Piasere, ed. 199–214.
Myers-Scotton, Carol. 1993. Duelling languages. *Grammatical structure in code-switching.* Oxford: Clarendon Press.
Newbold, F. R. S. 1856. The Gypsies of Egypt. *Journal of the Royal Asiatic Society of Great Britain and Ireland* 1856: 285–312.
Oranskij, I. M. 1977. *Folklor i jazyk gissarskix Parja Sredneja Azija.* Moscow: Akademija Nauk.
Pallas, Peter. 1781. *Neye nordische Beiträge zur physikalischen und geographischen Erd- und Völkerbeschreibung*, 3. St Petersburg.
Paspati, Alexandre G. 1870 [reprint 1973]. *Etudes sur les Tchinghianés ou Bohémians de l'Empire Ottoman.* Osnabrück: Biblio.
Pasquali, Pietro Settimio. 1935. Romani words in Italian slangs. *JGLS*, third series, 14: 44–51.
Patkanoff, K.P. 1907/1908. Some words on the dialects of the Transcaucasian Gypsies. *JGLS*, new series, 1: 229–57; 2: 246–66, 325–34.
Payne, Doris, and Immanuel Barshi, eds. 1999. *External possession.* Amsterdam: John Benjamins.
Payne, John R. 1995. Inflecting postpositions in Indic and Kashmiri. In: Plank, ed. 283–98.
1997. The Central Asian Parya. In: Akiner and Sims-Williams, eds. 144–53.
Petropoulos, Elias. 1971. *Kaliarda.* Athens: Nefeli.
Piasere, Leonardo, ed. 1996. *Italia Romaní* I. Roma: Centro d'Informazione e Stampa Universitaria.
1999. Italia Romaní II. Roma; Centro d'Informazione e Stampa Universitaria.
Pischel, Richard. 1883. Die Heimath der Zigeuner. *Deutsche Rundschau* 36: 353–75.
Pischel, Richard. 1900. *Grammatik der Prakrit-Sprachen.* Straßburg: Trübner.
Pistor, Jutta. 1998. Berwick-upon-Tweed: Romani words in an English dialect. In: Matras, ed. 231–42.
Plank, Frans. 1995. (Re-)Introducing Suffixaufnahme. In: Plank, ed. 3–110.
Plank, Frans. 2000. Foreword. In: Elšík and Matras, eds. 1–7.
ed. 1995. *Double case. Agreement by Suffixaufnahme.* New York: Oxford University Press.
Pobożniak, Tadeusz. 1964. *Grammar of the Lovari dialect.* Crakow: Państwowe wydawnictwo naukowe.
Poplack, Shana. 1980. Sometimes I'll start a sentence in English y termino en español: toward a typology of code-switching. *Linguistics* 18: 581–618.

Pott, August. 1844–5. *Die Zigeuner in Europa und Asien. Ethnographisch-linguistische Untersuchung vornehmlich ihrer Herkunft und Sprache.* Halle: Heynemann.

1846. Über die Sprache der Zigeuner in Syrien. *Zeitschrift für die Wissenschaft der Sprache* 1: 175–86.

Puchmayer, Anton Jaroslaw. 1821. *Románi Čib, das ist: Grammatik und Wörterbuch der Zigeuner Sprache, nebst einigen Fabeln in derselben. Dazu als Anhang die Hantýrka oder die Čechische Diebessprache.* Prague: Fürst-erzbischöflichen Buchdruckerey.

Puxon, Grattan. 1979. Romanès and language policy in Jugoslavia. *International Journal of the Sociology of Language* 19: 83–90.

Quindalé, F. [= Francisco de Sales Mayo.] 1867. *El gitanismo.* Madrid: V. Suarez.

Raffler-Engel, W. von, ed. 1975. *Child language today.* London.

Ramirez-Heredia, Juan de Dios. 1993. Gramática gitana. *I Tchatchipen* 2: 41–62; 3: 46–63; 4: 44–63.

Rao, Aparna. 1976. Histoire d'un mulo. *Etudes Tsiganes* 22: 1–3.

1995. Marginality and language use: the example of peripatetics in Afghanistan. *JGLS*, fifth series, 5: 69–95.

Réger, Zita. 1979. Bilingual Gypsy children in Hungary: explorations in 'Natural' second-language acquisition. *International Journal of the Sociology of Language* 19: 59–82.

1999. Teasing in the linguistic socialization of Gypsy children in Hungary. *Acta Linguistica Hungarica* 46: 289–315.

Reichenbach, Hans. 1947 [reprint 1963]. *Elements of symbolic logic.* New York: Macmillan.

Reiter, Norbert, Uwe Hinrichs, and Jeřina van Leeuwen-Turnocová, eds. 1994. *Sprachlicher Standard und Substandard in Südosteuropa und Osteuropa.* Berlin/Wiesbaden: Harrassowitz.

Rijkhof, Jan. 1998. Bystander deixis. In: Matras, ed. 51–67.

Román, Mercedes. 1995. El dialecto Gitano-Espanol, Calo: análisis semántico del léxico conservado en la provincia de Valladolid. *Neuphilologische Mitteilungen* 96: 437–451.

Ross, M. 1996. Contact-induced change and the Comparative Method. In: Durie and Ross, eds. 180–217.

Roussakov, Alexandre Yu. 2000. North Russian Romani dialect: on interference phenomena in syntax. Paper presented at the Fifth International Conference on Romani Linguistics, Sofia. 14–17 September 2000.

Rozwadowski, Jan. 1936. *Wörterbuch des Zigeunerdialekts von Zakopane.* Crakow: Polska Akademja Umiejęności.

Ruch, Martin. 1986. Zur Wissenschaftsgeschichte der deutschsprachigen 'Zigeunerforschung' von den Anfängen bis 1900. PhD Dissertation, Universität Freiburg.

Rüdiger, Johan Chr. Chr. 1782. [1990]. *Von der Sprache und Herkunft der Zigeuner aus Indien. In: Neuester Zuwachs der teutschen, fremden und allgemeinen Sprachkunde in eigenen Aufsätzen*, 1. Stück. Leipzig. 37–84. Hamburg: Buske.

Rusakov, Alexandre, and Olga Abramenko. 1998. North Russian Romani dialect: Interference in case system. *Grazer Linguistische Studien* 50: 109–33.

Salmons, Joe. 1990. Bilingual discourse marking: code switching, borrowing, and convergence in some German-American dialects. *Linguistics* 28: 453–80.

Salo, Matt T., ed. 1990. *100 years of Gypsy studies.* New York: The Gypsy Lore Society.

Sampson, John. 1910. Jacob Bryant. Being an analysis of his Angloromani vocabulary, with a discussion of the place and date of collection and an attempt to show that Bryant, not Rüdiger, was the earliest discoverer of the Indian origin of the Gypsies. *JGLS*, new series, 4: 162–94.

1923. On the origin and early migrations of the Gypsies. *JGLS*, third series, 2: 156–69.

1926 [reprint. 1968]. *The dialect of the Gypsies of Wales, being the older form of British Romani preserved in the speech of the clan of Abram Wood.* Oxford: Clarendon Press.

1927. Notes on Professor R. L. Turner's 'The position of Romani in Indo-Aryan'. *JGLS*, third series, 6: 57–68.

Sandry, Géo, and Marcel Carrère. 1953. *Dictionnaire de l'argot moderne.* Paris: Dauphin.

Schmid, Wolfgang P. 1963. Das zigeunerische Abstraktsuffix *-ben/-pen*. *Indogermanische Forschungen* 68: 276–83.

1968. Zur Bildung der Abstrakta in den Zigeunerdialekten Europas. In: Brekle and Lipka, eds. 210–16.

Sebba, Mark. 1997. *Contact languages. Pidgins and creoles.* London: Macmillan.

Sechidou, Irene. 2000. A Greek variety of a Mixed Romani Dialect. Paper presented at the Fifth International Conference on Romani Linguistics, Sofia, 14–17 September 2000.

Sergievskij, M. V. 1931. *Cyganski Jazyk.* Moscow: Centraljnoe Izdateljstvo Narodov SSSR.

Shibatani, Masayoshi. 1976. *Causativization.* New York: Academic Press.

Smart, Bath C. 1862–3. *The dialect of the English Gypsies* (Appendix to the Transactions of the Philological Society for 1862–1863). Berlin: Asher, and Co.

Smart, Bath C., and Crofton, Henry Thomas. 1875. *The dialect of the English Gypsies.* London: Asher, and Co.

Soravia, Giulio. 1972. Italian influences on the dialect of the Gypsies of Abruzzi. *JGLS*, third series, 51: 34–9.

1977. *Dialetti degli Zingari italiani.* (= Profilo dei dialetti italiani, 22.) Pisa: Consiglio Nazionale delle Ricerche.

1988. Die alcune etimologie zingariche. *Archivo Glottologico Italiano* 73: 1–11.

Soulis, George C. 1961. The Gypsies in the Byzantine Empire and the Balkans in the later Middle Ages. *Dumbarton Oak Papers* 15: 143–65.

Sowa, Rudolf von. 1887. *Die Mundart der slovakischen Zigeuner.* Göttingen: Vandenhoeck und Ruprechts Verlag.

Spears, Arthur A., and Donald W., eds. 1997. *The structure and status of pidgins and creoles.* Amsterdam: Benjamins.

Stolz, Christel, and Thomas Stolz. 1996. Funktionswortentlehnung in Mesoamerika. Spanisch-amerindischer Sprachkontakt Hispanoindiana II. *Sprachtypologie und Universalienforschung* 49: 86–123.

Streck, Bernhard. 1996. *Die Ḥalab.* Munich: Trickster Verlag.

Štrukelj, Pavla. 1980. *Rom na Slovenskem.* Ljubljana: Cankarjeva Zalozba.

Sulán, Béla. 1963. Probleme der Argotforschung in Mitteleuropa. *Innsbrucker Beiträge zur Kulturwissenschaft* 18: 5–14.

Sutherland, Anne. 1975. *Gypsies. The hidden Americans.* Prospect Heights: Waveland.

Tagare, Ganesh V. 1948 [reprint 1987]. *Historical grammar of Apabhraṃśa.* Delhi: Motilal Banarsidass.

Tálos, Endre. 1999. Etymologica Zingarica. *Acta Linguistica Hungarica* 46: 215–68.

Tauber, Elisabeth. 1999. Tenkreh tu kao molo ke ǵam ti mangel? In: Piasere, ed. 59–70.

Thesleff, Arthur. 1912. Report on the Gypsy problem. Part II. *JGLS*, new series, 5: 255–69.

Thieroff, Rolf, and Joachim Ballweg, eds. 1994. *Tense systems in European languages.* Tübingen: Niemeyer.

1994. Inherent verb categories and categorizations in European languages. In: Thieroff and Ballweg, eds. 3–45.

1995. More on inherent verb categories in European languages, in: Thieroff, ed. 1–36.

ed. 1995. *Tense systems in European languages II.* Tübingen: Niemeyer.

Thomason, S. G. 1997. A typology of contact languages. In: Spears and Spears, eds. 71–88.

Thomason, S. G., and T. Kaufman. 1988. *Language contact, creolization, and genetic linguistics.* Berkeley: University of California Press.

Tipler, Derek. 1957. Specimens of modern Welsh Romani. *JGLS*, third series, 36: 9–24.

Tong, Diane. 1983. Language use and attitudes among the Gypsies of Thessaloniki. *Anthropological Linguistics* 25: 375–85.

Toropov, Vadim. 1994. *Krymskij dialekt tsiganskogo jazyka.* Ivanovo: A-grif.

Torrione, Margarita. 1989. *Diccionario caló-castellano de don Luis Usoz y Rio: un manuscrito del siglo XIX.* Perpignan: Université de Perpignan, Publications du Centre de Recherches Ibériques et Latino-Américaines, 1.

Treimer, Karl. 1937. *Das tschechische Rotwelsch. Entstehung und Schichten.* Heidelberg: Carl Winter.

Triandaphyllidis, Manolis. 1924. Eine griechisch-zigeunerische Geheimsprache, *Zeitschrift für vergleichende Sprachforschung auf dem Gebiet der indogermanischen Sprachen* 52: 1–42.

Trudgill, Peter, ed. 1984. *Language in the British Isles.* Cambridge: Cambridge University Press.

Turner, Ralph L. 1926. The position of Romani in Indo-Aryan. *JGLS*, third series, 5: 145–89.

1927. The position of Romani in Indo-Aryan: a reply to Dr J. Sampson. *JGLS*, third series, 6: 129–38.

1928 [1975]. Romani les and Sanskrit tásya. In: Turner, 1975: 310–18.

1932. So-called prothetic V- and Y- in European Romani. *JGLS*, third series, 11: 115–20.

1959. Transferance of aspiration in European Romani. *Bulletin of the School of Oriental and African Studies* 22: 491–8.

1975. *Collected papers. 1912–1973.* London: Oxford University Press.

Uhlik, Rade. 1941. Bosnian Romani: a vocabulary A–F. *JGLS*, third series, 20: 100–40.

1954. Ciganizmi u Šatrovačkom argou i u sličnim govorima. *Istorija i etnografija* 9: 5–31.

1965. A gimlet-maker's fairy tale. *JGLS*, third series, 44: 11–37.

Valet, Joseph. 1991. Grammar of Manush as it is spoken in the Auvergne. In: Bakker and Cortiade, eds. 106–31.

Valtonen, Pertti. 1972. *Suomen mustalaiskielen etymologinen sanakirja.* Helsinki: Soumalaisen kirjallisuuden seura.

van den Eijnde, Alexander. 1991. Romani vocabulary in Swedish slang. In: Bakker and Cortiade, 185–92.

van der Auwera, Johan. ed. 1998. *Adverbial constructions in the languages of Europe.* Berlin: Mouton de Gruyter.

van der Voort, Hein. 1991. The Romani dialects of the Finnish Gypsies. In: Bakker and Cortiade, eds.

van Hout, Roeland, and Pieter Muysken. 1994. Modeling lexical borrowability. *Language Variation and Change* 6: 39–62.

Vekerdi, József. 1971b. Statistisches zum Wortschatz des Zigeunerischen. *Acta Linguistica Academiae Scientiarum Hungaricae* 21: 129–34.

1971a. The Gurvari Gypsy dialect in Hungary. *Acta Orientalia Academiae Scientiarum Hungaricae* 24: 381–9.

1981. On the social prehistory of the Gypsies. *Acta Orientalia Academiae Scientiarum Hungaricae* 35: 243–54.

1983. *A magyarországi cigány nyelvjárások szótára.* (= Tunolmányok, 7.) Pécs: Janus Pannonius Tudományegyetem Tanárképző Kara.

1984. The Vend Gypsy dialect in Hungary. *Acta Linguistica Academiae Scientiarum Hungaricae* 34: 65–86.

Velidi, Zeki. 1950–5. *Symbolae in Honorem Z. V. Togan.* Istanbul.

Ventcel', Tatjana V., and Lev N. Čerenkov. 1976. Dialekty cyganskogo jazyka. *Jazyki Azii i Afriki* I. Moscow: Nauka. 283–332.

Wagner, Max L. 1937. Stray notes on Spanish Romani, Chapter 2: Cryptolalic formations in other Romani dialects. *JGLS*, third series, 16: 27–32.

Ward, H. Gordon. 1947. On some Romani and Shelta words in British slang. *JGLS*, third series, 26: 73–75.

1936. Romani words in Swedish slang. *JGLS*, third series, 15: 78–85.

Weinreich, Uriel. 1953. *Languages in contact: findings and problems.* The Hague: Mouton.

Wentzel, Tatjana W. 1980. *Die Zigeunersprache (Nordrussischer Dialekt).* Leipzig: Enzyklopädie.

Windfuhr, Gernot. 1970. European Gypsy in Iran: A first report. *Anthropological Linguistics* 12: 271–92.

Wink, André. 1990. *Al-Hind. The making of the Indo-Islamic world.* Volume 1. Leiden: Brill.

Wogg, Michael, and Dieter W. Halwachs. 1998. *Syntax des Roman.* (Arbeitsbericht 6 des Projekts Kodifizierung und Didaktisierung des Roman.) Oberwart: Verein Roma.

Wolf, Siegmund A. 1958. Völker- und geographische Namen im Romani (Zigeunersprache). *Beiträge zu Namensforschung* 9: 180–8.

Wolf, Siegmund A. 1960a. Etymologisches zu einigen zigeunerischen Stammesnamen. *Beiträge zur Namensforschung* 11: 162–70.

1960b. Zur Frage einer normierten Zigeunersprache (Basic Romani). *Phonetica* 5: 204–9.

1985. *Deutsche Gaunersprache. Wörterbuch des Rotwelschen.* Hamburg: Buske.

Wood, Manfri Frederick. 1973. *In the life of a Romany Gypsy.* London: Routledge and Kegan Paul.

Woolner, Alfred C. 1913–14. The Indian origin of the Gypsies in Europe. *Journal of the Panjab Historical Society* 2: 136–41.
1915. Studies in Romani philology I: Personal pronouns. *JGLS*, second series, 9: 119–28.
1928. Aśoka and the Gypsies. *JGLS*, third series, 7: 108–11.
Wurr, Zazie, ed. 2000. *Newo Ziro – Neue Zeit? Wider die Tsiganomanie.* Kiel: Agimos.

Index of dialects

Index of names

Index of subjects

ablative, 42, 44, 87, 88, 89, 92, 93, 94, 113, 188, 221
accusative, 48, 70, 71, 82, 85, 87, 174, 175, 176, 214, 242
  see also oblique, independent
acquisition
  of Romani, 238, 240
  of Para-Romani, 244
active participle, 44, 122, 148, 155, 156, 225, 226
adjectival participle *see* active participle
adjectives, 1, 60, 120, 121, 123, 133
  borrowing of, 193, 196, 197, 203, 209, 211
  derivation, 23, 42, 74, 76–8
  inflection, 42, 63, 66, 72, 73, 89, 90, 91, 94–6
  position of, 97, 105, 165, 166–7, 190
adverbial clauses
  anteriority, 187–9
  posteriority, 188
  simultaneity, 160, 162, 188
  see also conditional
adverbs, 5, 22, 42, 70, 79, 88, 91, 120, 214
  of place/location, 44, 109, 111, 165, 196, 209, 211, 222, 247
  of reversal and repetition, 197, 213
  phasal, 197, 199, 210, 211, 212, 213
affricates, 49, 50, 51, 52–3, 55, 58, 224
agentive
  derivation marker, 5, 76, 84, 86, 170, 204
  verb form, 147–8
agglutinative, 45, 78, 79, 87, 117, 152, 156
agreement, of adjectives, 44, 94, 101, 142, 143, 155, 207
aktionsart, 117, 118, 121, 156, 158, 159, 172, 193, 202, 203, 211, 212, 213
animacy, 72–3, 82, 85–7, 113, 170, 177, 178
Apabhraṃśa, 44, 69, 125
Arabic, 16, 18, 25, 38, 80, 129, 180
archaism, 33, 34, 36, 46, 48, 85, 102, 107, 116, 117, 125, 133, 145, 174, 175, 215, 216, 217, 222, 223, 234, 236, 237
areal development, 48, 49, 59, 96, 113, 149, 175, 190, 196, 198–9, 229
argot, 1, 2, 243, 246, 249
  see also secret language; slang
Armenian, 13, 18, 21, 23, 24, 25, 26, 27, 28, 29, 35, 52, 75, 114, 196
Aromanian, 242
  see also Balkan Romance
Aśokan inscriptions, 33
aspiration, 30, 31, 35, 36, 49, 50, 52, 54, 57, 126, 254, 257
  transfer of, 30, 35, 39, 40, 41, 48, 52
athematic grammar, 19, 22, 63, 71, 73, 74, 79, 81, 82, 83, 84, 85, 95, 128, 160
auxiliaries, 44, 45, 118, 125, 126, 128, 138, 141, 145, 157, 158, 242
Awadhi, 43, 125
Azerbaijanian, 209

Bahlawān, 15
Balkan Romance, 115, 130, 195
Balkanisms, 23, 97, 113, 157, 179, 199, 206
Baluchi, 23
benefactive, 87, 88, 94, 178
Bengali, 32, 43, 44
Bhojpuri, 43
bilingualism, 134, 135, 191, 201, 238, 241, 242, 245
  bilingual texts, 252, 254, 255, 256
bodyparts, terms for, 27, 85
broadcasting, in Romani, 240, 258
Bulgarian, 249
Burushaski, 24

Cant, 246
case layers
  analytic formation of, 78–9, 82, 91–3
  Layer I, 44, 63, 64, 79, 80–5, 92, 94, 96
  Layer II, 44, 45, 48, 53, 63, 64, 70, 79, 82, 85, 87–90, 92, 93, 98, 99, 105, 252